# WHAT AMERICA'S SMALL COMPANIES PAY THEIR SALES FORCES... AND HOW THEY MAKE IT PAY OFF

Dartnell is a publisher serving the world of business with books, manuals, newsletters, and training materials for executives, managers, supervisors, salespeople, financial officials, personnel executives, and office employees. Dartnell also produces management and sales training videos and audiocassettes, publishes many useful business forms, and many of its materials and films are available in languages other than English. Dartnell, established in 1917, serves the world's business community. For details, catalogs, and product information, write to:

THE DARTNELL CORPORATION
4660 N Ravenswood Ave
Chicago, IL 60640-4595, U.S.A.
Or phone (800) 621-5463 in U.S. and Canada
www.dartnellcorp.com

This publication is designed to provide accurate and authoritative information in regard to the subject matter covered. It is sold with the understanding that the publisher is not engaged in rendering legal, accounting, or other professional service. If legal advice or other expert assistance is required, the services of a competent professional person should be sought.

*—From a Declaration of Principles jointly*
*adopted by a Committee of the American Bar*
*Association and a Committee of Publishers.*

© Copyright 1997
in the United States, Canada, and Britain by
THE DARTNELL CORPORATION

ISBN 0-85013-270-3

Library of Congress Catalog Card Number 97-65285

Printed in the United States of America by The Dartnell Press, Chicago, IL 60640-4595

# CONTENTS

# LISTING OF FIGURES

# ACKNOWLEDGMENTS

**M**any people contributed their time and effort to *What America's Small Companies Pay Their Sales Forces ... And How They Make It Pay Off*. The author wishes, first, to thank all survey participants, whose help and cooperation made the survey portion of this book possible. In addition, the author wishes to acknowledge the considerable data preparation work of Ron Metz and Annette Salapatek.

Special thanks to Hal Fahner, Vice President of Corporate Marketing, Blue Cross & Blue Shield of Florida, Inc., who freely contributed his ideas and allowed them to be incorporated in this book, and to Charles Schlom, whose ground-breaking work in territory design and management adds a new understanding to the topic. Special thanks, too, to the many Dartnell authors, who, over the years, have contributed to the storehouse of knowledge that this book builds on.

Additional thanks to the Dartnell team members who contributed their time and effort to this project: Biff Johnson, information systems manager; Megan Mulligan, production manager; Andrew Epstein, creative director; Amy Flammang, page formatting; Annie Chesney, survey coordination and tabulation of supplemental survey results; Dave Palomares, promotion coordinator; and Anne Garry, who checked final pages.

# ABOUT THE AUTHOR

**C**hristen P. Heide, executive editor for sales and marketing publications at The Dartnell Corporation, is also the author of *Dartnell's 29th Sales Force Compensation Survey* (1996), *Dartnell's 28th Sales Force Compensation Survey* (1994), and *Dartnell's 27th Sales Force Compensation Survey* (1992). He is a respected speaker and writer on the topics of sales compensation and sales force management. His articles have appeared in such publications as *Advertising Age* and *Marketing News*, and he is widely quoted in the business press as a sales and marketing authority. Heide is an expert on contemporary issues in compensation and has been a featured sales compensation speaker at several national conferences. He recently appeared on *Inc.* magazine's "Annual Growing The Company Conference" program, where he spoke on using sales incentives to boost sales performance. He is the editor of Dartnell's *Sales and Marketing Executive Report* and a former board member of Sales and Marketing Executives of Chicago.

## THE DARTNELL CORPORATION

One of the world's leading producers and distributors of business information and training materials, Dartnell has been a recognized source for the best in sales training and information for more than 75 years. Sales managers have counted on the Dartnell Sales Force Compensation Survey for current, accurate data since 1929. Dartnell offers books, manuals, newsletters, audiocassettes, and films and videos for diverse business audiences on a variety of important business topics.

# FOREWORD

Ignorance is an invitation for exploitation. In the years since I started *Selling Power* magazine, I have come to realize that the profession of selling occupies a small space between two raging rivers. One of these rivers is called Ignorance. After graduating from school, some people slowly get swept away by the tides of ignorance. Driven by the pursuit of pleasing experiences, they begin to drift and miss valuable opportunities for learning and growing. They often pretend that they know it all, or sell you on the idea that there is nothing new in this world.

On the other side, there exists a river of Information. People who enter this river are often swept away by the raging currents — acting confused, spending money impulsively on the wrong resources, pursuing the wrong opportunities, or forming relationships that lead to financial disaster.

The solid space between the two rivers is like an island refuge that allows access to the seasoned sales executive. That's where you find rare sales achievers who despise ignorance and who have harnessed the power of information.

When I started my own business, I was excited and inspired by the many possibilities and opportunities around me, but I was also overwhelmed by the many challenges that I faced. From the very beginning of hiring, training, and motivating our sales staff, I struggled to come up with a compensation plan that worked for the employee, the customer, and the business. There was a multitude of misleading adages that often influenced the decision making process, such as "We pay what the market will bear," "In sales, you write your own paycheck," or "Salespeople will do anything for a buck." To find a path to what's right and what's fair to the employee and the company (affordable yet motivating, exciting but not crazy) requires good insights. How could I evaluate all requirements to meet my company's objective? How could I translate these requirements into meeting the goals set by our sales team?

Every good manager knows the impact of a good compensation plan on the company's bottom line. Every good manager also knows just how difficult it is to revise an established plan, especially after the company has reached a new sales record. What if your compensation plan is based on last year's success, and next year a recession is threatening to wipe out all gains?

From making decisions about setting salaries to figuring out incentive plans and territory designs, I realized just how vital this question is in determining the ultimate success or failure of any enterprise. Eventually, I learned the answers to my questions and was able to come up with a format (using Dartnell's compensation surveys as a guide) that worked for us. Recounting my experiences wouldn't benefit others. Why is this? Just as no two successful companies are exactly alike, neither are successful compensation plans. Each one is unique.

No one knows this better than Chris Heide. Sitting at the top of the "information food chain" of Dartnell, Heide has researched the subject for many years and gained unique access to the compensation plans of his client companies. This book does not pretend that there is one magic formula for success. Heide recognizes that what works for IBM may not prove to be profitable for everyone else. Instead, this book embraces the individual nature of businesses and supplies managers with the information and strategies they need to be able to make informed decisions.

The first part of the book offers valuable insights about the basics of sales compensation plans, including territory designs, quotas, and incentive plans. After you've gotten the basics covered, Chapter 7 shows you how to keep it all running smoothly. The second part of the book highlights the results of Dartnell research studies and provides a fascinating and useful look at the data of other businesses that will help you manage your own sales team. You'll find out what you need to know in order to answer all your questions about how to draft your own successful compensation plan, or even how to fine-tune the one you've already got.

Scratch the surface of any successful sales organization, and you will find a solid compensation plan underneath. Nothing helps you more on your way to success than knowing what you're doing and seeking new knowledge that will empower you to become more successful. At some point in time, we have each taken a dive into the river of Ignorance, but that doesn't mean we have to stay there. With the help of *What America's Small Companies Pay Their Sales Forces … And How They Make It Pay Off*, you will have a good chance of reaching that coveted "middle ground" between the two rivers.

— Gerhard Gschwandtner
Publisher and Founder
*Selling Power*

# OVERVIEW OF *WHAT AMERICA'S SMALL COMPANIES PAY THEIR SALES FORCES... AND HOW THEY MAKE IT PAY OFF*

This book came about as a result of many customer requests for a book that would answer basic sales compensation questions. Most of these requests came from owners or sales managers of companies with under $5 million in annual sales who were about to hire their first salesperson, draft their first sales compensation plan, or adjust a plan that was not working.

What they needed, they said, was a working knowledge of how to go about drafting a plan and putting the numbers to it. What they did not want was complicated theory that was hard to understand and impossible to put to use. In short, they wanted something they could understand and something that would work. As one individual said: "I've got plenty of time to get complicated, but I've got to understand the basics first."

To meet this need, we envisioned a book that would be divided into two parts: part one would cover sales compensation planning basics — the pros and cons of the three basic plans, and a thorough discussion of incentive plan design, territory design, quota setting basics, and the like.

Part two would concentrate on the results of Dartnell research studies. In part two we would include our latest compensation figures for companies with under $5 million in annual sales. To round out the picture, we would also include benchmark performance figures on expenses, benefits, and training; data on how salespeople spent their time; and other data of interest to anyone managing a sales force.

This is that book. In the more than 65 years that Dartnell has tracked sales compensation and sales performance issues, our aim has always been to provide sales and marketing executives with an indispensable tool to improve the productivity of their sales forces as well as the bottom lines of their companies. We think you will agree that *What America's Small Companies Pay Their Sales Forces...And How They Make It Pay Off* delivers on this promise.

## WHAT THIS BOOK *CAN* DO FOR YOU

This book can give you the basics of setting up a compensation plan for your company. Even if you have a compensation plan in place, this book will provide you with the information to evaluate and fine-tune your plan. If you are not 100 percent satisfied with your plan, or wonder if you could be getting better results, this book will help.

In addition, our extensive survey sections in part two enable you to compare your company's figures with our survey averages. You'll be able to see how your company compares with other companies with under $5 million in annual sales. Here you'll also find figures for answering those tough questions, such as how much time and money to spend on training, what to provide in the way of benefits, and what constitutes "normal" turnover.

In short, this book can give you the tools you need to make your company more profitable.

## WHAT THIS BOOK *CAN'T* DO FOR YOU

This book doesn't attempt to provide "ready-to-use, one-size-fits-all" compensation plans that you can just "plug in" and use. While we do provide sample job descriptions and sample compensation plans used by other companies, these should be regarded as "idea starters."

In conversations with Dartnell customers, we are often asked for a sample plan, job description, or other document "just to get the creative juices flowing." It is hoped that the job descriptions and compensation plans we have provided will give you that "creative spark."

Readers are encouraged to pull ideas from this book and try them out. Discard any ideas that are inappropriate for your company or particular situation. Of course, feel free to adapt, modify, or change any of these ideas to better suit your company.

A word about our survey data: As noted elsewhere, survey data is based on extremes and should be applied with good judgment. You should not change pay scales or business practices that are working in your company solely on the basis of our research findings. Every company has its own idiosyncrasies, place in the market, and other differences that make it unique. Use our survey data to update your knowledge of today's sales dynamics; you will be sure to uncover new trends and ideas that could be applied to your company to improve its success. Again, use good judgment and up-to-date figures from your own company before making widespread changes.

# FREQUENTLY ASKED QUESTIONS

H ere are some of the questions we receive regularly at Dartnell from people wrestling with designing a sales compensation plan. We've included them here as a quick overview of some of the more important issues in sales compensation.

We suggest you read through this quick "FAQ" sheet — the answers to some of your most pressing problems are likely to appear here.

**Question No. 1:** "I'm an entrepreneur and while my business is growing, it has the potential to grow at a faster rate. How can I tell when it is time to hire a salesperson?"

**Answer:** This is really a mathematical problem. We'll work through the math one step at a time. This isn't a difficult concept, but it's a very important one. Be sure you're clear on this concept before moving, on as many of the basics of compensating salespeople build on this discussion.

Ready? Let's go!

Let's say that right now you are making a net profit of $180,000 on $600,000 in sales. If you were to hire a salesperson who cost you $50,000 a year in compensation and expenses, and there was no increase in sales volume, you would reduce your net profit to $130,000. What you need to do, of course, is increase sales volume to more than cover your risk — your risk being committing the extra expense of hiring a salesperson.

Here's how to look at the problem: If you need to sell 100,000 units at $6 each to net $180,000, then your margin is 30 percent. That is, you make 30 cents on each dollar of total revenue. (Thirty percent of $600,000 in revenue equals $180,000.)

Now how many more units do you need to sell to "break even," or cover your additional expense ($50,000) of hiring a salesperson? To break even on your risk, you'll need to make a new net profit of $230,000 (Your original net profit of $180,000 plus the $50,000 cost of hiring a salesperson.)

Here's the math: At 30 percent margin, you need $166,667 more in sales for a new total sales volume of $766,667. (Thirty percent of $166,667 equals $50,000 — the amount of new revenue needed to generate an additional $50,000 in profit.) This translates into 27,778 more units that you need to sell. ($166,667 in new revenue needed divided by a unit cost of $6 equals 27,778 units.) Therefore, if you add $50,000 in additional expenses, you need to sell a new total of 127,778 units or nearly 28 percent more. (Old unit volume of 100,000 plus 27,778 new units to be sold.)

What this means is you need a sales volume increase of nearly 28 percent just to break even or generate the same amount of net profit.

Now consider this: If your $50,000 salesperson can generate a 50 percent increase in sales to $900,000 or 150,000 units at $6 each and 30 percent profit per unit, net profit climbs to $220,000 — approximtely a 22 percent increase in profit.

If you believe you are not covering the potential territory well and that if you could spend *full time* at sales you could generate twice your $600,000 volume, the picture gets rosier:

$1,200,000 in sales volume means $360,000 in profit before compensating your salesperson. (200,000 units at $6 each with 30 percent profit per unit equals $360,000.) If you had to pay $50,000 to get a good performing salesperson to produce $900,000 in sales, then you would probably spend more on sales compensation to generate $1,200,000 in sales.

Now that you understand this concept, work on it with your accountant. Remember also to recognize any other expenses that increase with volume to get to the real new net profit.

**Question No. 2:** "I'm thinking of hiring my first sales rep. I know how to hire an accountant or a production manager. But I don't know how to hire a salesperson. Would I be better off hiring a sales manager and letting him or her take care of the entire selling function?"

**Answer:** Take another look at the financial analysis above. The volume and profit would have to go up enough to cover the additional expense of the sales manager and any salesperson hired.

Also consider cash flow, since some portion of the compensation plan for each person will be salary, benefits, and expenses paid before the sale is made. Usually a smaller potion of the cost is the commission and/or bonus paid after you get new higher volume. An alternative is to find a capable sales recruiter who understands the sales function and who you can trust.

**Question No. 3:** "I'd like my company to grow and am thinking about getting some help in making sales. Should I hire a salesperson, or can I get results cheaper by using a telesalesperson or an independent manufacturers' rep?"

**Answer:** Wrong question. The answer is in the arithmetic for question Nos. 1 and 2 above. Your question revolves around the net profit generated by the additional sales produced by the sales producer and the need to cover the fixed and front-end expenses of a salesperson.

The independent rep approach is attractive to many mostly because of the variable expense of sales — you don't pay until you get the sale. However, you give up much of the control of the person's activities, which may erode your margin. Bear in mind that you may not get the coverage of the market that you should, you may not get the best customers, and the independent rep may take your customers to another company if you have a falling out. (See page 7 for an in-depth discussion on independent reps.)

Inside sales or telephone sales looks cheaper, but the quality and intensity of coverage may not be enough to increase sales sufficiently. Perform the same analysis outlined in question No. 1 above.

**Question No. 4:** "Your point about the difficulty of controlling an independent manufacturers' rep is well taken. But what about a commission-only salesperson? That seems to me to be the way to go, since I don't have to pay for sales until I get them."

**Answer:** Take a look at our discussion of the pros and cons of various pay plans beginning on page 18. Remember that you still face the same problem of control over the salesperson's activities when you use this plan. And coverage, too, may not be adequate for your needs — a commission-only salesperson may tend to focus on easy or marginal sales or expend just the amount of effort needed to satisfy his or her financial needs. While it may sound like a good deal to pay only for the sales you get, ask yourself if you can afford not to get the sales you need.

Here's a side issue that you may want to think about: A commission-only plan attracts both the best and worst sales applicants. Here's why:

- High-performing salespeople who want to maximize their earnings prefer to work on a commission-only plan. These plans generally offer unlimited earnings and encourage the salesperson to sell as much volume as possible. These individuals have complete confidence in their ability to get the selling job done and don't need the security of a "base" or "salary." These individuals are also highly independent and have a tendency to "play by their own rules."

- Poorer-performing salespeople are drawn to the commission-only plan for completely different reasons, a major reason being an inability to get hired by a firm paying a salary plus incentive, since these companies tend to hire more selectively. Many commission-only firms, believing they don't pay for sales efforts until the sale is made, use the "mirror test" in hiring salespeople — that is, if the individual is breathing (can fog a mirror), he or she is brought on board. After all, this person isn't really costing the company anything, right?

Wrong. And here are a few quick reasons why: 1.) A poor performing salesperson won't bring in the sales you need, which creates a loss of opportunity; 2.) This individual can give your firm a bad name in the marketplace by creating a poor impression on accounts called on and leads followed up on; 3.) An unqualified hire will demoralize any better-performing salespeople that might have been, usually accidentally, hired (Who wants to be associated with a group that includes losers?); 4.) All these reasons will cause sales management to spend valuable resources trying to manage people who can't do the job, which will make the task of moving the firm forward almost impossible — to say the least.

**Question No. 5:** "I need to draft a sales compensation plan for my company. What's the first thing I need to do?"

**Answer:** Two things are the first thing:

1. Make sure the plan makes money for you from a cost standpoint; that is, that the profit from the sales gives you a satisfactory increase in additional profit above the additional acquisition cost of getting the business;
2. Make sure you tell the sales force the same thing with your compensation plan that you told yourself and your banker in your initial business plan. In other words, use your compensation plan to control quality and profitability of accounts as well as unit and dollar volume. (See page 29 for a full discussion of this important issue.)

**Question No. 6:** "I need to put together a sales compensation plan. What's the single biggest thing I need to watch out for?"

**Answer:** This question shows that there are a variety of ways to ask the same thing. The answer to this question is conceptually the same as the answer to question No. 5. Take a look at what you are really asking. Chances are you'll find the answer by rephrasing the question.

**Question No. 7:** "What's the best base salary/incentive pay split?"

**Answer:** There is no single right answer here. Our survey data for companies with under $5 million in annual sales shows that, on average, for companies paying salespeople on a combination plan, 54 percent of total pay is salary and 46 percent is incentive. For additional survey data on this topic, see page 125.

**Question No. 8:** "How do I determine what pay plan — straight salary, straight commission, or combination plan — I should use?"

**Answer:** See our discussion of the pros and cons of these three plans on page 18. However, here's something to keep in mind: Companies within the same industry tend to all pay their salespeople similarly; that is, they use the same type of pay plan. See our survey data on page 123 to see what plan companies in a variety of industries use.

**Question No. 9:** "I'd like to hire a salesperson to help me sell but am not sure of the sales growth possibility for my product. Is there an easy way to project total sales in a territory? I don't have much historical data to work with."

**Answer:** Don't forget to look at your business plan; certainly that document contains information about sales potential for your product or service. Also, we'd bet the farm that you do have some data you can put to use. Be creative in looking for it. What you need to do is develop a system for capturing the data you need.

And what about companies selling competitive products? They may have made predictions in the trade press about *their* prospects for the future.

You also need to perform a territory audit. Our discussion on how to go about this begins on page 33.

**Question No. 10:** "My margins are slim — about 6 percent. Companies selling similar products pay their salespeople 10 percent commission. How can I compete?"

**Answer:** Okay, okay — we threw this one in to see if you were paying attention. But if this *were* your situation, you would be *the* high-cost producer by at least 4 percent. If your competitors are willing to operate at breakeven, they have to have 4 percent more margin than you do to pay 10 percent commission just to break even! Again, the analysis in question No. 1 will keep you on the right track.

**Question No. 11:** "I'm not getting the sales results I need. I know that salespeople are motivated by money, so I'm thinking of increasing the amount of incentive I pay to get the results I need. What do you think of this idea?"

**Answer:** You're lucky you bought this book. We have included a complete discussion of incentive design practices beginning on page 29. But in answer to your question, take a look at our survey data in the second half of the book to see how your pay practices compare with other companies in your general industry. If you're far and away in the low-paying category, you may not be attracting the sales talent you need. Remember: Compensation cannot make up for lack of skill. In other words, paying someone more to do a job he or she can't perform in the first place will get you nowhere.

**Question No. 12:** "What if I have a question that isn't answered in this book?"

**Answer:** Give us a call at Dartnell. The author can be reached at (800) 621-5463, ext. 3142. He'll do his best to find an answer to your question (and probably include it in the next edition of this book).

# PART ONE — BASIC CONSIDERATIONS

# DO YOU REALLY NEED ADDITIONAL SALES REPRESENTATION?

**B**efore getting started, ask yourself if you *really need* additional sales representation. If you are making a comfortable income and don't want to add to the complexity of your business, you may be better off maintaining the status quo. There are always tradeoffs to consider.

Here's a related example: The owners of a small trucking company determined they could add trucks and expand their business. Over a short period of time they increased their fleet from four trucks to 20 trucks. While the business grew, so did the complexities of managing it. With 20 trucks on the road, the owners spent most of their time keeping track of the trucks and managing cash flow. They had no time for themselves and began arguing about finances. The situation was going from bad to worse when they decided to take a good, hard look at the numbers.

What they determined, much to their surprise, was that they could make the same amount of profit operating eight trucks as they were making operating 20 trucks!

By eliminating 12 trucks, they were able to make the same profit — at much reduced stress levels.

The point: Growth for the sake of growth is not necessarily what's best for your company — or for you.

Here are some other considerations: Your business plan is an indispensable document; refer to it often, as it contains nuggets of information that can help you decide the direction of your company. All too often, this document ends up filed away and corporate decisions are made that do not reflect the best interests of the firm. In other words, companies lose track of their main objectives and grow in directions they cannot support or afford.

Or it may well be that the products your company produces can best be sold through direct mail, advertising, or some other method that does not involve hiring a salesperson. (Think about, for example, the many products that are manufactured to be sold exclusively through infomercials.)

## DETERMINE YOUR SITUATION

Perform a thorough assessment of your company, listing total assets, expenses, obligations, product line and margins, position in the marketplace, strengths and weaknesses, prospects for future growth, current profit level, and any other measures that will help you make an informed decision. In other words, make sure you don't buy more trucks than you need to get the job done!

Here's another situation: Let's say you are the sole owner/employee of your business. After 20 years of producing and selling your product(s), you'd like to slow down and have someone else take care of maintaining existing accounts and calling on new accounts.

Again, do the financials based on the guidance found in this book. Remember, you'll have to produce and sell more to cover the additional expense of hiring someone. If your financial analysis shows that you will have to produce more than you are comfortably able to produce, you might want to consider other options, such as accepting reduced income in exchange for more free time. (Small graphic design, advertising, and corporate communications firms are just some of the types of companies this could apply to.)

What you want to avoid is working harder (and taking on more risk) to produce the same, or even reduced, profit.

The key is to know what you are getting into before investing any time and money in what could be a losing proposition.

If your financial analysis supports a decision to hire sales representation, you'll need to acquaint yourself with typical job duties of sales representatives, as well as the pros and cons of independent manufacturers' representatives. If you decide to hire a direct salesperson, you'll want to study the principal objectives of a salesperson's compensation plan at the end of this chapter.

## TYPICAL JOB DUTIES: SALES REPRESENTATIVE

One of the most important documents and links in clear communications in a sales organization is the position description. It is essential to successful sales operations and provides a clear understanding of what the employer wants the employee to do. The nature of the job, the knowledge deemed essential, and the exact duties and responsibilities should be written out carefully and serve as a basis for the sales personnel program. The program should be, in fact, a blueprint for not only building, but also for activating salespeople and all other personnel in the sales department.

Following are typical generic position descriptions for salespeople. These position descriptions may serve as a "jumping off" place when writing your own sales job description. Feel free to "mix and match" criteria to suit your own organization.

One idea: Highlight the items of critical importance to your company, keeping the final job description as simple as possible. Focus on the "must perform" responsibilities to keep your objectives firmly in front of you. Emphasizing too many responsibilities results in nothing being done well.

Since responsibilities and duties can change frequently, position descriptions should be reviewed annually for updating. (For actual company job descriptions, see page 69.)

## TYPICAL SALES POSITION DESCRIPTIONS
## TITLE: SALES REPRESENTATIVE
## PRIMARY RESPONSIBILITIES

Responsible for soliciting orders, selling the company's products, and representing the company in accordance with its policies and in the area assigned; for maintaining an awareness of local competitive conditions, and for reporting them back promptly to management.

### DUTIES

1. To maintain and increase the sales volume of assigned accounts or territories.
2. To aggressively solicit orders from present and prospective customers for the products assigned.

3. To provide useful and practical service to customers.
4. To aggressively seek new customers.
5. To seek new uses and applications for company products with present and prospective customers.
6. To assist present and prospective customers in adapting company products to their own requirements and specifications.
7. To aggressively carry out merchandising programs as directed.
8. To authorize "return" goods in accordance with company policy.
9. To resolve customer complaints in accordance with company policy, and to advise management promptly of any situations beyond his or her scope of authority.
10. To comply with all company policies, instructions, and directives for the fulfillment of company objectives and for maximum profitable sales.
11. To be alert to competitive products and merchandising practices, and to keep management informed concerning them.
12. To prepare sales audits and analyses of present and prospective customers in accordance with company procedures and instructions.
13. To assist in developing sales forecasts, territory potentials, workload analyses, call programs, and routes.
14. To maintain up-to-date customer record books and other records in accordance with company instructions.
15. To prepare and submit call and expense reports as required.
16. To submit any special reports regarding the operation of the territory, acceptance of products, or competitive conditions as may be requested.
17. To recommend the addition of new products to the line and the modification or deletion of present products from the line as appropriate.
18. To attend and participate in sales meetings, training programs, conventions, and trade shows as directed.
19. To maintain an awareness of likely candidates for the sales force and to call any such candidates to the attention of the branch manager.
20. To assist in the field training of any salesperson as requested.
21. To cooperate with all personnel in the branch, department, division, and other divisions on the execution of company programs.

## CUSTOMER-RELATED RESPONSIBILITIES

1. Analyzes customer's needs and formulates solutions by utilizing all resources made available by the company.
2. Offers service and looks for ways to help the customer do a better job.
3. Provides information to customers on new and current products, back orders, general order status, current pricing structure, and company policy changes, and anticipates customers' future needs.
4. Achieves prompt, mutually satisfactory solutions to customer complaints.
5. Keeps promises and appointments. Exercises courtesy at all times.
6. Takes active part in customer sales meetings and trade shows.

## KNOWLEDGE, TRAINING, AND EXPERIENCE RECOMMENDED

1. Minimum five years' field sales experience, or three years if related field.
2. Minimum two years' college.

## TITLE: SALES REPRESENTATIVE
## PRIMARY RESPONSIBILITIES

The sales representative is the company's primary contact with accounts and prospects in a geographic sales territory. He or she is primarily responsible for promoting the sale of the division's consumer products through established customers in accordance with approved sales policies and programs. He or she initiates and maintains the continuing sales relationships with approved accounts, calling on them in a regular and consistent manner.

He or she is also responsible for achieving in his or her territory the sales and marketing objectives for all consumer product lines.

### DUTIES

1. Contact all approved accounts and prospects in an established territory, or enumerated in a specific assignment, on a regular and clearly defined basis.
2. Sell and service existing accounts for all products in accordance with the company's established sales policies.
3. Develop accurate knowledge of the buying and selling methods and practices of each account in the territory in order to tailor individual sales approaches for each account.
4. Develop accurate knowledge and maintain appropriate records of competitive sales activity within the territory and with each account that would affect the division's sales efforts and policies.
5. Identify and approach each qualified prospective account in the territory to determine whether or not it would be a satisfactory outlet for the division's products.
6. Encourage wholesale and retail accounts to advertise and promote the division's products to increase the effectiveness of the company's advertising program at the local level. Work with account ad managers, sales promotion personnel, and merchandisers in setting up ads and promotions to take full advantage of the company ad allowances, seasonal specials, etc.
7. Assist each active account in the maintenance of optimum inventory levels of the division's products and the establishment of ordering points and order quantities that fit each account.
8. Take part in customer sales meetings, whenever possible and advisable, to increase the knowledge of sales personnel and to promote the display and sale of products.
9. Handle the quality problems that arise in the field with each distributor and retail chain in a manner that is fair and equitable to both the customer and the company.
10. Service selected retail accounts on a regular basis as directed by the regional manager, even though buying is handled in another territory.
11. Identify incentive merchandising prospects and develop into active accounts, calling upon the premium sales manager for assistance where necessary.
12. Maintain appropriate territorial records as required by sales management and submit required reports regarding conditions in the territory on a regular basis.
13. Take part in distributor trade shows where such attendance can result in further penetration of the market by the division.
14. Represent the company at national or regional trade shows as required and directed by the regional manager.

## MANUFACTURERS' REPRESENTATIVES

While we touched briefly on manufacturers' agents in our Q&A section (page xv), the following covers this topic in greater detail. It may well be that hiring a direct sales-person is not the answer for your company, or only part of the answer — your financial analysis will help you here. As noted in the data section of this book, approximately 25 percent of companies with under $5 million in annual sales participating in our survey use manufacturers' reps solely or to augment the efforts of the company's direct sales force. In some industries (food products, furniture and fixtures, machinery, and primary metal products), 100 percent of survey respondents say they use manufacturers' agents. (See Figure 107 for survey data.)

Here are some things to consider:

Sales agents are important as a marketing channel for manufacturers in a variety of businesses requiring specialized attention, as in the case of technical products, food products, engineering component systems, or institutional applications.

In some lines of business, manufacturers depend on independent agents as their main channel of distribution. In other industries, small companies have not reached the stage of developing their own sales organizations, and they also operate through manufacturers' agents.

Usually a new company just starting in business employs agents as the quickest and most economical way to establish itself on a nationwide basis. Still other companies produce low-cost items, the total volume of which would not support the cost of field representatives. In these cases, manufacturers' sales agents can make definite and valuable contributions to the solution of the sales problems of their principals.

To determine whether using manufacturers' agents is a viable alternative, consider:
- How can agents help achieve the company's sales and marketing goals?
- To what extent does management wish to control the sales force?
- Can the firm offer agents sufficient support and technical training?
- How quickly must the market be penetrated?

When a decision is made to hire agents, gather information by interviewing candidate agencies. Determine how long the agency has been in business; the owner's background and expertise; the experience, responsibilities, and number of employees; the compatibility of the agent's other product lines; and the number of manufacturers the agency represents. Also consider the agency's gross sales; participation in trade shows; and methods of compensation.

According to the Manufacturers' Agents National Association (MANA), Laguna Hills, California, there are a number of pros and cons to be aware of when considering manufacturers' agents.

## BENEFITS OF AGENCY SELLING

Agency sales are attractive because they:
1. **Provide predictable sales costs.** The manufacturer and agent agree in advance on a set commission. Through good times and bad, it remains the same for the life of the agreement; with the direct sales method, costs may go sky-high just when sales are floundering. Knowing the costs of sales up front — a percentage of the unit price — obviously eliminates many planning and pricing headaches.
2. **Lower sales costs.** Current Dartnell research suggests that the average direct sales-person costs his or her company $60,000 to $70,000 per year. To average total cash

compensation of $50,000, add average field expenses of $12,000 and average benefit cost of $4,000. (See Figure 1, Dartnell Profile: The American Sales Professional in Companies with Under $5 Million in Annual Sales — National Averages.) Many newly formed manufacturers, with a minimum of financial resources and little or no market penetration, have relied on the agent for market coverage.

3. **Reduce administrative overhead.** Internal costs of administering the sales payroll and furnishing various backup services for direct salespeople are reduced when the switch is made to a sales agency — and, of course, costs of administrative personnel will continue to rise.

4. **Eliminate the costs of training and turnover in sales personnel.** The training period for the agent will be minimal and largely related to learning about your product. Whenever you hire a new direct salesperson, you can estimate that he or she will miss thousands of dollars in sales that an established agent would have brought in. There is no way to recover these sales once they are lost. In addition, the manufacturer must pay the salesperson a salary plus expenses long before that individual is able to produce.

5. **Give immediate access to the market.** With the agent, manufacturers have an experienced salesperson in the territory immediately. He or she will be very familiar with the area and have a number of good prospects ready to consider the new line. Also, in the sales agent, the new manufacturer finds immediate geographical sales coverage. By employing an agent, the manufacturer can concentrate on production and product-line expansion, rather than incurring financial risk and expenses associated with establishing a company sales office.

6. **Provide a highly experienced sales force.** Studies show that today's agents are highly educated and trained and often have several years of experience as sales managers or senior salespersons that predates their establishment of or working for agencies. The agent has no base salary to rely on and can't afford to slack off at any time; the agent must sell to live and must make sales time count.

7. **Provide sales forecasting equal or superior to that of a direct sales force.** The volume of future sales is no less predictable with agents than with direct salespeople; in fact, it may be better, since so many of today's agents use sales analysis and forecasting methods that are often more sophisticated than those of the manufacturers they represent.

8. **Provide a broader sales context for your product.** Because he or she sells several related items (none of them competitive with yours, of course), the agent calls on a wider variety of prospects and customers and in so doing, he or she often finds applications for products denied the single-line salesperson.

9. **Add marketing flexibility at less cost.** Sales agents can increase your volume by selling outside your present marketing territory — and you'll pay them only when they produce, by commission. Agents can also sell a new line without conflicting with your present sales organizations. There are numerous ways that manufacturers' agents can fit into your marketing picture. Many companies use both direct salespeople and agents and find that the two sales forces are completely compatible.

10. **Increase sales.** Many manufacturers have switched from direct salespeople to agents and enjoyed increased sales. Selling through agencies is not for every manufacturer. But it may well be the method — used in whole or in part — to give your company the cost effectiveness and added sales impetus it needs.

## DISADVANTAGES OF THE AGENT

Some of the major disadvantages of selling through agents or agencies are as follows:
1. Lack of control, often considered to be the most limiting factor.
2. Lack of a full-time effort.
3. Limited direct factory contact with customers.
4. Reluctance of some agencies to provide service beyond selling. Service start-up and other services are frequently needed and must be supplied by the factory.

Manufacturers' agents usually think in terms of immediate sales. Many have little interest in building for the future, particularly if the company is likely to take its account away from them at some time in the future. They sell hardest those items that are easy for them to sell and on which they will obtain the greatest and quickest return.

A company buying their services may find its products offered as a secondary item or as an afterthought, the agent concentrating on his primary account. The agent is likely to ask himself or herself: "Why should I cut the selling time on my good accounts to promote a new one, particularly since my net sales commissions would remain exactly the same?"

For example, suppose the agent spends 75 percent of his time on Company A's product and 25 percent on Company B's, and his or her income is $100,000 a year. Now Company B urges him to spend half the time on its product. If the agent does so, and sales of B products rise while sales of A products fall, and income remains at $100,000, there is no incentive for the agent to change work patterns and habits.

Since the main worry of some agents is that a company will take away its account and put in its own salesperson, they may try to guard against this by deliberately holding down their sales, so as not to build too attractive a "plum" for the company. Other agents are very secretive about their accounts and discourage management visits to their areas. They refuse to furnish mailing lists, insist that all customer dealings go through them, and make use of every possible means to protect "their" accounts.

Because agents are independent operators, and therefore individualists in the first place, they are often slow to enter wholeheartedly into company programs. They frequently believe they know a better way or feel that "the program is a waste of my time." Customer audits, scheduled routes, daily reports, and campaign programs are difficult to install unless such activities are clearly provided for in the agency agreement.

If your financial analysis suggests you hire a direct salesperson, you'll want to read through the following principal objectives of a salesperson's compensation plan.

## WHAT TO LOOK FOR IN A MANUFACTURERS' REP

In some areas in which sales volume doesn't justify a company salesperson, a rep may, in some instances, be the only means of distributing the product.

### WHAT TO LOOK FOR IN A REP

Treat a candidate rep the same way you would treat a prospective employee. Look at the individual's past performance and check references. Many manufacturers say that "word of mouth" is one of the best approaches. Get recommendations from the salespeople of other noncompeting companies. Ask your own customers for their views. Above all, don't be hasty in the selection of your rep — he or she will be representing you, your product, and your company.

And remember, there's no sure-fire way to select the best rep for you. Look for the same characteristics in a rep as you would look for in a company salesperson. Look for someone who will to be thorough. You need someone who has the ability to move into a saturated area and get the job done.

## PRINCIPAL OBJECTIVES OF A SALESPERSON'S COMPENSATION PLAN

1. To be consistent with marketing objectives.
2. To increase sales.
3. To increase gross profit.
4. To have sales expenses decline as a percent of sales and gross profit dollars as sales volume increases.
5. To have Company salesperson's total compensation relatively consistent with competition's total compensation. (Use the survey data in Part 2 of this book to help you determine this.)
6. To minimize turnover of salespeople.
7. To alleviate seasonal influences on salesperson's income flow.
8. To alleviate cyclical influences on salesperson's income flow.
9. To maintain the relationship between the income of the salespeople and other Company personnel.
10. To provide equal treatment (not necessarily the same compensation levels) of all salespeople in various markets, territories, and/or branches.
11. To provide continuous motivation for salespeople to:
    (a) Maximize sales with existing accounts.
    (b) Maximize gross margin with existing accounts.
    (c) Open new accounts.
12. To make it easy for management to:
    (a) Understand the plan.
    (b) Hire salespeople.
    (c) Add and/or subtract products from the line.
    (d) Realign existing territories and create new ones.
    (e) Reassign accounts.
    (f) Control salespeople's cost in relation to sales and gross profit.
    (g) Control travel and entertainment expenses.
    (h) Calculate and administer compensation levels.
13. To make it easy for salespeople to:
    (a) Understand the plan.
    (b) Estimate incentive earnings per order, month, etc.
    (c) Maintain a continuing positive attitude toward increasing sales in their territories.
    (d) Maintain a continuing positive attitude toward increasing gross profit in their territories.
    (e) Maintain a continuing positive attitude toward the Company.
14. To maintain existing compensation levels at existing sales and gross profit levels.
15. To provide a mathematical formula for calculating incentive payments.
16. To have incentive payments include a commission.
17. To have incentive payments include a bonus.
18. To have salespeople sell a "balanced line."
19. To generally have the salespeople increase their market penetration in order to earn more money.

In a nutshell, you want your compensation plan to:
- Support your business plan.
- Achieve profit objectives.

- Motivate salespeople.
- Attract top performers.
- Retain top performers.

Is this too tall an order for most companies? Far from it, according to data from *Dartnell's 29th Survey of Sales Force Compensation 1996-1997*. We asked companies of all sizes how well their compensation plan supported these criteria. Here are the results:

## MOTIVATING SALESPEOPLE

| RESPONSES | PERCENT OF RESPONSES |
| --- | --- |
| VERY EFFECTIVE | 22.2% |
| EFFECTIVE | 47.9 |
| SOMEWHAT EFFECTIVE | 22.2 |
| NOT EFFECTIVE | 4.2 |
| NOT SURE | 1.4 |
| NO ANSWER | 2.1 |
| TOTAL | 100% |

## RETAINING TOP PERFORMERS

| RESPONSES | PERCENT OF RESPONSES |
| --- | --- |
| VERY EFFECTIVE | 31.9% |
| EFFECTIVE | 36.1 |
| SOMEWHAT EFFECTIVE | 22.9 |
| NOT EFFECTIVE | 6.3 |
| NOT SURE | 0.7 |
| NO ANSWER | 2.1 |
| TOTAL | 100% |

## ATTRACTING QUALIFIED SALESPEOPLE

| RESPONSES | PERCENT OF RESPONSES |
| --- | --- |
| VERY EFFECTIVE | 15.3% |
| EFFECTIVE | 35.4 |
| SOMEWHAT EFFECTIVE | 36.8 |
| NOT EFFECTIVE | 8.3 |
| NOT SURE | 0.7 |
| NO ANSWER | 3.5 |
| TOTAL | 100% |

## ATTAINING COMPANY GOALS

| RESPONSES | PERCENT OF RESPONSES |
| --- | --- |
| VERY EFFECTIVE | 20.8% |
| EFFECTIVE | 46.5 |
| SOMEWHAT EFFECTIVE | 25.0 |
| NOT EFFECTIVE | 4.9 |
| NOT SURE | 0.7 |
| NO ANSWER | 2.1 |
| TOTAL | 100% |

When you combine the totals for "very effective" and "effective," it is easy to see how well these companies are meeting the challenge of designing effective compensation plans.

With these principles understood, we're now ready to move on to the next section, Compensation Plan Basics.

# COMPENSATION PLAN BASICS

**Y**ears ago, I talked at length with a former sales manager who firmly believed that when it came to salespeople, money didn't motivate. What I think he meant to say was that money doesn't do the entire job of motivating salespeople.

Salespeople, perhaps more than individuals in any other profession, attach great importance to monetary rewards. This was borne out dramatically in a recent Dartnell study.

When we asked whether or not salespeople were satisfied with their earnings, we thought the results would be a simple matter to interpret. What emerged instead was a look at how salespeople feel about money, their careers, and themselves.

The survey question was straightforward: "Overall, are you satisfied with your earnings? Yes; No; Please explain." The final tabulations of nearly 1,000 responses revealed that 47.3 percent of responding salespeople are satisfied with their earnings while 52.7 percent say they are *dissatisfied* with earnings.

While it may at first appear that salespeople, as a group, feel they are underpaid, a look at individual responses provides a different picture that can be summarized as follows: Salespeople measure their success (and often their personal sense of well-being) by constantly increasing their earnings from one year to the next.

Consequently, to be satisfied with earnings is to become complacent. Many survey respondents say that while they are earning "top dollar," they cannot afford to be satisfied. As one salesperson put it: "If you're satisfied with your earnings, then you're very near retirement." This sentiment is typical and serves to summarize the feelings of many respondents.

Respondents make it very clear that money is a yardstick by which success, career growth, personal growth, and self-esteem are all measured. Even those reps at the lower end of the economic scale are willing to work hard *if* the potential for increased earnings is there. If your compensation plan does not now attach significance to the great importance salespeople (and sales managers) put on monetary rewards, you might want to consider this in your next compensation plan revision.

## TYPICAL SURVEY RESPONSES

Following are representative survey responses:
- "I am compensated well, but would prefer more incentives."
- "We always want more."
- "Want growth. Haven't reached the top of the mountain yet."
- "Satisfied for right now, yes, but overall I expect to be more valuable in the next two years."
- "Never have been satisfied, never will be."
- "I am very competitive and always trying to exceed my past earnings."
- "Satisfied, but each year I target a reasonable, but higher, plateau."
- "In sales you could always be making more money."
- "Come on! Is anyone ever really satisfied? More is always better."
- "I've only been involved in this area of selling for two years, but my earnings are increasing yearly. I'm satisfied, but want to keep growing."

- "I am comfortable, but I continually strive for more."
- "Once you're satisfied you lose the incentive to achieve what you're capable of achieving."
- "I guess the correct answer is no, I'm not satisfied. I always want more, but I'm pleased with present earnings."
- "Enough is never enough! Sell, sell, and sell more!"
- "To be satisfied would be to get complacent — I'm always looking to grow".
- "Never satisfied; do not want to grow stale."
- "When I become satisfied with my earnings I won't have goals."
- "To be strong at sales you should always want more."
- "No salesperson will ever be happy because we could always sell more."

These survey results — and these representative comments — should convince you that when it comes to designing compensation plans, you're moving into emotionally charged waters.

## A QUICK REVIEW

In the last chapter, we covered some of the principal objectives of a sales compensation plan. You might want to review that material before moving ahead.

Building on that discussion, all the various objectives of compensation plans can be reduced to five major categories:

1. *Income and Security.* A compensation plan won't work unless it provides an adequate income for acceptable work. The need for salespeople to feel financially secure and the desire among sales managers to provide minimum income figures represent part of the general trend toward companies using combination (salary plus incentive) plans.

2. *Incentives.* More and more companies are using incentives to compensate their salespeople. According to Dartnell survey results, nearly 64 percent of companies with under $5 million in annual sales use a combination plan to compensate their senior salespeople. (See Figure 6, page 121.) Certainly, a good compensation plan should encourage salespeople to expend their efforts along lines that are consistent with the best interests of the company. For the incentive to achieve desired results, it must be understandable to everyone affected by the plan.

3. *Flexibility.* A plan for compensating salespeople should be designed to work during periods of fluctuations in business conditions — at least during the ranges in sales *reasonably* to be expected. This may mean emphasizing the fixed salary element to making the incentive element relatively low. It is likely that no plan that has a high incentive element will work equally well in periods of good business and bad business unless the margin of fluctuations in the company's business is relatively narrow — or, of course, unless executives and salespeople are really prepared to accept wide fluctuations in earnings.

4. *Economy.* From the standpoint of cost, the compensation plan should increase sales efforts at costs that are competitive or better. Costs include (a) payments to salespeople, (b) travel and other expenses, and (c) the expense of operating the plan, which sometimes is substantial.

5. *Fairness.* The objective of the compensation plan should be fairness, not only in the eyes of the employer, but also from the viewpoint of the salespeople. The plan should, by its nature and its administration, contribute to building morale.

Now, to go from the general to the specific, one or two key strategic and tactical objectives might be selected from a list looking something like this:

1. To increase the company's return on investment
2. To increase sales volume:
    a. Across the board
    b. Primarily in certain profitable products (improved product mix)
3. To increase profits:
    a. As a dollar amount
    b. As a percentage of sales
4. To increase market share
5. To make the company more competitive in the marketplace.

These potential objectives are not mutually exclusive.

## TACTICAL OBJECTIVES

Given the key strategic objective, how can the plan assist in its attainment? To succeed, the compensation plan will need to do more of the following (although some may not be applicable in particular cases):

1. Motivate the sales force. This is a must.
2. Be competitive with compensation plans that may lure sales reps away.
3. Be fair to both the sales force and the company.
4. Reinforce successful sales habits or behavior patterns on the part of the sales force.
5. Provide for stability of sales.
6. Reduce or control the sales/expense ratio.
7. Be flexible with respect to the following:
    a. Apply to missionary territories as well as established territories.
    b. Provide for changes in territories.
    c. Provide for changes in the size or character of the sales force.
    d. Provide for changes in product emphasis.
    e. Be effective in recessions as well as boom times.
    f. Avoid the necessity of frequent changes.
8. Make it possible to recruit, train, and retain the desired type of salespeople. Building loyalty and morale, sometimes cited as a possible objective, is a subordinate objective in reducing turnover.

## OBJECTIVES INVOLVING BEHAVIORAL CHANGE

The compensation plan, if it is to achieve its key objective, must encourage the sales force to perform in an effective way. These desired work habits might include such activities as prospecting, running dealer or distributor meetings, doing promotional work, minimizing expenses, and so on. (See Figures 90–97 for further discussion of this point.)

The plan should ultimately reward the salesperson who does whichever of these tasks are applicable to the company:

1. Stresses the most profitable products.
2. Concentrates on the most profitable customers.
3. Does across-the-line selling.
4. Performs supporting or nonselling tasks such as promotion, missionary work, and customer service.
5. Cooperates with other salespeople, other levels of the sales force, and other company departments.

6. Keeps headquarters informed of his or her own activities and of market conditions.
7. Makes effective sales calls, using the best applicable professional techniques.
8. Allocates his or her time among large and small customers, among customers and prospects, among products, among selling and nonselling functions, in such a way as to maximize results.
9. Applies appropriate selling efforts during all seasons.

See page 29 for an in-depth discussion on the use of incentives.

## OBJECTIVES OF THE SALESPEOPLE

Finally, if the compensation plan is to motivate salespeople to do what the company wants, the plan should give salespeople as much as possible of what *they* want.

Here are some of the sales force objectives to keep in mind:
1. Potential after-tax incentive payments large enough to justify the extra effort.
2. Incentive payments reasonably frequent and prompt.
3. Where applicable, a good balance between security (base pay) and incentive.
4. Rewards based on individual performance, and only on factors under the salesperson's control.
5. Income that does not fluctuate greatly when the salesperson is performing consistently.
6. No ceiling on earnings under normal conditions.
7. Compensation commensurate with sales results.
8. Opportunity for advancement without financial loss.
9. Incentives based on clear measurements of accomplishment, without arbitrary factors.
10. Salesperson not unduly penalized by inaccuracies in establishing quotas.
11. Salesperson not unduly penalized by differences in potential of assigned territories or accounts.

## ELEMENTS OF THE PLAN

To achieve these objectives, a wide variety of component features or elements are available for incorporation in the plan. Some of these elements are designed to contribute to adequacy and security; others add to incentive flexibility. Some are designed to influence costs favorably; others contribute toward smooth administration. The more complex plans simply combine more single elements, or more variations of single elements, than do the simpler plans.

Here's a list of these elements:
A. Salary: monetary compensation at an agreed rate for definite time periods, usually paid at the end of each period. The salary may constitute the entire salesperson's compensation or a fixed portion of total compensation.
B. Commission: monetary compensation that is usually a percentage of sales or profit, but occasionally a fixed money payment per case, barrel, ton, or some other unit of product. The commission element in compensation must include a base, a rate or rates, and a starting point.
C. Special payments for sales operations: payments in the nature of piece rates on tasks rather than commissions on results. In this category fall flat payments per call or payments per new customer secured. To the extent that these payments are estimated by size of customers' purchases, they resemble commissions and

are sometimes called commissions. Other bases for special payments are demonstrations, putting up counter or window displays, special promotional work, and so on.

D. Bonus payments: usually lump-sum payments over and above contractual earnings, for extra effort or merit or for results beyond normal expectation. Bonuses that vary directly with sales or profit results, however, are really commissions.

E. Special prizes: monetary amounts or valuable merchandise to reward the winners of sales contests and other competitions. Practices vary from those firms that never use sales contests to those firms in which there is continuous use and nearly every salesperson expects to get some compensation from this source during the year.

F. Profit sharing: a share of the profits of the business as a whole, figured on the basis of earnings, retail sales, profits of an area, or other factors. Sometimes profit sharing is intended to build up a retirement fund.

G. Expense allowances: provision for travel and other business expenses, which becomes an important part of any compensation plan. No agreement for outside sales work is complete without an understanding as to whether the company or the salesperson is to pay the travel and other business expenses incurred by him or her in connection with his or her work, and, if the company is responsible, just what the arrangements should be. (See Figures 72–85 for data on what expenses companies with under $5 million in annual sales generally pay for.)

H. Benefits: pensions, group insurance, health insurance, and so on. More and more often these are given to salespeople as a matter of policy and become a definite part of the compensation plan. (See Figure 86 for a listing of benefits paid for by companies with under $5 million in annual sales.)

I. Administrative provisions: devices and procedures to ensure carrying out the chosen plan and provide for smooth operation. For instance:
   1. Special credits for particularly desired performance.
   2. Provision for splitting credits or commissions between two or more salespeople involved with a particular sale.
   3. Measurement of salespeople's performance and the keeping of records relating to compensation.
   4. Notification of salespeople as to earnings.
   5. Installation procedures for new plans or changes in established plans.
   6. Procedures and policies for the revision of salary, commissions, bonuses, or other elements.
   7. Dates and frequency of payments made to salespeople, together with special provisions necessitated by particular plans.

## Implementing the Objectives

Obviously, the value of a specific element or combination of elements depends on the objectives sought. First you need to have a clear idea of the tasks you want to compensate salespeople for; otherwise you'll likely find your salespeople resisting or failing to perform satisfactorily those tasks that are not well rewarded by the plan. Next the problem is to determine what particular features will help you attain your particular objectives.

Here's something to keep in mind: The effect that certain features will have is never clear-cut. Combined with other features, they are bound to overlap in their influence on the salesperson. *The net result is that almost every plan is a compromise.* You must weigh the advantages and disadvantages of each of the elements in an effort to find the particular combination that seems on balance to be best suited for your purposes.

Now, let's go on to the next step and look at the basic pay plans available and the advantages and disadvantages of each.

## THE THREE BASIC COMPENSATION PLANS

There are three basic compensation plans: salary, commission, and combination (salary plus incentive) plans.

### SALARY PLAN

This kind of plan, in which salespeople are paid fixed rates of compensation, may also include occasional additional compensation in the form of discretionary bonuses, sales contest prizes, or other short-term incentives. The plan works well when your main objective is "account servicing." Secondary objectives of increasing sales from existing accounts and opening new accounts require special incentive treatment.

The salary plan is appropriate where it is difficult to evaluate who really makes the sale, where a salesperson's contribution cannot be accurately separated from the efforts of others in the company such as inside personnel and technical service people. Sales of technical products commonly involve this form of team selling. When management finds it difficult to develop adequate measures of performance against which an equitable bonus or commission can be paid, a salary plan is generally used.

The position description for a sales engineer on salary with an industrial equipment manufacturer illustrates the difficulty of measuring sales performance for incentive reward. The field engineer calls on distributors. Duties include the following:

- Developing and executing sales and product training programs for the distributor's sales forces.
- Doing missionary work with selected manufacturers and major oil companies to encourage them to recommend his or her products to their dealers and mention them in their service and installation manuals.
- Participating in national and local trade shows; conducting occasional training programs for trade groups and associations.
- Suggesting ideas for new products and promotional programs; recommending changes or improvements in existing products.

Many durable goods industries experience cyclical sales patterns, which make a salary plan more compatible with the salesperson's efforts and avoid the sharp swings in income that can occur in a commission plan.

After close examination of the salary plans of many companies, the following basic advantages and disadvantages of the salary plan approach have come to light.

The salary plan has advantages for both salespeople and their companies because it:
- Assures a regular income.
- Develops a high degree of loyalty.
- Makes it simple to switch territories or quotas or to reassign salespeople.
- Ensures that nonselling activities will be performed.
- Facilitates administration.
- Provides relatively fixed sales costs.

However, the salary plan has its disadvantages, in that it:
- Fails to generate a balanced sales mix because salespeople concentrate on products with greatest customer appeal.
- Provides little, if any, financial incentive for the salesperson.
- Offers few reasons for putting forth extra effort.
- Favors salespeople who are the least productive.
- Tends to increase direct selling costs over other types of plans.
- Creates the possibility of salary compression where new trainees may earn almost as much as experienced salespeople.

The two lists do not necessarily cancel each other out. Every compensation plan is a compromise. Determination of marketing and sales objectives, which will in turn determine the role of the sales force, will help you decide whether the salary plan is best for achieving your goals. Most companies with under $5 million in annual sales do not use this plan. In our current survey, just 10 percent of responding companies say they use a salary-only plan. (See Figure 6.)

## COMMISSION PLAN

In this type of plan, salespeople are paid in direct proportion to their sales. The plan works well at the start of a new business, when the market possibilities are very broad and highly fragmented. In such situations, territory boundaries are usually rather fluid and difficult to define. Therefore, quota and customer assignments are difficult to determine, making other types of compensation plans too costly or too complex to administer.

When management wants to maximize incentive, regardless of compensation levels in other company functions, or prefers a predictable sales cost in direct relationship with sales volume, the commission plan is appropriate. However, use of the straight commission approach has declined in popularity over the past several years. Just 26 percent of companies with under $5 million in annual sales responding to our survey say they use this plan. (See Figure 6.)

Following are the advantages of the straight commission plan:
- Pay relates directly to performance and results achieved.
- System is easy to understand and compute.
- Salespeople have the greatest possible incentive.
- Unit sales costs are proportional to net sales.
- Company's selling investment is reduced.

The disadvantages of this plan are as follows:
- Emphasis is more likely to be on volume than on profits.
- Little or no loyalty to the company is generated.
- Wide variances in income between salespeople may occur.
- Salespeople are encouraged to neglect nonselling duties.
- Some salespeople may be tempted to "skim" their territories.
- Service aspect of selling may be slighted.
- Problems arise in cutting territories or shifting people or accounts.
- Pay is often excessive in boom times and very low in recession periods.
- Salespeople may sell themselves rather than the company and stress short-term rather than long-term relationships.
- Highly paid salespeople may be reluctant to move into supervisory or managerial positions.
- Excessive turnover of sales personnel occurs when business turns bad.

If a commission plan is used, the disadvantages must be offset. To accomplish this, some elements of guarantee must be added to the compensation package, especially for new salespeople. These can include guaranteeing a monthly minimum income, generous draws, and starting new people on a salary-plus-commission plan until commissions reach a desired level. The effect of possible personal economic fluctuations should be balanced by strong, security-oriented fringe benefit packages including medical and dental insurance, pensions, and educational assistance. These stabilizing elements should help in recruiting and keeping personnel.

### COMBINATION PLAN

This type of plan includes all variations of salary plus other monetary incentive plans. The variations include base salary plus commission on all sales, salary plus bonus on sales over quota, salary plus commission plus bonus, and so on.

There are many good reasons for installing a salary-plus-incentive plan. It provides more incentive than a salary plan and provides better control of the incentive or variable income than is possible with the commission plan. Also, the much greater degree of flexibility with a wide variation in incentives to work with allows you to develop practically tailor-made plans for each salesperson.

But these plans have liabilities, too. Salary-plus-incentive plans tend to be more complex than the other two methods. Thus, they involve more paperwork, control, and administrative work. They need more frequent revision because of the interaction of the elements that comprise the total plan.

The most important determination in building a sound salary-plus-incentive plan is the split between the fixed portion (salary) and the variable portion (incentive). The split is usually determined on the basis of historical sales performance and compensation records. Competitive analysis of other company programs, the base salary needed to keep good people, and an estimate of incentive potential should also be considered.

The average percentage split reported in our Dartnell study among companies with under $5 million in annual sales was 54 percent base salary and 46 percent incentive. (See Figure 8.) The "best" salary/compensation split continues to be a matter of hot debate, however. In a recent Dartnell study, we asked sales managers from all sizes of companies what they thought the split should be. Here are the results of that study:

**QUESTION: WHAT PROPORTION OF BASE SALARY AND INCENTIVE PAY DO YOU BELIEVE WORKS BEST (FOR EXAMPLE, 60 PERCENT BASE/40 PERCENT INCENTIVE; 70 PERCENT BASE/30 PERCENT INCENTIVE, ETC.)?**

| RESPONSES | PERCENT OF RESPONSES |
|---|---|
| 60/40 | 19.5% |
| 70/30 | 16.2 |
| 0/100 | 14.0 |
| 80/20 | 9.1 |
| 40/60 | 7.0 |
| 30/70 | 7.0 |
| 50/50 | 5.6 |
| VARIES | 4.2 |
| 100/0 | 3.5 |
| 20/80 | 2.8 |
| 75/25 | 2.8 |
| 90/10 | 2.1 |
| 65/35 | 1.4 |
| 25/75 | 1.4 |
| 45/55 | .7 |
| 85/15 | .7 |
| 35/65 | .7 |
| 67/33 | .7 |
| UNSURE | .6 |
| TOTAL | 100% |

The following selected responses shed additional light on this often hotly debated issue:

- "40/60. Higher incentive gives sales force more opportunity for income advancement."
- "40/60. Good producers make more. Others strive to grow or replace themselves."
- "Varies. Depends where in career employee is."
- "80/20. In the trucking industry, there are many variables that can impact the numbers, both positive and negative."
- "70/30. Need to cover base with minimal compensation to attract good personnel and keep turnover low."
- "80/20. You must respect your sales force first with a decent salary package. Incentives are just icing on the cake, acknowledging their competence."
- "70/30. Incentive...sell more, make more."
- "90/10. We sell continued support to existing customers."
- "20/80. Nature of this business."
- "30/70 to 50/50. Salespeople need to have a large account."
- "65/35. Experience."
- "30/70. 30 percent pays the basic bills to keep a roof over a salesperson's head, and the 70 percent is an individual opportunity to excel."
- "25 percent base, 75 percent incentive or commission. If they are not producing, what's the reason to pay them?"
- "100 percent base with bonus on profit and growth. Again, consistency can impact account retention, and that is key in our business. Also, not all ace producers are income driven (highs and lows)."
- "90/10. We should move to 80/20 or 70/30. Our base is very strong and enables us to make long-term decisions."
- "100 percent commissions. Self-motivated people will profit."
- "75/25. Salespeople need motivation from outside sources — not many are very self-motivated."

- "40/60. Ability to move much higher in personal income."
- "70/30. Too much incentive and there is a loss of non-financial focus like service."
- "60/40. We have need for bringing in new customers as well as retaining old ones, and we need high commission incentive."
- "50/50. It covers the essentials; the rest is up to the sales generated."
- "70/30. Compensating for incentives can develop the wrong behaviors."
- "80/20. This provides a solid base which sustains the force, even during slow business periods."
- "60/40. Opportunity to materially affect income through performance."
- "75/25. Good professional salespeople like to be rewarded fairly. Proper sales planning helps them grow their base."
- "30/70. More incentive to sell."
- "100 percent base. Fired if you don't perform. Focus on customer vs. self."
- "80 base/30 incentive. Our sales process is more relationship selling, and the larger base allows for security while still giving the individual incentive to grow his business."
- "67 base/33 incentive. Rewards for focusing on strategic issues."
- "30 base/70 incentive. Don't let them get too complacent."
- "Unsure...Sales force is primarily salaried."
- "Our people are independent. Paid on all bonuses."
- "60 salary/40 bonus. Need to give security and push to perform."
- "100 percent incentive. Company exercises little control over activities."
- "Base plus 50 percent potential."
- "50/50. The ability to make more money makes some excited."
- "70 base/30 incentive. Base takes care of needs. May be enough there to make the rep not have to worry about those areas."

Structuring the salary portion of the plan requires establishing salary grades for the sales force. The three grades used in the Dartnell study are entry level salesperson, intermediate (one to three years of sales experience), and senior salesperson (more than three years of sales experience). Each salary grade should be supported by a job description and each salesperson assigned according to experience and ability.

In the incentive portion of the combination plan, three basic forms of reward can be considered: a commission, a bonus, and a commission plus bonus.

*Commission* incentives are the most popular. Companies pay by one or more of these typical methods:

1. A fixed commission on all sales.
2. At different rates by product category.
3. On sales above a determined goal.
4. On product gross margin.

The rationale of paying commissions on gross margin dollars is the assumption that such an arrangement will motivate salespeople to improve both product and customer mix and therefore to improve territory gross margin.

A good example of a sound compensation plan incorporating the elements of base salary and incentive pay of a percentage of gross profit and gross sales generated in a territory is one set up by the sales executive of an electrical component manufacturer.

In his plan, a base salary level is determined on a discretionary basis. Gross profit is defined as the difference between the selling price of an item and the cost of purchasing the goods, freight to transport, and labor and/or materials that must be added to make the goods salable as represented to the buyer, and other costs directly related to the transaction. Gross sales are those of new and/or used equipment invoiced to a buyer within a period of a calendar month.

Each territory has a minimum requirement for gross profits and gross sales. The following three-step formula is applied. (Data in this example have been simplified to better illustrate the principles involved.)

**Step 1:  Sales volume up to $18,000 a month.**
Base salary plus 7 percent of gross profits plus 1/2 percent of gross sales.

**Step 2:  Sales volume from $18,000 to $25,000 a month.**
Base salary plus 9 percent of gross profits plus 1/2 percent of gross sales.

**Step 3:  Sales volume over $25,000 a month.**
Base salary plus 10 percent of gross profits plus 1/2 percent of gross sales.

Base salary is paid every two weeks. The earned percentage of gross profits and gross sales is paid monthly.

One great advantage of an incentive based on commission is the frequency and regularity of the reward, usually monthly. Salespeople are more quickly motivated to keep or exceed performance levels with the rapid tie-in between performance and reward.

*Bonus* incentives are usually paid as a percentage of salary and vary by goal performance levels. Bonuses are paid on a variety of sales results, but gross margin goals are used most frequently. Other factors used as a measure for bonus goals are market share, product mix, new accounts, nonsales activities, higher unit sales, and increased sales from existing accounts. Some companies simply make bonus payments on a discretionary basis.

Goals may be based on an analysis of the potential of the territory and expected performance against the potential. They may be developed from a moving average of historical sales or gross margin for two or three years plus a one-year forecast averaged into the moving base.

Bonus payments should be structured to begin at the 70 percent- to 75 percent-of-goal level to motivate salespeople to achieve goals. A lower threshold level works against sustained sales effort. Conversely, by not receiving bonuses until sales effort of 100 percent goal is achieved, many people become discouraged along the way. While payment rates may be uniform both under and over the 100 percent goal, increasing the rate beyond the 100 percent mark adds an additional incentive with a lower cost factor.

Because bonus incentives are usually paid quarterly, it is not recommended that the full amount be paid when due. Withholding a small percentage due each quarter until the end of the year avoids a possible overpayment for the total year bonus. A proper adjustment is made with the final quarter payment.

A bonus incentive plan is more difficult to establish and administer than a commission incentive. Also, rewards paid on a quarterly basis are not as effective motivators as weekly or monthly commission payments.

Another variation of the combination plan is one that pays *salary, commission,* and *bonus*. While this approach offers more flexibility than the other two types, it is more complex and more difficult to administer than any other plan.

Here are the elements of a good salary, commission, and bonus plan used by a fabricated metal products company:

1. Base salary, company car, and all business expenses.
2. A 5 percent commission, based annually and paid quarterly, on all sales volume over predetermined sales base.

3. A bonus on attainment of quota. Annual quota is divided in two parts: first six calendar months and last six calendar months. If quota is attained for the first half, bonus of 1 percent of all sales during that period is paid in July. This is repeated for the second half, with bonus paid in January.
4. If quotas for both halves of the calendar year are attained, an additional bonus of 1/2 percent of all sales for the year is paid. Thus, a total of 1 1/2 percent of annual sales is paid as a bonus.
5. If quota for either of the six month periods is not achieved but annual quota is achieved, 1/2 percent for the year is paid but not the 1 percent for period in which quota is not achieved.
6. "House" or "divisional manager" accounts are excluded from quota, commission, and bonus calculations.

Advantages of the combination plan:
- Offers participants the advantages of both salary and commission.
- Provides greater range of earnings possibilities.
- Gives salespeople greater security because of steady base income.
- Makes possible a favorable ratio of selling expense to sales.
- Compensates salespeople for all activities.
- Allows a greater latitude of motivation possibilities so that goals and objectives can be achieved on schedule.

Disadvantages of the plan:
- Is often complex and difficult to understand.
- Can, where low salary and high bonus or commission exist, develop a bonus that is too high a percentage of earnings; when sales fall, salary is too low to retain salespeople.
- Is sometimes costly to administer.
- Can, unless a decreasing commission rate for increasing sales volume exists, result in a "windfall" of new accounts and a runaway of earnings.
- Has a tendency to offer too many objectives at one time so that really important goals can be neglected, forgotten, or overlooked.

Other policies besides direct compensation have an impact on both the salesperson's total pay package and the company's financial position. These are sales expenses and extra incentive plans.

## EXPENSE PRACTICES

The need for keeping a tight rein on sales-generated expenses, which have a direct effect on profits, is always important. With the cost of sales calls constantly rising and with increased field expenses, companies must periodically examine their expense policies and procedures and make adjustments in order to draw that ideal fine line at which expenses are kept under proper control and reimbursement to salespeople is fair and reasonable. (See page 65 for a discussion of the average cost of a sales call and how you can determine your own sales call costs.)

## ADDITIONAL INCENTIVES

No matter how well a compensation plan is formulated and executed, another dimension is necessary to achieve best results. These are the incentives that make a salesperson work harder all around. Let's consider the unique aspects of the salesperson's job: limited personal contact with his or her manager; extended periods of travel that brings loneliness and inconvenience; decisions that require a high level of motivation (when to make the first call of the day, how many calls to make, objectives to be achieved on each call, when to quit for the day); and emotional swings between the elation of obtaining a large order and the frequent frustrations of orders lost to competitors and missed shipping dates.

Motivation calls for creating a climate in which the salesperson can motivate himself or herself with the incentives provided by management. These incentives can be financial, nonfinancial, or a combination of the two.

## FINANCIAL INCENTIVES

Short-term sales competitions are popular. Costs are predictable, results are usually successful, and rewards are immediate. Competitions usually run for one or two months, but some as short as a week can produce results. The awards that are most favored are money, trips, merchandise, and personal recognition.

A successful sales contest should include these basic elements: well-defined objectives, simple rules, short duration, goals attainable by most salespeople, inclusion of spouse and families when possible, and a follow-through program to sustain enthusiasm.

Contests are like a double-edged sword. Improperly used or used for the wrong reasons, they can create dissension and dissatisfaction within the ranks. Properly used, these contests can create a competitive atmosphere that will stimulate sales and provide additional rewards.

In addition to the usual objectives of increased sales volume, more sales calls, new accounts, and so forth, contests can serve to build off-season business, stimulate various dealer tie-ins, revive dead accounts, and reduce costs.

## NONFINANCIAL INCENTIVES

Techniques that principally provide salespeople recognition, status, and a sense of group belonging are generally referred to as "psychic income."

Over the years, as the role of the salesperson has been redefined and enlarged, many companies have conferred more meaningful titles on members of their sales forces to improve their status with customers, to give them personal status symbols, and to more aptly describe their functions. Companies commonly use such titles as regional, area, or zone manager, field sales engineer, account executive, and staff associate.

Other productive ways to recognize individual good performance or encourage effectiveness are awards, honorary job titles, publicity, personal letters or telephone calls of commendation, face-to-face encouragement, and individual help with responsibilities.

## BENEFITS

The cost of maintaining medical, accident, life, and dental insurance programs on a personal basis is significant, so benefits constitute an important part of the "total income" of every company employee, including the sales force.

Adding up the costs of personal use of the company or leased car, memberships, and educational expense assistance that many companies provide, a basic benefit package would cost a salesperson a minimum of $5,000 a year, and that's no doubt a conservative figure.

## SUMMARY

Combination plans dominate the compensation package makeup despite the complexity of administration and control. The disadvantages are far overshadowed by the flexibility in providing meaningful incentive pay tied more directly to sales performance — that is, applying commission and bonus to single and/or multiple sales goals. In addition, a combination plan provides the salesperson with a greater range of earnings possibilities based on a steady base income.

In Dartnell studies over recent years, the subject of "profitability of sales" keeps coming up. While sales executives should never lose sight of their primary objectives — to increase sales — top management pressure for profitable sales increases. It demands new rules and definitions of the cost of doing business in a given sales territory.

The trend toward obtaining profitable sales, as opposed to sheer sales volume, could increase the prevalence of defining a sales territory as a profit center with the salesperson as the sales and profit producer in the territory. The overall effect would be to increase the influence of a profit factor in the salesperson's compensation package.

(See Figure 98 for data on how the profitability of the sale is working its way into compensation planning and design.)

Throughout this book we have emphasized that there is a certain portion of every sales dollar available to compensating a salesperson for making a sale. This compensation can take the form of salary, commission, expenses, benefits, and so on. Hal Fahner has kindly allowed us to reprint his comprehensive article on compensation plan design. It follows below. (Figures have been simplified to illustrate the concepts involved.)

## DEVELOPING A SALES COMPENSATION PLAN BY WORKING BACKWARD
### BY HAL FAHNER
### VICE PRESIDENT OF CORPORATE MARKETING
### BLUE CROSS & BLUE SHIELD OF FLORIDA, INC.

### XYZ COMPANY

| | |
|---|---|
| NET SALES | $3,400,000 |
| COST OF GOODS SOLD SELLING, ADMINISTRATIVE, AND GENERAL EXPENSE (EXCEPT SALES FORCE SALARY AND COMMISSION) | $454,400 |
| | $681,600 |
| COMPANY GOAL IS 15 1/2 PERCENT NET PROFIT BEFORE TAXES (THAT'S $526,600) | $526,600 |
| LEAVING $155,000 FOR SALES FORCE SALARY AND COMMISSION (THAT'S 4 1/2 PERCENT) | $155,000 |

Using the foregoing figures, we might install the following compensation plan:

$12,000 salary
0 commission on first $100,000
1 percent commission on second $100,000
2 percent commission on third $100,000
4 percent commission on fourth $100,000
5 percent commission on fifth $100,000
6 percent commission on sixth $100,000

Which would produce the following earnings for a salesperson:

| Sales | Salary | Commission | Total Compensation | Sales Force Compensation as % of Sale |
|---|---|---|---|---|
| $100,000 | $12,000 | 0 | $12,000 | 12.% |
| $200,000 | $12,000 | $1,000 | $13,000 | 6.5% |
| $300,000 | $12,000 | $3,000 | $15,000 | 5.% |
| $400,000 | $12,000 | $7,000 | $19,000 | 4.75% |
| $500,000 | $12,000 | $12,000 | $24,000 | 4.80% |
| $600,000 | $12,000 | $18,000 | $30,000 | 5.% |

If sales performance went something like this with 10 salespeople:

| | Total Sales | Total Sales Force Compensation |
|---|---|---|
| Two salespeople $100,000 | $200,000 | $24,000 |
| One salesperson $200,000 | $200,000 | $13,000 |
| Three salespeople $300,000 | $900,000 | $15,000 |
| One salesperson $400,000 | $400,000 | $19,000 |
| One salesperson $500,000 | $500,000 | $24,000 |
| Two salespeople $600,000 | $1,200,000 | $60,000 |

Then company total sales would be $3,400,000, the company's net profit before taxes would be 15.5 percent or $526,000, and sales force compensation would be 4.5 percent.

Could we get to the same place with any other compensation plan? Let's try a lower base salary, start commissions on the first dollar of sales with higher commissions, and see if total compensation can be kept at 4.5 percent:

$10,000 salary
1 percent commission on first $100,000
1 percent commission on second $100,000
3 percent commission on third $100,000
3 percent commission on fourth $100,000
4 percent commission on fifth $100,000
6 percent commission on sixth $100,000

| Sales | Salary | Commission | Total Compensation | Sales Force Compensation as % of Sale |
|---|---|---|---|---|
| $100,000 | $10,000 | $1,000 | $11,000 | 11.% |
| $200,000 | $10,000 | $2,000 | $12,000 | 6.% |
| $300,000 | $10,000 | $5,000 | $15,000 | 5.% |
| $400,000 | $10,000 | $8,000 | $18,000 | 4.5% |
| $500,000 | $10,000 | $12,000 | $22,000 | 4.5% |
| $600,000 | $10,000 | $18,000 | $28,000 | 4.5% |

How about that!

But let's say we had to have a higher base salary to attract the quality candidate we need. Can we juggle the commission schedule and stay under 4.5 percent total for salary and commission?

$15,000 salary
0 commission on first $100,000
0 commission on second $100,000
1 percent commission on third $100,000
2 percent commission on fourth $100,000
4 percent commission on fifth $100,000
6 percent commission on sixth $100,000

| Sales | Salary | Commission | Total Compensation | Sales Force Compensation as % of Sale |
|---|---|---|---|---|
| $100,000 | $15,000 | 0 | $15,000 | 15.% |
| $200,000 | $15,000 | 0 | $15,000 | 7.5% |
| $300,000 | $15,000 | $1,000 | $16,000 | 5.75% |
| $400,000 | $15,000 | $3,000 | $18,000 | 4.5% |
| $500,000 | $15,000 | $7,000 | $22,000 | 4.5% |
| $600,000 | $15,000 | $13,000 | $28,000 | 4.5% |

The point is that we can determine the amount we have available to pay salespeople at a realistic, attainable total volume and work out many different compensation plans to suit our situation.

Work this concept through using your own company's figures and see what different scenarios you come up with.

This section has provided you with the basics of compensation plan design. Always keep in mind that whatever level of compensation you pay at, the actual amounts paid must always be firmly rooted in your company's financial picture.

In the next section we'll present a simple, but powerful, concept for designing your incentive plan.

# INCENTIVE PLAN DESIGN

Earlier we touched on the subject of profit and why making profit for the company wasn't a prime motivator for salespeople. As one frustrated person recently posted on the Internet: "How about someone in sales who really understands what the definition of true PROFIT is and learns how to make some of it for the company they work for instead of just trying to make enough to cover their own needs?"

Figure 98 (How Commissions are Determined) takes a look at how many companies are considering the profitability of the sale in calculating compensation. While nearly half the companies with under $5 million in annual sales pay commissions on the basis of sales volume only, 16 percent determine commissions strictly on the profitability of the sale. Another 30 percent base commissions on a combination of sale volume and profitability.

Profitability of sales is not a matter to be taken lightly; without profits, everyone would be out of a job. So how can salespeople be motivated to go after the most profitable business?

Hal Fahner, Vice President of Corporate Marketing at Blue Cross & Blue Shield of Florida, Inc., addressed this problem in an article for *Dartnell's Sales & Marketing Executive Report* entitled "Designing Incentive Plans That Work." Since this article so clearly explains the procedure for designing incentive plans, we are reprinting it here in its entirety:

As long as there have been salespeople, business managers and accountants have been designing sales incentive compensation plans that pay salespeople for selling more without regard to profit margin, the desired product mix, and the long-term objectives of the corporation in the marketplace.

We can't go on like this! It *is* possible to design incentive plans for salespeople that pay them for doing exactly what the corporation wants done: for carrying out marketing's responsibility for the achievement of the end results stated in the corporate business plan.

The total incentive plan for our salespeople is usually partially designed for us by our industry. That is, competition is often the biggest single factor influencing our method of paying our salespeople. If a large base salary, company car and expenses, and small commission is the norm in our industry, our plan will probably have those characteristics. If our industry has always offered a small draw, large commissions, and no expense reimbursement, we will probably continue that basic pattern.

## WHAT A COMPENSATION PLAN SHOULD ACCOMPLISH

Your compensation plan should enable you to attract better qualified sales candidates than your competition and allow you to retain your proven, effective, productive people. The compensation plan should provide your salespeople with the assurance of some regular income and provide incentive to reach top performance. And the compensation plan should offer an incentive to your sales force to prospect for and sell to your most desirable and profitable accounts.

The incentive plan should discourage your salespeople from bringing in accounts that you consider undesirable because these customers buy low margin items, are not liable to reorder and become steady customers, buy small amounts — or whatever criteria you use to describe desirable and undesirable accounts.

The incentive plan should encourage the sales force to sell the high-margin items in the product line and sell the total product mix the company has targeted in its annual business plan.

For instance, if the company business plan calls for the following mix of products in its annual volume...

| PRODUCT | VOLUME | PERCENT OF TOTAL REVENUE |
|---|---|---|
| PRODUCT A | $10MM SALES | 50% |
| PRODUCT B | $ 5MM SALES | 25% |
| PRODUCT C | $ 2MM SALES | 10% |
| PRODUCT D | $ 1.5MM SALES | 7.25% |
| PRODUCT E | $ 1.0MM SALES | 5% |
| PRODUCT F | $ 0.5MM SALES | 2.5% |

... the incentive plan should line up with the company business plan and reward the sales force for selling that mix of products.

If the incentive plan pays the same for all products, the sales force will sell the products that are easiest to sell, regardless of the profit margin or the product mix the company desires.

If the incentive plan pays the same for all accounts, the sales force will pursue the prospects who are easiest to sell to whether they buy high-margin or low-margin goods, are slow to pay or prompt, or are desirable or undesirable accounts by the company's criteria.

## HOW TO REWARD PROFITABLE SELLING

If we want to pay our salespeople to sell profitable and desirable business, how do we do it?

First, we must define very specifically what we want — what our targets are. What target markets do we want to go after? What products do we want emphasized?

The second step is to look at these goals through the salesperson's eyes and design the incentive portion of the total compensation plan to pay the sales force for reaching those goals. If you see varying degrees of desirability in potential accounts, then classify them formally in order of desirability. If some of your products are loss leaders; if others are established and almost sell themselves; and if others are your stars of the near future for which you must establish a customer base — pay the sales force accordingly.

Once you have classified your categories of prospective and existing accounts as, for instance, Class I (most desirable), Class II (average), and Class III (least desirable), you have the beginning of a system to control the profitability of your sales force.

Now classify your products. For example: Class A products (high profit, stars of the future), Class B products (bread and butter, heart of the line), and Class C products (low margin, may be popular with some customers due to hard-to-find features but low total gross volume to the company).

## REMEMBER THE GOAL

It is important to remember that *desirability to the company* is the criteria to use in putting both prospects/customers and products in ascending/descending commission categories. That is, the difficulty of the sale is not the main determinant of commission.

In the example above, the Class I customers are probably high-volume buyers and visible to your competitors. Therefore, they are probably more difficult for your sales force to sell as regular repeat customers than Class III customers, who probably buy small amounts and are not hotly pursued by your competitors.

So, in paying your salespeople more for Class I accounts, you are probably paying them more for making more difficult sales. However, if one of your salespeople has a Class I account that is easy to sell to — a real sweetheart — don't resent paying extra for an easy sale. Instead, count your blessings.

Remember, we are paying extra to ensure that we sell profitable products to profitable, desirable accounts. The degree of difficulty of the sale is incidental. Profitability is what we are after with incentive pay.

## MAKE SURE YOUR INCENTIVE REALLY CONTROLS SALES EFFORT

We now have customers classified as Class I, Class II, and Class III. We have our products classified as Class A, Class B, and Class C. How much should you differentiate the commission amount or percentage between each to ensure that the sales force will concentrate on the most profitable accounts and products?

Here is one way of looking at the consequences of doing what the company wants or ignoring what the company wants as seen through the salesperson's eyes:

| PRODUCT CATEGORIES | CUSTOMER CATEGORIES | | |
|---|---|---|---|
| | I | II | III |
| CLASS A | 150% | 125% | 100% |
| CLASS B | 125% | 100% | 75% |
| CLASS C | 100% | 50% | 25% |

The illustration above shows that a salesperson who sells a middle-of-the-road average margin product to a middle-of-the-road average prospect (Class B product, Class II Customer — middle of the grid) will make the average (100%) commission.

However, the salesperson who sells to the account most wanted by the company (Class I) and sells them the product the company most wants to sell (Class A) makes half again as much as on an average sale (150%).

The salesperson who ignores the company's goals and calls on marginal accounts (Class III) and just takes orders for the low-margin commodity items in the line (Class C) will receive a commission that is only 25 percent of what is paid for an average sale.

There must be a dramatic difference in the economic consequences to encourage your sales force to sell your most desirable products to your target accounts.

If you believe this incentive concept can help your company reach business plan objectives, here is a summary of a few things to keep in mind:
- Define your target market.
- Create specific, clear criteria for each class of account.
- Categorize your products for commission/bonus purposes.
- Look at the situation through the eyes of your salespeople. Be sure you are telling them the same thing with your incentive plan as you are saying to them with your words. That is, make sure your incentive plan reinforces what you tell the sales force about their objectives and the company's objectives.
- Fine tune your incentive plan. After you make adjustments, test the effect on your base of accounts, product mix, and profits as well as the effect on your salespeople's total earnings.

This approach really works! Your salespeople will sell what/who you pay them to sell. Make sure your targets are really what you want.

# TERRITORY DESIGN

**A**ny discussion of sales compensation design should include a discussion of sales territory design. One of the best sources of sound territory design practices is Charles C. Schlom's book, *Planning and Managing Sales Territories: How to Focus Sales Efforts for Top Performance in Today's Markets*, published by Dartnell. This section draws from that book.

First, however, we'll explain how to use the *cost approach* in designing territories.

As with compensation plan design, you start with product cost sheets and your company's P&L statement.

Consider cost first. The best method is to *find out what you can afford* before you do anything else. Visit your accountant, study the balance sheet and statement — not market size, market share, etc. What is the good of working out a logical sales organization if you can't afford it?

You should determine exactly how much it costs to make the product. Then determine how much money is invested in the business and how much profit is necessary. Now you can find out how much sales cost you can afford.

The cost method, highly simplified, works like this:

After a thorough examination of your business plan, balance sheet, etc., you decide you can afford, say, a 5 percent sales cost. If your projected sales are $5 million, that gives you $250,000 for the field sales force. If the type of salesperson you need costs $50,000, you can afford 5 salespeople. Each territory should produce about $1,000,000 in sales. ($1,000,000 x 5 territories = $5,000,000, your company's total annual projected sales volume.) At this point, you know roughly how many territories you will need and what is expected from them in general. (To be completely accurate, however, you will need to subtract sales management costs, as well as any other sales costs, from the amount you have available. This example was simplified to illustrate the basic principles involved.)

## EVALUATE FOUR BASIC AREAS

To design a territory, evaluate four basic areas:
1. **Your products.** How many products do you have? Are they simple or complicated? Are they suited to one market or to a variety of markets? Do they change quickly or slowly over the years?
2. **Your markets.** What is your market potential? — Or how much could you sell if you sold every customer? What is your market size? — Or how much of your product is being sold today? You know what your share of the market is now. Consider the types of markets you deal with. Are there many different specialized markets for different products or product lines, or do you have just one basic market? What are the characteristics of your markets? Are rural and urban markets different? Check your historical pattern and consider market trends.
3. **Your distribution.** Do you have different channels of distribution for different products or product lines? Where are your distributors located? How big are they? How much territory do they cover? Are they financially sound and well managed? Do they have the physical facilities to handle your products? Do they have the personnel who can do a good job for you? What is the historical pattern? Which types

of distribution and which specific distributors have worked best in the past? Find out why some have prospered and others have not done too well. Your territories will be smaller in problem areas that require more of your attention.

4. **Your salespeople.** You already know about how many you need and how much to pay them. But how to pay them? Salary, commission, or a combination plan? Are your salespeople order takers or true professionals? Order takers require closer supervision and smaller territories. Are they across-the-board people who sell your entire line, or do you have specialists? If you have specialists, you could have over-lapping territories or more than one person in a single territory. How long do your salespeople stay with the company? Go over the past performance of each person.

There are a few remaining factors that do not fit into any of these categories. Boundaries, for instance. Would you rather use political, natural, or market areas as a basis for territory boundaries? And what time cycle is permissible? How long should a salesperson leave any account unserviced? Weather can play a significant role also. The location of your sales offices and distribution points should not be overlooked.

## BUILD FROM THE BOTTOM

Remember that territories are built from the bottom up, by putting together small bits and pieces. Divide or lump them together as necessary.

Once formed, sales territories still require constant attention. They should never be considered as static. As any of the factors change, so — perhaps — should the territory.

Adjust the factors and methods discussed to fit your company needs. How much weight you give the different items, what sources you use to get your facts, and the effort you can bring to bear on the problem will vary widely. But three basic points will apply to all:

1. Use the cost approach — do only what you can really afford.
2. Build your territories bit by bit.
3. Make a detailed analysis — consider all factors on an individual basis.

With concept understood, you'll find the material from Charles Schlom's book, referenced above, especially helpful. Suggestion: As you look through the following material, highlight those points that are particularly pertinent to your company or your situation. After you have completed this section, construct a "worksheet" out of the questions you highlighted and answer them before proceeding. That way, you'll have before you the answers you need to develop a thriving territory.

## WHAT IS A TERRITORY?

A sales territory is usually thought of as a geographic entity containing groups of prospects and customers within specific boundaries. However, it is primarily one segment of a company's total market.

A sales territory can be thought of as a franchise from which must come enough dollars to be profitable to management, who underwrites it, and to the salesperson responsible for working it.

A sales territory, to be workable and profitable, must be clearly defined in terms of the following factors:

- Specific objectives.
- Boundaries, whether geographical; political, by market or trade area; by company production or distribution facilities; by the existence of competitive plants or

shipping locations, as a reflection of the rail movement of goods; by operating areas of key distributors, etc.

- Potential on which it is possible to capitalize.
- Planning so that results will be achieved.
- Coverage to ensure that all important prospects and customers can be seen on schedule.

Such clarity of definition provides management with a specific marketing unit it can use to plan and control field operations. It helps to identify prospects and customers with the potential necessary for continued growth and development. Finally, it produces information with which to clarify and evaluate accounts, so that sales contacts can be adjusted to the needs imposed by the market and competition. Without a clear definition, neither the manager nor the sales rep can get organized. Both become slaves to chaos and confusion.

Below, and on the following pages, you will find a concentrated overview of the total planning process. You'll find in reading through the balance of this section that we've presented a wealth of information, which at times may appear overwhelming. Because of the importance of this material, you may want to digest it over a period of time. You may find it necessary to read this material over several times before thoroughly understanding it.

The best way to define answers to questions concerning factors vital to success in every territory is to learn as much as possible about the following:

1. Profitability
   - Is the territory increasing in its market share? Or is it remaining static?
   - What has been the trend in profits within the territory, and do any individual causes seem to have drastically helped or hurt earnings?
   - What does it cost to operate this territory efficiently?
   - What is the potential in this territory if we could sell every product?

2. Markets
   - How many markets are there within the territory, and how big are they?
   - Is there just one basic market, or are there many highly specialized ones?
   - Are the markets within the territory predominantly urban? Rural? Combination?
   - In which markets can we expect to be the strongest or the weakest in the territory?
   - Who are our competitors in the territory? Rank them by characteristics and strengths.
   - Have any major shifts in competitive activities been detected? Is the division of markets among suppliers fairly stable?
   - Are there any environmental factors that seem to be of critical importance? What are they?
   - Are there major voids in the company's information base that might make a sound analysis of the territory difficult — or impossible?
   - What are the most important strengths and weaknesses of the territory, and what key influences, present or future, must be taken into account?

3. Products
   - How many products or product lines do we sell in this territory?
   - What is their acceptability?
   - How adaptable are they? Do they fit only one type of market or many?
   - Do they change from year to year (automobiles), or do they tend to remain fairly static (screwdrivers)?

- What is the product's history of profitability?
- How much product can this territory be reasonably expected to absorb?
4. Customers
   - How many are there in the territory?
   - What number of prospects have been identified?
   - How many customers have the potential for becoming key accounts?
   - How efficiently are customers being covered at the present time? With what frequency? Is the present system effective, or will it require major revisions?
   - What is our image among customers? Prospects?
   - What is our reputation in the trade?
   - Does potential exist for increasing sales to present customers?
   - What kinds of people or firms comprise the best customers and prospects in this territory?
5. Sales reps
   - What will it cost to put a sales rep in the territory as far as compensation, expenses, etc., are concerned?
   - How are the sales reps paid? Commission? Salary? Combination?
   - Is the sales rep in the territory a real selling "pro" or just another order-taker? What kind of sales rep is required for best results?
   - Can the sales rep sell the complete line or only some of the products?
   - How long has the rep been with the company? How long is the rep likely to remain with the company?
6. Problems
   - Was the previous sales rep in the territory so strong or so weak that the sales assignment was adjusted to fit?
   - Were key accounts, distributors, or new business development assignments tailored to fit the rep previously working the territory?
   - Were sales and distribution plans arranged long ago when the company lacked many of its present products and services?
   - Is there no clear line of demarcation between large and small accounts?
   - Are there too many divided responsibilities between the company and key accounts?
   - Has there been a failure to classify customers, so that sales and servicing policies and activities are difficult or impossible to apply?
   - Has the company's reputation suffered in the territory due to actions of previous sales reps?

**Identifying the Situation: Territory Analysis**
A. The starting point to gaining objective answers to questions relating to profitability, products, etc., is to conduct an analysis of the territory to identify and determine the amount of potential in that submarket. Knowing exactly where you are in a territory is the jumping-off point to determining where it is possible to go.
B. A good analysis will also give you a comprehensive picture of conditions within a territory by revealing the following:
   1. Population concentrations.
   2. Extent of purchasing power.
   3. Need for products your sales reps sell.
   4. Types of accounts utilizing your company's products.

5. Amount of available business.
6. Prospects and their locations.
7. Classifications of customers and prospects who might buy more or offer less sales resistance than others.
8. Competitive sales reps, lines, products, and companies.

C. Analysis can be no better than the information sources you use. Here are some of the sources available to you in analyzing and planning territorial activities.
1. Personal contacts:
   - Observation
   - Company controllers
   - Chambers of commerce, etc.
2. Newspapers, publications, and other media:
   - Trade papers, books, periodicals
   - Company house organs, etc.
3. Lists, directories, and records:
   - *Moody's Manual*
   - Predicasts
   - Government reports
   - Bureau of the Census
   - Directories of corporations
   - Company records and reports
   - Correspondence, etc.

D. Steps in conducting a territory analysis:
1. List important facts about territory as they relate to profits, markets, products, accounts, sales reps, and problems.
2. Arrange facts in order of importance.
3. Check for possible trends, changes, and problems.
4. Note conditions affecting territory's needs, wants, requirements, and opportunities.
5. Compare data from territory with that analyzed for other territories under your jurisdiction.
   - What does the data suggest?
   - Where is the territory strong/weak in comparison with the other territories?
   - What immediate or long-range actions are suggested?
6. Outline briefly possible courses of action regarding the territory as they relate to:
   - Sales reps
   - Management
   - Customers/prospects.
7. Keep analyzed data handy for quick reference as territorial plans are developed.
8. Pass along data of immediate interest to other departments within company and to management.

E. At the conclusion of your analysis, a better understanding of the following should be achieved:
1. Territorial geography:
   - Area and boundaries
   - Major metro centers
   - Location of counties
   - Transportation networks

- Topographical characteristics
- Climate.

2. Prospects/customers:
   - Locations/concentrations
   - Needs, wants, and preferences
   - Limitations
   - Size of various types of operations
   - Potential, etc.
3. Economic conditions:
   - Level of general business activities
   - Growth factors/trends/potential
   - Employment/extent of depressed areas
   - Construction starts
   - Population growth or decline.
4. Competition:
   - Names/numbers/concentrations
   - Capabilities/aggressiveness/limitations
   - Services offered
   - Products sold
   - Pricing/profitability/volume
   - Installations/facilities/headquarters.
5. Use of our products:
   - Type(s) preferred
   - Current/projected usage
   - Pricing/terms
   - Servicing
   - Distribution
   - Facilities/installations, etc.
F. The analysis should also permit you to do the following:
   1. Determine possibilities for achieving additional volume on products presently sold in this territory.
   2. Define opportunities for stimulating sales to new groups of accounts or to middlemen.
   3. Detect problems or dangers that would have remained concealed or unknown unless an analysis had been made.
   4. Detail any unusual differences between the territory analyzed and others within the district or company — and the reasons why.

**Targeting Potential**

A. With analysis completed, it is then possible for the manager to sit down with the sales rep and together establish some realistic, specific, and achievable objectives, including the following:
   1. Coverage of the territory.
   2. Grading of each specific account in the territory in terms of its potential revenue and profit.
   3. Grading of each product in the line with respect to its profitability, and the contribution it makes to the sale of other products.
   4. Business development activities.
      - Prospecting

- New account development
- Servicing activities, etc.
5. Utilization of time and effort.
   - Number of accounts to be covered
   - Number of calls to be made
   - Duration of calls
   - Travel time required.
B. Out of the analysis and the establishment of objectives, it should be possible for the manager and sales rep to determine the following:
   1. The number of key accounts in the territory.
      - Generally few in number; it is not unusual to find the top 10 customers worth almost as much as all the others combined.
      - Their value is so high that losing just one would be a major setback in the territory.
   2. Unprofitable accounts.
      - Those that represent an actual loss to the company when the true cost of serving them is calculated.
      - Some, however, will have a potential that greatly exceeds their present purchases.
      - The manager may want to advise the sales rep to convert such customers to different sales service and distribution coverage through agents, distributors, brokers, etc. — or by mail or phone.
   3. Regular accounts.
      - Level of purchases below that of key accounts, but whose present or future worth warrants a regular sales program.
   4. Unclassified accounts.
      - Require further analysis and investigation before true potential can be accurately ascertained.

**How Do We Get There?**

A. By this time your sales rep ought to have a reasonably clear understanding of what the territory is all about — or know enough to at least ask some probing questions about any areas that remain unclear.
   These include the following:
   1. Company sales coverage policy.
   2. Key customers by size, type, and location.
      - Identification of influencers, specifiers, and decision makers.
      - Types of calls that predominate.
      - Description of any personal attributes needed by the sales rep.
      - Sales programs required.
      - Sales support necessary.
   3. Functions of any distributors, brokers, junior sales reps, technical representatives, etc., within the territory.
   4. Description of any company-operated installations.
   5. Summary of any public warehousing arrangements or other sources of supply and services.
   6. Logistical arrangements that affect the rep's ability to service customers.
   7. Territory size and boundaries as well as geography.

8. Significant situations in adjoining territories that may affect the rep's operations and responsibilities.
9. Programs currently in operation.
10. Problems and opportunities.
B. It is at this point you can begin development of a comprehensive plan of action with which to achieve territorial objectives.
   1. Assistance in plan preparation, recommendations, and review are the responsibility of the manager.
   2. Plan development, implementation, and follow-through are the responsibility of the sales rep.
C. Before developing a comprehensive program, it's important to review the following:
   1. Any programs already launched in the territory.
      - Some development work is usually going on in a territory — especially one that is already established.
      - Based on analysis and objectives, manager/sales rep must decide to either pursue or drop these programs.
   2. The maintenance of current sales.
      - Identified key and regular accounts must continue receiving selling efforts so that each customer receives required attention.
      - Regular sales programs, campaigns, and promotions for accounts.
D. The following are the functions of the program by which objectives are achieved:
   1. Detail tactics necessary for accomplishing each objective.
   2. Determine possible alternative courses of action for use when and where needed.
   3. Develop essential information as well as resources required for carrying out action plan.
   4. Devise checkpoints for measuring progress or lack of it.
   5. Define results expected, and how they are to be attained.
E. Program development steps:
   1. Tactical development.
      - Clarify each program's importance.
      - Define purpose of each program.
      - Establish standards of performance.
      - Estimate costs.
      - Name each program for quick identification.
      - Develop a program for each objective.
   2. Support required.
      - List resources and personnel available.
      - Review fact base developed during analysis for information.
   3. Checking results.
      - Prepare schedule of periodic program reviews.
      - Establish deadlines for each program.
      - Check accomplishments against objectives.
      - Create alternatives should changes occur.
F. Programs should be designed to do the following:
   1. Maintain and/or increase sales and profits with key and regular customers.
   2. Transfer unprofitable accounts to other sales/service arrangements.
   3. Follow up on any programs that have already been launched.
   4. Exploit special situations or remedy critical problems.

5. Correct any sales deficiencies.
6. Capitalize on opportunities revealed through analysis of the territory.

**What Does it Take to Stay on Target?**
A. Because opportunities can spring up requiring immediate action; because problems can suddenly emerge; because trends can cause objectives and programs to veer off on a tangent, territorial plans need continuous review and revision.
B. Review the following with sales reps:
   1. Objectives and deadlines for programs.
   2. New information affecting customers, coverage, programs, etc.
   3. Developing trends.
   4. Comments from customers (and prospects).
   5. Programs in action.
   6. Competitive activities.
   7. Problems.
C. Assist sales reps with changes necessary by helping to do the following:
   1. Identify revisions necessary in programs.
   2. Take action.
      - What?
      - How?
      - When?
      - Why?
   3. Evaluate results.

**Implementation — Key to Action**
A. Territory coverage.
   1. Territorial coverage involves putting the territory plan into action.
      - It is the activities aspect of the selling job.
      - It includes sales calls, travel time, account servicing activities, etc.
      - Territorial coverage must be accomplished within the framework of a territory plan in order to optimize the sales rep's time.
   2. In planning for coverage of accounts, it's helpful to know the approximate time it takes for each of your sales reps to cover his or her territories once.
      - One way to estimate begins with determining the total number of accounts in the territory and how many days it will take to contact each account.
      - Another estimating method indicates the total number of accounts each sales rep can contact within a given period.
   3. Figuring out cost per call (techniques/formulas for):
      - Direct costs
      - Costs per working hour
      - Costs per call hour.
   4. Once each sales rep knows about how long it will take to make one swing through the territory, the manager can work with him or her — or see to it that appropriate forms or file cards are prepared on which the following information is included:
      - Account name, number, address, phone, etc.
      - Classification of account by potential.
      - Potential within account for each product or product line.

- Current sales.
- Deciders, influencers, and specifiers. For example, for specialized, engineered products, a purchasing agent might sign the purchase order but be the least important individual in the purchase decision; engineering staff members might be the primary influence.
- Special information, etc.

5. As your reps prepare for calls, information on computer printouts, cards, or forms can be handled in the following ways:
   - Checked to learn which ones must be seen immediately and which ones can be seen at a later date.
   - Placed in the order sales reps plan to call on accounts, thus streamlining routing and eliminating excess travel.
   - Inspected to see on whom to call within each account.
   - Reviewed for key facts about account as calls are prepared.
   - Evaluated to ensure proper balance of calls between customers and prospects.

6. During calls, reps can use information to do the following:
   - Check basic facts about account and personnel to be seen
   - Note observations for immediate or future use in planning
   - Identify changes in facilities, personnel, product lines, etc.

7. After calls:
   - Note down new information on cards or forms.
   - Return to file in same order as drawn.
   - Note dates on which accounts were seen. This will eliminate confusion with other accounts in same area who are to be contacted at different dates and times.
   - Transcribe information onto appropriate records and reports.

B. Plotting moves on maps.
1. Maps are indispensable to effective territory coverage.
   - The sales rep can't visualize the market, know geographic factors affecting customer accessibility, or lay routes that facilitate travel convenience without a graphic representation of the sales area.
   - Maps make it easy for sales reps to prearrange the order of their stops in order to work out a logical sequence of cities, places, prospects, and customers to be visited.
2. The master map of each territory can indicate the following:
   - Active accounts (key, regular, and prospective)
   - Competitive headquarters, facilities, etc.
   - Communication facilities
   - Company branch offices, plants, labs, service centers, etc.
   - Key information centers (newspapers, TV stations, etc.)
   - Location of accounts currently sold and serviced by competitors
   - Proposed sites of customer plant expansions, etc.
   - Subterritories
   - Territorial boundaries
   - Transportation nets
   - Trade areas and market centers.

3. Evaluate routes. Check to be sure sales reps have done the following:
   - Identified and numbered accounts on map based on sequence of scheduled calls.
   - Check to see that backtracking, crisscrossing, or otherwise wasting time traveling is kept to a minimum.
   - Apply the principle for efficient routing: a straight line is more economical. Since this isn't always possible, be sure your sales reps straighten travel lines as much as possible.
   - Make sure routing is done at the same time call schedules are prepared.

## Take the Pulse in Each Territory

A. Exercise your manager's prerogative by evaluating periodically each sales rep's territorial responsibilities, including the following:
   1. Accounts worth more calls or fewer calls.
   2. Accounts to whom the company wants to sell — and how much.
   3. Rechecking for accuracy the number of account categories in the territory.
   4. Efficiency with which the sales rep handles work loads, travel time, calls, etc.
   5. Percent each territory has of the company's volume, etc.
B. After each territory has been analyzed and evaluated, the manager summarizes to obtain the same information for the district as a whole.
C. You can then more effectively direct your sales reps to do the following:
   1. Check objectives developed for each of their territories.
      - Are they still realistic and achievable?
      - Which ones are being achieved on schedule? Which ones are not?
      - What changes or revisions will be necessary to keep objectives on target?
      - What additional steps will be required of the manager? Sales reps in other territories? Members of company management? Other departments?
      - What new objectives are needed?
   2. Consult records, reports, correspondence, personal observations in the field, customer contacts, etc.
      - What accounts will require greater frequency of contact? Which ones less?
      - Are call costs, time expenditures, etc., worth it? What changes are needed now? Later?
      - What additional services should be provided? Within what limits?
   3. Review their modes of travel.
      - Check maps to hold down excessive travel.
      - The car is usually the most suitable — Stress that urgency of a call or importance of an account takes precedence over distance or expenses of travel.
   4. Evaluate prospecting procedures used by each of your sales reps.
      - Do they have specific criteria for qualifying prospects?
      - How are prospects located, identified, or evaluated? What changes may be necessary in these procedures?
      - What sources yield best results? How effectively are they being utilized?
      - Do their records, files, maps, etc., provide means for noting pertinent facts observed and obtained about prospects?
   5. Examine expenses in relation to sales.
      - What are the major costs incurred in the territories?

- What are the reps now spending for transportation, hotel/motel accommodations, meals, entertainment, etc.?
- Where should more be spent to stimulate sales?
- How does each rep's territory coverage affect sales and sales expense?

6. Compare overall performance against plans.
   - Coverage plans do not automatically come to fruition.
   - Plans must be carried out completely if they are to succeed.
   - Compare each rep's planned performance against actual performance on a periodic basis.
   - Find out if each has been able to increase the number of calls on prospects with genuine potential.
   - Have selling interviews increased?
   - Has each rep been able to increase the number of customers seen because of better coverage patterns and routing routines used?
   - Have reps been able to raise the dollar value of their selling time?

D. Devise daily/weekly schedules and priorities.
   1. Before implementing a rep's plans and activities, as a manager you want all of your reps to ask themselves the following questions:
      - What results do I need today? Tomorrow? Next week? Six months hence?
      - What do my customers expect from me, from the company I represent?
      - What does the company, my manager, require of me, so that their goals and objectives can be realized?
   2. This approach will help each of your sales reps to do the following:
      - Focus on priorities.
      - Maintain working communications with you and the company.
      - Determine major job responsibilities.
      - Estimate the time required for handling the really important jobs.
      - Correctly structure time outlays.
      - Prepare for emergencies.
   3. To encourage your reps to do more of what is important in their territories, get them to do the following:
      - Schedule around key events.
        - Note what they are.
        - Group sales calls and selling activities.
      - Organize activities.
        - Keep related tasks together.
        - Indicate activities that will depend on the activities and/or actions of others.
      - Prepare an informal schedule.
        - Estimate the time each activity will take.
      - Set deadlines.
        - Cut out overlapping or redundant activities.
      - Evaluate schedule periodically.
      - Plan what to do when any of the following occur:
        - You have to split prosperous territories.
        - The veteran is "milking," rather than working, the territory.
        - Shifts in population, new products, increased competition, changes in the economy — or other factors — dictate territory adjustments or realignment.

**Help Your Reps in Managing Their Territories**

A. Require that long-range strategies be worked out for each account, including the following:
   1. A statement of objectives.
   2. Selling tactics to be employed.
   3. Number of calls to be made.
   4. Specific objectives for each call, etc.

B. Each call should result in a step closer toward the long-range objective that is getting a stated share of the account's business.
   1. That's why you cannot allow your rep's plans to remain merely good intentions.
   2. Supervise continually! Work with them systematically! Keep in close touch between contacts via the phone or correspondence. See to it that each rep does the following:
      • Carries out plans so that the sales value of each customer can be realized.
      • Carries out plans so that the best possible coverage patterns can also be used as guides in scheduling calls.
      • Carries out plans so that each sales rep knows who to see, where, and when.
      • Carries out plans so that each sales rep's personal as well as territorial objectives are accomplished.

# CHAPTER 5

# QUOTA-SETTING BASICS

The setting of quotas is an imprecise science at best; often quotas are simply a best "guesstimate" of what a particular territory and salesperson are capable of producing.

While we won't delve here into every nook and cranny of the philosophy of quota setting, we will cover the rudimentary basics and familiarize you with some of the issues involved.

First, however, let's take a look at how many salespeople meet and exceed quota.

In a recent Dartnell survey, we asked:

**WHAT PERCENTAGE OF YOUR SALESPEOPLE CONSISTENTLY MEET QUOTA, DO NOT MEET QUOTA, EXCEED QUOTA?**

The data tabulations confirm what most of us suspected all along — that just 20 percent of salespeople consistently perform at the top.

| RESPONSES | PERCENT OF SALESPEOPLE |
|---|---|
| SALESPEOPLE WHO EXCEED QUOTA | 20% |
| SALESPEOPLE WHO MEET QUOTA | 50 |
| SALESPEOPLE WHO DO NOT MEET QUOTA | 30 |
| TOTAL | 100% |

You might want to keep this data in mind as we move through the basics of setting quotas.

## SETTING SALES QUOTAS

The sales quota is a key measurement of a salesperson's performance. You can make sales quotas as equitable as possible to both the sales rep and the company by considering these basic fundamentals:

- **Determination of share of the market your company wants, both nationally and in each market area.** You need knowledge of what the total industry is doing, along with projections of expected growth. Utilize data from industry and trade associations, government sources, published trade journal surveys. Adjust for regional and seasonal differences in product use and need. The factor of industry market penetration is probably the biggest single influence in establishing a quota from the company viewpoint. Each quota should reflect how rapidly your company can reasonably expect to increase its penetration.
- **Local territory conditions.** Some salespeople may have territories that are enjoying a local economic boom, while other territories are not. In either event, these conditions must be taken into account if quotas are to be equitable.
- **How well a territory is managed.** Poor management, even in a prime market, may force you to set lower quotas than penetration and industry sales might indicate. The comparison of such figures also gives you an insight into whether your present management, in any given area, is strong or weak.
- **New product introductions, planned product diversification, and product discontinuances are factors that should be reflected in the quota.** You can be certain that you have set equitable quotas if your weaker sales reps fail to attain them and if your better reps reach or exceed them. If everyone exceeds quotas,

they're set too low. If no one achieves them, you've set them too high. In either case, it's "back to the drawing board" for another look at the factors you used.

While the views of your reps should be included in establishing quotas, limit their authority in final decisions.

Finally, make periodic status checks to adjust quotas for product price adjustments, new products, or other developments during the quota period.

## DARTNELL RESEARCH STUDIES

According to Dartnell research, most companies base quotas on dollar volume (40 percent of responding companies), the potential of the territory (24 percent), and unit volume (19 percent). Less important considerations were the number of new accounts opened (5 percent), calls made (3 percent), and services rendered (2 percent).

A majority of the companies (80 percent) attempted to achieve balanced-line selling when they carried a varied product line. Various methods were used: 14 percent relied on commission variations, while 11 percent used a quota system.

The methods used to determine the amount of time to be devoted to each account were usually based on potential (24 percent). Other factors were also significant. They included the individual salesperson's discretion, the size of the account, population, market trends, the cost-revenue ratio, the grade of the account, present dollar volume, the dealer volume and importance, and the percentage ratio.

One of our survey respondents offered the following comments on his company's program: "Quotas must be challenging, obtainable, and rewardable. They must be fair to the salesperson, to sales management, and to the company, and must support the overall company goals and objectives. When the final quota is settled on, other reward-able nonsales objectives, such as product mix, prospecting, and management training, are agreed upon. The participating salesperson is often more demanding on himself or herself than is management. This can be a strong self-motivating force."

This respondent included a description of his company's plan, which is included here:
- The salesperson receives a 100 percent bonus if quota is achieved.
- The salesperson receives a base salary for obtaining 80 percent of the established quota and then can earn up to the full bonus (20 percent of the base salary) by achieving the last 15 percent of his or her quota. This is the regular bonus for attaining the sales quota and represents 80 percent of his or her total bonus.
- The remaining 20 percent can be earned through the completion of various non-sales quotas, which are not standard but tailored to each salesperson to encourage growth.
- Up to 25 percent additional bonus can be earned by exceeding quota by 25 percent.

## SOME QUESTIONS ABOUT QUOTAS

Sales and marketing people are far from agreement on how to set up and administer a quota system. But in most companies, the following factors are considered in establishing or revising quotas:
- The amount of last year's sales
- The trend in the territory over the past several years
- Economic trends (regional or national)
- Movement of current or potential customers into or out of the territory
- Competitive conditions
- Customers' buying habits

- The company's advertising programs
- New product introductions.

Some companies request each salesperson to make an analysis of his or her major accounts and potential customers and then reconcile them with management estimates in order to arrive at equitable totals.

As a general rule, you have set equitable quotas for salespeople if your weaker salespeople fail to attain them and if your better salespeople either reach them or slightly exceed them.

If a quota is properly and fairly established, it should be the best single measuring stick you can use to evaluate a salesperson. A salesperson's quota that is equitable for him or her and for the company provides the best basis for a salesperson's earnings, as well as the best measuring stick to qualify him or her for advancement. As such, it provides management with an essential tool for continued growth and sets up for the salesperson an attainable goal that he or she can achieve with justifiable pride. See Exhibit 1, below, for an example of a working quota.

## EXHIBIT 1

**WORKING QUOTA**

| DEALER | | BINDERS | FLOPPY DISKS | PHONE INDEXES | CALCULATORS |
|---|---|---|---|---|---|
| WARD'S OFFICE SUPPLY AMES, IOWA | ESTIMATE | 100 | 25 | 50 | 50 |
| | YOUR PERSONAL SALES | | | | |
| | | | | | |
| WEAVER STATIONER NEWTON, IOWA | ESTIMATE | | WILL NOT HANDLE AGAIN | | |
| | YOUR PERSONAL SALES | | | | |
| | | | | | |
| DOYLE'S DUBUQUE, IOWA | ESTIMATE | 75 | 50 | 75 | |
| | YOUR PERSONAL SALES | | | | |
| | | | | | |
| FISHER & MARSHALL DAVENPORT, IOWA | ESTIMATE | 310 | | 15 | 5 |
| | YOUR PERSONAL SALES | | | | |
| | | | | | |
| ESTELLE'S SHOP MUSCATINE, IOWA | ESTIMATE | | NO GOOD | | |
| | YOUR PERSONAL SALES | | | | |
| | | | | | |
| | TOTAL | 485 | 75 | 140 | 55 |

BY LISTING ALL ACCOUNTS IN A TERRITORY AND THEN HAVING EACH INDIVIDUAL SALESPERSON ESTIMATE WHAT HE OR SHE FEELS EACH ACCOUNT SHOULD BUY DURING THE YEAR, AND BY THEN AVERAGING THESE ESTIMATES WITH POTENTIAL QUOTA, A SATISFACTORY WORKING QUOTA CAN BE ESTABLISHED.

Note: Probably one of the greatest handicaps to basing quotas on management esti-mates (or the "wishful thinking" of management) of total sales is the likelihood that salespeople can't or won't perform as management expects them to perform. If man-agement sets its production schedules and operating budgets on such anticipated sales figures and the salespeople fall down, the company will likely suffer losses.

## A Combination of Methods

Probably the safest method to follow in setting quotas is to work from both ends, from the top down and from the territories up, and then compromise to reach the final figure.

As management prepares its figures based on economic and market studies, the branch managers conduct customer audits with their individual salespeople. Every attempt is made by the branch managers to obtain realistic sales goals, influenced by the characteristics of the salespeople and their individual customers. The sales goals of all the territories are totaled and compared with management's initial quota; if these are reasonably close, management's quota stands.

Working from both ends is a practical method. For unless the branch managers and salespeople can sell the quota on paper, they can hardly be expected to sell it in fact. If top management's initial quota is higher than the field force honestly feels it can pro-duce, management's quota had best be lowered, or new plans projected by the force that will make the achievement realistic. Conversely, if the estimate of the field force is high, its program should be searchingly examined; if it still looks reasonable, top man-agement should raise its sights, if practicable.

# CHAPTER 6
# PUTTING IT ALL TOGETHER

**B**y now you should have a firm understanding of what you should take into consideration when designing a sales compensation plan. This is not to say that the task that lies before you is easy; indeed, it's one of the most difficult aspects of managing your company to "get right."

And you're not alone; countless sales executives wrestle every day with a multitude of problems related to sales compensation. Here are selected results from a recent Dartnell study that will bring you up to date on what other people, like you, are thinking about.

## QUESTION 1: WHAT ARE THE TOUGHEST SALES COMPENSATION ISSUES FACING YOU OVER THE NEXT YEAR?

| RESPONSES | PERCENT OF RESPONSES |
|---|---|
| COMMISSION-RELATED ISSUES | 17.9% |
| COMPETITIVE COMP PROGRAM | 9 |
| MOTIVATING SALESPEOPLE | 8 |
| CHANGE IN COMPENSATION PLAN | 8 |
| INCENTIVE/BONUS PROGRAMS | 7 |
| DECREASING SALES/PROFITS | 6.3 |
| PAY FOR PERFORMANCE | 6.3 |
| HOW TO STRUCTURE PLAN | 5.6 |
| KEEPING HIGH ACHIEVERS | 5.6 |
| INCENTIVES FOR NEW ACCOUNTS | 3 |
| TEAM-BASED SELLING | 3 |
| CREATING A FAIR COMP PLAN | 3 |
| FAIR BENEFIT PLANS | 2.4 |
| SETTING REALISTIC SALES TARGETS | 2.4 |
| RECRUITING QUALITY PEOPLE | 2.4 |
| MAKING QUOTAS | 1.5 |
| HANDLING PEAKS AND VALLEYS | 1.5 |
| RECRUITING ENTRY LEVEL REPS | 1.5 |
| TRACKING INDIVIDUAL EFFORTS | .8 |
| COMPENSATION OF NEW REPS | .8 |
| RISING COST OF BEING ON THE ROAD | .8 |
| INDUSTRY/CHANNEL CHANGES | .8 |
| GETTING MORE SUPPORT | .8 |
| TYING INSIDE SUPPORT TO EXPENSES | .8 |
| DEALING WITH LOSS OF PEOPLE DUE TO OUTSOURCING | .8 |
| TOTAL | 100% |

Selected responses from survey participants:
- "Nonmotivated employees that do not produce."
- "How to maintain the loyalty and optimism of good sales personnel during periods when sales are temporarily down due to market or other conditions beyond the control of the individual salesperson, without maintaining a compensation level higher than that justified by sales productivity."
- "Keeping compensation level of sales force at a good, effective level of motivation, and competitive with industry."
- "Balancing sales cycle, which is very long, with compensation tools that keep motivation high."
- "Keeping sales team motivated through incentives rather than commissions. Knowing what really motivates each person."

- "Spiffing salespeople so that they sell what we want them to sell and not making the spiff part of the pay plan."
- "How to compensate top producers without making them so high in their range that you overprice your talent for the territory."
- "Using a base salary that is high enough to attract good people without making them so comfortable that they don't feel the need to sell."
- "Balancing salary (for standard duties) with incentive for encouraging new business production."
- "Establishing equitable earnings for effort and contribution with seniority and territory changes taken into account."
- "How to reward sales that don't actually produce income for up to a year after the sale then may be extremely profitable or may not."
- "Relating pay to production."
- "How to accurately define 'pay for performance.'"
- "Designing a comp. system that will leverage individual efforts with team efforts."
- "The company car — how to offer it as a business tool, but charge for it to comply with IRS."
- "Ensuring that each person's individual effort is tracked."
- "For our commission paid sales reps, the rising cost of being on the road in a difficult economic climate."
- "Setting realistic sales targets."
- "Reductions in product pricing is approaching a crisis period in cost of sales. Can't justify direct salespeople when comparing their cost versus sales revenue generated."
- "The accuracy and fairness in quota setting."
- "Erosion of gross profit percentage."
- "Matching upper management's expectations with a plan that works for the salespeople."
- "The fact that multiple people are involved in each sale."
- "Recruiting quality people."
- "Sales compensation based on percent of product contribution over budget goal."
- "We are looking to establish a retail sales force, and it will be difficult to establish compensation packages."
- "High potential college grads who have a lower income need who reach a comfort zone with little effort."
- "Developing a fair commission schedule that encourages growth in various conditions."
- "Finding the correct balance between base pay and commission on profits."
- "Transitioning previously salaried staff to commission."
- "Compensation of new products commission vs. core products. How to get sales reps to sell growth products with low margins when they earn more by selling small amounts of core products."
- "Splitting on some way of sharing commission between salespeople and technical support people assisting with the sale."
- "Maintaining 100 percent commission vs. having to establish a base to attract the quality employees I need."
- "Transition of rookie to a performer on commission."

- "The amount of commission for each sale and the commission formula for one-time sales vs. repeat business."
- "Development of new sales commission payment plan."
- "Commissions. There is a downward trend in our industry to lower commissions."
- "Providing the proper commission program to a mature sales staff in a declining market segment as we develop new products and programs. Without a realistic opportunity for growth, I may lose my best people."
- "Balance between commission and salary."
- "Lower than anticipated sales volume does not permit paying higher commission rates; very soft economy."
- "Put salesmen on commission instead of salary and commission."
- "Ease of formulation of commission."
- "Bringing in qualified people to work on draw vs. commission."
- "Commission program; currently do not offer and would like to initiate."
- "Salespeople who only look at the commission amount and not the quality, quantity, or other factors about the product they are selling."
- "Our outbound sales department is not compensated with commissions. Our reps are paid straight hourly wage. We found commissions paid to reps caused excessive competition, unfair practices, and attitude problems, and this behavior had significantly lowered our profits."
- "Fair and manageable sales incentive plan — allowing salesperson to be highly rewarded for high achievement."
- "Keeping incentives meaningful."
- "Keeping up with competitors in terms of pay, incentives, and benefits."
- "Setting bonus percentage."
- "Learning to develop incentive pay based on quality of sales."
- "How to create an incentive plan that focuses our salesmen on growing their sales."
- "Maintaining and motivating salespeople yet reducing cost of sales."
- "Competing with the rising compensation for salespeople in other fields."
- "Remaining competitive while giving the salespeople a performance-based incentive."
- "Structuring compensation to meet both sales goals and total company goals. Making sure we are compensating for the effort we want."
- "Developing a team compensation plan vs. individual."
- "The fact that our compensation program for sales is so much different than that of the competition."
- "Making sure we compensate key producers in pay and additional nonhard items (flex time, etc.) to retain the best long-term producers."
- "Determining proper comp in relation to level of sales. Do we increase comp with increased sales or decrease it?"
- "Fairness in proper compensation for top producers while keeping compensation at a level to keep lesser producers while remaining profitable."
- "Another new compensation program this year. The program is based on net profits totally, which is a change from the program last year."
- "Retaining good salespeople, as margins shrink and sales income continues to slide due to competitive pressure."
- "To make sure I'm paying enough to the producers to keep them from going to my competitors."

- "Retaining long-term sales professionals on commission only."
- "Profits are low, overhead is high — reorganizing."
- "Repeat sales. Our reps are paid to get new business. We do not address the long-term relationship after the sale."
- "We have ongoing reorganization within the company."
- "Attracting quality candidates in a relatively tight labor market."
- "Getting our salesmen to really buy into the new compensation plan."
- "How to compensate salespeople for selling to new accounts and targeted accounts."
- "Developing a package attractive enough to entice new recruits."
- "Health insurance and other fringe benefits. How much to cover; should salespeople pay future increases, etc."

### QUESTION 2: IF YOU COULD CHANGE ONE THING ABOUT YOUR SALES COMPENSATION PLAN, WHAT WOULD IT BE?

| RESPONSES | PERCENT OF RESPONSES |
|---|---|
| ESTABLISH/IMPROVE BONUS/ INCENTIVE PROGRAM | 16.9% |
| PAY FOR PERFORMANCE | 14.2 |
| LOWER BASE/HIGHER COMMISSION | 13.2 |
| OTHER | 11.3 |
| LARGER BASE, LOWER COMMISSION | 9.4 |
| REWARDS FOR NEW ACCOUNTS | 9.4 |
| SIMPLIFY COMP PROGRAM | 8.5 |
| EQUAL COMP PROGRAM FOR ALL | 4.7 |
| COMPENSATION SHOULD PARALLEL COMPANY PROFITABILITY | 4.7 |
| ALL INCENTIVE/NO SALARY | 3.8 |
| CHANGE IN PAYROLL SCHEDULE | 1.9 |
| SALARY ONLY/NO COMMISSION | 1.9 |
| MORE EMPHASIS ON CUSTOMER SATISFACTION | 0.1 |
| TOTAL | 100% |

Selected responses from survey participants:
- "Pay incentives quarterly instead of yearly. Account manager gets reward several times."
- "Increase 401(k) contribution (matching). Often salespeople are interested only in bringing home more. I would like to lower total household incomes should salespeople desire."
- "Lower base salary, increased commission. To highly reward a long sales cycle, to encourage long-lasting relationships."
- "Offer standard sales commission for reps and live with it. The more they sell, the more they make, even if it's more than the CFO. They're the life blood of a company. As long as they prospect and service, the reps should be rewarded. Too much turnover is beginning, and this may keep that from occurring."
- "I would increase the commission and lower the base salary. It would tie income closer to production."
- "Higher commission for loyal, long-term reps. Commitment and import to growth."
- "Would prefer to pay commissions on gross margin rather than on the sales. Improve cost of sales."
- "We pay our full-time salespeople a salary. I would like to change the compensation to include some type of commission. I believe it would stimulate sales."

- "Switching from fixed salary only to lower fixed bonus incentive. Believe lower fixed salary plus compensation results in more effective results."
- "Base it on profitability. Our markets are softening and the sales staff will be under greater pressure to obtain sales, perhaps causing them to cut prices too quickly."
- "I would tie compensation directly to profitability of the company rather than individual productivity or performance. Sales compensation that outpaces profit is a burden on the company, which limits its growth and progress and can even threaten the survival of the organization."
- "Let eagles soar. More incentive for excellent performance."
- "Lower the commission and moderate salary and expenses as an alternative. Our business runs on a three- to five-year cycle: lots of strategic work before the P.O. with many people."
- "Increase base pay and incorporate team incentives. To attract and retain quality people to the job, which in turn would increase dept. performance."
- "Larger base to start — slowly switching to larger commissions. Incentive to continue growth while offering a competitive salary initially."
- "Lower guarantee and commission."
- "Higher base, lower incentives. Better retention, recruiting, and customer service."
- "Change from straight commission for more security."
- "Make it more attractive to help recruiting and hiring. 100 percent commission reduces applicant pool."
- "We just changed. We no longer pay a percentage of the gross profit, but pay an $800 salary, a bonus based on unit sales, and a cash voucher based on documentation of new prospects, appointments, demonstrations, write-ups, sales, and repeat sales."
- "Change from a salary/commission to a salary/bonus program. Current salary/commission does not drive salespeople to focus on achieving quotas."
- "Go to a base plus bonus. Establish longer term relationships with salespeople."
- "Paying a year-end bonus or having residuals."
- "More incentives — bonuses — especially for a first-time sale. It takes an extreme amount of effort to win a new customer, and I believe this should be recognized separately."
- "Higher bonus for strategic results."
- "Retention bonuses."
- "More frequent 'performance' bonuses. It keeps incentive high; also allows for income consistency for sales reps."
- "Bonus tied into annual budget."
- "Initiate a commission program or incentive program to reward productivity on a more frequent basis. Right now currently on a yearly bonus plan."
- "No bonus plan, no retirement plan, no 401(k), nothing. Only DOSM gets bonus; entire staff should be compensated — company always uses team effort, so why no team bonus?"
- "Offer better incentive plans. Leads to more involvement from sales force. The sales process may be the same but the final incentives could vary, thus adding new elements to the sales process."
- "Further incentivize promotional programs with added commission. Increase sales in specialized areas of product line."
- "I would institute a healthy incentive to reach goals. It would motivate the

'driven' reps and offer a positive reinforcement of their behavior in terms they understand most — money."

- "Remove existing 'cap' on sales incentive plan to reward for higher achievement."
- "Commissions for new accounts to financially motivate salespeople to prospect."
- "Target reward for specific efforts/results."
- "Better incentive program. Reward for performance. Too much overhead with not enough results."
- "More incentive for new accounts. We need to grow our market share."
- "Eliminate commissions and have annual bonus. Administration of program is complicated due to contracts and timing issues."
- "Even out the peaks and valleys. Our plan is fairly complicated, which requires a lot of management."
- "Addition of client satisfaction data. This would allow us to reward client awareness."
- "Based on performance, not company profits. Sales vs. profitability and reorganization."
- "Adequately compensate those who are most productive."
- "Increase in percentage paid to reps as they continue to grow their company product after five years, after seven years, after 10 years. They deserve to share in the continuing success that they are helping their company obtain, and there is the loyalty of staying with the company for the long term."
- "To more accurately reflect effort, not just sales. Time and effort is spent targeting new customers, but this doesn't always meet with success."
- "Tie it closer to profitability vs. revenue. It's cheaper to keep customers than to get new ones."
- "More emphasis on activity numbers."
- "Get rid of rep residual that encourages reps to stay close to old customers. Some reps can live on it for a short period. It does not give them the drive to sell more."
- "Pay less on inherited business. They did nothing to generate it."
- "More variable incentive tied to results rather than sales activity. This would help more quality people get into the business."
- "Pay incentive commission to those reps' agencies that sell on value-added criteria rather than price. Don't need order takers — need imaginative sales effort."
- "Eliminate salary — increase commission bonus. This would reward the salesperson for results."
- "Put everyone on straight commission."
- "Free up dollars to bring in a more experienced rep. Can make impact quicker."
- "Upper management that does not like to see salespeople make almost as much as they do though the salesman has an outstanding year. The more a salesman sells and makes, the more successful the company is. If salespeople are successful, the managers above them should also do very well."
- "Make market share a part of the commission plan. This would be better overall."
- "Pay on profit margin percentages."
- "Simplification. Too much time wasted explaining the details and administering it."
- "Make it simple. Simple is easier for everyone to figure out and keep up with what is going on."
- "I would like to simplify the program and not use different percentages for each product line. It would simplify bookkeeping."

- "Simplify, simplify, simplify. Anything that takes more than one page to explain is not motivational."
- "Salary adjustment to reflect industry standards. Our salary structure is not competitive with the marketplace. Hiring good quality people is difficult."
- "Make it easier to track new business. Lots of manual effort, new business comes quietly, not immediately noticed."
- "Commission based on a sliding scale. If price is reduced or increased, salesperson should share positive or negative."
- "Be able to amend/alter plan in midstream. Complication leads to error."
- "Create forecast that is more realistic."
- "More attainable quota. This would increase self-esteem and provide more compensation."
- "To change from a gross profit plan to a net receivable plan. Over the past three years, several accounts have filed bankruptcy after we paid our people on those accounts."
- "Tailor compensation based on each rep's individuality. Different forms of compensation motivate people differently."
- "Tracking all orders in territories. Some jobs fall between the cracks, and proper commissions are not paid."
- "Longer grace period for beginning salespeople. It takes six months for them to build a good monthly goal."

## QUESTION 3: DO YOU INCLUDE INCENTIVES FOR SALES ACTIVITIES (FOR EXAMPLE, NUMBER OF CALLS, TYPES OF ACCOUNTS CONTACTED, ADDITIONAL PRODUCTS OFFERED TO EXISTING ACCOUNTS, LEVEL OF CUSTOMER SATISFACTION, ETC.) AS WELL AS END RESULTS?

| RESPONSES | PERCENT OF RESPONSES |
|---|---|
| INCLUDE INCENTIVES FOR SALES ACTIVITIES | 24.6% |
| DO *NOT* INCLUDE INCENTIVES FOR SALES ACTIVITIES | 75.4 |
| TOTAL | 100% |

Just 24.6 percent of respondents say they include incentives for sales activities as well as for end results, down significantly from results two years ago, when 35 percent of respondents told us they included activity incentives. However, all companies in this year's survey that include such incentives also report increased sales from this practice. In our survey of two years ago, 14 percent of companies using activity incentives said they did not receive additional sales from these incentives.

## QUESTION 4: WHAT END RESULTS DO YOU WANT TO PRODUCE THROUGH YOUR SALES INCENTIVE PROGRAM (FOR EXAMPLE, VOLUME, PROFIT, TARGET ACCOUNTS)?

| RESPONSES | PERCENT OF RESPONSES |
|---|---|
| VOLUME/GROWTH | 30.5% |
| ALL OF THE ABOVE | 24.4 |
| PROFIT | 19.1 |
| LONG-TERM ACCOUNTS | 17.6 |
| IMPROVED CUSTOMER RELATIONS | 3.8 |
| TARGET ACCOUNTS | 2.3 |
| OTHER | 1.5 |
| NEW CUSTOMERS | .8 |
| TOTAL | 100% |

While nearly 25 percent (24.4%) of responding companies are seeking multiple objectives, it's interesting to note that a significant number of responding companies are focusing on a single objective, such as increased profit. If the results you are getting from your incentive program are hard to track and/or difficult to measure, perhaps a more focused approach will yield the results you are looking for. Often, when we try to accomplish too much, we dilute our efforts and end up with an unwieldy plan.

**QUESTION 5: DO YOU INVOLVE FIELD SALES MANAGEMENT AND/OR THE SALES FORCE IN THE DESIGN OF YOUR SALES INCENTIVE PLAN?**

| RESPONSES | PERCENT OF RESPONSES |
|---|---|
| ALL REPS ARE ASKED THROUGH MEETINGS/ DISCUSSIONS/SURVEYS | 83.8% |
| TASK FORCE IS CREATED/TEAMS | 6.4 |
| OTHER | 5.5 |
| REPS NOT ASKED. DECISIONS ARE MADE AT ANOTHER LEVEL | 4.3 |
| TOTAL | 100% |

It is encouraging to note that fewer than 5 percent (4.3%) of responding companies do not seek input from their sales reps when designing their sales incentive plan. Often the best way to get "buy in" from your reps is to include them in the decision-making process. If you don't know what motivates your reps, ask them!

Here are some selected responses from survey participants:

- "Group meeting, committee."
- "Task force — feedback and communications before implementation."
- "Discussion prior to implementation."
- "Solicit ideas."
- "Focus groups, live and telephone."
- "Ask salespeople what motivates them."
- "We ask the sales force what they would like."
- "Open discussions with regional sales managers each year."
- "Ask what motivates them."
- "We design the plan with their input."
- "Roundtable discussions."
- "Get their ideas. We will use something they come up with."
- "I explain goals and basic outline to the sales team, then ask how we can achieve."
- "Ask for input on ways to up sales while remaining profitable."
- "We all meet four times a year to review incentive plans."
- "They help design the overall program."
- "We involve our sales managers in support of our sale efforts for all of our reps."
- "Create ownership in plan by dialoguing with them about what they need."
- "Roundtable brainstorming."
- "Simply ask for suggestion/recommendation."
- "In-person discussion."
- "We elicit feedback and ideas."
- "We involve them in discussions on not only their personal goal but also the needs of the company. We work together with management to strike a balance."
- "Discuss benefits with both individual and company. Make it win-win for everyone."

- "Ask how they would like to be paid."
- "All sales management is involved in designing the components."
- "Overall perfection is provided by executive management — sales manager develops plan details and budgets."
- "Management has designed the plan."

## QUESTION 6: WHAT EFFECT, IF ANY, HAS THE ECONOMY HAD ON THE DESIGN OF YOUR SALES COMPENSATION PLAN OVER THE LAST TWO YEARS?

The majority of respondents say the economy has had no effect on the design (or redesign) of their compensation plans.

| RESPONSES | PERCENT OF RESPONSES |
| --- | --- |
| NONE | 59.2% |
| OTHER | 18.2 |
| VERY LITTLE | 8.3 |
| COMPENSATION HAS GONE DOWN | 6.8 |
| COMPENSATION HAS GONE UP | 4.5 |
| STRONG ECONOMY — CAPS REMOVED | 1.5 |
| NEEDS TO BE/HAS BEEN WRITTEN | 1.5 |
| TOTAL | 100% |

Selected responses from participants who said they did change their compensation plan due to changes in the economy:
- "Just changed plans, and the slowdown makes it appear as though we socked it to them."
- "We used to have a guarantee paid out every 3 months — instead we use a weekly draw now."
- "A better economy has allowed us to stretch our efforts and compensate more for them — very positive effects."
- "More attention being paid to health insurance and other fringes."
- "In Sioux Falls, SD, the economy is great. We have had to look at other areas for retention of good people."
- "Salespeople want more flexibility in work hours."
- "We are a wholesale company, and people are consuming fewer alcoholic beverages or are buying less expensive products."
- "With flat sales, struggle to get motivation."
- "Threaten change, but lot of foot dragging because of fear of upsetting sales force."
- "We had to curtail incentives because of reduced profitability."
- "We've made it richer to keep our good people in the face of a consolidating market — turnover kills productivity."
- "Pressure for lower prices has cut into profits  Sales individuals were paid the same commission rate regardless of profit. Obviously, we had to address the profit issue by looking at overall sales compensation."
- "It has made it slightly more incentive-oriented."
- "It has affected the company car, streamlined expenses (sales team used for sales incentives with their accounts)."
- "Very little. Both major teamster's strike and competition going out of business left us with plenty of market to target."

**QUESTION 7: HOW MUCH INFLUENCE DOES YOUR SALES COMPENSATION PLAN HAVE IN DIRECTING THE DAY-TO-DAY ACTIVITIES OF YOUR SALESPEOPLE?**

Do your salespeople perform the tasks that you want them to perform? Or do they pretty much follow their own inclinations? A well-designed compensation plan enables you to exert influence to encourage those sales behaviors that help attain your company goals. The data below provides a look at the influence compensation plans exert on the activities of salespeople.

| RESPONSES | PERCENT OF RESPONSES |
|---|---|
| GREAT INFLUENCE | 26.4% |
| MODERATE INFLUENCE | 31.9 |
| SOME INFLUENCE | 32.6 |
| NO INFLUENCE | 2.1 |
| NOT SURE | 0.7 |
| NO ANSWER | 6.3 |
| TOTAL | 100% |

**QUESTION 8: HOW MANY MAJOR CHANGES HAVE YOU MADE IN YOUR SALES COMPENSATION PLAN IN THE LAST FIVE YEARS?**

| RESPONSES | PERCENT OF RESPONSES |
|---|---|
| NONE | 16.7% |
| ONE | 18.1 |
| TWO | 21.5 |
| THREE | 19.4 |
| FOUR | 8.3 |
| FIVE | 3.5 |
| SIX | 2.8 |
| SEVEN | 0.7 |
| EIGHT | 0.7 |
| MORE THAN EIGHT | 2.8 |
| NO ANSWER | 5.5 |
| TOTAL | 100% |

Here are selected participant responses that describe the change(s) they made to their compensation plans:

- "Hired a remote salesman with 20 percent bonus possibility."
- "Increased percentage of bonus."
- "More emphasis on sales profits rather than sales volume."
- "Readjusted commission structure."
- "1. New approach to contests; 2. changed percent of commissions; 3. varied awards."
- "1. Gone to all upfront commissions to a mix including residuals; 2. increased quotas."
- "Commission based to salary based to take pressure off new salespeople."
- "1. Straight percent; 2. Based on target categories (new business, etc.); 3. New company budget."
- "1. New management; 2. Consolidation/standardization."
- "1. Top down/bottom up selling; 2. Added a team award."
- "1. Gone from a contractual force to full-time; 2. Adjusted commission threshold to include and reward larger accounts (formerly was based on number of sales vs. dollars)."
- "1. Expenses tied to compensation; 2. But gross margin is determining factor for compensation."
- "1. Quarterly bonus program; 2. Annual bonus program."

- "Reduced incentives on percent of total and increased base salary."
- "1. Modified commission. If job is discounted, sales shares cut; 2. Pay commission on prepayment instead of waiting until entire dollar amount is collected."
- "1. Volume margin percent relationship — margins perceived as eroding; 2. Deterrent to channel switch — no pay for one year — Turf battle."
- "1. New products; 2. Penalty for not meeting objective; 3. Lower rates for renewal."
- "Bounced back and forth between profit and sales growth."
- "1. Lower base, more bonus/commission; 2. Payment of incentives quarterly instead of annually."
- "1. Bonus commission for new accounts; 2. Bonus commission for reviving old accts."
- "1. Changed commission percent to graduate higher with plan; 2. Changed commission rates based on higher margin products."
- "1. Raised base salary, decreased commission; 2. Revised quota, increased commission."
- "Adding profitability into plan."
- "1. Changed the base; 2. Changed the commission rate; 3. Deleted draws."
- "1. Rate of commissions — too low; 2. Threshold for calculation of additional incentive — too high."
- "1. Based on company performance — not individual; 2. Increased commission incentive for performance."
- "1. Added commission on three different accessory offerings; 2. Offered an additional product line for them to sell; 3. Made the earning and payment of a commission tied to customer follow-up follow-through. Penalties for abandonment."
- "We review our compensation plan yearly and make adjustments as needed."
- "Varied base and incentive."
- "1. Paid best performer more; 2. Flex time."
- "1. Added products and added incentive; 2. Added team compensation; 3. Modified base vs. variable percentage."
- "1. Changes in the strategic plan; 2. Changes in caliber of sales individual."
- "1. Created interest in new products; 2. Focused on training; 3. Added more ways to make money."
- "We increased the base and lowered commission. Reason: it prevents a salesperson's income from dipping below monthly household expenses. The result is a more satisfied salesperson."
- "Scaled down from a 'vacation' super trip to a less expensive continuing education training as incentive."
- "1. Target specific customers — additional incentive; 2. Attract salespeople — labor market is becoming tight; 3. Retain salespeople — labor market is becoming tight."
- "Reduced compensation for lower producers."
- "1. Increased bases for everyone in company; 2. Added extra incentives for top management."
- "More incentives added."
- "Added quarterly yearly bonuses."
- "1. Developed more aggressive bonus to provide greater incentive; 2. "Changed bonus from monthly to quarterly to ensure program wasn't abused."
- "Changed from flat percent on all business less percent monthly; if qualifying quota is reached, additional percent is paid on all business generated that quarter."

- "1. From base plus commission to salary; 2. Salary back to base plus commission."
- "1. 1993-94 eliminated commissions — went to straight hourly wage; 2. 1994-95 reduced sales force from 50 to 10 sales reps; 3. 1995-96: increased hourly wage to compensate for inflation and competition."
- "1. Paying on net profit; 2. Not compensating for maintenance or gross sales; 3. Payment by performance objective."
- "1. Introduced bonus plan; 2. Widened bonus and size potential."
- "1. Increased commission on company-manufactured products twice; 2. Changed formula splitting on turnover and net profit twice; 3. Changed formula for sales managers twice."
- "Items that were included in figuring the cost of the job were increased, thereby reducing commissions earned."
- "1. Provided a base salary that is based on territory volume; 2. Provided incentive over and above base."
- "1. Higher cap on incentive; 2. Incentive for number of accounts closed."
- "Increased bonuses on first-time orders to get more new business."
- "Eliminated quarterly bonus and replaced it with progressive bonus."
- "1. Higher commission on some products; 2. Commission on average month instead of initial 30 days."
- "1. Increased salary percent of total comp (to retain talent); 2. Reduced annual bonus potential (lower profitability); 3. Raised standard for annual bonus (lower profitability)."
- "1. Restructured commission tiers — too easy to reach goals; 2. Restructured override plan and retired former sales mgr."
- "More comp time."
- "Lowered commission rate — increased profits."

As you can see, there are many questions and problems, and just as many answers. It is hoped that *What America's Small Companies Pay Their Sales Forces ... And How They Make It Pay Off* will provide you with the guidance you need to answer these and other problems as they arise.

By way of review, here are some guidelines you can use that will help you develop your compensation plan and manage your company:

1. Define the objectives for the sales organization, both long-run and short-run.
2. Define policies and sales plans that will make others more productive.
3. Provide the resources that will help the organization to focus attention upon its objectives.
4. Make sure that everyone in the sales organization from top to bottom is crystal clear on their objectives, including quotas and standards of performance.
5. Manage compensation and other rewards in such a way that people go in your direction because they want to go.
6. Think about strategies (multiyear objectives), as well as immediate sales operations.
7. Think in terms of multiyear spans of time, as well as the immediate quotas and targets for the month ahead.
8. Relate to the outside world and to those social, economic, and political influences that can have a long-run impact on your business.

9. Allocate your resources in ways that will produce the highest yield.
10. Manage change, both in response to pressures and in anticipation of things that will be needed but aren't yet present.
11. Teach management to your subordinate managers. You know that the rate at which your organization grows is in direct proportion to the rate at which your people grow, not only in selling but in managing sales.
12. Interpret your organization to top management, and top management to your organization.
13. Constantly appraise and evaluate your organization, making adaptive moves to keep it going toward its goals.
14. Provide the selection guidelines for bringing new people aboard and adequate training programs to bring them up to your standards. Use systems to motivate them to go in the right direction, remain with you, persist in their efforts, and constantly grow in professional competence.

# STAYING ON TRACK

**A**t Dartnell we regularly receive requests on how to determine the cost of an average sales call, how to figure out how much a salesperson's time is really worth, and how to determine what *really* happens when you cut price.

Here are some helpful formulas for keeping you, your salespeople, and your company on track.

## THE "AVERAGE" COST OF A SALES CALL: WHAT DOES IT MEAN TO YOU?

Readers of this book who would like to determine "benchmark" figures for the average cost of a sales call in their particular industry can easily do so by using data from the survey portion of *What America's Small Companies Pay Their Sales Forces…And How They Make It Pay Off*.

Quite simply, the average cost of a sales call is calculated by dividing the average annual total cost of keeping your typical senior salesperson in the field by the total number of sales calls he or she makes per year. Average annual total expenses are determined by adding together data for total compensation, field expenses, and benefits.

For example, let's say you want to determine the average cost of a sales call for a top-performing senior salesperson selling business services. Consult Figure 71 to determine the average cost of field expenses ($11,375) and the average cost of benefits ($3,562). See Figure 62 for third-quartile total cash compensation figures ($60,000). Add these figures together to determine total annual expenses to keep this salesperson in the field ($11,375 + $3,562 + $60,000 = $74,937). See Figure 104 to determine the average number of sales calls made per day by salespeople selling business services (2.6). To determine the total number of sales calls made per year, multiply the average number of calls made per day (2.6) by the average number of workdays in a year. While the average number of workdays varies by company, most salespeople work approximately 225 days a year. Multiplying 2.6 by 225 gives us the total number of sales calls made per year (585). Divide the total annual costs ($74,937) by total annual sales calls (585) to determine the average cost of a sales call, in this case, $128.09.

## THE SURVEY AS A WHOLE

When we perform the same calculation for the survey as a whole, combining all levels of salespeople, all sizes of companies, and the entire range of industries, our average cost of a sales call is approximately about one-third the amount frequently quoted by other research groups. This is understandably confusing.

## MAKING SENSE OF IT ALL

To make some sense out of this, let's begin by taking a look at the Dartnell questionnaire. Basically, the Dartnell questionnaire asks the respondent to combine total compensation and total field expenses plus benefits and divide that amount by the total number of sales calls made per year. All computations are compiled on a per rep basis. To compute the number of sales calls made each year by each rep, respondents are asked to multiply the average number of sales calls per day by 225 days — the average number of days worked by most salespeople.

For example, let's say my "average senior salesperson" makes a total of $60,000 in salary and commissions per year. Let's also say that it costs me an additional $15,000 per year in expenses. This includes travel reimbursement, lodging, etc. I also spend another $8,000 in benefits for this individual on health insurance and the like. That gives me a total of $83,000, or what it costs per year to keep that rep in the field. This hypothetical rep makes about four calls per day, or 900 calls per year. Dividing $83,000 by 900 gives me $92.22 — the cost of an "average" sales call in my particular business.

Here's another approach that gets to the real crux of the matter. Let's say that I accept the frequently quoted figure of $295 as the cost of an "average" sales call. Let's further assume that my average rep makes an average of three calls per day. Multiplying 3 by 225 gives us 675 sales calls per year for each rep. Now if we multiply $295 by 675, we get a total of $199,125 — the total cost to keep a senior sales rep in the field on a per year basis.

Most people would agree that they do not spend an average of nearly $200,000 to keep one of their salespeople in the field. Working the "cost of an average sales call" formula backward can give you a better insight into the reasonableness of the figure.

When all is said and done, the figure given for the cost of an average sales call only makes sense when it is compared with how profitable those sales calls are. Any company concerned with rising selling costs should take a look at what it is getting for those costs.

Here's a procedure for companies to follow to determine what they are getting for the money they spend on sales calls:

1. Determine the average cost of a sales call for your particular business using the Dartnell formula.
2. Determine the average number of calls required for your salespeople to make a sale.
3. Determine the average dollar amount of an "average" sale.
4. Multiply the answer to #1 above by the answer to #2.
5. Divide the answer to #3 above by the answer to #4 above.

Your answer to #5 is the number of dollars of total revenue generated for every dollar spent on sales call costs. If this figure falls within the defined objectives of your company — great! If not, determine where the problem lies.

## DO YOUR SALESPEOPLE KNOW HOW MUCH THEIR TIME IS WORTH?

You can conduct this quick analysis at a sales meeting for all your salespeople, or you can ask individual salespeople to make the calculations on their own.

In either case, the resulting figures dramatically highlight the value of the salesperson's time.

- Determine from your own company's data approximately how much it costs to maintain a sales representative in the field.
- This figure is revealed at the start of the exercise, and participants are asked to complete the following worksheet.
- Once the calculations are completed, the group is encouraged to discuss what the figures mean in their particular situations.

# WORKSHEET

It costs approximately $___ per year for your organization to maintain a sales-person in the field. This figure includes total compensation, benefits, travel and entertainment expenses, and any other related costs.

Using this cost figure as a reference point, make the following calculations:

1. Estimate how many days per year you actually work. Consider weekends, vacation, sickness, emergencies, meetings, etc. (An average is around 225 days per year.)
2. The cost of your time is $____ per working day.
3. If you average _____ calls per day, your average cost per call is $_____.
4. Estimate how much time you spend during an average day in face-to-face selling: _____ hours.
5. The cost of your face-to-face selling time is $____ per hour.
6. The total forecast for your territory is $_____ per year.
7. To meet forecast, you must generate an average of $_____ in sales each working day.
8. On this basis, your face-to-face selling time is worth $ ____ per hour.
9. Select a typical customer. Your forecast for that customer is $ _____ per year.
10. As a rough guide, you should spend _____ days with that customer (including travel time).
11. Your forecast for _____ (select a product) is $ _____ per year. You should spend around _____ days on that product in the coming year.

Following this procedure, you can estimate roughly how much time should be allocated to each customer and each product, and how much you have to produce in any given period of time to meet forecast.

## DISCOUNTING PRICE: A LOSER'S GAME

When was the last time you heard a salesperson say "If we cut the price, we can sell more"? Here's a chart you might want to share with your salespeople to show them in no uncertain terms why it is important that they sell their products and services at full price. (Or you might want to ask them if they can make up the difference in volume!)

## EXHIBIT 2

### YOU MUST SELL MORE TO BREAK EVEN

TO FIND THE PERCENTAGE OF INCREASE IN UNIT SALES YOU WILL NEED TO EARN THE SAME GROSS PROFITS WHEN YOU CUT A PRICE, LOOK IN THE COLUMN HEADED "PRESENT GROSS PROFIT"

| IF YOU CUT YOUR PRICE | AND YOUR PRESENT GROSS PROFIT IS | | | | | | | |
|---|---|---|---|---|---|---|---|---|
| | 5% | 10% | 15% | 20% | 25% | 30% | 35% | 40% |
| 1% | 25.0% | 11.1% | 7.1% | 5.3% | 4.2% | 3.4% | 2.9% | 2.6% |
| 2 | 66.6 | 25.0 | 15.4 | 11.1 | 8.7 | 7.1 | 6.1 | 5.3 |
| 3 | 150.0 | 42.8 | 25.0 | 17.6 | 13.6 | 11.1 | 9.4 | 8.1 |
| 4 | 400.0 | 66.6 | 36.4 | 25.0 | 9.0 | 15.4 | 12.9 | 11.1 |
| 5 | — | 100.0 | 50.0 | 33.3 | 25.0 | 20.0 | 16.7 | 14.3 |
| 6 | — | 150.0 | 66.7 | 42.9 | 31.6 | 25.0 | 20.7 | 17.6 |
| 7 | — | 233.3 | 87.5 | 53.8 | 38.9 | 30.4 | 25.0 | 21.2 |
| 8 | — | 400.0 | 114.3 | 66.7 | 47.1 | 36.4 | 29.6 | 25.0 |
| 9 | — | 1000.0 | 150.0 | 81.8 | 56.3 | 42.9 | 34.6 | 29.0 |
| 10 | — | — | 200.0 | 100.0 | 66.7 | 50.0 | 40.0 | 33.3 |
| 11 | — | — | 275.0 | 122.2 | 78.6 | 57.9 | 45.8 | 37.9 |
| 12 | — | — | 400.0 | 150.0 | 92.3 | 66.7 | 52.2 | 42.9 |
| 13 | — | — | 650.0 | 185.7 | 108.3 | 76.5 | 59.1 | 48.1 |
| 14 | — | — | 1400.0 | 233.3 | 127.3 | 87.5 | 66.7 | 53.8 |
| 15 | — | — | — | 300.0 | 150.0 | 100.0 | 75.0 | 60.0 |
| 16 | — | — | — | 400.0 | 177.8 | 114.3 | 84.2 | 66.7 |
| 17 | — | — | — | 566.7 | 212.5 | 130.8 | 94.4 | 73.9 |
| 18 | — | — | — | 900.0 | 257.1 | 150.0 | 105.9 | 81.8 |
| 19 | — | — | — | 1900.0 | 316.7 | 172.7 | 118.8 | 90.5 |
| 20 | — | — | — | — | 400.0 | 200.0 | 133.3 | 100.0 |
| 21 | — | — | — | — | 525.0 | 233.3 | 150.0 | 110.5 |
| 22 | — | — | — | — | 733.3 | 275.0 | 169.2 | 122.2 |
| 23 | — | — | — | — | 1115.0 | 328.6 | 191.7 | 135.3 |
| 24 | — | — | — | — | 2400.0 | 400.0 | 218.2 | 150.0 |
| 25 | — | — | — | — | — | 500.0 | 250.0 | 166.7 |

EXAMPLE: YOUR PRESENT GROSS MARGIN IS 25 PERCENT AND YOU CUT YOUR SELLING PRICE 10 PERCENT. LOCATE 10 PERCENT IN THE LEFT-HAND COLUMN. NOW FOLLOW ACROSS THE COLUMN HEADED 25 PERCENT. YOU FIND YOU WILL NEED TO SELL 66.7 PERCENT MORE UNITS TO EARN THE SAME MARGIN DOLLARS AS AT THE PREVIOUS PRICE.

THIS "LOOK BEFORE YOU CUT PRICES!" TABLE HAS BEEN USED BY MANY COMPANIES TO DISCOURAGE PRICE CUTTERS.

Keep these charts and formulas handy. And "work the math" from time to time to see how you're staying on track.

# JOB DESCRIPTIONS AND COMPENSATION PLANS

Sometimes we need to take a look at what has gone before to help us organize our thinking. It is for this reason that we have included selected job descriptions and compensation plans to help you begin the process of drafting your own plans. Note that job descriptions frequently include the basics of the compensation plan.

Eric Schafer, Sales Manager at Data Security, Inc., Lincoln, Nebraska, kindly sent us the following job descriptions and compensation table for inclusion in *What America's Small Companies Pay Their Sales Forces…And How They Make It Pay Off*. Job descriptions from other companies are also included in this section.

---

### JOB DESCRIPTIONS FOR SALES POSITIONS AT DSI, INC.

**Primary Responsibilities:** Inside sales of tape degausser products and services to Department of Defense and commercial broadcasters over the telephone using extensive database for lead tracking.

**Duties:**
1. Data Collection
2. Purging
3. First Calls
4. Second Calls
5. Third Calls
6. Sales
7. Projects
8. Travel

**Entry Level Sales Rep:** A salesperson with less than one year of sales experience.
  Base Salary:  $19,000
  Expected Sales: $100,000
  Possible Commissions: $3,000
  Upper Quartile: $25,000 with bonus.

**First-Year Intermediate Sales Rep:** A salesperson in his or her second year of sales.
  Base Salary: $20,000
  Expected Sales; $150,000–$200,000
  Possible Commissions: $6,000
  Upper Quartile: $29,000

**Second-Year Intermediate Sales Rep:** A salesperson in his or her third year of sales.
  Base Salary: $20,000
  Expected Sales: $200,000–$250,000
  Possible Commissions: $7,500
  Upper Quartile: $31,000

**First-Year Senior Sales Rep:** A salesperson in his or her fourth year of sales.
  Base Salary: $20,000
  Expected Sales: $300,000
  Possible Commissions: $10,000
  Upper Quartile: $33,500

---

**Second-Year Senior Sales Rep:** A salesperson in his or her fourth year of sales.
Base Salary: $20,000
Expected Sales: $300,000–$400,000
Possible Commissions: $12,000
Upper Quartile: $36,000

**Sales Trainer:** Typically has three years' sales experience. Responsible for training entry level salespeople. Can also maintain a Third-Year Intermediate Sales Rep territory.
Base Salary: $22,500
Expected Sales: $300,000–$400,000
Possible Commissions: $12,000
Upper Quartile: $39,000

**National Account Manager:** Typically has five years of sales experience. Sells to major accounts/programs with a central purchasing point. Also maintains a Senior Sales Rep territory.
Base Salary: $22,500
Expected Sales: $300,000–$400,000
Possible Commissions: $12,000
Upper Quartile: $39,000

**International Sales Manager:** Typically has five years of sales experience. Works with Distributors to promote sales of products in foreign countries. Receives a 1 percent commission on all International Sales. Also maintains a Senior Sales Rep territory.
Base Salary: $22,500
Sales Rep Expected Sales: $300,000–$350,000
Possible Commissions: $11,000
International Sales: $80,000–$100,000
Possible Commissions: $1,000
Upper Quartile: $39,000

**Sales Manager:** Typically has five years' sales experience. Trains and manages entry, intermediate, and senior sales reps. Works with Distributors to promote sales of products in United States. Also maintains a Senior Sales Rep position.
Base Salary: $25,500
Sale Rep Expected Sales: $300,000–$400,000
Possible Commissions: $12,000
Upper Quartile: $55,000

### SALES COMPENSATION TABLE, DATA SECURITY, INC., LINCOLN, NEBRASKA

| SALES REP | BASE SALARY | EXPECTED SALES (MIN.) | EXPECTED SALES | POSSIBLE COMMISSION | BONUS | UPPER QUARTILE |
|---|---|---|---|---|---|---|
| TRAINEE | $14,560 | — | $33,000 | $1,000 | $1,000 | $16,560 |
| ENTRY LEVEL | $19,000 | — | $100,000 | $3,000 | $3,000 | $25,000 |
| INTERMEDIATE 1 | $20,000 | $150,000 | $200,000 | $6,000 | $3,000 | $29,000 |
| INTERMEDIATE 2 | $20,000 | $200,000 | $250,000 | $7,500 | $3,500 | $31,000 |
| SENIOR 1 | $20,000 | — | $300,000 | $10,000 | $3,500 | $33,500 |
| SENIOR 2 | $20,000 | $300,000 | $400,000 | $12,000 | $4,000 | $36,000 |
| SALES TRAINER | $22,500 | $300,000 | $400,000 | $12,000 | $4,500 | $39,000 |
| NATIONAL ACCOUNT | $22,500 | $300,000 | $400,000 | $12,000 | $4,500 | $39,000 |
| INTERNATIONAL | $22,500 | $380,000 | $450,000 | $12,000 | $4,500 | $39,000 |
| SALES MGR. | $25,000 | $300,000 | $400,000 | $12,000 | $17,500 | $55,000 |

## JOB DESCRIPTION: ACCOUNT EXECUTIVE

The Account Executive's primary function is selling advertising space in the *Greater Baton Rouge Business Report* and related special projects. In keeping with this objective, an Account Executive's activities should be directed toward establishing new accounts and growing existing accounts.

The Account Executive establishes and maintains an ongoing professional business relationship with clients by understanding their business objectives, monitoring their development and growth, and clearly presenting the benefits of the Business Report's services to assist our clients in the attainment of their business objectives. This relationship should include addressing and resolving account problems in a professional, timely, and fair manner.

Tasks associated with these objectives include consistently calling on assigned accounts, prospecting for new business, developing ad ideas with the client, communicating with agencies (providing timely information on special reports, editorial focus, and seasonal promotions), processing insertion orders, art specifications, and account information, keeping records and, when necessary, assisting with collections. Ongoing duties include submitting weekly run sheets, verifying ad dummy and price information, preparing color and hit list forms, as well as ad and price changes, meeting with the sales manager weekly, attending the weekly staff and sales meetings, entertaining clients, presenting promotional items and gifts supplied by the Business Report, and participating in company events such as the annual Business Expo and publisher's luncheons.

The Account Executive is responsible for overseeing the quality and accuracy of his/her clients' advertisements. To accomplish this, the Account Executive monitors and proofreads ads developed or altered by Lunar Graphics, receives, inspects, and traffics agency-generated artwork, and participates on a rotating basis in checking all advertising pages in the upcoming issue.

The Account Executive promotes a positive image for the Business Report in the business community by attending functions of special interest and community events. He/she maintains a professional appearance and manner in the office and out in the field.

The Account Executive participates in a continuing personal program of professional development. This program includes training courses, motivational seminars, and a reading program of literature in assigned categories.

The Account Executive reports to the Sales Manager. After a training period, compensation is composed solely of commission and bonuses. Work hours are as necessary to service the clients and meet specified company goals, typically 8:00 a.m.–5:00 p.m., Monday through Friday.

### Performance Criteria for Account Executives

1. Account Executives are assigned an account list of up to 100 accounts. These accounts belong to Business Report and are assigned with confidence that the Account Executive will consistently call on and service each client or prospect. Accurate records reflecting client/prospect contact must be kept and available to review by the Sales Manager. Success in servicing these accounts will result in sales with the associated commission and bonuses, as well as periodic verbal written and official recognition of achievement. Failure to evidence consistent and appropriate contact with assigned accounts will result in lack of sales, informal or formal training, consultation, or corrective action provided by the Sales Manager or loss of account assignments.

2. Account Executives are given personal sales goals for each issue of Business Report. Compensation and recognition will result from meeting or exceeding goals. Continued lack of success in reaching sales goals will result in corrective action, possibly leading to termination of employment.

3. Account Executives are required to abide by the policies and carry out the duties and procedures outlined in the Sales Handbook. The Sales Manager notes consistency, or lack thereof, on the part of the Account Executive in fulfilling this criterion. Continuing verbal recognition and critique is provided informally at weekly one-on-one meetings.

## JOB DESCRIPTION: ASSOCIATE ACCOUNT EXECUTIVE
## PROFESSIONAL DEVELOPMENT AND RECOGNITION

The first task of an Associate Account Executive is to thoroughly learn Louisiana Business' mission, policies, and procedures along with the technical aspects of advertising sales such as ad design concepts, ad production, and ad sales techniques through successful completion of the two-week training program.

An Associate Account Executive will immediately assume responsibility for a sales territory of prospects and, at the discretion of the Advertising Director, contract clients. This territory's responsibility is to represent its individual division by selling advertising programs, maintaining and servicing accounts as appropriate, and attending special interest, community, and civic functions.

An Associate Account Executive should, under the guidance of and as evaluated by the Advertising Director, successfully complete the training program and achieve an initial level of sales goals over a three-month initial period.

Note: The Associate Account Executive title is an *internal* company designation that reflects an employee's initial need for orientation and training for the position of Account Executive. Such an "Associate" will be referred to as an Account Executive when dealing with customers, listed on our masthead, or identified on business cards.

Upon successful completion of these objectives, the Associate Account Executive is *eligible* for promotion to the level of Account Executive.

This associate position includes the following compensation and perks:

1. Initial Salary Periods: The Advertising Director will establish the amount of salary based on past individual sales experience and expected sales goal performance. This salary is a minimum income for this initial period, and Account Executives can earn additional compensation to the extent regular commissions/bonuses on their sales exceed such salary. At the end of this initial period, Account Executives will be paid straight commission on collected sales as described in their individual Position Results Description.

This initial salary period varies by division (Business Report/ROUGE/Special Projects) due to differing sales times. These initial salary periods are as follows:
   - Business Report: three complete selling cycles, i.e., between three and four months.
   - ROUGE: two complete selling cycles, i.e., between four and six months.
   - Special Projects: three months.

2. $75 car allowance: Note: this is treated as salary/earned income on your paycheck. You are responsible for maintaining proper income tax records for the deductibility of your business auto expenses.

3. Name listed on masthead after the second month at discretion of Advertising Director.

4. Business cards provided.

5. Participation in bonus programs. Note that such bonuses are earned income and taxable to the employee.

6. Benefits as listed in the Employee Handbook.

Each salesperson is expected to deal with customers with the highest ethical and professional standards. Without exception, the integrity of our rate cards, policies, and procedures must be consistently and accurately communicated to customers.

# JOB DESCRIPTION: CORPORATE PROJECTS
## SENIOR ACCOUNT EXECUTIVE
## PROFESSIONAL DEVELOPMENT AND RECOGNITION

An Account Executive is eligible for promotion to Senior Account Executive after establishing a record of consistent successful sales attainment and performing at an "exceeds" level of performance as evaluated by the appropriate manager for at least one year.

The Senior Account Executive's basic job is to perform all the functions of an Account Executive for his/her assigned accounts. (See attached Account Executive job descriptions.)

Additionally, a Senior Account Executive is expected to achieve a "satisfactory" level of performance in the following areas:

- Maintain a consistent record of attaining higher sales goals.
- Assist Corporate Projects Sales Manager in the training of Associate Account Executives and in the ongoing development of Account Executives.
- Assist the Corporate Projects Sales Manager in the management of special projects.
- Project Preparation/Sales Preparation.
- Prospecting and dividing leads.
- Checking issue at Lunar.

This is truly an exclusive position that reflects a very high degree of professional sales attainment. This exemplary individual reflects outstanding knowledge, initiative, motivation, and results accumulated through much experience.

Because such an individual has a demonstrable record of achievement, there are not the required office hours and call sheet accountability as with Associates and Account Executives.

All of a Senior Account Executive's business activities should be dedicated to the attainment of personal and team sales goals and to the development of a professional staff.

This position includes the following additional compensation and perks:

1. $50.00 per month car phone reimbursement.
2. Business cards with "Corporate Projects, Senior Account Executive" printed.
3. Masthead change to Corporate Projects, Senior Account Executive.

## JOB DESCRIPTION: OUTSIDE SALES

**Broad Function**

To maintain and grow the assigned sales territories to their fullest possible production capabilities while at the same time promoting the Company image of being the most customer oriented company in our business. To show the customer *we care*!

**Principal Responsibilities**

1. Organize and plan territory.
2. Continuously work to maintain and increase product knowledge.
3. Assure regular contact with customers.
4. Develop new customers consistently by ongoing work in the field.
5. Develop and meet goals mutually set for territory with sales manager or store manager.
6. Assist local store or sales manager as requested for any special store projects.
7. Maintain cooperative attitude toward other employees.
8. Keep management informed of any conditions in the field that are pertinent to (Co. Name) present or future operations.
9. Maintain all required paperwork in a current and orderly fashion. (Call reports, expense reports, special reports, territory, customer work files, etc.) Provide VP/sales any requested information pertaining to your territory, plans or work.
10. Strive for professionalism — our customers deserve nothing less.
11. Responsible to Store Manager.

EMPLOYEE NAME _____  WEEK ENDING _____  PAGE _____ OF _____

| DATE | DESCRIPTION; DESTINATION; PURPOSE; CONTACT; ETC. | CAR MILEAGE & OPERATING EXPENSES | | | | | | OTHER BUSINESS EXPENSES | | | | |
|---|---|---|---|---|---|---|---|---|---|---|---|---|
| | | BUSINESS MILEAGE | GAS | OIL/LUBE | TOLLS/ PARKING | OTHER | DESCRIBE | ENTER- TAINMENT | FARES | LODGING | MEALS | OTHER |
| | | | | | | | | | | | | |
| | | | | | | | | | | | | |
| | | | | | | | | | | | | |
| | | | | | | | | | | | | |
| | | | | | | | | | | | | |
| | | | | | | | | | | | | |
| | | | | | | | | | | | | |
| | | | | | | | | | | | | |
| | | | | | | | | | | | | |
| | | | | | | | | | | | | |
| | | | | | | | | | | | | |
| TOTAL ALL OTHER PAGES | | | | | | | | | | | | |
| TOTALS | A | | | | | | | | | | | |

| | | |
|---|---|---|
| ODOMETER READING END OF WEEK | | |
| MINUS ODOMETER READING PRIOR REPORT | | |
| TOTAL MILES | | |
| MINUS BUSINESS MILES — BLOCK A | | |
| EQUALS PERSONAL MILES TRAVELED | | |

BLOCK B — PERSONAL AUTO REIMBURSEMENT
BLOCK C — PERSONAL USE OF COMPANY AUTO

X _____ = B _____
X _____ = C _____

| | |
|---|---|
| TOTAL ALL COLUMNS | |
| PLUS BLOCK B | |
| MINUS BLOCK C | |
| TOTAL EXPENSES | |

NOTE: RETAIN receipts for all lodging. RETAIN receipts for transportation and single expenditures of $10.00 or more.

ATTACH RECEIPTS TO BACK OF REPORT

# JOB DESCRIPTION: SALESMAN

A. Conceptual sales to mid/top management. Selling the benefits of a system of Monitoring, Supervising, and Control of drivers and vehicles. Result: *COST REDUCTIONS*

B. Direct Sales to all types of Commercial Fleets as well as Police, School Bus, and Public Utilities.

C. Other sales through Truck Dealers, Truck Lessors, and Automotive Service Dealers.

Territory:  Defined/Exclusive based on truck/tractor/bus and total fleet registrations. Many existing customers. Travel required.

Compensation:  Weekly Salary and Company Paid Expenses, plus graduated Commissions paid the 15th of the following month. Also, Quarterly Bonus. Hospitalization, Dental, Major Medical, Disability, Life Insurance, Pension Plan company paid.

Eight-week training period at home office, regional office, and in the field.

Sales Generated:  50% from heavy advertising program (LEADS).
40% from intelligent prospecting new accounts.
10% referrals from existing customers and dealers.

## Applicant Requisites:

A. Current and past *successful* sales background — any field.

B. Intelligent/responsible self-starting individual.

C. Experienced organizing territory and sales calls planning. Weekly reports required.

D. Excellent references and capable of working with a recognized high-caliber regional and national sales team.

Specific circumstances may require a business expense not mentioned above. Approval for reimbursement must be obtained in advance from the National Sales Manager.

## Commission Schedule:

A monthly commission of 7% will be paid to you on net sales in excess of $22,000 per month. For example, if your sales are $30,000 for the month, you will be paid a commission of 7% on the $8,000 difference between $22,000 and $30,000 = $560 commission.

In addition, you will be paid a monthly achievement commission for maintaining a sales level above $17,000 per month on a monthly average basis. It will be assumed that average monthly sales for the prior 12 months were $17,000 per month for a total of $204,000. If your sales for the first month under this plan were to be $30,000, then the new total for the prior 12 months' average would be changed to: $204,000 - 17,000 = $187,000 + $30,000 = $217,000 ÷ 12 = 18,083 per month, and you would be paid a bonus commission of 7% on the difference between the original average of $17,000 per month and the new average of $18,083 per month. 7% of $1,083 amounts to $75.81. Your total commission for this one month example would be $635.81.

In addition, you will be paid a quarterly bonus on all sales above $66,000 per quarter. For example, if your quarterly sales were to be $70,000, you will be paid 10% on the $4,000 different between $66,000 and $70,000. Therefore, your quarterly commission would be $400.

There will be an annual bonus of 20% based on the increase in average monthly net sales for the year, as compared to the average monthly net sales for the previous year. The previous year's sales are assumed to be an average of $17,000 per month, for an annual total of $204,000. On the assumption that your total net sales for this year will be $420,000 for an average of $35,000 a month, you will be paid on the difference between $17,000 and $35,000, which is $18,000, and your annual bonus, at 20%, would be $3,600.

**Computer Hardware:**

Sales of this equipment, whether made by the Company or the computer manufacturer, is not included in commissionable sales, and no commissions will be paid thereon.

**Computer Services:**

Charts sent in for IP-15 evaluation printouts or accident analysis are not included in commissionable sales, and no commissions are paid thereon. FMS cartridges sent in for printouts are not included in commissionable sales, and no commissions are paid thereon.

## SALESPERSONS OPERATIONAL POLICY

Welcome to the Company. In a growing organization such as ours, adherence to set policies is a must in order to assure a smooth-running operation. From time to time, improvements, modifications, discontinuations, or changes must be made in order to build a better organization.

I. Remuneration policies
  (a) Salespersons are paid twice monthly, on the 15th and 30th of each month.
  (b) Auto allowance — the Company provides a $200 per month auto allowance. The Salesperson is responsible for furnishing auto insurance, fuel, and repairs.
  (c) Insurance — Company-paid health and life insurance ($10,000).
  (d) Vacation — Sales personnel vacation schedule is in accordance with the employee handbook.
  (e) Expenses — no phone, parking, or miscellaneous expenses are to be paid. A maximum of 1/2% of total sales per month will be reimbursed by the Company for entertainment expenses. Any extraordinary expense per diem.

II. Areas of responsibility
  (a) Sales — Customers
    1. Regular prospecting.
    2. Regular call-back schedule to existing customers, on a weekly, biweekly, or mutually agreed upon time frame, to best service the individual customer.
    3. Credit—Salesperson is responsible for supplying credit information on new accounts, also to promptly assist in the collection of overdue accounts.
    4. Estimates—Salesperson alone is responsible for getting price from the estimator to the customer and following all the quotations to customers with a written proposal.
    5. When a job is brought in, complete responsibility for following the job through; being sure all proofs are delivered on time, corrections are made, customers are informed of progress of job and of delivery date. (All changes or corrections to job will not be made unless they are in writing!)

6. Follow-up after job is delivered ... are they satisfied with job, any problems, etc.? Feedback to Company.

7. Prompt return of artwork to customer is essential.

(b) Salesperson Responsibility in Job Estimating

1. Sales personnel should request a quotation, filling out a job spec sheet complete with stock description and layout. If information is incomplete, job spec sheet will be returned, to be completed. No verbal specs or explanations will be accepted.

2. Estimates — job spec sheet will be returned to Salesperson with prices posted — computer runouts will *NOT* be give to Sales.

(c) Sales Responsibility to Order and Production Department

1. Job orders will not be accepted without a job spec sheet. If the job has been quoted, use the same job spec sheet estimate is on, mark as order, and attach a copy of written quotation, as well as computer quote from the file. If information is missing, job spec sheet will be returned to sales from order department or production control, i.e., date ordered, date wanted, proof date.

2. Delivery dates — general rule — 11 working days for new orders, and 6 working days for exact repeats. This is based on camera-ready art. Rush delivery dates decided on a per job basis.

3. Proof dates — if proof is not returned within one day, or mutually agreed upon time frame, original delivery date will not hold. A new delivery date will be scheduled upon return of the proof. All proofs *must* be signed before production is started.

4. Change orders — use the change order/proof approval 3/P form, take to production officer. Customer to be charged for all work prior to change order.

5. Cancellations — for any cancellations, customer is to be charged for all material and labor performed up to the time of cancellation.

III. General

(a) A weekly itinerary will be turned in each Monday.

(b) A Sales quota will be set for each Salesperson on an annual and monthly basis. Salespersons will be evaluated on a continuous basis.

(c) Office hours — 8:00 a.m. to 4:30 p.m. It is not necessary to report to the office before starting calls. We do, however, require you to phone in three times a day: early morning, noon and midafternoon.

(d) Business cards, stationery, samples, selling aids, etc., will be supplied by the Company upon request.

(e) Training period — per individual, as to office and shop procedures, selling in the field.

(f) All amendments to this policy will be made in writing. They should be placed in Sales folder immediately upon receipt.

(g) It is mandatory that all Salespeople adhere strictly to these policies. Keep this book handy and refer to it often, as any deviation from set policies will be cause for disciplinary action.

(h) General Sales meetings will be held on occasion. Attendance is required. Reasonable advance notice will be given.

**Compensation Package**

1. Base salary — $20,000 per year.
2. 7% commission on sales over quota ($250,000 per calendar year).
3. Full Health and $10,000 Life Insurance.
4. $200/month car allowance.
5. Expenses.
6. Paid vacation and holidays.

   a. The base salary serves as payment for the fulfillment of the minimum responsibilities established for this position.
   b. Sales personnel are responsible for maintaining a monthly quota of $20,835/$250,000 annually.
   c. Sales personnel must make quota within an agreed-upon time frame.

Type of work produced by the company: 1/color, 2/color, short run 4/color, price lists, booklets, newsletters, and carbonless forms.

**Compensation Package — Training Program**

1. Base salary — $11,250.
2. 3.5% commission on sales to $250,000 per calendar year.
   7.0% commission on sales over $250,000 per calendar year.
3. Full Health and $10,000 Life Insurance.
4. $200/month car allowance.
5. Expenses.
6. Paid vacation and holidays.

   a. The base salary serves as payment for the fulfillment of the minimum responsibilities established for this position.
   b. Sales personnel are responsible for maintaining a monthly quota of $20,835/$250,000 annually.
   c. Sales personnel must make quota within an agreed-upon time frame.

Type of work produced by the Company: 1/color, 2/color, short run 4/color, price lists, booklets, newsletters and carbonless forms.

# JOB DESCRIPTION: SALES REPRESENTATIVE

I. Basic Function:

Responsible for providing sales coverage and developing best possible market penetration for all products to present and prospective accounts in his assigned territory in accordance with the Company's policies and programs.

II. Organizational Relationships:

Reports to: Regional or District Sales Manager

Supervises: None

III. Duties and Responsibilities:

A. Company

1. To reflect both in his personal demeanor and professional integrity the true image of the company he represents to his customers and prospects.
2. To maintain and increase sales volume with established accounts and to aggressively seek new customers by formulating and following planned sales strategies and company marketing programs to ensure optimum profitable sales penetration in his assigned territory.
3. To be sensitive to the current individual needs of customers and prospects, and to help them attain their goals through the proper utilization of the Company's products and services.
4. To understand and administer customer service, in accordance with Company policy, in a mutually beneficial manner, to ensure lasting goodwill between the customers and the Company.
5. To seek new uses and applications for Company products with present and prospective customers.
6. To assist present and prospective customers in adapting Company products to their own requirements and specifications.
7. To aggressively carry out marketing programs as directed.
8. To authorize "return" goods in accordance with Company policy.
9. To adjust customer complaints in accordance with Company policy, and to advise management promptly of any situations beyond his scope of authority.
10. To comply with all Company policies, instructions, and directives for the fulfillment of Company objectives and for maximum profitable sales.
11. To be alert to competitive products and marketing practices, and to keep management informed concerning them.
12. To participate actively in the development of sales forecasts.
13. To maintain up-to-date customer and territory records in accordance with Regional/District Managers' instructions.
14. To prepare and submit call and expense reports as required.
15. To submit special reports regarding the operation of the territory, acceptance or rejection of products, and competitive conditions beneficial to other salesmen and Company operations.
16. To recommend the addition of new products and the modification or deletion of present products to the line as appropriate.
17. To attend and participate in sales meetings, training programs, conventions, and trade shows as directed.
18. To attend and participate in allied trade meetings and organizational activities.

19. To participate actively in Market or Product Test Programs as directed.
20. To maintain an awareness of likely candidates for the sales force and to call any such to the attention of the Regional Manager.
21. To participate actively in territory and self-development programs.
22. To cooperate with all personnel in the region, department, division, and other divisions in the execution of programs and policies, to achieve overall Company objectives.
23. To assume the obligations of good citizenship and to participate in worthwhile community activities as a public relations asset to the Company.

B. Customer
1. Analyzes customer's needs and formulates solutions, by utilizing all resources made available to him by the Company.
2. Offers service; looks for ways that he and the Company can help the customer do a better job.
3. Provides information to customers on new and current products, back orders, general order status, current pricing structure, Company policy changes, and anticipates customers' future needs.
4. Achieves prompt, mutually satisfactory solutions to customer complaints.
5. Keeps promises, appointments. Exercises courtesy at all times.
6. Takes active part in customers' sales meetings and trade shows.

IV. Principal Working Relations:
1. Works with the Sales Administration Manager — in providing service to customer accounts.
2. Cooperates with Market Managers as directed by Regional or District Manager.
3. Cooperates with National Accounts Managers as directed by Regional or District Manager.
4. Cooperates with the Company as directed by Regional or District Manager.
5. Cooperates with personnel as directed by Regional or District Manager.

V. Knowledge, Training, and Experience Recommended:
1. Minimum five years' field sales experience, or three years in related field.
2. Minimum two years of college.

## JOB DESCRIPTION: ACCOUNT MANAGER

**Accountability Objective**

Under the direction of the District Manager, responsible for maximizing the sale of products by maintaining and implementing effective sales and service techniques with an emphasis toward producing new accounts.

**Dimensions**

Sales Volume —

**Nature and Scope**

Responsible for continually leading in the production of new accounts of industries concerned with the efficient utilization of water and energy. Promotes the application and benefit of products with current and prospective customers in order to increase sales and develop a more beneficial customer rapport. Capable of selling company products in all groups in order to expand current penetration with existing customers and seek new applications for existing products. Develops up-to-date selling skills and maintains basic sales ability through constant practice and upgrading. Through review of trade publications, search for new facilities being built, customer contracts, referrals, chamber of commerce data, and knowledge of existing potential, calls on such industries and applies proven sales techniques.

Responsible for providing current customers with competent technical service in all major applications. Establishes role as an authority on new technical developments and reinforces it through continuing education and making information and assistance available to customers. As required, conducts various field tests and may occasionally send samples to research facilities for analysis. With the aid of a test kit, develops strategies and effective technical service. Periodically discusses with a member of a supporting staff the strong and weak points of the individual's sales presentation or technical service.

Develops a formal Personnel Development Report on each member of the supporting staff and submits it to the District Manager and discusses the report with the individual on which the report was written. This report provides data on the individual's ability to sell, technical knowledge, appearance, and rapport with the customer. Coaches sales staff but does not provide counseling advice.

Calls on national accounts within an assigned area and coordinates sales efforts between various sales districts. Acts as a liaison between the Company and customer. Provides the District Manager with information pertaining to product requirement, acceptability, competitive markets and prices. Communicates Company policy to the supporting staff and ensures compliance.

Assists the District Sales Manager in conducting District Sales Meetings. Attends conventions, exhibits, and meetings in order to stay abreast of industry trends.

**Principal Accountabilities**

1. Responsible for the sale and service of a variety of products.
2. Applies an experienced background in determining customer needs, seeking new product application, and recommending changes in customer equipment or chemical dosages.

3. Provides motivation to a supporting staff and continually advises the supporting staff concerning the achievement of predetermined sales goals.
4. Calls on national accounts within an assigned area and ensures coordination of sales and service efforts toward the accounts.
5. Trains and develops the supporting staff by accompanying them on various trips and by preparing Personnel Development Reports.
6. Attends conventions, exhibits, and seminars in order to stay abreast of industry trends.
7. Supports management in all areas of responsibilities.
8. Maintains state of technology current and complete, and reviews, comments on, or corrects service reports for customers as directed by District Manager.

## JOB DESCRIPTION: DISTRICT REPRESENTATIVE II

**Accountability Objective**

Under the direction of a District Manager, and with the occasional assistance of a District Representative I, responsible for continual development and application of effective sales and technical service techniques to maximize the sale of products.

**Dimensions**

Sales Volume —

**Nature and Scope**

Completes the initial training program and acquires competent sales and technical service techniques. Responsible for calling on and selling Company products to customers who are concerned with the efficient utilization of water and energy. Expands current penetration with existing customers and seeks new applications for existing products. Responsible for improving those contact skills which will ultimately lead to increased sales volume and more beneficial customer rapport.

With assistance of a District Representative I, responsible for servicing and maintaining existing customers; however, the majority of time is devoted to the development of new business with existing or prospective customers. Acquires new accounts through reviewing various publications, seeking new facilities, customer contact, referrals, Chamber of Commerce data, and knowledge of existing opportunities.

Responsible for being competent in technical service as well as in sales. Periodically conducts field tests and may occasionally send samples to Company research facilities for further analysis. Through technical service calls with existing customers, determines the effectiveness of present products and makes any necessary adjustments. May provide a customer with a written report outlining the analytical conclusions and recommendations for changes in equipment design, chemical dosages, and/or chemical techniques. May be called upon by a new or existing customer to provide technical assistance on equipment or products for facility.

Maintains a close contact with the District Manager in order to review customer sales and service calls, inform the District Manager of key personnel changes in customer plants, report significant changes in competitive pricing or products, seek direction, and occasionally discuss a personal development or problem. Coordinates sales and service efforts between corporate headquarters and other district offices when applicable. Acts as a liaison between customers and the Company.

Prepares an annual sales forecast for approval by the District manager. Operates within a controlled expense budget.

Attends professional meetings and conferences in order to enhance professional abilities. Attends workshop sessions and continually reviews training material for self-development.

Stays abreast of all product trends and marketing techniques within the industry and the Company. Assists research and product managers in conducting field tests and market studies with customers.

**Principal Accountabilities**

1. Expands current product penetration with existing customers and continually seeks new accounts.

2. Maximizes the sale of Company products through the effective use of sales techniques and technical service skills.
3. Participates in field tests and market studies with Research and Marketing personnel.
4. Coordinates sales and service activities with corporate headquarters and other district offices.
5. Keeps abreast of changing technology and competitive markets and products.

# JOB DESCRIPTION: DISTRICT REPRESENTATIVE I

**Accountability Objective**

Under the direction of the District Manager and Area Manager, responsible for maximizing the sale of Company products by maintaining and implementing effective sales and service techniques.

**Dimensions**

Sales Volume —

**Nature and Scope**

Responsible for seeking new accounts of industries concerned with the efficient utilization of water and energy. Promotes the application and benefit of company products with current and prospective customers to increase sales and develop a more beneficial customer rapport. Reviews trade publications, searches for new facilities being built, customer contacts, referrals, Chamber of Commerce data, and knowledge of existing potential. Calls on such industries and applies proven sales techniques. Expands current penetration with existing customers and seeks new applications for existing products.

Responsible for providing current customers with a competent technical service. Conducts various field tests and service calls and may occasionally send samples to Company research facilities for analysis as required; conducts analyses using a test kit to determine existing conditions and what corrective chemicals are required. Determines the effectiveness of present products and makes any necessary adjustments. Provides customers with a written report outlining the analytical results, suggestions on equipment design changes, minor or major changes in chemical dosages, or changes in chemical techniques. May be called upon by a new or existing customer to provide technical assistance on equipment or products for a new facility.

Acts as a liaison between customers and the Company. Maintains close contact with a District Manager and/or Area Manager at least once a week to review customer sales and service calls, inform the District Manager of key personnel changes in customer plants, report any significant changes in competitive pricing or products, seek direction on how to undertake a particular sales situation, and occasionally discuss a personal development or problem. Regularly submits competitive surveys to maintain awareness of competitive activity and to seek new business opportunities.

Stays abreast of all product trends within the industry and maintains familiarity with marketing techniques of the Company and competitive products. Participates with research and product managers in conducting field tests and market studies with customers.

Assists the District or Area Manager in training a new District Representative II. May be assigned a District Representative II to expose him/her to testing techniques, interpreting results, explaining processes and equipment, correct sales and service techniques, and product application.

Prepares an annual sales forecast for approval by the District Manager. Controls expenses within budget.

Attends professional meetings and conferences in order to enhance professional abilities. Attends workshop sessions and reviews training material for self-development.

Responsible for improving those contact skills which will ultimately lead to increased sales volume and more beneficial customer rapport.

**Principal Accountabilities**

1. Increases sales by developing new accounts and expanding penetration with existing customers. Seeks new applications for existing products.
2. Provides competent technical service and establishes excellent customer relationships to assure continued growth.
3. Coordinates sales and service activities between corporate headquarters and district offices.
4. Participates in field tests and market studies.
5. Keeps abreast of changing technology and competitive markets and products.
6. Assists in the training and development of District Representatives II's.

# JOB DESCRIPTION: DISTRICT REPRESENTATIVE TRAINEE

## Accountability Objective

Responsible for the acquisition of effective sales skills through the completion of the Company's Sales Training Manual, through familiarization with products and philosophy, and through the training by and exposure to successful sales personnel.

## Dimensions

Indeterminate

## Nature and Scope

Responsible for the acquisition of those skills necessary to contribute effectively to the profitability of the Company. Demonstrates a knowledge of the fundamentals of water chemistry through the completion of numerous exercises in the Company's Salesman's Training Manual. These exercises include reading assignments and questions concerning such areas as water preparation, pollution control, process chemicals, and marketing services.

Completes exercises in coordination with visits to customer plants. Accompanies various district personnel on sales and service calls to customer operations to gain exposure to plant operations.

Responsible for some handling of the district's service calls to contribute to the profitability of the district. Calls on customers and recommends changes in chemical dosage, flow rates, or equipment to assist in maximizing customer satisfaction and profitability.

Attends the Company's New Salesmen's School at corporate headquarters to learn effective sales techniques, Company products and applications, and general chemical applications.

Responsible for improving customer contact skills. Maintains familiarity with competitive prices and products to stay abreast of new developments. Coordinates with marketing personnel to provide feedback on marketing operations or to request assistance from various marketing personnel.

## Principal Accountabilities

1. Responsible for the successful completion of the Company's Salesman's Training Manual.
2. Visits customer plants with various district personnel to become familiar with customer operations.
3. Handles some of the assigned district's service calls.
4. Attends the New Salesmen's School at corporate headquarters.
5. Implements effective sales strategies and techniques to contribute efficiently to Company profitability and growth.

# SALES INCENTIVE COMPENSATION PLAN

A. Purpose

The purpose of the Sales Incentive Compensation Plan (SICP) is to provide incentive to increase Division sales by way of a quarterly commission payment for all credited sales in a participant's assigned territory. An annual bonus award opportunity is also provided based upon the results against the Division's annual operating plan and individual performance against specific written measurable objectives.

B. Participants

Individual Sales Engineers must be recommended by the Vice President, Sales and the Division President and approved by the Chief Operating Officer.

C. Award Opportunity

Each participant will be paid 1/8 of 1% (.00125) of all credited sales in his assigned territory on a quarterly basis. An annual bonus award pool will also be formed by taking 10% of the total of the salary grade midpoints of all participant Sales Engineers. The distribution of this pool, if any, will depend upon the following factors:

- If the Division achieves less than seventy-five percent (75%) of its overall pre-tax profit annual plan, no award pool will be formed. Division performance close to annual plan targets would generally provide for 50% of the maximum award pool to be available for distribution, while performance of 125% or greater would allow the maximum award pool to be available for distribution to participants.
- Both the bookings and billings plan will have to be met or exceeded for any of the pool to be distributed.
- Individual performance against specific written measurable objectives must be such as to warrant a bonus payment.

Note: Distribution of all or part of the annual bonus award pool, subject to the above guidelines, will be discretionary on the part of the Vice President, Sales and the Division President and subject to the approval of the Chief Operating Officer.

D. Annual Award Determination

Assuming an award pool is available for distribution, the following procedure is used to calculate an award recommendation:

1. At the beginning of the fiscal year, each participant and Manager must establish mutually acceptable objectives that support or compliment the Division objectives. These individual objectives define special programs or tasks that require performance above and beyond that of normal job duties.
2. These objectives, which typically are two to six in number, are then weighted to the nearest 5 percent in order of importance and priority so that all the weighted percentages will total to 100 percent.

3. Near the close of the fiscal year, the results achieved for each objective are reviewed, discussed, and rated on the following basis:

| Rating | Points | Definition |
| --- | --- | --- |
| Truly Exceptional | 2.0 to 3.0 | Reflects an unusually high level of achievement relative to the objective. Significantly exceeded expectations in terms of quality and quantity. |
| Exceeds Expectations | 1.0 to 2.0 | Indicates the successful achievement of the objective. Consistently peformed above normal expectations. |
| Meets Expectations | .5 to 1.0 | Relates to an acceptable level of performance consistent with normal expectations relative to the achievement of the objective. |
| Below Expectations | 0 | Designates an unacceptable level of performance wherein the incumbent failed to achieve acceptable results in relation to the objective. |

4. The rating points assigned each objective are then multiplied by its weighted percentage of importance/priority t determine the objective's weighted points. These weighted points are then totaled for each participant.

The total weighted points for all participants are then added together to form a grand total. This grand total, when divided into the dollars available in the award pool, will determine the value of one point. This value, times each individual's total points, will determine the recommended award. Exhibit I shows an example individual award calculation.

E. Administration — Annual Bonus Award Pool

Shortly after the completion of each fiscal year, the Vice President, Sales will make a first-cut annual award recommendation for each participant. All first-cut award recommendations, along with a summary of the results achieved by the participant for each objective, shall be submitted for review by the Division President, the President and Chief Operating Officer, the Vice President and General Counsel (Chief Personnel Officer), and the Director of Compensation. Each recommendation will be reviewed against each individual participant's award calculation to ensure it is fair and consistent with compensation policy guidelines.

Final award recommendations will be developed after audited Division and Corporate results are known. All annual incentive award recommendations must be approved by the Chief Operating Officer before actual awards are granted.

F. Miscellaneous Considerations
1. No commission is paid on shipping or cancellation charges, bad debts or returned goods, etc.
2. Sales Engineers may be added or deleted at any time. Sales territories may be revised at Management's discretion. Where this has an effect on territory assignments or commission opportunity, the Vice President, Sales will determine the most equitable approach to such changes.
3. The Vice President, Sales will also determine the proper distribution of commission payments for credited sales involving more than one party.

4. A participant must be an employee at fiscal year end to be eligible for any annual bonus award. Exception is made for normal retirement or approved early retirement where such awards may be determined on a pro rata basis.

5. The Company may, at its discretion, amend or discontinue this Plan at any time.

G. Timing and Form of Annual Bonus Award Payments

Awards, if approved, are normally paid in cash to participants after the close of the fiscal year and before the close of the calendar year in which such fiscal year ends.

H. Duration of Participation

Participants are recommended and approved on an annual basis. No participation beyond that is intended or implied.

# EXAMPLE
## INDIVIDUAL AWARD CALCULATION

| | OBJECTIVES | | RESULTS ACHIEVED | |
|---|---|---|---|---|
| No. | WEIGHTED IMPORTANCE/ PRIORITY | DESCRIPTION | COMMENTS | |
| 1. | 45% | SELL A MINIMUM OF "X" MACHINES IN ASSIGNED TERRITORY. | MET QUOTA AND SOLD "Y" ADDITIONAL MACHINES. | |
| 2. | 30% | REDUCE PERSONAL SALES EXPENSE PER MACHINE SOLD BY 10% | REDUCED PERSONAL SALES EXPENSE BY 8% PER MACHINE SOLD. | |
| 3. | 15% | DEVELOP FIVE NEW ACCOUNTS. | DEVELOPED NINE NEW ACCOUNTS. | |
| 4. | 10% | REVIVE TWO LOST ACCOUNTS. | REVIVED THREE LOST ACCOUNTS. | |
| | 100% | | | |

| OBJECTIVE No. | WEIGHTED IMPORTANCE/ PRIORITY | | RATING RESULTS* | | WEIGHTED POINTS |
|---|---|---|---|---|---|
| 1. | 45% | X | 1.6 | = | 72.0 |
| 2. | 30% | X | .5 | = | 15.0 |
| 3. | 15% | X | 2.5 | = | 18.0 |
| 4. | 10% | X | 1.8 | = | 142.5 |

| *RATING | | POINTS |
|---|---|---|
| TRULY EXCEPTIONAL | = | 2.0 TO 3.0 |
| EXCEEDS EXPECTATIONS | = | 1.0 TO 2.0 |
| MEETS EXPECTATIONS | = | .5 TO 1.0 |
| BELOW EXPECTATIONS | = | 0 |

ASSUME ALL 8 PARTICIPANTS TOGETHER HAVE A TOTAL OF 880 POINTS.

ASSUME ANNUAL BONUS AWARD POOL = $30,000.

VALUE OF ONE POINT = $30,000/800 = $34.09

PARTICIPANT IN ABOVE EXAMPLE WITH 142.5 POINTS X $34.09/POINT = $4,858 RECOMMENDED AWARD.

# SALES INCENTIVE COMPENSATION PLAN (SICP)
## OBJECTIVES EVALUATION FOR FY_____

Name: _____ Title: _____

Division: _____ Location: _____

Approvals:

    Date:_____ Participant: _____ Manager: _____

    Final Approval Level: Date: _____ Signature: _____

    Column 1 should be completed at the beginning of the fiscal year when objectives are established. Column 2 should be completed at the close of the fiscal year when the performance against objectives is evaluated. Additional pages may be attached, if necessary.

| MAJOR OBJECTIVES: | % WEIGHTED IMPORTANCE | RESULTS ACHIEVED: |
|---|---|---|
| | | |

# SALES INCENTIVE COMPENSATION PLAN (SICP)
## OBJECTIVES EVALUATION FOR FY _____ (CONTINUED)

Name: _____  Title: _____

| MAJOR OBJECTIVES: | % WEIGHTED IMPORTANCE | RESULTS ACHIEVED: |
|---|---|---|
|  |  |  |

# SALES INCENTIVE COMPENSATION PLAN

## AWARD CALCULATION

| OBJECTIVES | RESULTS ACHIEVED |
|---|---|
| | |

| OBJECTIVE NO. | WEIGHTED IMPORTANCE/ PRIORITY % | x | RESULTS RATING | = | WEIGHTED POINTS |
|---|---|---|---|---|---|
| | | | | | |

APPROVALS:

DATE: _____ PARTICIPANT: _____ MANAGER: _____

| RESULTS RATING | | | POINTS |
|---|---|---|---|
| TE | = | TRULY EXCEPTIONAL | = 2.0 TO 3.0 |
| EE | = | EXCEEDS EXPECTATIONS | = 1.0 TO 2.0 |
| ME | = | MEETS EXPECTATIONS | = .5 TO 1.0 |
| BE | = | BELOW EXPECTATIONS | = 0 |

1. TOTAL WEIGHTED POINTS _____

2. VALUE OF ONE POINT $ _____

3. RECOMMENDED AWARD $_____

(1.x 2.)

# WHAT THE COMPANY EXPECTS OF ITS SALES STAFF

To represent the Company well and honorably. To complete agreed sales assignments with efficiency, integrity, and profitability to the Company.

All orders shall have signed Purchase Orders of the client or an order confirmation of the Company completed by the sales rep and signed and dated by the client showing quantity, description, and price quoted.

A. Each order shall be entered promptly upon receipt of all details from the client and in the way designated by the Company for entering all orders.

B. The sales rep shall lend all help to production people as requested to permit smooth and proper flow of each order.

C. A proof for final okay by the customer shall be presented and signed and dated by the customer. The only exception to this will be as follows:

- When a finished sample and complete negatives are supplied by the client.
- When a complete and comprehensive hand drawing, exact in spacing and complete in copy, is signed by the customer as his complete approval to proceed.
- When the order is a repeat of a previous order done by the Company and on which no alteration or change of any kind is made.

D. No sale is completed until paid for. Sales credit and payment of bonus or commission may be reversed if the account is not paid in 90 days. Nonpayment will require a deduction from any credit, bonus, or commission paid to the sales representative.

The only time the sales rep will not be affected is if nonpayment is due to an order delivered not as ordered and the sales rep has played no part in the creation of the error. The sales rep is always required to give his or her complete effort to solve a customer dispute, despite its cause, and to obtain payment to the Company.

Should nonpayment be due to a bankruptcy of a client, the sales rep will receive no credit of any kind for the sale and all commissions and/or bonuses will be reversed, but the sales rep will have no other penalty (no charge-back against profitability). The sale, its costs and, of course, remuneration, whether paid or unpaid, shall disappear from the sales territory record.

E. The sales rep will be responsible for providing a means of transportation within and to his/her territory.

F. Any expense incurred by the rep in carrying out of his/her work in the territory for entertainment, promotion, or living shall be within the policy of the Company or it will be subject to the approval of the sales manager prior to any commitment of the Company to reimburse.

G. Punctuality and full attendance at all announced Company meetings is expected of each rep.

H. Prompt filing by each rep of all requested reports, plans, and sales/client-related details required by the Company from time to time.

I. All clients and customers served by a Company sales rep are the clients and customers of the Company, and the Company retains the right to reassign such clients and customers to another rep when the company feels it will be beneficial to the client or the Company to do so.

J. The legal courtesy of leaving the Company with clean hands. (All details, materials, listings, and records pertaining to the Company — client-related materials used while serving the Company and its clients—remain at the Company upon departure of a sales rep for any reason whatsoever.)

# PART TWO — SURVEY DATA

# SURVEY DATA

This, the second part of *What America's Small Companies Pay Their Sales Forces...And How They Make It Pay Off*, focuses on our survey data where you'll find hard-to-find sales compensation and sales management information. This data is compiled in an easy-to-use, reader-friendly format to help you easily find the particular information you need. In this part of the book you'll find a wealth of facts, figures, and commentary that will enable you to create a complete picture of today's sales compensation practices.

Nearly 300 companies employing a total of more than 2,000 salespeople participated in this study.

To make it easy for users of this survey to see exactly what kinds of companies are represented, we have listed survey participants by four-digit Standard Industrial Classification (SIC) codes. This listing begins on page 271.

## MORE THAN COMPENSATION DATA

In addition to providing comprehensive sales compensation figures, we have included research data to answer such questions as:

- What field expense items are companies with under $5 million in annual sales likely to pay for? (See page 204.)
- What benefits are usually provided?
- How much do these companies spend on training for their new and experienced salespeople? (See pages 229 and 231.)
- Do companies base commissions strictly on sales volume, profitability of the sale, a combination of those measures — or some other measures? The answers are here. (See page 249.)
- Who is most likely to be hired when a job opening occurs — an entry level, intermediate, or senior level rep? Why? (See page 251.)
- How do salespeople divide their time between selling and nonselling activities?

## SURVEY METHODOLOGY

Since sales issues are often significantly influenced by industry type, we have segmented the data by industry (SIC) code. However, we have found that many issues also tend to be driven by other broader groupings. Thus, in addition to industry groupings, we have also segmented much of the data by type of buyer (industry, consumers, retailers, and wholesalers/distributors/jobbers) and by type of product or service sold. Data for an organization that sells to several buyer types (or that sells a combination of products and services) is reported under each type for that grouping, but only once in the overall survey results. We believe that these additional groupings will improve the usefulness of the survey results, especially for those industries with thin representation.

Often a small amount of representative information is better than none at all. However, in order to ensure the confidentiality of the responses of any individual participant, we do not report data for any particular category with fewer than seven companies submitting information.

## SURVEY POSITIONS

We asked survey participants to match positions in their sales force to the 10 positions described in the questionnaire. Matches are based primarily on the positions' responsibilities, as well as on reporting relationships and frequently used titles. (Position descriptions can be found on pages 108 and 109.)

## ABOUT THE SURVEY DATA

The collection of data for this book took place during 1996. Base salary data is effective as of January 1, 1996. Incentives, which were earned in 1995, may have been paid in 1996.

## COMPENSATION DATA

Participants were asked to report the average level of base salary, annual incentive, and total cash compensation for each survey position. For positions with more than one individual in the position, we asked each survey respondent for the third quartile and highest levels as well. In general terms, the average, third quartile, and highest figures reflect those compensation levels paid to the average, better, and best performing salespeople in a sales force. (For an in-depth discussion of the terminology used in this survey, see page 108.)

The following charts provide data on responding companies:

## CHART 1

**BREAKDOWN OF RESPONDING COMPANIES**

|  | PERCENTAGE OF COMPANIES |
|---|---|
| **COMPANY SIZE** | |
| UNDER $5 MILLION | 100.0% |
| **PRODUCT OR SERVICE** | |
| CONSUMER PRODUCTS | 32.1 |
| CONSUMER SERVICES | 32.5 |
| INDUSTRIAL PRODUCTS | 45.2 |
| INDUSTRIAL SERVICES | 42.5 |
| OFFICE PRODUCTS | 20.6 |
| OFFICE SERVICES | 26.2 |
| COMBINED PRODUCTS | 19.4 |
| COMBINED SERVICES | 22.6 |
| **TYPE OF BUYER** | |
| CONSUMERS | 75.2 |
| DISTRIBUTORS | 33.7 |
| INDUSTRY | 39.9 |
| RETAILERS | 45.0 |
| COMBINED | 57.0 |
| **AREA OF DISTRIBUTION** | |
| LOCAL | 15.1 |
| REGIONAL | 34.7 |
| NATIONAL | 25.9 |
| INTERNATIONAL | 24.3 |

# CHART 2

PERCENTAGE OF RESPONDENTS FROM FOUR REGIONAL AREAS

| | PERCENTAGE OF RESPONDENTS |
|---|---|
| EAST | 18% |
| MIDWEST | 34 |
| WEST | 23 |
| SOUTH | 25 |

## NOTE TO USERS OF THIS SURVEY

All users of the data are invited to suggest improvements that will make future editions even more useful tools for assessing sales force effectiveness. Please direct your comments and observations to:

The Dartnell Corporation
4660 N Ravenswood Ave
Chicago, IL 60640-4595
Telephone: (800) 621-5463
e-mail: cheide@dartnellcorp.com

# HOW TO USE THIS SURVEY

We strongly suggest you read through this material before trying to use or apply the data. This section explains how the data tables were constructed, provides an example of how to use the data, and defines the terminology used in this survey.

## HOW THE DATA TABLES ARE CONSTRUCTED

The data tables in this survey are self-explanatory; however, here are some guidelines you can use when analyzing compensation figures for your organization. Additional guidelines are presented in front of each series of compensation tables in the survey. Compensation data for position levels covered in this survey is presented in a variety of ways to enable you to look at those separate segments of the data that are most pertinent to your own situation.

## FIGURES 10 TO 19

Figures 10 to 19 provide average total cash compensation by plan type and all plans used. If you are analyzing compensation paid on an all-incentive plan or all-salary plan, these tables provide a complete picture of total compensation paid. These tables also include data for salary and incentive compensation for those salespeople on a combination plan.

Bear in mind, however, that compensation data for combination plans on this series of tables includes figures that encompass our entire range of responses. In other words, for users of combination plans, these tables report data that includes *all levels of salespeople regardless of ability and all companies regardless of whether they are average-paying or higher-paying companies*. Additional compensation tables provide further breakouts for those companies using a combination plan.

## FIGURES 20 TO 29

Figures 20 to 29 provide average total cash compensation figures for *average*, *better*, and *best* performers. Additionally, this data is reported for typical paying (*"median"*) companies and higher paying (*"third quartile"*) companies. (See page 108 for definitions of the above italicized words and terms.) These tables provide average total cash compensation broken out by product or service sold, type of buyer, and industry for average, better, and best performers in median and third quartile ranges. While these tables will give you total cash compensation figures, you will still need to break the total cash compensation figure into its base salary and incentive components. Figures 30 to 39 will help you determine base salary levels for combination plans.

## FIGURES 30 TO 39

After you have determined total cash compensation for those positions paid on a combination plan, use Figures 30 to 39 to determine average base salary. These figures are again broken out by product or service sold, type of buyer, and industry for average, better, and best performers. The difference between average total cash compensation and average base salary is the average amount incentive paid.

### FIGURES 40 TO 47

Figures 40 to 47 focus on average sales volume for average, better, and best performers and the percentage premium paid to better and best performers. These tables are discussed in greater detail elsewhere in this report.

### FIGURES 48 TO 57

To compare sales compensation and volume levels for the average of the median range of responses, you will want to consult Figures 48 to 57. These tables provide average total cash compensation for all plans combined and sales volume figures broken out for product or service sold, type of buyer, and industry for average, better, and best performers.

### FIGURES 58 TO 67

In order to provide a look at the higher range (third quartile) responses, we have included Figures 58 to 67, which examine the relationship between total cash compensation for all plans combined and sales volume for the third quartile level. If your company is higher paying, you will want to consult these tables for a look at the upper range of survey responses.

Finally, in each section in which data tables appear, a breakout of the data is provided by type of products or services sold and by type of buyer of those products or services, as well as by specific industry group wherever possible. Often a small amount of representation is better than none at all. However, in order to ensure the confidentiality of the responses of any individual participant, we do not report data for any particular category with fewer than seven companies submitting information.

### PUTTING THE DATA TO WORK — AN EXAMPLE

So what does all this mean to us? The following example may help clarify any concepts that remain unclear.

Example: You're a sales manager for a company selling business services. You want to see if your senior salespeople are being compensated at, above, or below the industry average. You use a combination plan (base salary plus incentive) for your senior salespeople.

How to proceed: There are several ways or combinations of ways to approach this problem. You may decide, for example, that you're interested in taking a look at how companies in other industries compensate their senior salespeople so that you can get a general idea of prevailing compensation levels. This step will enable you to see whether your particular industry is higher or lower paying than the general average for companies with under $5 million in annual sales.

Looking at Figure 14, you see that other firms pay their senior salespeople who are on a combination plan $32,300 in salary and another $15,600 in incentive for a total of $47,900. You see also in Figure 14 that there is a breakout for business services. (General classifications of types of companies represented in the industry breakouts can be found on page 271.) Here you note that senior reps on a combination plan earn $34,300 in salary and $15,400 in incentive for a total of $49,700 — a little higher than the median pay for companies under $5 million in annual sales. Remember, however, that the figures on this table encompass our entire range of responses and include all levels of salespeople regardless of ability and all companies regardless of whether they are average-paying or higher-paying companies.

We need to see if we can refine the data a bit. Moving to Figure 24, Average Total Cash Compensation for Senior Sales Reps, you see that senior salespeople in companies with under $5 million in annual sales earn between $46,000 and $94,000 annually. This gives us the range of responses from average performer to best performer. In other words, this is the compensation a senior salesperson on a combination plan could expect to earn in a company with annual sales of $5 million or less, depending, of course, on the variables of industry, geographic location, salesperson ability, and so on.

When you look at the breakout for business services, you see a total compensation range of $50,000 to $60,000 annually. Looking at Figure 24, you can easily see the progression of compensation from average performer to best performer. You now have two "benchmarks" to work with.

You now need to determine how much compensation takes the form of salary. Looking at Figure 34, Average Base Salary and Total Compensation for Senior Sales Reps, you find that base salary is $33,000 annually. (Note: This series of tables — Figures 30–39 — covers the median range of total survey responses.) The difference between average total cash compensation and base salary is the amount of incentive paid. If we look at figures for the average performer selling business services, we find that a typical pay plan would consist of $33,000 a year in base salary and $14,800 in incentive ($47,800 - $33,000 = $14,800).

Should you want to check on the average percent salary and average percent incentive for your industry, Figure 8 will provide that information. In this case, we see that in business services, an average of 44.1 percent of total annual compensation is incentive. This is in line with our other findings ($33,000 + 44.1% = $47,553).

If your company is "higher paying," you'll want to take a look at Figure 62, Sales Compensation and Volume Levels — 3rd Quartile — Senior Sales Reps. This table provides a look at the higher range of responses.

A word of caution: Survey results are generated from a collection of widely varying responses and are therefore based on extremes. The data presented here is intended to provide guidelines as to prevailing practices and emerging trends.

Your figures will differ based on the particular idiosyncrasies of your own company, its geographic location, and other factors. In looking at the range of data, however, you will be able to determine how your company compares with other companies of similar size in a similar industry. Use your own judgment when applying these figures to your own organization.

As mentioned previously, all the data tables contained in this survey are self-explanatory. Many of the tables that do not deal directly with compensation data include a brief commentary noting findings from other Dartnell research. It is suggested that all this data be considered carefully when making judgments based on the material in this survey.

It is not uncommon for us to receive calls from individual salespeople wanting to know exactly how much they should be making in their particular company — or how much of a raise they should ask for during their annual review. No survey can provide that kind of specific information.

All companies of similar size in a similar industry do not pay their salespeople exactly the same. If that were the case, you'd already know how much everyone in your industry was paying for each survey position. While this may seem obvious, it's worth mentioning if only to remind users of this survey that all data contained in this survey should be applied with good judgment.

## TERMINOLOGY USED IN THIS SURVEY

The following explanations of terminology used in this survey will help you more fully understand the data configurations presented.

- **Average** — Average, when used in connection with dollar amounts, always refers to the average of the median range. In all other instances, average figures represent true averages of responses received.
- **Median** — The median is the figure that is in the middle of all values arranged from lowest to highest; that is, half of the set of numbers fall above the median and half fall below it. The advantage of using the median is that it is not affected by extremes at either the high or low end of the range and thus provides a truer picture of the data.
- **Median range** — The median range is the middle 50 percent of responses; that is, those responses that fall between the 25th and 75th percentile of the entire range of responses.
- **Third quartile** — The third quartile is also referred to as the 75th percentile. It is the figure that is higher than 75 percent of all figures reported, but lower than 25 percent of the figures reported. Third-quartile figures enable us to look at the higher range of the data reported.
- **Better performer** — Better performers are those individuals who rank in the top 25 percent of their respective sales forces.
- **Best performer** — Best performers are those individuals who rank at the top of the survey sample. Compensation figures for best performers represent the top end of the scale in any particular breakout of the data. Similarly, sales volume data given for the best performer is generated from highest reported figures.
- **N/R** — An N/R entry in the data tables indicates that although data was received, the figure is not released due to insufficient sample size.
- **0.0** — A 0.0 entry in the data tables indicates that no data was received for that data category.
- **Salary-only plan** — A salary-only plan compensates the individual on the basis of a fixed yearly amount.
- **Incentive-only plan** — An incentive-only plan compensates the individual an agreed-upon amount on the successful completion of certain tasks and activities. Earnings are based entirely on the performance of the individual.
- **Combination plan** — A combination plan is a combination of the salary and incentive plans. An individual on this plan is paid an annual sum in the form of salary but earns additional (incentive) compensation on the basis of performance.

We suggest you refer to these definitions whenever data or explanations in the text seem unclear.

## POSITION DESCRIPTIONS

The following position definitions are used throughout this survey.
1. **Top Marketing Exec.** — Typical title: Vice President of Marketing. Directs marketing functions and may oversee international operations, as well as field marketing support and field service. Reports to CEO, President, or Division President.
2. **Top Sales Exec.** — Typical title: Vice President of Sales. Directs U.S. sales, has minimal marketing responsibilities, and may oversee field service. Reports to CEO, President, Division President, or Top Marketing Executive.

3. **Regional Sales Manager** — Manages specific region, industry, product, or distributor sales. Reports to Top Sales Executive.
4. **District Sales Manager** — Manages a more limited region, industry or product segment. reports to Regional Sales Manager.
5. **Senior Sales Rep** — A salesperson with three or more years of sales experience.
6. **Intermediate Sales Rep** — A salesperson with one to three years of sales experience.
7. **Entry Level Sales Rep** — A salesperson with less than one year of sales experience.
8. **National or Major Account Sales Manager** — Segments accounts and develops account strategies. Manages only National or Major (Key) Account Reps. Reports to Top Sales Executive.
9. **National Account Rep** — Sells to national customers. Typically requires at least seven years of industry-specific experience. Reports to National Account Sales Manager.
10. **Major (Key) Account Rep** — Sells to major (key) accounts with a central purchasing point. Reports to National Account Sales Manager.

## SECTION 2
# CURRENT LEVELS OF PAY

How much are sales and marketing professionals in companies with under $5 million in annual sales paid? How are they most likely to be paid — straight salary, straight commission, or a combination of the two? And if they're paid on a combination plan, what percent is likely to be salary and what percent is likely to be incentive? This section has the answers to all these questions and more.

Figure 1, *The Dartnell Profile of The American Sales Professional in Companies with Under $5 Million in Annual Sales*, summarizes major findings from our study. The chart below includes data for national averages and is intended to provide a "snapshot" look at salespeople in smaller companies. Data for your company will vary depending on geographic location, industry, position in the marketplace, and other factors.

## FIGURE 1

**DARTNELL PROFILE: THE AMERICAN SALES PROFESSIONAL IN COMPANIES WITH UNDER $5 MILLION IN ANNUAL SALES— NATIONAL AVERAGES**

|  |  | FURTHER DETAIL PROVIDED IN |
|---|---|---|
| • 76.3% ARE MALE |  | FIGURE 100, PAGE 253 |
| • 23.7% ARE FEMALE |  | FIGURE 100, PAGE 253 |
| • 53.5% HAVE A COLLEGE DEGREE |  | FIGURE 101, PAGE 255 |
| • SALES CALLS PER DAY | 3.1 | FIGURE 104, PAGE 261 |
| • NUMBER OF CALLS TO CLOSE | 3.8 | FIGURE 104, PAGE 261 |
| • FIELD EXPENSES COST | $12,016 | FIGURE 71, PAGE 203 |
| • VALUE OF BENEFITS | $4,023 | FIGURE 40, PAGE 163 |
| • ANNUAL SALES VOLUME (SENIOR REP) | $461,300 | FIGURE 99, PAGE 249 |
| • AUTOMOBILES* |  |  |
| – COMPANY OWNED | 35.3% | FIGURE 72, PAGE 206 |
| – COMPANY LEASED | 25.9% | FIGURE 73, PAGE 207 |
| – PERSONAL (MILEAGE) | 58.1% | FIGURE 74, PAGE 208 |
| • SPENDS ON AVERAGE 46.9 HOURS PER WEEK AS FOLLOWS: |  | FIGURE 103, PAGE 259 |

| TASK | PERCENT OF WEEKLY TIME |
|---|---|
| – SELLING FACE TO FACE | 28.4% (12.9 HOURS) |
| – SELLING OVER THE PHONE | 28.8 (13.1 HOURS) |
| – ADMINISTRATIVE TASKS | 14.7 (6.7 HOURS) |
| – WAITING / TRAVELING | 16.1 (7.3 HOURS) |
| – SERVICE CALLS | 12.0 (5.4 HOURS) |

| • COSTS TO TRAIN (NEW HIRE) | $5,291 | FIGURE 88, PAGE 227 |
|---|---|---|

*TOTAL EXCEEDS 100% DUE TO MULTIPLE RESPONSES

Figure 2 presents median cash compensation for three levels of salespeople in companies with under $5 million in annual sales.

## FIGURE 2

| POSITION | MEDIAN 1996 TOTAL CASH COMPENSATION |
|---|---|
| SENIOR REP | $50,000 |
| INTERMEDIATE REP | $39,000 |
| ENTRY-LEVEL REP | $25,000 |

You'll also find complete data tables for current levels of pay for the 10 survey positions broken out by product or service sold, type of buyer, and industry. In addition, compensation data is broken out for most positions by average, better, and best performer. (For a discussion of the terminology used in this survey and a description of positions surveyed, see pages 108 and 109.)

Positions surveyed include:
- Top marketing executive.
- Top sales executive (note that since most companies have only one top marketing and/or top sales executive, there is no better or best performer).
- Regional sales manager.
- District sales manager.
- Senior sales rep.
- Intermediate rep.
- Entry level sales rep.
- National/Major account manager.
- National account rep.
- Major (Key) account rep.

Before using these tables, be sure to read the suggestions on how to use this survey. The data tables in this section are comprehensive and may appear confusing. To help you, additional suggestions for using each series of tables are also presented in this section.

Other tables in this section include data on projected earnings and merit increases for senior sales representatives, the type of compensation plan used, and the base salary/incentive split used to determine total compensation.

The compensation tables can be summarized as follows:
- Figures 10–19 exhibit the average pay levels for each of the 10 sales positions surveyed by plan type and all plans combined. For positions that you compensate on an all-salary or all-incentive plan, these tables provide all the data you need. For those paying on a combination plan, these tables provide salary, incentive, and total cash compensation figures for the entire range of survey respondents. If you use a combination plan, you'll want to consult the more comprehensive data tables in this section for additional breakouts that will more closely represent your particular company.
- Figures 20–29 exhibit average total cash compensation for average, better, and best performers for most positions surveyed. Since most companies have only one top marketing and/or one top sales executive, there are no better or best performers in that position. Use these tables to determine average total cash compensation for those positions paid on a combination plan.

- Figures 30–39 exhibit average base salary and average total compensation for all plans for average, better, and best performers in the positions surveyed. Use these tables to determine the base salary for those individuals paid on a combination plan.

This survey provides extensive breakouts of the data to enable you to look at the data in a variety of ways; for example, median and third-quartile figures for average, better, and best performers. These breakouts give you the opportunity to examine the segment of the data that is most relevant to you and also enable you to make extensive comparisons of the data.

## FIGURE 3—PROJECTED SENIOR SALESPERSON
## EARNINGS IN 1997 — INCREASES

**Figure 3** shows that nearly 90 percent (88.1%) of responding companies predict that their senior salespeople will earn an average of 13.1 percent more in 1997 than in 1996 and that these increases will come primarily from increases in sales volume. Fewer than 10 percent (9.6%) of the companies say increased earnings will come about through changes in their compensation plans.

By contrast, although 90.7 percent of companies with more than $5 million in annual sales predict higher senior sales rep earnings (9.8% higher) in 1997, nearly 20 percent (17.3%) say the increased earnings will come through a change in their sales compensation plans. As you review these figures, bear in mind that changes in compensation plans can often lead to increases in productivity. Whether the salespeople in your company will earn more based on increased sales volume under their existing plan or whether changes in the compensation plan will help drive increases in sales volume, remember that increases in compensation need to be based on increases in productivity if you are to maintain your competitive edge. The high level of optimism in both large and small companies is most encouraging.

# FIGURE 3

## Projected Senior Salesperson Earnings in 1997—Increases

| | Percentage of Firms Predicting Higher Earnings in 1997 | Percentage Higher | Percentage of Firms Indicating Change In Compensation Plan |
|---|---|---|---|
| **COMPANY SIZE** | | | |
| Under $5 Million | 88.1% | 13.1% | 9.6% |
| **PRODUCT OR SERVICE** | | | |
| Consumer Products | 85.1 | 14.8 | 10.3 |
| Consumer Services | 87.2 | 13.7 | 13.6 |
| Industrial Products | 87.6 | 14.9 | 9.8 |
| Industrial Services | 91.0 | 13.3 | 7.1 |
| Office Products | 86.3 | 17.4 | 8.7 |
| Office Services | 84.8 | 14.7 | 8.1 |
| **TYPE OF BUYER** | | | |
| Consumers | 84.4 | 12.1 | 12.1 |
| Distributors | 83.3 | 14.1 | 9.0 |
| Industry | 88.0 | 13.2 | 8.4 |
| Retailers | 83.1 | 13.3 | 7.1 |
| **INDUSTRY** | | | |
| Amusement & Recreation Services | 50.0 | 12.5 | 0.0 |
| Business Services | 89.1 | 11.9 | 7.7 |
| Electronics | 83.3 | 16.2 | 33.3 |
| Fabricated Metals | 83.3 | 12.0 | 0.0 |
| Food Products | 100.0 | 11.3 | 0.0 |
| Furniture and Fixtures | 80.0 | 12.0 | 0.0 |
| Health Services | 75.0 | 13.3 | 0.0 |
| Holding & Other Investment Offices | 80.0 | 10.0 | 0.0 |
| Hotels & Other Lodging Places | 100.0 | 7.0 | 25.0 |
| Instruments | 83.3 | 14.8 | 0.0 |
| Insurance | 100.0 | 8.5 | 11.1 |
| Machinery | 100.0 | 11.7 | 0.0 |
| Manufacturing | 100.0 | 18.7 | 0.0 |
| Office Equipment | 81.8 | 25.6 | 22.2 |
| Pharmaceuticals | 87.5 | 12.9 | 0.0 |
| Printing and Publishing | 100.0 | 14.1 | 8.3 |
| Retail | 69.2 | 6.4 | 13.3 |
| Wholesale (Consumer Goods) | 72.7 | 10.1 | 9.1 |
| Wholesale (Industrial Goods) | 91.7 | 11.2 | 8.3 |
| **OVERALL** | **88.1%** | **13.1%** | **9.6%** |

## FIGURE 4—PROJECTED SENIOR SALESPERSON EARNINGS IN 1997—DECREASES

Fewer than 12 percent (11.9%) of responding companies predict that their senior sales representatives will earn less in 1997 than in 1996. Of these, nearly 30 percent (29.3%) say these decreases will come from changes in their sales compensation plans. In other words, the majority of companies (70.7%) encountering unfavorable business conditions do not tinker with their compensation plans.

Larger companies report similar data: Of the 9.3 percent predicting lower earnings for their experienced salespeople in 1997, one-fourth (26.6%) say these decreases will come from changes in their sales compensation plans.

We all know that all companies do not experience continued growth through all economic cycles. Eroding margins, increased competition, aging product lines, and the like can take their toll. But what is interesting to note is the apparent reluctance on the part of companies both large and small to adjust their compensation plans downward in response to these changing conditions. If your company is experiencing declining market share or price erosion or is feeling any other pressures on its bottom line, remember that adjusting your compensation plan downward can be potentially demotivating, to put it mildly. Any solution you look for should address long-term needs, not short-term results. Your goal is to generate a professional, skilled, motivated, and productive sales team. Regardless of market conditions, you still need to compete for, and retain, the best people.

# FIGURE 4

**PROJECTED SENIOR SALESPERSON**
**EARNINGS IN 1997 — DECREASES**

| | PERCENTAGE OF FIRMS PREDICTING LOWER EARNINGS IN 1997 | PERCENTAGE LOWER | PERCENTAGE OF FIRMS INDICATING CHANGE IN COMPENSATION PLAN |
|---|---|---|---|
| **COMPANY SIZE** | | | |
| UNDER $5 MILLION | 11.9% | 9.2% | 29.3% |
| **PRODUCT OR SERVICE** | | | |
| CONSUMER PRODUCTS | 14.9 | 9.5 | 35.5 |
| CONSUMER SERVICES | 12.8 | 9.8 | 32.4 |
| INDUSTRIAL PRODUCTS | 12.4 | 9.3 | 24.1 |
| INDUSTRIAL SERVICES | 9.0 | 9.7 | 26.3 |
| OFFICE PRODUCTS | 13.7 | 10.0 | 27.3 |
| OFFICE SERVICES | 15.2 | 9.2 | 30.8 |
| **TYPE OF BUYER** | | | |
| CONSUMERS | 15.6 | 10.1 | 30.8 |
| DISTRIBUTORS | 16.7 | 9.9 | 35.7 |
| INDUSTRY | 12.0 | 9.8 | 27.6 |
| RETAILERS | 16.9 | 9.7 | 35.3 |
| **INDUSTRY** | | | |
| AMUSEMENT & RECREATION SERVICES | 50.0 | 4.0 | 0.0 |
| BUSINESS SERVICES | 10.9 | 8.9 | 36.4 |
| ELECTRONICS | 16.7 | 15.0 | 40.0 |
| FABRICATED METALS | 16.7 | 5.0 | 0.0 |
| FURNITURE AND FIXTURES | 20.0 | 10.0 | 0.0 |
| HEALTH SERVICES | 25.0 | 10.0 | 0.0 |
| HOLDING & OTHER INVESTMENT OFFICES | 20.0 | 0.0 | 0.0 |
| INSTRUMENTS | 16.7 | 0.0 | 0.0 |
| OFFICE EQUIPMENT | 18.2 | 15.0 | 16.7 |
| PHARMACEUTICALS | 12.5 | 11.0 | 50.0 |
| RETAIL | 30.8 | 10.0 | 25.0 |
| WHOLESALE (CONSUMER GOODS) | 27.3 | 3.0 | 0.0 |
| WHOLESALE (INDUSTRIAL GOODS) | 8.3 | 7.0 | 0.0 |
| **OVERALL** | **11.9%** | **9.2%** | **29.3%** |

## FIGURE 5 — AVERAGE PERCENT MERIT INCREASE

The average 1995 merit increase for salespeople averaged 5.8 percent, down from the 7.3 percent increase projected by respondents to our 1994 survey. (1995 is the most recent year for which complete data is available.) Projections for 1997 are more modest: 6.0 percent. It is interesting to note that since 1989, the first year Dartnell began collecting data on merit increases, projections by smaller companies (under $5 million in annual sales) have consistently been more optimistic than projections by companies with over $5 million in annual sales. What's more, actual merit increases in smaller companies have equaled or exceeded merit increases paid by their larger counterparts. For example, merit increases in larger companies were 4.5 percent in 1995. As noted above, merit increases in smaller companies were 5.8 percent in 1995, or 1.3 percent more. The following graphic provides historical data on merit increases in companies with under $5 million in annual sales.

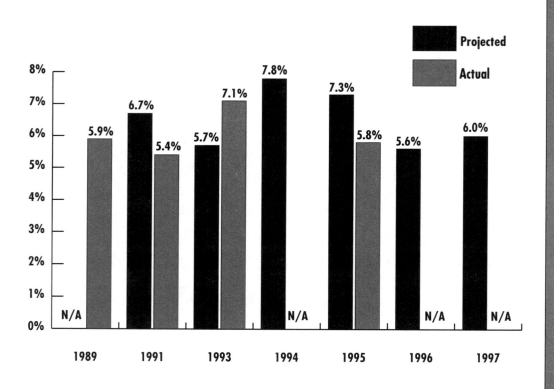

# FIGURE 5

**AVERAGE PERCENT MERIT INCREASE**

| | 1995 | PROJECTED 1996 | PROJECTED 1997 |
|---|---|---|---|
| **COMPANY SIZE** | | | |
| UNDER $5 MILLION | 5.8% | 5.6% | 6.0% |
| **PRODUCT OR SERVICE** | | | |
| CONSUMER PRODUCTS | 5.8 | 5.6 | 6.2 |
| CONSUMER SERVICES | 6.3 | 6.1 | 6.0 |
| INDUSTRIAL PRODUCTS | 6.2 | 5.9 | 6.4 |
| INDUSTRIAL SERVICES | 5.7 | 5.6 | 5.7 |
| OFFICE PRODUCTS | 5.5 | 5.4 | 6.0 |
| OFFICE SERVICES | 5.4 | 5.6 | 5.8 |
| **TYPE OF BUYER** | | | |
| CONSUMERS | 6.7 | 5.9 | 5.9 |
| DISTRIBUTORS | 5.6 | 5.9 | 6.4 |
| INDUSTRY | 5.7 | 5.9 | 6.2 |
| RETAILERS | 4.9 | 5.3 | 5.6 |
| **INDUSTRY** | | | |
| AMUSEMENT & RECREATION SERVICES | 6.3 | 4.0 | 4.5 |
| BUSINESS SERVICES | 5.9 | 5.5 | 5.6 |
| ELECTRONICS | 8.6 | 8.6 | 9.0 |
| FABRICATED METALS | 7.0 | 5.3 | 4.7 |
| FOOD PRODUCTS | 3.0 | 4.3 | 4.0 |
| FURNITURE AND FIXTURES | 6.3 | 8.0 | 6.0 |
| HEALTH SERVICES | 4.8 | 3.7 | 4.0 |
| HOLDING & OTHER INVESTMENT OFFICES | 3.0 | 3.0 | 3.0 |
| HOTELS & OTHER LODGING PLACES | 7.2 | 6.8 | 7.0 |
| INSTRUMENTS | 4.0 | 4.2 | 4.3 |
| INSURANCE | 3.5 | 4.0 | 4.0 |
| MACHINERY | 7.7 | 7.5 | 7.5 |
| MANUFACTURING | 5.0 | 4.7 | 6.5 |
| OFFICE EQUIPMENT | 5.7 | 5.4 | 6.0 |
| PHARMACEUTICALS | 3.7 | 4.3 | 5.5 |
| PRINTING AND PUBLISHING | 5.6 | 5.5 | 5.9 |
| RETAIL | 5.4 | 6.0 | 6.8 |
| WHOLESALE (CONSUMER GOODS) | 7.0 | 6.8 | 8.0 |
| WHOLESALE (INDUSTRIAL GOODS) | 5.1 | 5.6 | 6.5 |
| **OVERALL** | **5.8%** | **5.6%** | **6.0%** |

# FIGURE 6—TYPE OF COMPENSATION PLAN USED FOR SENIOR SALES REPRESENTATIVES

The combination plan (base salary plus an incentive) continues to be the most popular pay plan, used by 63.6 percent of responding companies. The combination plan is the plan of choice among larger companies, too, with more than 80 percent (80.5%) of companies with over $5 million in annual sales using the plan. Among smaller companies, 10 percent use the "salary only" plan and one-fourth (26.4%) use the "incentive only" plan. Over the years, companies both large and small have increasingly favored the combination plan. Here's a summary of how the combination plan in companies with under $5 million in annual sales has gained ground over the years:

|      | Salary Only | Incentive Only | Combination Plan |
|------|-------------|----------------|------------------|
| 1990 | 12.0%       | 40.0%          | 48.0%            |
| 1992 | 8.0         | 32.0           | 60.0             |
| 1994 | 12.7        | 31.6           | 55.7             |
| 1996 | 10.0        | 26.4           | 63.6             |

The number of companies using the "salary only" plan has remained relatively stable, while the number of companies using the "incentive only" plan has shown a steady decline. We expect the number of companies using the combination plan to increase as sales executives learn how to use this plan to drive sales performance and company profitability.

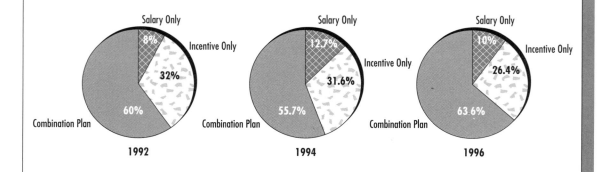

120

# FIGURE 6

**SENIOR SALES REP: COMPENSATION PLAN TYPE USED**

| | PERCENTAGE OF COMPANIES USING | | |
| | SALARY ONLY | INCENTIVE ONLY | COMBINATION PLAN |
|---|---|---|---|
| **COMPANY SIZE** | | | |
| UNDER $5 MILLION | 10.0% | 26.4% | 63.6% |
| **PRODUCT OR SERVICE** | | | |
| CONSUMER PRODUCTS | 15.2 | 15.2 | 69.6 |
| CONSUMER SERVICES | 11.6 | 32.6 | 55.8 |
| INDUSTRIAL PRODUCTS | 11.8 | 20.6 | 67.6 |
| INDUSTRIAL SERVICES | 12.3 | 22.8 | 64.9 |
| OFFICE PRODUCTS | 16.0 | 20.0 | 64.0 |
| OFFICE SERVICES | 19.4 | 12.9 | 67.7 |
| **TYPE OF BUYER** | | | |
| CONSUMERS | 12.9 | 22.6 | 64.5 |
| DISTRIBUTORS | 14.3 | 11.1 | 74.6 |
| INDUSTRY | 9.3 | 24.3 | 66.4 |
| RETAILERS | 14.0 | 14.0 | 72.0 |
| **INDUSTRY** | | | |
| AMUSEMENT & RECREATION SERVICES | 0.0 | 0.0 | 100.0 |
| BUSINESS SERVICES | 4.2 | 20.8 | 75.0 |
| ELECTRONICS | 25.0 | 0.0 | 75.0 |
| FABRICATED METALS | 0.0 | 50.0 | 50.0 |
| FOOD PRODUCTS | 50.0 | 0.0 | 50.0 |
| FURNITURE AND FIXTURES | 0.0 | 50.0 | 50.0 |
| HEALTH SERVICES | 0.0 | 33.3 | 66.7 |
| HOLDING & OTHER INVESTMENT OFFICES | 0.0 | 100.0 | 0.0 |
| HOTELS & OTHER LODGING PLACES | 0.0 | 0.0 | 100.0 |
| INSTRUMENTS | 20.0 | 0.0 | 80.0 |
| INSURANCE | 0.0 | 75.0 | 25.0 |
| MACHINERY | 0.0 | 25.0 | 75.0 |
| MANUFACTURING | 0.0 | 60.0 | 40.0 |
| OFFICE EQUIPMENT | 0.0 | 33.3 | 66.7 |
| PHARMACEUTICALS | 0.0 | 0.0 | 100.0 |
| PRINTING AND PUBLISHING | 12.5 | 12.5 | 75.0 |
| RETAIL | 9.1 | 9.1 | 81.8 |
| WHOLESALE (CONSUMER GOODS) | 0.0 | 42.9 | 57.1 |
| WHOLESALE (INDUSTRIAL GOODS) | 0.0 | 42.9 | 57.1 |
| **OVERALL** | **10.0%** | **26.4%** | **63.6%** |

# FIGURE 7—METHODS OF COMPENSATION

The data on this table provide the percentage of responding companies using either straight salary, incentive only, or combination pay plans to compensate the sales positions covered in this survey. When you compare the data on this table with the data on Figure 6, keep in mind that the data tables report on different segments of the sales force; that is, Figure 6 refers to senior salespeople only, and **Figure 7** includes all positions surveyed. The data can be easily understood more by remembering, for example, that some companies use a straight salary plan to compensate their new hires and move them over to a combination plan after they have completed training. By the same token, a company may pay most company sales positions on a combination type basis, yet have a significant number of senior salespeople compensated on an "incentive only" plan. These two tables, taken together, help us see the dynamics and variations in sales compensation plans.

## METHODS OF COMPENSATION (FOR ALL POSITIONS COMBINED) 1990–1994
### (SEE FIGURE 7 FOR CURRENT DATA)

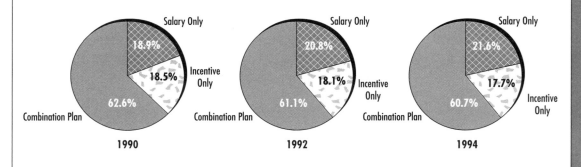

# FIGURE 7

**METHODS OF COMPENSATION**

|  | PERCENTAGE OF COMPANIES USING | | |
|---|---|---|---|
|  | STRAIGHT SALARY | INCENTIVE ONLY | COMBINATION PLAN |
| **COMPANY SIZE** | | | |
| UNDER $5 MILLION | 21.6% | 15.8% | 62.6% |
| **PRODUCT OR SERVICE** | | | |
| CONSUMER PRODUCTS | 26.0 | 9.2 | 64.8 |
| CONSUMER SERVICES | 19.9 | 19.1 | 61.0 |
| INDUSTRIAL PRODUCTS | 24.7 | 12.2 | 63.1 |
| INDUSTRIAL SERVICES | 23.3 | 11.2 | 65.5 |
| OFFICE PRODUCTS | 20.7 | 14.0 | 65.3 |
| OFFICE SERVICES | 24.1 | 7.9 | 68.0 |
| **TYPE OF BUYER** | | | |
| CONSUMERS | 20.9 | 16.1 | 63.1 |
| DISTRIBUTORS | 18.7 | 8.3 | 73.0 |
| INDUSTRY | 21.0 | 13.8 | 65.2 |
| RETAILERS | 22.3 | 8.7 | 69.0 |
| **INDUSTRY** | | | |
| AMUSEMENT & RECREATION SERVICES | 25.0 | 0.0 | 75.0 |
| BUSINESS SERVICES | 17.5 | 13.8 | 68.7 |
| ELECTRONICS | 40.0 | 0.0 | 60.0 |
| FABRICATED METALS | 3.3 | 13.3 | 83.3 |
| FOOD PRODUCTS | 16.7 | 0.0 | 83.3 |
| FURNITURE AND FIXTURES | 22.8 | 33.4 | 43.8 |
| HEALTH SERVICES | 36.0 | 11.2 | 52.8 |
| HOLDING & OTHER INVESTMENT OFFICES | 30.0 | 20.0 | 50.0 |
| HOTELS & OTHER LODGING PLACES | 12.5 | 0.0 | 87.5 |
| INSTRUMENTS | 25.0 | 0.0 | 75.0 |
| INSURANCE | 5.0 | 70.0 | 25.0 |
| MACHINERY | 23.2 | 25.0 | 51.8 |
| MANUFACTURING | 4.1 | 24.1 | 71.8 |
| OFFICE EQUIPMENT | 12.5 | 8.3 | 79.2 |
| PHARMACEUTICALS | 17.9 | 0.0 | 82.1 |
| PRINTING AND PUBLISHING | 18.5 | 7.7 | 73.8 |
| RETAIL | 27.2 | 12.5 | 60.3 |
| WHOLESALE (CONSUMER GOODS) | 24.9 | 14.8 | 60.3 |
| WHOLESALE (INDUSTRIAL GOODS) | 18.2 | 23.7 | 58.1 |
| **OVERALL** | **21.6%** | **15.8%** | **62.6%** |

## FIGURE 8 — BASE SALARY/INCENTIVE SPLIT

How do companies using the combination plan split total compensation into its primary components: salary and incentive? The average base salary/incentive split is 53.7 percent salary and 46.3 percent incentive. In larger companies, this ratio is 59.7 percent salary and 40.3 percent incentive. The base salary/incentive split in companies with under $5 million in annual sales has remained relatively constant over the years, as can be seen by the graphic on this page. In larger companies, there has been a trend to reduce the percentage of base salary as part of the entire compensation package, enabling these companies to put more money into incentive programs while at the same time reducing fixed expenses. It is expected that smaller companies will follow suit. In the years ahead, it is likely that both large and small companies will reduce the percentage of base salary as part of total pay in an effort to further reduce fixed costs and pay these monies out as incentives instead. As we move toward the year 2000, look for inventive and creative uses of incentives to become much more common than they are today.

**BASE SALARY/INCENTIVE SPLIT (AS A PERCENT OF TOTAL COMPENSATION) 1990 – 1994**
**(SEE FIGURE 8 FOR CURRENT DATA)**

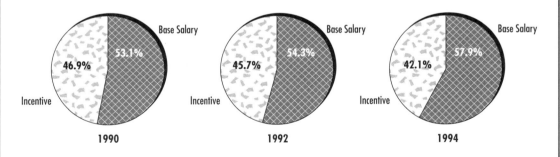

# FIGURE 8

## Base Salary/Incentive Split

| | Average Percent Salary | Average Percent Incentive (Commission, Bonus) |
|---|---|---|
| **Company Size** | | |
| Under $5 Million | 53.7% | 46.3% |
| **Product or Service** | | |
| Consumer Products | 57.7 | 42.3 |
| Consumer Services | 56.0 | 44.0 |
| Industrial Products | 55.3 | 44.7 |
| Industrial Services | 57.9 | 42.1 |
| Office Products | 58.4 | 41.6 |
| Office Services | 59.5 | 40.5 |
| **Type of Buyer** | | |
| Consumers | 57.3 | 42.7 |
| Distributors | 58.6 | 41.3 |
| Industry | 54.5 | 45.5 |
| Retailers | 58.0 | 42.0 |
| **Industry** | | |
| Amusement & Recreation Services | 75.5 | 24.5 |
| Business Services | 55.9 | 44.1 |
| Electronics | 70.5 | 29.5 |
| Fabricated Metals | 54.2 | 45.8 |
| Food Products | 65.0 | 35.0 |
| Furniture and Fixtures | 41.0 | 59.0 |
| Health Services | 50.0 | 50.0 |
| Holding & Other Investment Offices | 49.4 | 50.6 |
| Hotels & Other Lodging Places | 68.8 | 31.2 |
| Instruments | 60.2 | 39.7 |
| Insurance | 18.9 | 81.1 |
| Machinery | 42.5 | 57.5 |
| Manufacturing | 39.4 | 60.6 |
| Office Equipment | 53.6 | 46.4 |
| Pharmaceuticals | 66.2 | 33.8 |
| Printing and Publishing | 65.2 | 34.8 |
| Retail | 51.7 | 48.3 |
| Wholesale (Consumer Goods) | 40.0 | 60.0 |
| Wholesale (Industrial Goods) | 47.0 | 53.0 |
| **Overall** | **53.7%** | **46.3%** |

## FIGURE 9—HOW SALES EXECS AND REPS ARE PAID

This survey covers 10 sales positions — from entry level salesperson to top marketing executive. How these positions are compensated in companies with under $5 million in annual sales can provide insight into the actual selling responsibilities of the position.

In looking at this data, remember that the more a particular position is compensated through the use of an incentive (commission), the more likely it is that that position carries responsibility for actually making sales. For example, nearly half (43.04%) of the top marketing executives in the survey receive commission pay, a strong indication that these individuals do have selling responsibilities.

**Figure 9** on the opposite page shows how the 10 sales positions in the Dartnell survey are compensated. Note that **Figure 9** carries the added information that the data is "incumbent weighted" — that is, final figures are based on the total number of people in each position represented in the survey. This table, then, provides us with an in-depth look at how the individuals represented in the survey are actually paid. Use this table to compare how similar positions in *your* company are paid.

Additionally, this table puts the prevalence of particular compensation plans in perspective. Comparing this data with the data in Figure 6, for example, we can see that although 10 percent of the companies in this survey use a "salary only" plan in compensating their senior sales reps, fewer than 5 percent (4.95%) of the senior sales reps in this survey are paid on a "salary only" basis. We can conclude, on the basis of this data, that a "salary only" pay plan is the *least favored* pay plan for senior sales reps in companies with under $5 million in annual sales.

# FIGURE 9

**How Sales Execs and Reps Are Paid in Companies with $5 Million or Less in Annual Sales (All Respondents) Incumbent Weighted**

| SURVEY POSITION | STRAIGHT SALARY | STRAIGHT COMM. | COMM. & BONUS | SALARY & COMM. | SALARY & BONUS | SALARY, BONUS, & COMM. |
|---|---|---|---|---|---|---|
| 1. Top Marketing Executive | 38.61% | 4.43% | 1.27% | 25.95% | 18.35% | 11.39% |
| 2. Top Sales Executive | 22.12% | 10.58% | 2.40% | 38.46% | 11.06% | 15.38% |
| 3. Regional Sales Manager | 18.87% | 1.89% | 1.89% | 40.57% | 16.98% | 19.81% |
| 4. District Sales Manager | 11.54% | 1.92% | 5.77% | 32.69% | 11.54% | 36.54% |
| 5. Senior Sales Rep | 4.95% | 38.46% | 2.20% | 34.43% | 3.66% | 16.30% |
| 6. Intermediate Sales Rep | 11.43% | 30.79% | 2.22% | 35.87% | 6.35% | 13.33% |
| 7. Entry Level Sales Rep | 28.88% | 22.32% | 0.44% | 39.82% | 4.38% | 4.16% |
| 8. Nat'l/Maj Account Manager | 31.58% | 0.00% | 0.00% | 36.84% | 5.26% | 26.32% |
| 9. National Account Rep | 26.09% | 13.04% | 0.00% | 26.09% | 17.39% | 17.39% |
| 10. Major (Key) Account Rep | 41.38% | 0.00% | 0.00% | 17.24% | 17.24% | 24.14% |

# FIGURE 9A

**How Sales Execs and Reps Are Paid in Companies of All Sizes (All Respondents) Incumbent Weighted**

| SURVEY POSITION | STRAIGHT SALARY | STRAIGHT COMM. | COMM. & BONUS | SALARY & COMM. | SALARY & BONUS | SALARY, BONUS, & COMM. |
|---|---|---|---|---|---|---|
| 1. Top Marketing Executive | 27.02% | 0.70% | 0.88% | 13.12% | 27.82% | 30.46% |
| 2. Top Sales Executive | 29.49% | 2.31% | 3.24% | 20.04% | 16.65% | 28.26% |
| 3. Regional Sales Manager | 23.09% | 2.22% | 0.48% | 25.32% | 25.10% | 23.62% |
| 4. District Sales Manager | 28.42% | 1.85% | 0.48% | 23.82% | 26.68% | 18.22% |
| 5. Senior Sales Rep | 4.29% | 6.59% | 0.49% | 41.35% | 29.56% | 17.73% |
| 6. Intermediate Sales Rep | 4.49% | 3.36% | 0.25% | 33.89% | 41.45% | 16.57% |
| 7. Entry Level Sales Rep | 3.00% | 2.87% | 0.29% | 60.75% | 21.40% | 11.70% |
| 8. Nat'l/Maj Account Manager | 61.23% | 0.06% | 0.18% | 17.24% | 2.93% | 18.36% |
| 9. National Account Rep | 9.89% | 0.73% | 0.18% | 50.73% | 14.65% | 23.81% |
| 10. Major (Key) Account Rep | 26.27% | 0.00% | 0.47% | 37.97% | 10.05% | 25.24% |

## FIGURES 10–19 — COMPENSATION TABLES: AVERAGE SALES COMPENSATION PAY LEVELS BY PLAN TYPE AND ALL PLANS COMBINED

The following tables (Figures 10–19) exhibit the average pay levels for each of the 10 sales positions surveyed by plan type and all plans combined. The positions surveyed are as follows:

- Top Marketing Executive
- Top Sales Executive
- Regional Sales Manager
- District Sales Manager
- Senior Sales Representative (three or more years of experience)
- Intermediate Sales Representative (one to three years of experience)
- Entry Level Sales Representative (less than one year of experience)
- National/Major Account Manager
- National Account Representative
- Major (Key) Account Representative.

A more detailed description of each of these positions can be found on pages 108 and 109.

These tables provide compensation data for those individuals paid on a combination plan, broken down by salary (base) pay and incentive pay; data for those paid on an all-incentive plan; and data for those paid on an all-salary plan. Average total cash compensation data for all plans is also provided. Note that the data on these tables includes the full range of responses for each position surveyed.

For those individuals on a salary-only or incentive-only plan, these tables provide a complete picture of average annual total compensation. However, for those individuals paid on a combination plan, you'll want to see Figures 20–39 for more extensive breakouts of the data.

# FIGURE 10

AVERAGE SALES COMPENSATION PAY LEVELS BY PLAN TYPE
AND ALL PLANS COMBINED ($000)/
TOP MARKETING EXECUTIVE

| | SALARY AND INCENTIVE | | | ALL-INCENTIVE PLAN | ALL-SALARY PLAN | AVERAGE TOTAL CASH COMPENSATION FOR ALL PLANS |
|---|---|---|---|---|---|---|
| | SALARY | INCENTIVE | TOTAL | | | |
| **COMPANY SIZE** | | | | | | |
| UNDER $5 MILLION | $65.1 | $28.9 | $94.0 | $108.6 | $79.4 | $75.1 |
| **PRODUCT OR SERVICE** | | | | | | |
| CONSUMER PRODUCTS | 63.0 | 31.4 | 94.4 | 150.0 | 107.4 | 76.4 |
| CONSUMER SERVICES | 63.8 | 22.2 | 85.9 | 142.3 | 63.8 | 73.9 |
| INDUSTRIAL PRODUCTS | 59.0 | 24.3 | 83.3 | 115.0 | 67.6 | 72.7 |
| INDUSTRIAL SERVICES | 62.4 | 24.3 | 86.6 | N/R | 59.5 | 68.5 |
| OFFICE PRODUCTS | 71.7 | 27.9 | 99.6 | 98.1 | 59.1 | 87.7 |
| OFFICE SERVICES | 72.4 | 40.0 | 112.4 | 55.0 | 128.4 | 80.3 |
| **TYPE OF BUYER** | | | | | | |
| CONSUMERS | 66.1 | 23.4 | 89.5 | 142.3 | 103.3 | 70.1 |
| DISTRIBUTORS | 59.6 | 34.0 | 93.6 | 129.2 | 98.0 | 77.4 |
| INDUSTRY | 67.4 | 28.7 | 96.1 | 73.1 | 66.2 | 75.5 |
| RETAILERS | 65.6 | 39.3 | 104.9 | 79.4 | 60.2 | 73.5 |
| **INDUSTRY** | | | | | | |
| BUSINESS SERVICES | 76.1 | 25.7 | 101.8 | 86.7 | 67.4 | 83.1 |
| ELECTRONICS | 50.0 | 15.0 | 65.0 | N/R | N/R | N/R |
| FOOD PRODUCTS | 102.5 | 13.0 | 115.5 | N/R | 1,000.0 | 410.3 |
| HEALTH SERVICES | 96.0 | 32.0 | 128.0 | N/R | 105.0 | 123.0 |
| HOLDING & OTHER INVESTMENT OFFICES | 65.0 | 153.0 | 218.0 | N/R | 90.0 | 175.3 |
| MANUFACTURING | 53.8 | 47.5 | 101.2 | N/R | 75.0 | 83.3 |
| OFFICE EQUIPMENT | 75.0 | 10.0 | 85.0 | N/R | 55.0 | 85.0 |
| PHARMACEUTICALS | 111.7 | 70.0 | 181.7 | N/R | 85.0 | 127.2 |
| PRINTING AND PUBLISHING | 97.5 | 39.2 | 136.7 | 80.0 | 75.0 | 98.3 |
| WHOLESALE (CONSUMER GOODS) | 60.0 | 18.8 | 78.8 | N/R | 61.0 | 68.5 |
| WHOLESALE (INDUSTRIAL GOODS) | 62.8 | 19.2 | 82.0 | 126.2 | 55.0 | 74.8 |
| **OVERALL** | **$65.1** | **$28.9** | **$94.0** | **$108.6** | **$79.4** | **$75.1** |

# FIGURE 11

**AVERAGE SALES COMPENSATION PAY LEVELS BY PLAN TYPE
AND ALL PLANS COMBINED ($000)/
TOP SALES EXECUTIVE**

| | | SALARY AND INCENTIVE | | ALL-INCENTIVE PLAN | ALL-SALARY PLAN | AVERAGE TOTAL CASH COMPENSATION FOR ALL PLANS |
| | SALARY | INCENTIVE | TOTAL | | | |
|---|---|---|---|---|---|---|
| **COMPANY SIZE** | | | | | | |
| UNDER $5 MILLION | $49.3 | $23.7 | $73.0 | $106.8 | $83.7 | $72.7 |
| **PRODUCT OR SERVICE** | | | | | | |
| CONSUMER PRODUCTS | 50.6 | 22.2 | 72.9 | 108.3 | 109.6 | 70.0 |
| CONSUMER SERVICES | 47.8 | 13.2 | 61.0 | 88.5 | 74.2 | 64.3 |
| INDUSTRIAL PRODUCTS | 46.7 | 22.2 | 68.9 | 107.2 | 70.0 | 75.1 |
| INDUSTRIAL SERVICES | 45.0 | 19.0 | 63.9 | 127.5 | 67.1 | 69.4 |
| OFFICE PRODUCTS | 53.6 | 26.4 | 80.0 | 118.3 | 73.3 | 84.0 |
| OFFICE SERVICES | 48.7 | 30.7 | 79.4 | 87.5 | 126.8 | 72.7 |
| **TYPE OF BUYER** | | | | | | |
| CONSUMERS | 46.0 | 19.9 | 66.0 | 88.5 | 118.8 | 66.7 |
| DISTRIBUTORS | 47.5 | 25.5 | 73.0 | 109.4 | 123.4 | 73.1 |
| INDUSTRY | 47.0 | 24.9 | 71.8 | 116.8 | 70.2 | 74.6 |
| RETAILERS | 44.7 | 28.7 | 73.3 | 84.2 | 64.2 | 63.6 |
| **INDUSTRY** | | | | | | |
| BUSINESS SERVICES | 52.1 | 21.0 | 73.1 | 145.0 | 68.1 | 72.7 |
| FABRICATED METALS | 28.0 | 38.9 | 66.9 | N/R | 40.0 | 57.9 |
| FOOD PRODUCTS | 37.5 | 46.5 | 84.0 | N/R | 87.9 | 86.0 |
| FURNITURE AND FIXTURES | 51.0 | 16.5 | 67.5 | 81.7 | 75.0 | 73.9 |
| MACHINERY | 65.0 | 12.5 | 77.5 | 100.0 | 100.0 | 97.5 |
| MANUFACTURING | 67.8 | 28.2 | 96.1 | 150.0 | N/R | 89.3 |
| OFFICE EQUIPMENT | 41.9 | 21.1 | 63.0 | N/R | 110.0 | 91.6 |
| PHARMACEUTICALS | 74.6 | 35.6 | 110.2 | N/R | 100.0 | 108.3 |
| PRINTING AND PUBLISHING | 50.4 | 19.5 | 69.9 | 80.0 | 53.0 | 78.8 |
| WHOLESALE (INDUSTRIAL GOODS) | 68.3 | 13.3 | 81.7 | 105.0 | 49.5 | 63.7 |
| **OVERALL** | **$49.3** | **$23.7** | **$73.0** | **$106.8** | **$83.7** | **$72.7** |

# FIGURE 12

| | SALARY AND INCENTIVE | | | | | |
| | SALARY | INCENTIVE | TOTAL | ALL-INCENTIVE PLAN | ALL-SALARY PLAN | AVERAGE TOTAL CASH COMPENSATION FOR ALL PLANS |
|---|---|---|---|---|---|---|
| **COMPANY SIZE** | | | | | | |
| UNDER $5 MILLION | $45.4 | $17.1 | $62.5 | $97.1 | $92.6 | $62.3 |
| **PRODUCT OR SERVICE** | | | | | | |
| CONSUMER PRODUCTS | 46.5 | 29.6 | 76.1 | 79.5 | 112.5 | 63.8 |
| CONSUMER SERVICES | 49.5 | 16.9 | 66.3 | 89.1 | 52.8 | 68.5 |
| INDUSTRIAL PRODUCTS | 42.6 | 10.3 | 52.9 | 81.0 | 56.8 | 61.8 |
| INDUSTRIAL SERVICES | 43.7 | 8.7 | 52.4 | N/R | 58.6 | 58.1 |
| OFFICE PRODUCTS | 45.5 | 18.0 | 63.5 | 150.0 | N/R | 60.5 |
| OFFICE SERVICES | 46.3 | 18.4 | 64.7 | N/R | 171.0 | 69.3 |
| **TYPE OF BUYER** | | | | | | |
| CONSUMERS | 49.6 | 13.0 | 62.6 | 89.1 | 124.9 | 64.7 |
| DISTRIBUTORS | 40.6 | 19.3 | 59.9 | 81.0 | 126.8 | 62.8 |
| INDUSTRY | 46.6 | 12.4 | 59.0 | 73.5 | 60.2 | 62.3 |
| RETAILERS | 52.5 | 16.4 | 68.9 | N/R | 54.3 | 62.5 |
| **INDUSTRY** | | | | | | |
| BUSINESS SERVICES | 56.0 | 11.9 | 67.9 | N/R | 43.0 | 62.3 |
| ELECTRONICS | 41.2 | 8.7 | 49.8 | N/R | N/R | 52.2 |
| FOOD PRODUCTS | 60.0 | 3.7 | 63.7 | N/R | N/R | 63.7 |
| INSURANCE | 65.0 | 15.0 | 80.0 | 129.2 | N/R | 112.8 |
| RETAIL | 37.5 | 4.2 | 41.8 | N/R | 32.0 | 41.8 |
| WHOLESALE (INDUSTRIAL GOODS) | 46.9 | 12.1 | 59.0 | 107.5 | 35.0 | 57.8 |
| **OVERALL** | **$45.4** | **$17.1** | **$62.5** | **$97.1** | **$92.6** | **$62.3** |

# FIGURE 13

**AVERAGE SALES COMPENSATION PAY LEVELS BY PLAN TYPE
AND ALL PLANS COMBINED ($000)/
DISTRICT SALES MANAGER**

| | SALARY AND INCENTIVE | | | ALL-INCENTIVE PLAN | ALL-SALARY PLAN | AVERAGE TOTAL CASH COMPENSATION FOR ALL PLANS |
| | SALARY | INCENTIVE | TOTAL | | | |
|---|---|---|---|---|---|---|
| **COMPANY SIZE** | | | | | | |
| UNDER $5 MILLION | $44.4 | $8.8 | $53.1 | $88.7 | $47.8 | $59.3 |
| **PRODUCT OR SERVICE** | | | | | | |
| CONSUMER PRODUCTS | 45.7 | 12.1 | 57.8 | 101.0 | N/R | 63.5 |
| CONSUMER SERVICES | 46.5 | 8.4 | 54.9 | 88.7 | 49.7 | 63.4 |
| INDUSTRIAL PRODUCTS | 40.1 | 6.0 | 46.2 | N/R | 40.0 | 48.5 |
| INDUSTRIAL SERVICES | 40.2 | 5.7 | 45.9 | N/R | 55.0 | 53.9 |
| OFFICE PRODUCTS | 44.0 | 9.2 | 53.2 | N/R | 30.0 | 48.2 |
| OFFICE SERVICES | 39.7 | 4.7 | 44.4 | N/R | N/R | 51.1 |
| **TYPE OF BUYER** | | | | | | |
| CONSUMERS | 46.2 | 9.5 | 55.8 | 88.7 | N/R | 66.4 |
| DISTRIBUTORS | 41.1 | 9.4 | 50.4 | N/R | N/R | 52.3 |
| INDUSTRY | 44.9 | 6.3 | 51.1 | 86.7 | 55.0 | 56.6 |
| RETAILERS | 43.4 | 10.9 | 54.4 | N/R | 62.5 | 57.1 |
| **INDUSTRY** | | | | | | |
| BUSINESS SERVICES | 47.7 | 4.2 | 52.0 | N/R | N/R | 52.9 |
| INSURANCE | 50.0 | 20.0 | 70.0 | 82.5 | N/R | 78.3 |
| RETAIL | 40.0 | 7.1 | 47.1 | N/R | N/R | 53.1 |
| **OVERALL** | **$44.4** | **$8.8** | **$53.1** | **$88.7** | **$47.8** | **$59.3** |

## FIGURE 14

AVERAGE SALES COMPENSATION PAY LEVELS BY PLAN TYPE
AND ALL PLANS COMBINED ($000)/
SENIOR SALES REP

| | SALARY | SALARY AND INCENTIVE | | ALL-INCENTIVE PLAN | ALL-SALARY PLAN | AVERAGE TOTAL CASH COMPENSATION FOR ALL PLANS |
| | | INCENTIVE | TOTAL | | | |
|---|---|---|---|---|---|---|
| **COMPANY SIZE** | | | | | | |
| UNDER $5 MILLION | $32.3 | $15.6 | $47.9 | $62.2 | $72.9 | $52.0 |
| **PRODUCT OR SERVICE** | | | | | | |
| CONSUMER PRODUCTS | 32.5 | 9.9 | 42.4 | 70.2 | 106.7 | 47.3 |
| CONSUMER SERVICES | 28.9 | 9.1 | 38.0 | 57.5 | 48.8 | 47.2 |
| INDUSTRIAL PRODUCTS | 34.8 | 19.4 | 54.2 | 55.4 | 34.1 | 52.4 |
| INDUSTRIAL SERVICES | 31.0 | 12.3 | 43.3 | 64.9 | 41.4 | 51.2 |
| OFFICE PRODUCTS | 39.3 | 18.1 | 57.3 | 45.6 | 29.6 | 50.6 |
| OFFICE SERVICES | 34.8 | 15.6 | 50.4 | 44.5 | 121.9 | 51.4 |
| **TYPE OF BUYER** | | | | | | |
| CONSUMERS | 28.8 | 10.2 | 39.0 | 67.5 | 101.3 | 47.6 |
| DISTRIBUTORS | 32.4 | 11.9 | 44.2 | 44.6 | 90.8 | 47.8 |
| INDUSTRY | 33.0 | 16.8 | 49.8 | 60.4 | 42.2 | 52.8 |
| RETAILERS | 32.2 | 13.3 | 45.5 | 56.0 | 41.7 | 47.6 |
| **INDUSTRY** | | | | | | |
| AMUSEMENT & RECREATION SERVICES | 24.0 | 6.5 | 30.5 | N/R | N/R | 34.0 |
| BUSINESS SERVICES | 34.3 | 15.4 | 49.7 | 56.8 | N/R | 51.4 |
| HEALTH SERVICES | 45.0 | 19.5 | 64.5 | 52.0 | N/R | 60.3 |
| INSTRUMENTS | 39.2 | 22.0 | 61.3 | N/R | 35.0 | 56.3 |
| MANUFACTURING | 32.5 | 9.2 | 41.8 | 80.1 | N/R | 58.4 |
| OFFICE EQUIPMENT | 28.8 | 11.8 | 40.6 | 60.0 | N/R | 42.8 |
| PHARMACEUTICALS | 38.8 | 11.4 | 50.2 | N/R | N/R | 56.7 |
| PRINTING AND PUBLISHING | 45.2 | 21.9 | 67.2 | 80.0 | 61.7 | 71.5 |
| RETAIL | 22.0 | 10.5 | 32.5 | 25.0 | 40.0 | 35.7 |
| WHOLESALE (CONSUMER GOODS) | 27.8 | 35.2 | 63.0 | 65.8 | N/R | 58.8 |
| WHOLESALE (INDUSTRIAL GOODS) | 36.1 | 13.3 | 49.4 | 54.9 | N/R | 53.2 |
| **OVERALL** | **$32.3** | **$15.6** | **$47.9** | **$62.2** | **$72.9** | **$52.0** |

133

## FIGURE 15

AVERAGE SALES COMPENSATION PAY LEVELS BY PLAN TYPE
AND ALL PLANS COMBINED ($000)/
INTERMEDIATE SALES REP

| | SALARY AND INCENTIVE | | | ALL-INCENTIVE PLAN | ALL-SALARY PLAN | AVERAGE TOTAL CASH COMPENSATION FOR ALL PLANS |
| | SALARY | INCENTIVE | TOTAL | | | |
|---|---|---|---|---|---|---|
| **COMPANY SIZE** | | | | | | |
| UNDER $5 MILLION | $24.2 | $14.3 | $38.5 | $40.2 | $36.0 | $36.9 |
| **PRODUCT OR SERVICE** | | | | | | |
| CONSUMER PRODUCTS | 23.3 | 10.3 | 33.6 | 33.0 | 49.5 | 36.4 |
| CONSUMER SERVICES | 21.1 | 8.3 | 29.4 | 34.7 | 35.8 | 34.6 |
| INDUSTRIAL PRODUCTS | 26.0 | 15.3 | 41.2 | 41.3 | 23.5 | 37.0 |
| INDUSTRIAL SERVICES | 23.9 | 11.1 | 34.9 | 51.5 | 37.0 | 37.6 |
| OFFICE PRODUCTS | 23.9 | 14.3 | 38.2 | 35.2 | 21.0 | 34.2 |
| OFFICE SERVICES | 23.6 | 21.0 | 44.6 | 32.0 | 42.8 | 38.2 |
| **TYPE OF BUYER** | | | | | | |
| CONSUMERS | 21.7 | 9.2 | 30.9 | 35.2 | 48.6 | 35.7 |
| DISTRIBUTORS | 24.1 | 14.8 | 38.9 | 40.4 | 44.2 | 36.2 |
| INDUSTRY | 24.6 | 14.9 | 39.5 | 38.0 | 32.4 | 37.4 |
| RETAILERS | 22.8 | 15.0 | 37.8 | 31.8 | 31.5 | 33.6 |
| **INDUSTRY** | | | | | | |
| BUSINESS SERVICES | 28.1 | 11.9 | 40.0 | 51.9 | 22.0 | 38.7 |
| FABRICATED METALS | 25.0 | 2.8 | 27.8 | 30.0 | N/R | 30.7 |
| FOOD PRODUCTS | 17.0 | 20.0 | 37.0 | N/R | 100.0 | 56.5 |
| HEALTH SERVICES | 20.0 | 20.0 | 40.0 | N/R | 37.5 | 38.3 |
| INSURANCE | N/R | N/R | N/R | 44.1 | N/R | 49.2 |
| OFFICE EQUIPMENT | 21.3 | 11.7 | 33.0 | N/R | N/R | 35.1 |
| PHARMACEUTICALS | 31.0 | 4.8 | 35.8 | N/R | N/R | 43.9 |
| PRINTING AND PUBLISHING | 23.0 | 13.2 | 36.2 | N/R | N/R | 33.4 |
| WHOLESALE (CONSUMER GOODS) | 21.6 | 19.4 | 40.9 | 39.7 | N/R | 46.0 |
| WHOLESALE (INDUSTRIAL GOODS) | 29.8 | 15.6 | 45.4 | 57.8 | 27.0 | 38.8 |
| **OVERALL** | **$24.2** | **$14.3** | **$38.5** | **$40.2** | **$36.0** | **$36.9** |

# FIGURE 16

| | SALARY AND INCENTIVE | | | | | |
| | SALARY | INCENTIVE | TOTAL | ALL-INCENTIVE PLAN | ALL-SALARY PLAN | AVERAGE TOTAL CASH COMPENSATION FOR ALL PLANS |
|---|---|---|---|---|---|---|
| **COMPANY SIZE** | | | | | | |
| UNDER $5 MILLION | $22.0 | $8.2 | $30.3 | $28.7 | $22.0 | $26.4 |
| **PRODUCT OR SERVICE** | | | | | | |
| CONSUMER PRODUCTS | 20.7 | 5.7 | 26.5 | 31.2 | 23.7 | 24.6 |
| CONSUMER SERVICES | 21.2 | 4.9 | 26.1 | 30.8 | 20.8 | 26.8 |
| INDUSTRIAL PRODUCTS | 23.1 | 7.1 | 30.2 | 32.7 | 19.9 | 26.0 |
| INDUSTRIAL SERVICES | 21.8 | 6.2 | 28.0 | 31.3 | 20.6 | 25.9 |
| OFFICE PRODUCTS | 21.6 | 8.2 | 29.8 | 31.0 | 15.5 | 23.8 |
| OFFICE SERVICES | 22.0 | 13.1 | 35.1 | N/R | 23.2 | 24.9 |
| **TYPE OF BUYER** | | | | | | |
| CONSUMERS | 19.5 | 4.6 | 24.1 | 30.7 | 24.1 | 25.5 |
| DISTRIBUTORS | 21.0 | 8.7 | 29.7 | 26.8 | 22.7 | 24.6 |
| INDUSTRY | 22.3 | 8.2 | 30.5 | 27.5 | 21.0 | 26.8 |
| RETAILERS | 21.3 | 8.1 | 29.4 | 27.4 | 19.9 | 23.9 |
| **INDUSTRY** | | | | | | |
| BUSINESS SERVICES | 26.1 | 10.4 | 36.5 | 18.2 | 17.0 | 27.9 |
| INSTRUMENTS | 25.8 | 13.2 | 39.0 | N/R | 25.0 | 34.3 |
| INSURANCE | 40.0 | 6.2 | 46.2 | 38.1 | N/R | 39.7 |
| MANUFACTURING | 17.2 | 10.3 | 27.5 | 23.0 | N/R | 29.0 |
| OFFICE EQUIPMENT | 16.1 | 5.6 | 21.7 | N/R | N/R | 21.0 |
| PHARMACEUTICALS | 27.7 | 7.6 | 35.3 | N/R | N/R | 34.7 |
| PRINTING AND PUBLISHING | 23.9 | 6.8 | 30.7 | N/R | N/R | 19.0 |
| RETAIL | 15.0 | 2.8 | 17.7 | 17.0 | 16.0 | 19.0 |
| WHOLESALE (CONSUMER GOODS) | 20.8 | 2.8 | 23.7 | 40.8 | N/R | 37.2 |
| WHOLESALE (INDUSTRIAL GOODS) | 24.9 | 4.1 | 29.1 | 34.5 | 23.5 | 25.8 |
| **OVERALL** | **$22.0** | **$8.2** | **$30.3** | **$28.7** | **$22.0** | **$26.4** |

# FIGURE 17

**AVERAGE SALES COMPENSATION PAY LEVELS BY PLAN TYPE
AND ALL PLANS COMBINED ($000)/
NAT'L/MAJ ACCOUNT MANAGER**

| | SALARY AND INCENTIVE | | | ALL-INCENTIVE PLAN | ALL-SALARY PLAN | AVERAGE TOTAL CASH COMPENSATION FOR ALL PLANS |
| | SALARY | INCENTIVE | TOTAL | | | |
|---|---|---|---|---|---|---|
| **COMPANY SIZE** | | | | | | |
| UNDER $5 MILLION | $62.3 | $14.4 | $76.8 | N/R | $40.2 | $58.4 |
| **PRODUCT OR SERVICE** | | | | | | |
| CONSUMER PRODUCTS | 72.7 | 19.6 | 92.3 | N/R | 40.0 | 54.6 |
| CONSUMER SERVICES | 111.0 | 15.3 | 126.3 | N/R | 30.0 | 82.3 |
| INDUSTRIAL PRODUCTS | 58.4 | 17.4 | 75.8 | N/R | 35.5 | 65.0 |
| INDUSTRIAL SERVICES | 63.3 | 18.6 | 82.0 | N/R | 35.5 | 73.2 |
| OFFICE PRODUCTS | 66.6 | 20.8 | 87.4 | N/R | 30.0 | 84.9 |
| OFFICE SERVICES | 57.8 | 19.9 | 77.7 | N/R | 30.0 | 69.9 |
| **TYPE OF BUYER** | | | | | | |
| CONSUMERS | 111.0 | 15.3 | 126.3 | N/R | 30.0 | 82.3 |
| DISTRIBUTORS | 42.7 | 14.7 | 57.4 | N/R | 40.0 | 53.0 |
| INDUSTRY | 71.7 | 11.2 | 82.9 | N/R | 37.0 | 62.8 |
| RETAILERS | 72.6 | 12.4 | 85.0 | N/R | 40.0 | 62.6 |
| **INDUSTRY** | | | | | | |
| BUSINESS SERVICES | 56.1 | 12.5 | 68.6 | N/R | N/R | 81.9 |
| PHARMACEUTICALS | 125.8 | 11.2 | 137.1 | N/R | 50.0 | 116.1 |
| **OVERALL** | **$62.3** | **$14.4** | **$76.8** | **N/R** | **$40.2** | **$58.4** |

## FIGURE 18

| | SALARY AND INCENTIVE | | | | | |
| | SALARY | INCENTIVE | TOTAL | ALL-INCENTIVE PLAN | ALL-SALARY PLAN | AVERAGE TOTAL CASH COMPENSATION FOR ALL PLANS |
|---|---|---|---|---|---|---|
| **COMPANY SIZE** | | | | | | |
| UNDER $5 MILLION | $50.1 | $12.4 | $62.5 | $51.5 | $34.0 | $58.8 |
| **PRODUCT OR SERVICE** | | | | | | |
| CONSUMER PRODUCTS | 53.6 | 14.2 | 67.8 | N/R | 34.0 | 58.3 |
| CONSUMER SERVICES | 53.6 | 12.5 | 66.1 | 53.0 | N/R | 57.7 |
| INDUSTRIAL PRODUCTS | 55.2 | 18.3 | 73.5 | 50.0 | 34.0 | 67.8 |
| INDUSTRIAL SERVICES | 53.9 | 16.2 | 70.1 | 51.5 | 26.0 | 59.1 |
| OFFICE SERVICES | 65.7 | 26.3 | 92.0 | 53.0 | N/R | 54.3 |
| **TYPE OF BUYER** | | | | | | |
| CONSUMERS | 55.3 | 13.8 | 69.1 | 53.0 | N/R | 56.5 |
| DISTRIBUTORS | 48.9 | 17.5 | 66.4 | N/R | 34.0 | 62.1 |
| INDUSTRY | 53.4 | 11.5 | 65.0 | 51.5 | 26.0 | 62.8 |
| RETAILERS | 48.4 | 12.1 | 60.5 | N/R | 34.0 | 58.8 |
| **INDUSTRY** | | | | | | |
| BUSINESS SERVICES | 58.6 | 13.1 | 71.7 | N/R | N/R | 78.7 |
| **OVERALL** | **$50.1** | **$12.4** | **$62.5** | **$51.5** | **$34.0** | **$58.8** |

# FIGURE 19

| | SALARY AND INCENTIVE | | | ALL-INCENTIVE PLAN | ALL-SALARY PLAN | AVERAGE TOTAL CASH COMPENSATION FOR ALL PLANS |
| | SALARY | INCENTIVE | TOTAL | | | |
|---|---|---|---|---|---|---|
| **COMPANY SIZE** | | | | | | |
| UNDER $5 MILLION | $38.8 | $11.9 | $50.7 | N/R | $43.3 | $46.8 |
| **PRODUCT OR SERVICE** | | | | | | |
| CONSUMER PRODUCTS | 45.3 | 12.7 | 58.0 | N/R | 50.0 | 53.0 |
| CONSUMER SERVICES | 45.5 | 10.3 | 55.8 | N/R | 48.9 | 40.4 |
| INDUSTRIAL PRODUCTS | 43.5 | 13.8 | 57.4 | N/R | N/R | 37.2 |
| INDUSTRIAL SERVICES | 33.4 | 16.2 | 49.6 | N/R | 44.2 | 43.8 |
| OFFICE PRODUCTS | 55.0 | 12.4 | 67.4 | N/R | N/R | 75.7 |
| OFFICE SERVICES | 45.0 | 12.7 | 57.7 | N/R | 48.9 | 49.7 |
| **TYPE OF BUYER** | | | | | | |
| CONSUMERS | 40.9 | 8.7 | 49.6 | N/R | 48.9 | 43.9 |
| DISTRIBUTORS | 39.4 | 10.1 | 49.5 | N/R | 43.3 | 46.0 |
| INDUSTRY | 40.0 | 11.4 | 51.4 | N/R | 44.2 | 52.1 |
| RETAILERS | 37.0 | 14.4 | 51.4 | N/R | 46.7 | 49.6 |
| **INDUSTRY** | | | | | | |
| BUSINESS SERVICES | 53.3 | 12.0 | 65.3 | N/R | N/R | 76.0 |
| PHARMACEUTICALS | 42.5 | 10.6 | 53.1 | N/R | 40.0 | 53.3 |
| **OVERALL** | **$38.8** | **$11.9** | **$50.7** | **N/R** | **$43.3** | **$46.8** |

# FIGURES 20–29 — COMPENSATION TABLES: AVERAGE TOTAL CASH COMPENSATION FOR AVERAGE, BETTER, AND BEST PERFORMERS (MEDIAN AND THIRD QUARTILE)

You'll want to use these tables to determine total cash compensation for those people paid on a combination plan. Remember, use Figures 10–19 to determine total cash compensation for those individuals on either a "salary only" or "incentive only" plan. Here's how this group of tables works:

Figures 20–29 show how much average, better, and best performers in various positions earn at typical-paying ("median") companies and higher-paying (third quartile) companies. The positions surveyed are as follows:

- Top Marketing Executive
- Top Sales Executive
- Regional Sales Manager
- District Sales Manager
- Senior Sales Representative (three or more years of experience)
- Intermediate Sales Representative (one to three years of experience)
- Entry Level Sales Representative (less than one year of experience)
- National/Major Account Manager
- National Account Representative
- Major (Key) Account Representative

Note: Since most companies have only one top marketing executive and/or one top sales executive, there is no better or best performer for that position. Therefore, data for these two positions encompasses the full range of responses received.

Here are some suggestions on how to use these tables:

1. Determine the relative level you should be paying at — median, above median, below median, highest, etc.
2. Determine the relative skill level of the person in the position for which you are analyzing compensation. Is this individual an average performer, a better performer, or a top (best) performer?
3. Select the comparison groups that are the most similar to your company. Potential comparison groups might be based on type of buyer, type of product or service sold, or industry.
4. Use the pay levels on the tables you've selected as guides when analyzing pay levels in your organization.
5. Remember that these data tables provide figures for total cash compensation. You will still need to break the total compensation you select into its base salary and incentive components. Figures 30–39 will help you determine salary levels for combined plans.

**FIGURE 20**

**AVERAGE TOTAL CASH COMPENSATION**
**TOP MARKETING EXECUTIVE**

|  | MEDIAN ($000) | 3RD QUARTILE ($000) |
|---|---|---|
| **COMPANY SIZE** | | |
| UNDER $5 MILLION | $75.0 | $100.0 |
| **PRODUCT OR SERVICE** | | |
| CONSUMER PRODUCTS | 75.0 | 100.0 |
| CONSUMER SERVICES | 69.0 | 101.0 |
| INDUSTRIAL PRODUCTS | 72.0 | 87.0 |
| INDUSTRIAL SERVICES | 64.0 | 95.0 |
| OFFICE PRODUCTS | 80.0 | 100.0 |
| OFFICE SERVICES | 80.0 | 100.0 |
| **TYPE OF BUYER** | | |
| CONSUMERS | 62.0 | 100.0 |
| DISTRIBUTORS | 80.0 | 100.0 |
| INDUSTRY | 75.0 | 100.0 |
| RETAILERS | 75.0 | 95.0 |
| **INDUSTRY** | | |
| BUSINESS SERVICES | 80.0 | 102.0 |
| HEALTH SERVICES | 106.0 | 140.0 |
| MANUFACTURING | 80.0 | 85.0 |
| OFFICE EQUIPMENT | 80.0 | 95.0 |
| PRINTING AND PUBLISHING | 100.0 | 115.0 |
| RETAIL | 45.0 | 60.0 |
| WHOLESALE (CONSUMER GOODS) | 60.0 | 100.0 |
| WHOLESALE (INDUSTRIAL GOODS) | 72.0 | 80.0 |
| **OVERALL** | **$75.0** | **$100.0** |

# FIGURE 21

**AVERAGE TOTAL CASH COMPENSATION**
**TOP SALES EXECUTIVE**

| | MEDIAN ($000) | 3RD QUARTILE ($000) |
|---|---|---|
| **COMPANY SIZE** | | |
| UNDER $5 MILLION | $70.0 | $100.0 |
| **PRODUCT OR SERVICE** | | |
| CONSUMER PRODUCTS | 65.0 | 85.0 |
| CONSUMER SERVICES | 63.0 | 85.0 |
| INDUSTRIAL PRODUCTS | 70.0 | 100.0 |
| INDUSTRIAL SERVICES | 65.0 | 100.0 |
| OFFICE PRODUCTS | 75.0 | 100.0 |
| OFFICE SERVICES | 65.0 | 100.0 |
| **TYPE OF BUYER** | | |
| CONSUMERS | 65.0 | 85.0 |
| DISTRIBUTORS | 70.0 | 100.0 |
| INDUSTRY | 70.0 | 100.0 |
| RETAILERS | 55.0 | 75.0 |
| **INDUSTRY** | | |
| BUSINESS SERVICES | 70.0 | 100.0 |
| ELECTRONICS | 32.0 | 78.0 |
| FURNITURE AND FIXTURES | 55.0 | 85.0 |
| MACHINERY | 95.0 | 100.0 |
| MANUFACTURING | 95.0 | 125.0 |
| PHARMACEUTICALS | 105.0 | 120.0 |
| PRINTING AND PUBLISHING | 75.0 | 100.0 |
| RETAIL | 50.0 | 60.0 |
| WHOLESALE (CONSUMER GOODS) | 40.0 | 50.0 |
| WHOLESALE (INDUSTRIAL GOODS) | 65.0 | 70.0 |
| **OVERALL** | **$70.0** | **$100.0** |

# FIGURE 22

**AVERAGE TOTAL CASH COMPENSATION**
**REGIONAL SALES MANAGER**

| | AVERAGE PERFORMER | | BETTER PERFORMER | | BEST PERFORMER | |
| --- | --- | --- | --- | --- | --- | --- |
| | MEDIAN ($000) | 3RD QUARTILE ($000) | MEDIAN ($000) | 3RD QUARTILE ($000) | MEDIAN ($000) | 3RD QUARTILE ($000) |
| **COMPANY SIZE** | | | | | | |
| UNDER $5 MILLION | $57.0 | $80.0 | N/R | N/R | $63.0 | $110.0 |
| **PRODUCT OR SERVICE** | | | | | | |
| CONSUMER PRODUCTS | 55.0 | 82.4 | N/R | 86.0 | 80.0 | 98.0 |
| CONSUMER SERVICES | 63.0 | 85.0 | 65.0 | 100.0 | 110.0 | 120.0 |
| INDUSTRIAL PRODUCTS | 55.0 | 70.0 | 55.0 | N/R | 80.0 | 98.0 |
| INDUSTRIAL SERVICES | 50.0 | 63.0 | 55.0 | 70.0 | 63.0 | 80.0 |
| OFFICE PRODUCTS | 55.0 | 70.0 | N/R | N/R | 80.0 | 98.0 |
| OFFICE SERVICES | 57.0 | 80.0 | 65.0 | 86.0 | 80.0 | 98.0 |
| **TYPE OF BUYER** | | | | | | |
| CONSUMERS | 55.0 | 80.0 | 60.0 | 95.0 | 98.0 | 120.0 |
| DISTRIBUTORS | 60.0 | 80.0 | N/R | N/R | 87.0 | 98.0 |
| INDUSTRY | 57.0 | 80.0 | N/R | N/R | 63.0 | 98.0 |
| RETAILERS | 55.0 | 80.0 | N/R | 86.0 | 60.0 | 110.0 |
| **INDUSTRY** | | | | | | |
| BUSINESS SERVICES | 50.0 | 70.0 | 55.0 | 86.0 | 62.5 | 98.0 |
| ELECTRONICS | 44.0 | 55.0 | 55.0 | 70.0 | N/R | N/R |
| FOOD PRODUCTS | 82.4 | N/R | N/R | N/R | N/R | N/R |
| INSURANCE | 85.0 | 90.0 | 100.0 | 110.0 | 165.0 | 225.0 |
| MACHINERY | 85.0 | 90.0 | N/R | N/R | N/R | N/R |
| PHARMACEUTICALS | 120.0 | 125.0 | N/R | N/R | 110.0 | 110.0 |
| PRINTING AND PUBLISHING | 70.0 | 80.0 | N/R | N/R | N/R | N/R |
| RETAIL | 30.0 | 51.5 | N/R | N/R | N/R | N/R |
| WHOLESALE (CONSUMER GOODS) | 30.0 | 53.0 | N/R | N/R | N/R | N/R |
| WHOLESALE (INDUSTRIAL GOODS) | 55.0 | 65.0 | N/R | 65.0 | 80.0 | 150.0 |
| **OVERALL** | **$57.0** | **$80.0** | **N/R** | **N/R** | **$63.0** | **$110.0** |

# FIGURE 23

**AVERAGE TOTAL CASH COMPENSATION**
**DISTRICT SALES MANAGER**

| | AVERAGE PERFORMER | | BETTER PERFORMER | | BEST PERFORMER | |
| --- | --- | --- | --- | --- | --- | --- |
| | MEDIAN ($000) | 3RD QUARTILE ($000) | MEDIAN ($000) | 3RD QUARTILE ($000) | MEDIAN ($000) | 3RD QUARTILE ($000) |
| **COMPANY SIZE** | | | | | | |
| UNDER $5 MILLION | $55.0 | $68.0 | $70.0 | $80.0 | N/R | $95.0 |
| **PRODUCT OR SERVICE** | | | | | | |
| CONSUMER PRODUCTS | 60.0 | 80.0 | N/R | 90.0 | 65.0 | N/R |
| CONSUMER SERVICES | 60.0 | 60.0 | 73.0 | 90.0 | 80.0 | 95.0 |
| INDUSTRIAL PRODUCTS | 48.0 | 60.0 | N/R | 73.0 | 45.0 | 87.0 |
| INDUSTRIAL SERVICES | 48.0 | 60.0 | 70.0 | 73.0 | N/R | 80.0 |
| OFFICE PRODUCTS | 40.0 | 66.0 | N/R | N/R | 28.0 | 28.0 |
| OFFICE SERVICES | 40.0 | 66.0 | 46.0 | 90.0 | 52.0 | N/R |
| **TYPE OF BUYER** | | | | | | |
| CONSUMERS | 60.0 | 70.0 | 73.0 | 90.0 | 80.0 | 95.0 |
| DISTRIBUTORS | 46.0 | 66.0 | N/R | 70.0 | 52.0 | N/R |
| INDUSTRY | 49.0 | 66.0 | 52.5 | 90.0 | 65.0 | N/R |
| RETAILERS | 60.0 | 68.0 | 70.0 | 90.0 | N/R | N/R |
| **INDUSTRY** | | | | | | |
| BUSINESS SERVICES | 46.0 | 66.0 | N/R | N/R | 52.0 | 60.0 |
| INSURANCE | 60.0 | 60.0 | 80.0 | 90.0 | 95.0 | 115.0 |
| MANUFACTURING | 41.0 | 68.0 | N/R | N/R | N/R | N/R |
| PHARMACEUTICALS | 80.0 | 95.0 | 110.0 | 110.0 | 160.0 | 160.0 |
| RETAIL | 60.0 | 60.0 | N/R | 73.0 | 28.0 | 87.0 |
| **OVERALL** | **$55.0** | **$68.0** | **$70.0** | **$80.0** | **N/R** | **$95.0** |

# FIGURE 24

**AVERAGE TOTAL CASH COMPENSATION**
**SENIOR SALES REP**

| | AVERAGE PERFORMER | | BETTER PERFORMER | | BEST PERFORMER | |
|---|---|---|---|---|---|---|
| | MEDIAN ($000) | 3RD QUARTILE ($000) | MEDIAN ($000) | 3RD QUARTILE ($000) | MEDIAN ($000) | 3RD QUARTILE ($000) |
| **COMPANY SIZE** | | | | | | |
| UNDER $5 MILLION | $46.0 | $60.0 | $50.0 | $65.0 | $60.0 | $94.0 |
| **PRODUCT OR SERVICE** | | | | | | |
| CONSUMER PRODUCTS | 43.0 | 53.0 | 55.0 | 72.0 | 60.0 | 85.0 |
| CONSUMER SERVICES | 40.0 | 50.5 | 50.0 | 67.0 | 60.0 | 85.0 |
| INDUSTRIAL PRODUCTS | 48.0 | 55.0 | 50.0 | 72.0 | 60.0 | 94.0 |
| INDUSTRIAL SERVICES | 45.0 | 60.0 | 50.0 | 65.0 | 60.0 | 80.0 |
| OFFICE PRODUCTS | 44.0 | 60.0 | 48.0 | 68.0 | 60.0 | N/R |
| OFFICE SERVICES | 44.0 | 65.0 | 45.0 | 68.0 | 50.0 | N/R |
| **TYPE OF BUYER** | | | | | | |
| CONSUMERS | 41.0 | 53.0 | 50.0 | 72.0 | 60.0 | 100.0 |
| DISTRIBUTORS | 41.0 | 60.0 | 45.0 | 65.0 | 57.0 | 75.0 |
| INDUSTRY | 46.0 | 60.0 | 50.0 | 67.0 | 60.0 | 94.0 |
| RETAILERS | 40.0 | 54.0 | 48.0 | 65.0 | 60.0 | 85.0 |
| **INDUSTRY** | | | | | | |
| AMUSEMENT & RECREATION SERVICES | 41.0 | 45.0 | N/R | N/R | N/R | N/R |
| BUSINESS SERVICES | 50.0 | 60.0 | N/R | N/R | 50.0 | 60.0 |
| ELECTRONICS | 30.0 | 36.0 | N/R | 47.0 | 55.0 | 55.0 |
| FABRICATED METALS | 65.0 | 70.0 | N/R | N/R | N/R | N/R |
| FOOD PRODUCTS | 40.0 | 50.0 | N/R | N/R | N/R | N/R |
| HEALTH SERVICES | 64.0 | 65.0 | N/R | N/R | N/R | N/R |
| INSTRUMENTS | 55.0 | 65.0 | N/R | 90.0 | 54.0 | 97.0 |
| INSURANCE | 34.0 | 50.0 | 50.0 | 75.0 | 60.0 | 126.0 |
| MACHINERY | 50.0 | 55.0 | 60.0 | 60.0 | 80.0 | 80.0 |
| MANUFACTURING | 46.0 | 55.0 | 55.0 | 65.0 | 75.0 | 85.0 |
| OFFICE EQUIPMENT | 50.8 | 60.0 | N/R | 60.0 | N/R | N/R |
| PHARMACEUTICALS | 53.0 | 60.0 | 60.0 | 60.0 | 95.0 | 95.0 |
| PRINTING AND PUBLISHING | 50.0 | 80.0 | N/R | N/R | 60.0 | 75.0 |
| RETAIL | 40.0 | 45.0 | 47.0 | 68.0 | 50.0 | N/R |
| WHOLESALE (CONSUMER GOODS) | 49.0 | 85.0 | 60.0 | N/R | 75.0 | 75.0 |
| WHOLESALE (INDUSTRIAL GOODS) | 43.0 | 60.0 | 55.0 | 75.0 | 70.0 | 100.0 |
| **OVERALL** | **$46.0** | **$60.0** | **$50.0** | **$65.0** | **$60.0** | **$94.0** |

# FIGURE 25

**AVERAGE TOTAL CASH COMPENSATION**
**INTERMEDIATE SALES REP**

| | AVERAGE PERFORMER | | BETTER PERFORMER | | BEST PERFORMER | |
|---|---|---|---|---|---|---|
| | MEDIAN ($000) | 3RD QUARTILE ($000) | MEDIAN ($000) | 3RD QUARTILE ($000) | MEDIAN ($000) | 3RD QUARTILE ($000) |
| **COMPANY SIZE** | | | | | | |
| UNDER $5 MILLION | $34.0 | $43.0 | $38.0 | $50.0 | $42.0 | $59.0 |
| **PRODUCT OR SERVICE** | | | | | | |
| CONSUMER PRODUCTS | 33.0 | 40.0 | 38.0 | 50.0 | 49.0 | 59.0 |
| CONSUMER SERVICES | 31.0 | 39.0 | 31.0 | 43.0 | 38.0 | 55.0 |
| INDUSTRIAL PRODUCTS | 36.0 | 41.0 | 40.0 | 52.0 | 55.0 | 62.0 |
| INDUSTRIAL SERVICES | 37.0 | 43.0 | 43.0 | 52.0 | N/R | 55.0 |
| OFFICE PRODUCTS | 38.0 | 40.0 | N/R | 54.0 | N/R | N/R |
| OFFICE SERVICES | 39.0 | 45.0 | N/R | 50.0 | N/R | 55.0 |
| **TYPE OF BUYER** | | | | | | |
| CONSUMERS | 33.0 | 40.0 | N/R | 45.0 | 38.0 | 55.0 |
| DISTRIBUTORS | 35.0 | 45.0 | N/R | 49.5 | N/R | 55.0 |
| INDUSTRY | 34.0 | 41.0 | 40.0 | 50.0 | 49.0 | 59.0 |
| RETAILERS | 32.0 | 40.0 | 33.0 | 45.0 | N/R | 55.0 |
| **INDUSTRY** | | | | | | |
| BUSINESS SERVICES | 35.0 | 46.0 | N/R | 54.0 | 38.0 | 55.0 |
| ELECTRONICS | 19.0 | 25.0 | 21.0 | N/R | N/R | N/R |
| HEALTH SERVICES | 40.0 | 45.0 | N/R | N/R | N/R | N/R |
| HOLDING & OTHER INVESTMENT OFFICES | 48.0 | N/R | 56.0 | N/R | N/R | N/R |
| INSTRUMENTS | 42.0 | 65.0 | 52.0 | N/R | 74.0 | 74.0 |
| INSURANCE | 30.0 | 40.0 | 40.0 | 60.0 | 50.0 | 75.0 |
| MACHINERY | 50.0 | N/R | N/R | N/R | N/R | N/R |
| MANUFACTURING | 36.0 | 40.0 | N/R | N/R | N/R | N/R |
| OFFICE EQUIPMENT | 27.0 | 31.0 | 35.0 | 55.0 | 40.5 | N/R |
| PHARMACEUTICALS | 33.0 | 50.0 | 43.0 | 50.0 | 55.0 | 70.0 |
| PRINTING AND PUBLISHING | 30.0 | 40.5 | N/R | N/R | N/R | 55.0 |
| RETAIL | 25.0 | 36.0 | 25.0 | N/R | 26.0 | 38.0 |
| WHOLESALE (CONSUMER GOODS) | 37.0 | 41.0 | 49.5 | 54.0 | N/R | 62.0 |
| WHOLESALE (INDUSTRIAL GOODS) | 40.0 | 45.0 | 45.0 | 45.0 | 59.0 | 60.0 |
| **OVERALL** | **$34.0** | **$43.0** | **$38.0** | **$50.0** | **$42.0** | **$59.0** |

# FIGURE 26

**AVERAGE TOTAL CASH COMPENSATION**
**ENTRY LEVEL SALES REP**

| | AVERAGE PERFORMER | | BETTER PERFORMER | | BEST PERFORMER | |
| --- | --- | --- | --- | --- | --- | --- |
| | MEDIAN ($000) | 3RD QUARTILE ($000) | MEDIAN ($000) | 3RD QUARTILE ($000) | MEDIAN ($000) | 3RD QUARTILE ($000) |
| **COMPANY SIZE** | | | | | | |
| UNDER $5 MILLION | $25.0 | $33.0 | $32.0 | $41.0 | $37.0 | $51.0 |
| **PRODUCT OR SERVICE** | | | | | | |
| CONSUMER PRODUCTS | 22.0 | 26.0 | 32.0 | 41.0 | 44.0 | 50.0 |
| CONSUMER SERVICES | 25.0 | 31.0 | 32.0 | 35.0 | 37.0 | 50.0 |
| INDUSTRIAL PRODUCTS | 25.0 | 33.0 | 26.0 | 41.2 | 45.0 | 53.0 |
| INDUSTRIAL SERVICES | 25.0 | 33.0 | 25.0 | 41.0 | N/R | 51.0 |
| OFFICE PRODUCTS | 22.0 | 25.0 | 33.0 | 41.0 | N/R | 45.0 |
| OFFICE SERVICES | 22.0 | 36.0 | N/R | 41.0 | N/R | N/R |
| **TYPE OF BUYER** | | | | | | |
| CONSUMERS | 25.0 | 30.0 | 30.0 | 35.0 | N/R | 50.0 |
| DISTRIBUTORS | 25.0 | 33.0 | N/R | 33.0 | N/R | N/R |
| INDUSTRY | 25.0 | 33.0 | 32.0 | 41.0 | 44.0 | 53.0 |
| RETAILERS | 22.0 | 30.0 | 24.0 | 35.0 | 25.0 | N/R |
| **INDUSTRY** | | | | | | |
| BUSINESS SERVICES | 26.0 | 36.0 | N/R | N/R | N/R | N/R |
| ELECTRONICS | 18.0 | 25.0 | N/R | N/R | N/R | N/R |
| INSTRUMENTS | 33.0 | 35.0 | 45.0 | 45.0 | 55.0 | 55.0 |
| INSURANCE | 28.0 | 40.0 | 35.0 | 47.5 | 45.0 | 55.0 |
| MANUFACTURING | 20.0 | 25.0 | 24.0 | 35.0 | N/R | N/R |
| OFFICE EQUIPMENT | 20.0 | 22.0 | N/R | 33.0 | N/R | N/R |
| PHARMACEUTICALS | 25.0 | 40.0 | 35.0 | 47.0 | 50.0 | 55.0 |
| PRINTING AND PUBLISHING | 16.0 | 22.0 | 16.0 | N/R | 16.0 | N/R |
| WHOLESALE (CONSUMER GOODS) | 26.0 | 37.0 | 32.0 | 41.2 | 37.0 | 49.7 |
| WHOLESALE (INDUSTRIAL GOODS) | 26.0 | 27.0 | N/R | 34.0 | 44.0 | 45.0 |
| **OVERALL** | **$25.0** | **$33.0** | **$32.0** | **$41.0** | **$37.0** | **$51.0** |

# FIGURE 27

**Average Total Cash Compensation**
**Nat'l/Maj Account Manager**

| | Average Performer | | Better Performer | | Best Performer | |
|---|---|---|---|---|---|---|
| | Median ($000) | 3rd Quartile ($000) | Median ($000) | 3rd Quartile ($000) | Median ($000) | 3rd Quartile ($000) |
| **Company Size** | | | | | | |
| Under $5 Million | $50.0 | $65.0 | $65.0 | N/R | N/R | N/R |
| **Product or Service** | | | | | | |
| Consumer Products | 50.0 | 60.0 | 65.0 | N/R | N/R | N/R |
| Consumer Services | 48.0 | 55.0 | 65.0 | N/R | N/R | N/R |
| Industrial Products | 60.0 | 90.0 | N/R | N/R | N/R | N/R |
| Industrial Services | 41.0 | 91.0 | 53.0 | N/R | N/R | N/R |
| Office Products | 90.0 | 91.0 | N/R | N/R | N/R | N/R |
| Office Services | 48.0 | 91.0 | 53.0 | N/R | N/R | N/R |
| **Type of Buyer** | | | | | | |
| Consumers | 48.0 | 55.0 | 65.0 | N/R | N/R | N/R |
| Distributors | 50.0 | 60.0 | 53.0 | N/R | N/R | N/R |
| Industry | 50.0 | 84.0 | 65.0 | N/R | N/R | N/R |
| Retailers | 55.0 | 65.0 | 65.0 | N/R | N/R | N/R |
| **Industry** | | | | | | |
| Business Services | 84.0 | 91.0 | N/R | N/R | N/R | N/R |
| Manufacturing | 50.0 | 90.0 | N/R | N/R | N/R | N/R |
| Pharmaceuticals | 55.0 | 60.0 | 65.0 | 65.0 | N/R | N/R |
| Wholesale (Industrial Goods) | 40.0 | 50.0 | N/R | N/R | N/R | N/R |
| **Overall** | **$50.0** | **$65.0** | **$65.0** | **N/R** | **N/R** | **N/R** |

## FIGURE 28

**AVERAGE TOTAL CASH COMPENSATION**
**NATIONAL ACCOUNT REP**

| | AVERAGE PERFORMER | | BETTER PERFORMER | | BEST PERFORMER | |
| --- | --- | --- | --- | --- | --- | --- |
| | MEDIAN ($000) | 3RD QUARTILE ($000) | MEDIAN ($000) | 3RD QUARTILE ($000) | MEDIAN ($000) | 3RD QUARTILE ($000) |
| **COMPANY SIZE** | | | | | | |
| UNDER $5 MILLION | $50.0 | $65.0 | N/R | N/R | N/R | N/R |
| **PRODUCT OR SERVICE** | | | | | | |
| CONSUMER PRODUCTS | 50.0 | 65.0 | N/R | N/R | N/R | N/R |
| CONSUMER SERVICES | 53.0 | 60.0 | N/R | N/R | N/R | N/R |
| INDUSTRIAL PRODUCTS | 50.0 | 80.0 | N/R | N/R | N/R | N/R |
| INDUSTRIAL SERVICES | 50.0 | 60.0 | N/R | N/R | N/R | N/R |
| OFFICE SERVICES | 53.0 | 80.0 | N/R | N/R | N/R | N/R |
| **TYPE OF BUYER** | | | | | | |
| CONSUMERS | 45.0 | 53.0 | N/R | N/R | N/R | N/R |
| DISTRIBUTORS | 45.0 | 80.0 | N/R | N/R | N/R | N/R |
| INDUSTRY | 50.0 | 80.0 | N/R | N/R | N/R | N/R |
| RETAILERS | 50.0 | 65.0 | N/R | N/R | N/R | N/R |
| **INDUSTRY** | | | | | | |
| BUSINESS SERVICES | 80.0 | 84.0 | N/R | N/R | N/R | N/R |
| PHARMACEUTICALS | 45.0 | 50.0 | N/R | N/R | N/R | N/R |
| **OVERALL** | **$50.0** | **$65.0** | **N/R** | **N/R** | **N/R** | **N/R** |

# FIGURE 29

FIGURE 29

**Average Total Cash Compensation**
**Major (Key) Account Rep**

| | Average Performer | | Better Performer | | Best Performer | |
|---|---|---|---|---|---|---|
| | Median ($000) | 3rd Quartile ($000) | Median ($000) | 3rd Quartile ($000) | Median ($000) | 3rd Quartile ($000) |
| **Company Size** | | | | | | |
| Under $5 Million | $45.0 | $65.0 | N/R | N/R | N/R | N/R |
| **Product or Service** | | | | | | |
| Consumer Products | 45.0 | 65.0 | N/R | N/R | N/R | N/R |
| Consumer Services | 40.0 | 45.0 | N/R | N/R | N/R | N/R |
| Industrial Products | 39.0 | 60.0 | N/R | N/R | N/R | N/R |
| Industrial Services | 35.0 | 75.0 | N/R | N/R | N/R | N/R |
| Office Products | 75.0 | 91.0 | N/R | N/R | N/R | N/R |
| Office Services | 32.0 | 80.0 | N/R | N/R | N/R | N/R |
| **Type of Buyer** | | | | | | |
| Consumers | 39.0 | 45.0 | N/R | N/R | N/R | N/R |
| Distributors | 40.0 | 75.0 | N/R | N/R | N/R | N/R |
| Industry | 40.0 | 80.0 | N/R | N/R | N/R | N/R |
| Retailers | 45.0 | 65.0 | N/R | N/R | N/R | N/R |
| **Industry** | | | | | | |
| Business Services | 84.0 | 91.0 | N/R | N/R | N/R | N/R |
| Office Equipment | N/R | N/R | N/R | N/R | N/R | N/R |
| Pharmaceuticals | 45.0 | 60.0 | N/R | N/R | N/R | N/R |
| **Overall** | **$45.0** | **$65.0** | **N/R** | **N/R** | **N/R** | **N/R** |

## Figures 30–39 — Compensation Tables: Average Base Salary and Total Compensation for Combined Plans (Marketing, Management, and All Sales Positions)

Once you have determined total cash compensation for the comparator groups you have selected, you need to break out the base salary and incentive components. The following group of tables allows you to do just that.

Figures 30–39 present average base salary levels for all bonus eligible individuals; in other words, those people in a combined compensation plan as opposed to a salary-only or an incentive-only plan. These tables will help you determine how much of the overall pay will take the form of salary for those people paid on a combined plan. Compensation figures are provided for average, better, and best performers broken out by size of company, product or service sold, type of buyer, and industry. Note: Since most companies have only one top marketing executive and/or one top sales executive, there is no better or best performer for that position. Therefore, data for these two positions encompasses the full range of responses received.

Here are some guidelines on how to use these tables:

1. Use these tables after you have used Figures 20–29, which presented figures for total compensation.
2. Determine the optimal compensation plan type for each position in your organization. Do not feel obligated to select the same plan type for each job.
3. For each position in a combined plan (salary plus incentive), use these tables to help determine base salary levels.

# FIGURE 30

**AVERAGE BASE SALARY AND TOTAL COMPENSATION**
**TOP MARKETING EXECUTIVE**

|  | AVERAGE BASE SALARY FOR BONUS ELIGIBLE INDIVIDUALS ($000) | AVERAGE TOTAL CASH COMPENSATION FOR ALL PLANS ($000) |
|---|---|---|
| **COMPANY SIZE** | | |
| UNDER $5 MILLION | $67.3 | $75.1 |
| **PRODUCT OR SERVICE** | | |
| CONSUMER PRODUCTS | 58.3 | 76.4 |
| CONSUMER SERVICES | 57.7 | 73.9 |
| INDUSTRIAL PRODUCTS | 59.7 | 72.7 |
| INDUSTRIAL SERVICES | 65.2 | 68.5 |
| OFFICE PRODUCTS | 69.4 | 87.7 |
| OFFICE SERVICES | 67.7 | 80.3 |
| **TYPE OF BUYER** | | |
| CONSUMERS | 58.6 | 70.1 |
| DISTRIBUTORS | 58.4 | 77.4 |
| INDUSTRY | 69.5 | 75.5 |
| RETAILERS | 60.6 | 73.5 |
| **INDUSTRY** | | |
| AMUSEMENT & RECREATION SERVICES | N/R | 57.7 |
| BUSINESS SERVICES | 79.8 | 83.1 |
| ELECTRONICS | 50.0 | 42.2 |
| FABRICATED METALS | 40.0 | N/R |
| FOOD PRODUCTS | 80.0 | N/R |
| HEALTH SERVICES | 92.0 | 123.0 |
| HOLDING & OTHER INVESTMENT OFFICES | 100.0 | 175.3 |
| HOTELS & OTHER LODGING PLACES | 30.0 | N/R |
| INSTRUMENTS | 45.0 | N/R |
| INSURANCE | N/R | N/R |
| MANUFACTURING | 60.0 | 83.3 |
| OFFICE EQUIPMENT | 75.0 | 85.0 |
| PHARMACEUTICALS | 92.5 | 127.2 |
| PRINTING AND PUBLISHING | 90.0 | 98.3 |
| RETAIL | 32.7 | 48.8 |
| WHOLESALE (CONSUMER GOODS) | 63.3 | 68.5 |
| WHOLESALE (INDUSTRIAL GOODS) | 60.0 | 74.8 |
| **OVERALL** | **$67.3** | **$75.1** |

# FIGURE 31

**AVERAGE BASE SALARY AND TOTAL COMPENSATION**
**TOP SALES EXECUTIVE**

| | AVERAGE BASE SALARY FOR BONUS ELIGIBLE INDIVIDUALS ($000) | AVERAGE TOTAL CASH COMPENSATION FOR ALL PLANS ($000) |
|---|---|---|
| **COMPANY SIZE** | | |
| UNDER $5 MILLION | $52.0 | $72.7 |
| **PRODUCT OR SERVICE** | | |
| CONSUMER PRODUCTS | 53.3 | 70.0 |
| CONSUMER SERVICES | 43.8 | 64.3 |
| INDUSTRIAL PRODUCTS | 48.7 | 75.1 |
| INDUSTRIAL SERVICES | 46.7 | 69.4 |
| OFFICE PRODUCTS | 46.8 | 84.0 |
| OFFICE SERVICES | 47.1 | 72.7 |
| **TYPE OF BUYER** | | |
| CONSUMERS | 45.9 | 66.7 |
| DISTRIBUTORS | 47.2 | 73.1 |
| INDUSTRY | 48.0 | 74.6 |
| RETAILERS | 47.9 | 63.6 |
| **INDUSTRY** | | |
| AMUSEMENT & RECREATION SERVICES | 36.0 | N/R |
| BUSINESS SERVICES | 52.9 | 72.7 |
| ELECTRONICS | N/R | 55.0 |
| FABRICATED METALS | 55.0 | 57.9 |
| FOOD PRODUCTS | 50.0 | N/R |
| FURNITURE AND FIXTURES | N/R | 73.9 |
| HOLDING & OTHER INVESTMENT OFFICES | 100.0 | N/R |
| HOTELS & OTHER LODGING PLACES | 16.5 | 36.2 |
| INSTRUMENTS | 75.0 | N/R |
| INSURANCE | N/R | 72.3 |
| MACHINERY | 65.0 | 97.5 |
| MANUFACTURING | 71.7 | 89.3 |
| OFFICE EQUIPMENT | 45.0 | 91.6 |
| PHARMACEUTICALS | 68.8 | 108.3 |
| PRINTING AND PUBLISHING | 36.0 | 78.8 |
| RETAIL | 25.0 | 50.8 |
| WHOLESALE (CONSUMER GOODS) | 30.0 | 45.0 |
| WHOLESALE (INDUSTRIAL GOODS) | 77.5 | 63.7 |
| **OVERALL** | **$52.0** | **$72.7** |

# FIGURE 32

**AVERAGE BASE SALARY AND TOTAL COMPENSATION**
**REGIONAL SALES MANAGER**

| | AVERAGE PERFORMER | | BETTER PERFORMER | | BEST PERFORMER | |
|---|---|---|---|---|---|---|
| | AVERAGE BASE SALARY FOR BONUS ELIGIBLE INDIVIDUALS ($000) | AVERAGE TOTAL CASH COMP. FOR ALL PLANS ($000) | AVERAGE BASE SALARY FOR BONUS ELIGIBLE INDIVIDUALS ($000) | AVERAGE TOTAL CASH COMP. FOR ALL PLANS ($000) | AVERAGE BASE SALARY FOR BONUS ELIGIBLE INDIVIDUALS ($000) | AVERAGE TOTAL CASH COMP. FOR ALL PLANS ($000) |
| **COMPANY SIZE** | | | | | | |
| UNDER $5 MILLION | $44.2 | $57.2 | $44.6 | N/R | $51.3 | $77.3 |
| **PRODUCT OR SERVICE** | | | | | | |
| CONSUMER PRODUCTS | 47.5 | 56.7 | 62.5 | 59.0 | 70.0 | 67.5 |
| CONSUMER SERVICES | 42.7 | 62.0 | 60.0 | 77.7 | 70.0 | 102.0 |
| INDUSTRIAL PRODUCTS | 35.3 | 57.4 | N/R | N/R | 37.3 | 78.9 |
| INDUSTRIAL SERVICES | 36.3 | 50.9 | 41.0 | 58.1 | 45.7 | 66.4 |
| OFFICE PRODUCTS | 50.0 | 53.1 | N/R | 56.0 | N/R | 89.0 |
| OFFICE SERVICES | 30.0 | 61.2 | N/R | 70.3 | 30.0 | 89.0 |
| **TYPE OF BUYER** | | | | | | |
| CONSUMERS | 41.4 | 59.5 | 60.0 | 68.8 | 70.0 | 102.0 |
| DISTRIBUTORS | 34.9 | 58.8 | N/R | N/R | N/R | 73.8 |
| INDUSTRY | 44.4 | 58.2 | N/R | N/R | 51.3 | 71.4 |
| RETAILERS | 42.6 | 57.4 | 51.7 | 57.8 | 61.0 | 79.6 |
| **INDUSTRY** | | | | | | |
| BUSINESS SERVICES | 54.2 | 56.3 | N/R | 62.0 | N/R | 73.5 |
| ELECTRONICS | 33.0 | 49.5 | 50.0 | N/R | N/R | N/R |
| FOOD PRODUCTS | 40.0 | N/R | N/R | N/R | N/R | N/R |
| RETAIL | 37.5 | 40.8 | N/R | N/R | N/R | N/R |
| WHOLESALE (INDUSTRIAL GOODS) | 35.0 | 53.8 | 35.0 | N/R | 43.0 | 93.5 |
| **OVERALL** | **$44.2** | **$57.2** | **$44.6** | **N/R** | **$51.3** | **$77.3** |

# FIGURE 33

**AVERAGE BASE SALARY AND TOTAL COMPENSATION**
**DISTRICT SALES MANAGER**

| | AVERAGE PERFORMER | | BETTER PERFORMER | | BEST PERFORMER | |
|---|---|---|---|---|---|---|
| | AVERAGE BASE SALARY FOR BONUS ELIGIBLE INDIVIDUALS ($000) | AVERAGE TOTAL CASH COMP. FOR ALL PLANS ($000) | AVERAGE BASE SALARY FOR BONUS ELIGIBLE INDIVIDUALS ($000) | AVERAGE TOTAL CASH COMP. FOR ALL PLANS ($000) | AVERAGE BASE SALARY FOR BONUS ELIGIBLE INDIVIDUALS ($000) | AVERAGE TOTAL CASH COMP. FOR ALL PLANS ($000) |
| **COMPANY SIZE** | | | | | | |
| UNDER $5 MILLION | $39.8 | $53.8 | $40.8 | $61.1 | $46.7 | $73.2 |
| **PRODUCT OR SERVICE** | | | | | | |
| CONSUMER PRODUCTS | 40.0 | 59.5 | 43.8 | 63.9 | 50.0 | 65.7 |
| CONSUMER SERVICES | 36.7 | 54.4 | 43.0 | 73.1 | 50.0 | 81.8 |
| INDUSTRIAL PRODUCTS | 32.0 | 47.3 | N/R | N/R | N/R | N/R |
| INDUSTRIAL SERVICES | 29.6 | 50.5 | 33.3 | 63.0 | 38.3 | 70.0 |
| OFFICE PRODUCTS | 38.0 | 48.2 | N/R | N/R | N/R | N/R |
| OFFICE SERVICES | 25.0 | 46.3 | 35.0 | 60.3 | 40.0 | N/R |
| **TYPE OF BUYER** | | | | | | |
| CONSUMERS | 37.5 | 58.0 | 42.5 | 73.1 | 50.0 | 81.8 |
| DISTRIBUTORS | 29.5 | 49.1 | 33.3 | 50.2 | 36.7 | 52.3 |
| INDUSTRY | 39.8 | 52.5 | 40.8 | 65.4 | 46.7 | 66.0 |
| RETAILERS | 35.8 | 54.4 | 45.0 | 68.7 | 51.7 | 70.0 |
| **INDUSTRY** | | | | | | |
| BUSINESS SERVICES | 41.7 | 49.0 | N/R | N/R | 40.0 | N/R |
| RETAIL | 37.5 | 48.0 | N/R | N/R | N/R | N/R |
| **OVERALL** | **$39.8** | **$53.8** | **$40.8** | **$61.1** | **$46.7** | **$73.2** |

# FIGURE 34

**AVERAGE BASE SALARY AND TOTAL COMPENSATION**
**SENIOR SALES REP**

| | AVERAGE PERFORMER | | BETTER PERFORMER | | BEST PERFORMER | |
|---|---|---|---|---|---|---|
| | AVERAGE BASE SALARY FOR BONUS ELIGIBLE INDIVIDUALS ($000) | AVERAGE TOTAL CASH COMP. FOR ALL PLANS ($000) | AVERAGE BASE SALARY FOR BONUS ELIGIBLE INDIVIDUALS ($000) | AVERAGE TOTAL CASH COMP. FOR ALL PLANS ($000) | AVERAGE BASE SALARY FOR BONUS ELIGIBLE INDIVIDUALS ($000) | AVERAGE TOTAL CASH COMP. FOR ALL PLANS ($000) |
| **COMPANY SIZE** | | | | | | |
| UNDER $5 MILLION | $29.2 | $45.9 | N/R | $50.9 | $29.5 | $64.0 |
| **PRODUCT OR SERVICE** | | | | | | |
| CONSUMER PRODUCTS | 25.6 | 42.7 | 29.2 | 54.7 | 30.5 | 56.4 |
| CONSUMER SERVICES | 21.8 | 39.1 | 23.0 | 50.4 | 26.0 | 56.6 |
| INDUSTRIAL PRODUCTS | 29.7 | 46.4 | N/R | 52.6 | N/R | 65.7 |
| INDUSTRIAL SERVICES | 29.8 | 45.1 | N/R | 49.5 | 24.0 | 57.6 |
| OFFICE PRODUCTS | 41.7 | 45.9 | 50.0 | 46.9 | 50.0 | 47.5 |
| OFFICE SERVICES | 22.4 | 45.1 | N/R | 46.5 | N/R | 53.4 |
| **TYPE OF BUYER** | | | | | | |
| CONSUMERS | 26.9 | 41.9 | 29.5 | 51.8 | 29.9 | 66.8 |
| DISTRIBUTORS | 27.0 | 42.7 | N/R | 46.9 | 25.3 | 56.8 |
| INDUSTRY | 30.0 | 46.7 | N/R | 52.4 | 31.2 | 64.0 |
| RETAILERS | 27.8 | 42.4 | 31.0 | 48.1 | 36.5 | 63.9 |
| **INDUSTRY** | | | | | | |
| AMUSEMENT & RECREATION SERVICES | 30.0 | 33.3 | N/R | N/R | N/R | N/R |
| BUSINESS SERVICES | 33.0 | 47.8 | N/R | N/R | N/R | 55.0 |
| INSTRUMENTS | 30.0 | 54.7 | 32.0 | 58.0 | 34.0 | 63.7 |
| MACHINERY | 40.0 | 52.5 | N/R | N/R | N/R | N/R |
| MANUFACTURING | 30.0 | 47.7 | N/R | 58.3 | N/R | N/R |
| OFFICE EQUIPMENT | 30.0 | 50.3 | N/R | N/R | N/R | N/R |
| PHARMACEUTICALS | 32.0 | 54.3 | 50.0 | N/R | 60.0 | N/R |
| WHOLESALE (CONSUMER GOODS) | 24.0 | 61.8 | 30.0 | N/R | 36.0 | N/R |
| WHOLESALE (INDUSTRIAL GOODS) | 41.2 | 45.6 | 51.0 | 52.6 | 55.0 | 70.0 |
| **OVERALL** | **$29.2** | **$45.9** | **N/R** | **$50.9** | **$29.5** | **$64.0** |

**FIGURE 35**

**AVERAGE BASE SALARY AND TOTAL COMPENSATION**
**INTERMEDIATE SALES REP**

| | AVERAGE PERFORMER | | BETTER PERFORMER | | BEST PERFORMER | |
|---|---|---|---|---|---|---|
| | AVERAGE BASE SALARY FOR BONUS ELIGIBLE INDIVIDUALS ($000) | AVERAGE TOTAL CASH COMP. FOR ALL PLANS ($000) | AVERAGE BASE SALARY FOR BONUS ELIGIBLE INDIVIDUALS ($000) | AVERAGE TOTAL CASH COMP. FOR ALL PLANS ($000) | AVERAGE BASE SALARY FOR BONUS ELIGIBLE INDIVIDUALS ($000) | AVERAGE TOTAL CASH COMP. FOR ALL PLANS ($000) |
| **COMPANY SIZE** | | | | | | |
| UNDER $5 MILLION | $23.1 | $34.5 | $27.5 | $37.3 | $32.1 | $41.9 |
| **PRODUCT OR SERVICE** | | | | | | |
| CONSUMER PRODUCTS | 20.5 | 33.9 | 29.4 | 38.2 | 33.7 | 47.0 |
| CONSUMER SERVICES | 19.7 | 31.0 | 20.0 | 33.3 | 24.2 | 41.2 |
| INDUSTRIAL PRODUCTS | 23.2 | 35.2 | 26.4 | 40.5 | N/R | 45.3 |
| INDUSTRIAL SERVICES | 24.9 | 36.0 | 30.6 | 41.0 | 33.3 | N/R |
| OFFICE PRODUCTS | 25.0 | 33.7 | N/R | N/R | N/R | N/R |
| OFFICE SERVICES | 22.7 | 36.6 | N/R | 36.7 | N/R | N/R |
| **TYPE OF BUYER** | | | | | | |
| CONSUMERS | 21.2 | 33.9 | 24.0 | N/R | 24.2 | 39.7 |
| DISTRIBUTORS | 23.1 | 35.1 | 33.0 | N/R | 42.5 | N/R |
| INDUSTRY | 23.4 | 34.6 | 27.5 | 39.3 | 32.5 | 43.0 |
| RETAILERS | 24.4 | 32.1 | 30.0 | 34.0 | 50.0 | N/R |
| **INDUSTRY** | | | | | | |
| BUSINESS SERVICES | 25.8 | 36.7 | N/R | 38.8 | N/R | 41.7 |
| ELECTRONICS | 20.0 | 22.0 | N/R | N/R | N/R | N/R |
| FABRICATED METALS | 24.0 | 27.3 | N/R | N/R | N/R | N/R |
| FOOD PRODUCTS | 25.0 | 58.0 | N/R | N/R | N/R | N/R |
| OFFICE EQUIPMENT | 25.0 | 29.0 | N/R | 41.7 | 25.0 | N/R |
| PHARMACEUTICALS | 23.2 | 38.7 | 36.7 | 42.0 | 52.5 | N/R |
| RETAIL | 17.3 | 24.4 | N/R | 25.0 | N/R | N/R |
| WHOLESALE (CONSUMER GOODS) | 18.0 | 36.7 | 24.0 | 47.2 | 30.0 | N/R |
| WHOLESALE (INDUSTRIAL GOODS) | 30.0 | 38.3 | 40.0 | N/R | 50.0 | 59.5 |
| **OVERALL** | **$23.1** | **$34.5** | **$27.5** | **$37.3** | **$32.1** | **$41.9** |

# FIGURE 36

**AVERAGE BASE SALARY AND TOTAL COMPENSATION**
**ENTRY LEVEL SALES REP**

| | AVERAGE PERFORMER | | BETTER PERFORMER | | BEST PERFORMER | |
|---|---|---|---|---|---|---|
| | AVERAGE BASE SALARY FOR BONUS ELIGIBLE INDIVIDUALS ($000) | AVERAGE TOTAL CASH COMP. FOR ALL PLANS ($000) | AVERAGE BASE SALARY FOR BONUS ELIGIBLE INDIVIDUALS ($000) | AVERAGE TOTAL CASH COMP. FOR ALL PLANS ($000) | AVERAGE BASE SALARY FOR BONUS ELIGIBLE INDIVIDUALS ($000) | AVERAGE TOTAL CASH COMP. FOR ALL PLANS ($000) |
| **COMPANY SIZE** | | | | | | |
| UNDER $5 MILLION | $19.6 | $25.4 | $20.5 | $28.7 | $27.0 | $36.2 |
| **PRODUCT OR SERVICE** | | | | | | |
| CONSUMER PRODUCTS | 16.5 | 22.5 | 22.5 | 29.7 | 28.5 | 39.0 |
| CONSUMER SERVICES | 16.3 | 23.9 | N/R | 29.4 | 20.0 | 33.8 |
| INDUSTRIAL PRODUCTS | 18.4 | 24.9 | N/R | 30.9 | 22.0 | 39.5 |
| INDUSTRIAL SERVICES | 19.8 | 25.7 | N/R | 27.6 | 20.0 | N/R |
| OFFICE PRODUCTS | 20.0 | 21.6 | N/R | 26.8 | N/R | N/R |
| OFFICE SERVICES | 22.0 | 23.8 | N/R | 26.5 | N/R | N/R |
| **TYPE OF BUYER** | | | | | | |
| CONSUMERS | 17.2 | 24.0 | N/R | 27.4 | 20.0 | 29.8 |
| DISTRIBUTORS | 19.9 | 24.2 | 20.0 | N/R | 24.0 | N/R |
| INDUSTRY | 19.9 | 25.7 | 20.5 | 30.9 | 27.0 | 40.0 |
| RETAILERS | 20.2 | 23.1 | N/R | 25.2 | N/R | N/R |
| **INDUSTRY** | | | | | | |
| BUSINESS SERVICES | 23.8 | 26.8 | N/R | 42.3 | N/R | N/R |
| MANUFACTURING | 20.0 | 22.5 | N/R | N/R | N/R | N/R |
| OFFICE EQUIPMENT | 15.0 | 21.0 | N/R | N/R | N/R | N/R |
| PHARMACEUTICALS | 18.0 | 28.3 | N/R | N/R | N/R | N/R |
| RETAIL | 14.8 | 20.1 | 15.0 | N/R | 20.0 | N/R |
| WHOLESALE (CONSUMER GOODS) | 18.0 | 31.5 | 20.0 | N/R | 24.0 | N/R |
| WHOLESALE (INDUSTRIAL GOODS) | 25.0 | 25.8 | 30.0 | N/R | 37.0 | N/R |
| **OVERALL** | **$19.6** | **$25.4** | **$20.5** | **$28.7** | **$27.0** | **$36.2** |

# FIGURE 37

**AVERAGE BASE SALARY AND TOTAL COMPENSATION**
**NAT'L/MAJ ACCOUNT MANAGER**

| | AVERAGE PERFORMER | | BETTER PERFORMER | | BEST PERFORMER | |
|---|---|---|---|---|---|---|
| | AVERAGE BASE SALARY FOR BONUS ELIGIBLE INDIVIDUALS ($000) | AVERAGE TOTAL CASH COMP. FOR ALL PLANS ($000) | AVERAGE BASE SALARY FOR BONUS ELIGIBLE INDIVIDUALS ($000) | AVERAGE TOTAL CASH COMP. FOR ALL PLANS ($000) | AVERAGE BASE SALARY FOR BONUS ELIGIBLE INDIVIDUALS ($000) | AVERAGE TOTAL CASH COMP. FOR ALL PLANS ($000) |
| **COMPANY SIZE** | | | | | | |
| UNDER $5 MILLION | $42.8 | $54.8 | N/R | N/R | N/R | N/R |
| **PRODUCT OR SERVICE** | | | | | | |
| CONSUMER PRODUCTS | 37.5 | 52.6 | N/R | N/R | N/R | N/R |
| CONSUMER SERVICES | 35.0 | 51.5 | N/R | N/R | N/R | N/R |
| INDUSTRIAL PRODUCTS | 47.3 | 65.0 | N/R | N/R | N/R | N/R |
| INDUSTRIAL SERVICES | 40.0 | 64.8 | N/R | N/R | N/R | N/R |
| OFFICE PRODUCTS | 60.0 | 76.3 | N/R | N/R | N/R | N/R |
| OFFICE SERVICES | 20.0 | 58.7 | N/R | N/R | N/R | N/R |
| **TYPE OF BUYER** | | | | | | |
| CONSUMERS | 35.0 | 51.5 | N/R | N/R | N/R | N/R |
| DISTRIBUTORS | 40.5 | 53.0 | N/R | N/R | N/R | N/R |
| INDUSTRY | 43.4 | 56.3 | N/R | N/R | N/R | N/R |
| RETAILERS | 38.8 | 55.6 | N/R | N/R | N/R | N/R |
| **INDUSTRY** | | | | | | |
| BUSINESS SERVICES | 40.0 | 70.7 | N/R | N/R | N/R | N/R |
| PHARMACEUTICALS | 37.5 | 55.0 | N/R | N/R | N/R | N/R |
| **OVERALL** | **$42.8** | **$54.8** | **N/R** | **N/R** | **N/R** | **N/R** |

# FIGURE 38

**AVERAGE BASE SALARY AND TOTAL COMPENSATION**
**NATIONAL ACCOUNT REP**

| | AVERAGE PERFORMER | | BETTER PERFORMER | | BEST PERFORMER | |
|---|---|---|---|---|---|---|
| | AVERAGE BASE SALARY FOR BONUS ELIGIBLE INDIVIDUALS ($000) | AVERAGE TOTAL CASH COMP. FOR ALL PLANS ($000) | AVERAGE BASE SALARY FOR BONUS ELIGIBLE INDIVIDUALS ($000) | AVERAGE TOTAL CASH COMP. FOR ALL PLANS ($000) | AVERAGE BASE SALARY FOR BONUS ELIGIBLE INDIVIDUALS ($000) | AVERAGE TOTAL CASH COMP. FOR ALL PLANS ($000) |
| **COMPANY SIZE** | | | | | | |
| UNDER $5 MILLION | $43.8 | $52.6 | $45.0 | $85.3 | $55.0 | N/R |
| **PRODUCT OR SERVICE** | | | | | | |
| CONSUMER PRODUCTS | 35.0 | 53.3 | 45.0 | N/R | 55.0 | N/R |
| CONSUMER SERVICES | 35.0 | 52.7 | 45.0 | N/R | 55.0 | N/R |
| INDUSTRIAL PRODUCTS | 50.0 | 57.3 | N/R | N/R | N/R | N/R |
| INDUSTRIAL SERVICES | 50.0 | 51.2 | N/R | N/R | N/R | N/R |
| **TYPE OF BUYER** | | | | | | |
| CONSUMERS | 35.0 | 49.0 | 45.0 | N/R | 55.0 | N/R |
| DISTRIBUTORS | 40.0 | 54.2 | N/R | N/R | N/R | N/R |
| INDUSTRY | 48.3 | 55.0 | N/R | 85.3 | N/R | N/R |
| RETAILERS | 38.3 | 55.0 | 45.0 | N/R | 55.0 | N/R |
| **INDUSTRY** | | | | | | |
| BUSINESS SERVICES | 60.0 | 74.7 | N/R | N/R | N/R | N/R |
| **OVERALL** | **$43.8** | **$52.6** | **$45.0** | **$85.3** | **$55.0** | **N/R** |

# FIGURE 39

**AVERAGE BASE SALARY AND TOTAL COMPENSATION**
**MAJOR (KEY) ACCOUNT REP**

| | AVERAGE PERFORMER | | BETTER PERFORMER | | BEST PERFORMER | |
|---|---|---|---|---|---|---|
| | AVERAGE BASE SALARY FOR BONUS ELIGIBLE INDIVIDUALS ($000) | AVERAGE TOTAL CASH COMP. FOR ALL PLANS ($000) | AVERAGE BASE SALARY FOR BONUS ELIGIBLE INDIVIDUALS ($000) | AVERAGE TOTAL CASH COMP. FOR ALL PLANS ($000) | AVERAGE BASE SALARY FOR BONUS ELIGIBLE INDIVIDUALS ($000) | AVERAGE TOTAL CASH COMP. FOR ALL PLANS ($000) |
| **COMPANY SIZE** | | | | | | |
| UNDER $5 MILLION | $37.2 | $45.1 | $45.0 | $65.0 | $55.0 | N/R |
| **PRODUCT OR SERVICE** | | | | | | |
| CONSUMER PRODUCTS | 32.3 | 50.0 | 45.0 | 88.3 | 55.0 | N/R |
| CONSUMER SERVICES | 28.5 | 33.8 | 45.0 | 80.0 | 55.0 | 88.3 |
| INDUSTRIAL PRODUCTS | 35.8 | 41.0 | N/R | N/R | N/R | N/R |
| INDUSTRIAL SERVICES | 29.2 | 43.5 | N/R | 67.5 | N/R | 68.3 |
| OFFICE PRODUCTS | 52.5 | 68.7 | N/R | N/R | N/R | N/R |
| OFFICE SERVICES | 20.0 | 44.2 | N/R | 80.0 | N/R | N/R |
| **TYPE OF BUYER** | | | | | | |
| CONSUMERS | 26.5 | 37.2 | 45.0 | 80.0 | 55.0 | 88.3 |
| DISTRIBUTORS | 34.2 | 45.1 | N/R | 80.0 | N/R | N/R |
| INDUSTRY | 40.4 | 49.5 | 45.0 | 65.0 | 55.0 | N/R |
| RETAILERS | 32.0 | 47.1 | 45.0 | 80.0 | 55.0 | 88.3 |
| **INDUSTRY** | | | | | | |
| BUSINESS SERVICES | 40.0 | 69.0 | N/R | N/R | N/R | N/R |
| PHARMACEUTICALS | 37.5 | 48.3 | 45.0 | N/R | 55.0 | N/R |
| **OVERALL** | **$37.2** | **$45.1** | **$45.0** | **$65.0** | **$55.0** | **N/R** |

# SECTION 3

# PAY AND PERFORMANCE

One of the things that makes sales compensation so intriguing is the continual search for that "perfect" pay plan—the one that drives salespeople to excel, but does not financially strain the resources of the company. Does such a plan exist? No—at least not for long. Changes in product lines, company priorities, and the make-up of the sales force itself put constant pressure on the sales compensation plan.

But that doesn't mean that we don't constantly try to find the one plan—or combination of plans—that will make our companies successful beyond our wildest dreams. The right plan—at the right time—can make all the difference in the world. With exactly the right plan we can point our salespeople in the direction we want them to take.

How much do salespeople earn compared with what they produce? How much more do top performers produce than their "average" counterparts? These are just two of the questions this section examines in detail:

- Figure 40 looks at the average annual sales volume for intermediate and senior sales representatives by average, better, and best performers.
- Figures 41–47 exhibit the compensation levels of better and best performers as a percentage increase over average performers.
- Figures 48–57 exhibit compensation levels and sales volume levels generated by average, better, and best performers.
- Figures 58–67 exhibit third-quartile compensation levels and sales volume levels generated by average, better, and best performers.
- Figure 68 exhibits top performers' productivity as compared to average performers' productivity.
- Figure 69 exhibits senior salesperson productivity by better and best performers.

While sales volume levels vary considerably by product or service sold, type of buyer, and industry, the data in this section provides "benchmark" figures you can use in comparing the productivity of your salespeople with salespeople in similar industries.

Geographic location, the company's position in the marketplace, and the effectiveness of its marketing programs can all have an effect on overall sales volume achieved. It is in these areas that larger companies often have an edge.

## FIGURE 40 — AVERAGE ANNUAL SALES VOLUME FOR INTERMEDIATE AND SENIOR SALES REPS

**Figure 40** presents average annual sales volume data for average, better, and best performers and looks specifically at the performance levels of intermediate and senior level salespeople. (For definitions of "average," "better," and "best" performers, see Terminology Used in This Survey on page 108.)

Sales volume levels for entry level salespeople, who may or may not have yet been assigned a territory, vary considerably and do not reflect the true potential of the individual. Intermediate and senior salespeople, on the other hand, provide "benchmark" data on average sales volume levels. Responses are broken out by product or service sold, type of buyer, and industry.

**Figure 40** provides a "quick view" look at some of the data covered in detail in this section. Additional tables in this section provide greater detail and should be consulted when comparing the sales volume levels of your salespeople with sales volume levels reported by participants in this survey.

Remember, average sales volume levels can vary considerably by different companies in the same industry. Additionally, geographic location, the company's position in the marketplace, and the effectiveness of its marketing programs can all have an effect on overall sales volume achieved. Readers of this survey are reminded to bear in mind that a wide range of responses was received from survey participants in answer to this question.

**FIGURE 40**

SALESPERSON'S ANNUAL SALES VOLUME
AVERAGE OF MEDIAN RANGE FOR INTERMEDIATE
AND SENIOR SALES REPS

| | AVERAGE PERFORMER ($000) | BETTER PERFORMER ($000) | BEST PERFORMER ($000) |
|---|---|---|---|
| **COMPANY SIZE** | | | |
| UNDER $5 MILLION | $359.3 | $364.3 | $483.6 |
| **PRODUCT OR SERVICE** | | | |
| CONSUMER PRODUCTS | 381.9 | 387.5 | 432.5 |
| CONSUMER SERVICES | 337.8 | N/R | 389.5 |
| INDUSTRIAL PRODUCTS | 382.4 | 453.2 | 518.3 |
| INDUSTRIAL SERVICES | 379.0 | N/R | 517.4 |
| OFFICE PRODUCTS | 434.3 | N/R | 589.8 |
| OFFICE SERVICES | 499.0 | N/R | 558.3 |
| **TYPE OF BUYER** | | | |
| CONSUMERS | 384.2 | N/R | 408.6 |
| DISTRIBUTORS | 349.8 | 371.9 | 523.1 |
| INDUSTRY | 371.4 | 410.2 | 509.5 |
| RETAILERS | 336.3 | N/R | 568.7 |
| **INDUSTRY** | | | |
| AMUSEMENT & RECREATION SERVICES | 506.2 | N/R | N/R |
| BANKING | 1,000.0 | 3,000.0 | 5,000.0 |
| BUSINESS SERVICES | 476.9 | N/R | N/R |
| CONSTRUCTION | 450.0 | N/R | N/R |
| EDUCATIONAL SERVICES | 700.0 | N/R | N/R |
| ELECTRONICS | 325.0 | 400.0 | 537.5 |
| FABRICATED METALS | 310.0 | N/R | 647.5 |
| FOOD PRODUCTS | 400.0 | N/R | N/R |
| FURNITURE AND FIXTURES | 196.2 | 254.2 | N/R |
| HEALTH SERVICES | 548.3 | N/R | 1,000.0 |
| HOLDING & OTHER INVESTMENT OFFICES | 489.0 | 700.0 | N/R |
| INSTRUMENTS | 500.0 | 700.0 | 866.7 |
| MACHINERY | 700.0 | 800.0 | 900.0 |
| MANUFACTURING | 222.0 | N/R | 203.0 |
| OFFICE EQUIPMENT | 256.7 | 315.0 | 375.0 |
| PRIMARY METAL PRODUCTS | 800.0 | N/R | N/R |
| PRINTING AND PUBLISHING | 370.0 | 545.0 | 601.8 |
| REAL ESTATE | 1,250.0 | 1,250.0 | 1,500.0 |
| RETAIL | 225.6 | 270.4 | 315.4 |
| WHOLESALE (CONSUMER GOODS) | 521.5 | N/R | N/R |
| WHOLESALE (INDUSTRIAL GOODS) | 397.5 | 460.0 | 533.3 |
| **OVERALL** | **$359.3** | **$364.3** | **$483.6** |

Salespeople, more than any other group of employees, can directly influence the amount of annual compensation they receive based on their own performance. Sales compensation plans, as we have seen, capitalize on the link between pay and performance to motivate salespeople to achieve their goals and the goals of their companies. Clearly, we need to pay top performers more than we pay average performers.

But while it's one thing to agree to pay better performers more, it's often quite another to agree on how much more. The following data tables shed some light on this issue. (For a definition of "better" and "best" performers, see Terminology Used in This Survey, page 108.)

Figures 41–47 show how much extra "better" and "best" performers are paid over and above what average performers are paid. (The "percentage premium" is the additional compensation paid to better and best performers expressed as a percentage increase over compensation paid to average performers.) The premiums paid to better and best performing salespeople were calculated as follows:

1.  The premiums reflect only those companies reporting average, third-quartile, and highest pay levels for positions with multiple individuals in those positions. (Since a company can have only one top marketing executive and one top sales executive, it can only report an average pay figure for that position.)
2.  Paired pay comparisons were used within each company to compute the premium for better and for best salespeople.
3.  For "better" salespeople: The premium reflects the average of the percent differences between the reported third-quartile level and the average pay level for each relevant position in each company.
4.  For "best" salespeople: The premium reflects the average of the percent differences between the reported highest pay level and the average pay level for each relevant position in each company.
5.  The premiums are expressed as percentage premiums above the pay levels for average performers.

# FIGURE 41

**Percentage Premium Paid to Better and
Best Performers (Compared to Average Performers)/
Regional Sales Manager**

| | Better Performers | Best Performers |
|---|---|---|
| **Company Size** | | |
| Under $5 Million | 22% | 64% |
| **Product or Service** | | |
| Consumer Products | 17 | 29 |
| Consumer Services | 27 | 103 |
| Industrial Products | 21 | 43 |
| Industrial Services | 25 | 73 |
| Office Products | 27 | 38 |
| Office Services | 30 | 93 |
| **Type of Buyer** | | |
| Consumers | 27 | 90 |
| Distributors | 23 | 66 |
| Industry | 26 | 67 |
| Retailers | 26 | 80 |
| **Industry** | | |
| Business Services | 27 | 53 |
| Insurance | 20 | 122 |
| Wholesale (Industrial Goods) | 19 | 54 |
| **Overall** | **22%** | **64%** |

# FIGURE 42

**PERCENTAGE PREMIUM PAID TO BETTER AND
BEST PERFORMERS (COMPARED TO AVERAGE PERFORMERS)/
DISTRICT SALES MANAGER**

|  | BETTER PERFORMERS | BEST PERFORMERS |
|---|---|---|
| **COMPANY SIZE** | | |
| UNDER $5 MILLION | 28% | 59% |
| **PRODUCT OR SERVICE** | | |
| CONSUMER PRODUCTS | 19 | 49 |
| CONSUMER SERVICES | 33 | 69 |
| INDUSTRIAL PRODUCTS | 13 | 32 |
| INDUSTRIAL SERVICES | 26 | 55 |
| OFFICE PRODUCTS | 8 | 17 |
| OFFICE SERVICES | 31 | 71 |
| **TYPE OF BUYER** | | |
| CONSUMERS | 28 | 62 |
| DISTRIBUTORS | 20 | 42 |
| INDUSTRY | 31 | 68 |
| RETAILERS | 29 | 69 |
| **INDUSTRY** | | |
| BUSINESS SERVICES | 40 | 71 |
| INSURANCE | 38 | 67 |
| PHARMACEUTICALS | 38 | 100 |
| RETAIL | 15 | 31 |
| **OVERALL** | **28%** | **59%** |

# FIGURE 43

**PERCENTAGE PREMIUM PAID TO BETTER AND
BEST PERFORMERS (COMPARED TO AVERAGE PERFORMERS)/
SENIOR SALES REP**

| | BETTER PERFORMERS | BEST PERFORMERS |
|---|---|---|
| **COMPANY SIZE** | | |
| UNDER $5 MILLION | 32% | 92% |
| **PRODUCT OR SERVICE** | | |
| CONSUMER PRODUCTS | 34 | 24 |
| CONSUMER SERVICES | 36 | 85 |
| INDUSTRIAL PRODUCTS | 30 | 65 |
| INDUSTRIAL SERVICES | 39 | 96 |
| OFFICE PRODUCTS | 38 | 196 |
| OFFICE SERVICES | 37 | 73 |
| **TYPE OF BUYER** | | |
| CONSUMERS | 36 | 89 |
| DISTRIBUTORS | 31 | 104 |
| INDUSTRY | 33 | 97 |
| RETAILERS | 41 | 158 |
| **INDUSTRY** | | |
| AMUSEMENT & RECREATION SERVICES | 14 | 29 |
| BUSINESS SERVICES | 37 | 63 |
| ELECTRONICS | 14 | 41 |
| FURNITURE AND FIXTURES | 17 | 33 |
| HOLDING & OTHER INVESTMENT OFFICES | 6 | 21 |
| INSTRUMENTS | 11 | 23 |
| INSURANCE | 43 | 117 |
| MACHINERY | 20 | 60 |
| MANUFACTURING | 43 | 103 |
| PHARMACEUTICALS | 13 | 79 |
| PRINTING AND PUBLISHING | 29 | 70 |
| RETAIL | 53 | 260 |
| WHOLESALE (CONSUMER GOODS) | 20 | 53 |
| WHOLESALE (INDUSTRIAL GOODS) | 35 | 73 |
| **OVERALL** | **32%** | **92%** |

# FIGURE 44

## PERCENTAGE PREMIUM PAID TO BETTER AND
## BEST PERFORMERS (COMPARED TO AVERAGE PERFORMERS)/
## INTERMEDIATE SALES REP

| | BETTER PERFORMERS | BEST PERFORMERS |
|---|---|---|
| **COMPANY SIZE** | | |
| UNDER $5 MILLION | 33% | 65% |
| **PRODUCT OR SERVICE** | | |
| CONSUMER PRODUCTS | 29 | 70 |
| CONSUMER SERVICES | 34 | 67 |
| INDUSTRIAL PRODUCTS | 37 | 70 |
| INDUSTRIAL SERVICES | 39 | 63 |
| OFFICE PRODUCTS | 31 | 75 |
| OFFICE SERVICES | 32 | 55 |
| **TYPE OF BUYER** | | |
| CONSUMERS | 33 | 67 |
| DISTRIBUTORS | 37 | 73 |
| INDUSTRY | 35 | 66 |
| RETAILERS | 39 | 78 |
| **INDUSTRY** | | |
| AMUSEMENT & RECREATION SERVICES | 14 | 29 |
| BUSINESS SERVICES | 24 | 47 |
| FURNITURE AND FIXTURES | 33 | 100 |
| INSTRUMENTS | 24 | 76 |
| INSURANCE | 42 | 88 |
| OFFICE EQUIPMENT | 29 | 43 |
| PHARMACEUTICALS | 29 | 112 |
| PRINTING AND PUBLISHING | 67 | 92 |
| RETAIL | 36 | 67 |
| WHOLESALE (CONSUMER GOODS) | 26 | 60 |
| WHOLESALE (INDUSTRIAL GOODS) | 24 | 64 |
| **OVERALL** | **33%** | **65%** |

# FIGURE 45

**PERCENTAGE PREMIUM PAID TO BETTER AND
BEST PERFORMERS (COMPARED TO AVERAGE PERFORMERS)/
ENTRY LEVEL SALES REP**

| | BETTER PERFORMERS | BEST PERFORMERS |
|---|---|---|
| **COMPANY SIZE** | | |
| UNDER $5 MILLION | 29% | 55% |
| **PRODUCT OR SERVICE** | | |
| CONSUMER PRODUCTS | 30 | 44 |
| CONSUMER SERVICES | 35 | 59 |
| INDUSTRIAL PRODUCTS | 41 | 64 |
| INDUSTRIAL SERVICES | 39 | 62 |
| **TYPE OF BUYER** | | |
| CONSUMERS | 34 | 58 |
| DISTRIBUTORS | 33 | 41 |
| INDUSTRY | 33 | 59 |
| RETAILERS | 43 | 67 |
| **INDUSTRY** | | |
| AMUSEMENT & RECREATION SERVICES | 15 | 31 |
| FABRICATED METALS | 67 | 67 |
| FURNITURE AND FIXTURES | 22 | 44 |
| INSTRUMENTS | 29 | 57 |
| INSURANCE | 24 | 88 |
| MANUFACTURING | 30 | 82 |
| PHARMACEUTICALS | 29 | 69 |
| RETAIL | 22 | 47 |
| WHOLESALE (CONSUMER GOODS) | 17 | 38 |
| WHOLESALE (INDUSTRIAL GOODS) | 26 | 63 |
| **OVERALL** | **29%** | **55%** |

# FIGURE 46

**PERCENTAGE PREMIUM PAID TO BETTER AND**
**BEST PERFORMERS (COMPARED TO AVERAGE PERFORMERS)/**
**NATIONAL ACCOUNT REP**

|  | BETTER PERFORMERS | BEST PERFORMERS |
|---|---|---|
| **PRODUCT OR SERVICE** | | |
| CONSUMER PRODUCTS | 24% | 49% |
| CONSUMER SERVICES | 24 | 49 |
| OFFICE PRODUCTS | 14 | 31 |
| OFFICE SERVICES | 14 | 31 |
| **TYPE OF BUYER** | | |
| CONSUMERS | 24 | 49 |
| RETAILERS | 24 | 49 |
| **INDUSTRY** | | |
| BUSINESS SERVICES | 14 | 31 |
| PHARMACEUTICALS | 33 | 67 |
| **OVERALL** | **22%** | **44%** |

# FIGURE 47

PERCENTAGE PREMIUM PAID TO BETTER AND
BEST PERFORMERS (COMPARED TO AVERAGE PERFORMERS)/
MAJOR (KEY) ACCOUNT REP

|  | BETTER PERFORMERS | BEST PERFORMERS |
|---|---|---|
| **COMPANY SIZE** | | |
| UNDER $5 MILLION | 28% | 74% |
| **PRODUCT OR SERVICE** | | |
| CONSUMER PRODUCTS | 25 | 60 |
| CONSUMER SERVICES | 28 | 74 |
| INDUSTRIAL PRODUCTS | 15 | 54 |
| INDUSTRIAL SERVICES | 27 | 77 |
| OFFICE PRODUCTS | 15 | 54 |
| OFFICE SERVICES | 27 | 77 |
| **TYPE OF BUYER** | | |
| CONSUMERS | 28 | 74 |
| DISTRIBUTORS | 27 | 77 |
| INDUSTRY | 28 | 74 |
| RETAILERS | 28 | 74 |
| **INDUSTRY** | | |
| BUSINESS SERVICES | 15 | 54 |
| PHARMACEUTICALS | 33 | 67 |
| **OVERALL** | **28%** | **74%** |

## FIGURES 48–57 — SALES COMPENSATION AND VOLUME LEVELS: AVERAGE OF THE MEDIAN RANGE (MARKETING, MANAGEMENT, AND ALL SALES POSITIONS)

Now that we've determined what percentage premium better and best performers earn over and above their average counterparts, how much more do they produce? (For a definintion of "better" and "best" performers, see Terminology Used in This Survey, page 108.)

Figures 48–57 show the relationship between pay and performance by comparing data for average total cash compensation for all plans combined with data for average annual sales volume. The data is broken out to include average performers, better performers, and best performers.

Again, since there is just one top marketing executive and/or top sales executive at any one particular company, there is no better and best performer for those positions.

Note: Sales volume figures for management positions frequently reflect a measure of overall job responsibility and do not necessarily reflect sales made. However, in smaller companies, the top marketing executive may make actual sales. In this survey, for example, an examination of the returned questionnaires indicated that indeed top sales and marketing executives did have direct sales responsibilities in many, if not most, of the companies with under $5 million in annual sales.

Also, as noted in our discussion of Figure 9, How Sales Execs and Reps Are Paid, a look at how the individuals in the various positions in this survey are actually compensated can provide a good indication of their selling responsibility. Individuals who receive all or a portion of their compensation in the form of commissions most often have direct selling responsibility.

# FIGURE 48

**Sales Compensation and Volume Levels**
**Top Marketing Executive**

| | Total Cash Compensation All Plans Combined Average ($000) | Sales Volume Average* ($000) |
|---|---|---|
| **Company Size** | | |
| Under $5 Million | $75.1 | $650.2 |
| **Product or Service** | | |
| Consumer Products | 76.4 | 500.0 |
| Consumer Services | 73.9 | 593.8 |
| Industrial Products | 72.7 | 584.5 |
| Industrial Services | 68.5 | 518.6 |
| Office Products | 87.7 | 683.0 |
| Office Services | 80.3 | 577.7 |
| **Type of Buyer** | | |
| Consumers | 70.1 | 600.6 |
| Distributors | 77.4 | 528.4 |
| Industry | 75.5 | 655.3 |
| Retailers | 73.5 | 470.6 |
| **Industry** | | |
| Amusement & Recreation Services | 57.7 | 260.0 |
| Business Services | 83.1 | 837.9 |
| Holding & Other Investment Offices | 175.3 | N/R |
| Manufacturing | 83.3 | N/R |
| Office Equipment | 85.0 | N/R |
| Pharmaceuticals | 127.2 | N/R |
| Printing and Publishing | 98.3 | N/R |
| Retail | 48.8 | 620.0 |
| Wholesale (Consumer Goods) | 68.5 | 755.0 |
| Wholesale (Industrial Goods) | 74.8 | 750.0 |
| **Overall** | **$75.1** | **$650.2** |

*Sales volume figures for this position are a measure of overall job responsibility and do not necessarily reflect actual sales made.

# FIGURE 49

**SALES COMPENSATION AND VOLUME LEVELS**
**TOP SALES EXECUTIVE**

| | TOTAL CASH COMPENSATION ALL PLANS COMBINED AVERAGE ($000) | SALES VOLUME AVERAGE* ($000) |
|---|---|---|
| **COMPANY SIZE** | | |
| UNDER $5 MILLION | $72.7 | $677.4 |
| **PRODUCT OR SERVICE** | | |
| CONSUMER PRODUCTS | 70.0 | 651.1 |
| CONSUMER SERVICES | 64.3 | 571.5 |
| INDUSTRIAL PRODUCTS | 75.1 | 702.7 |
| INDUSTRIAL SERVICES | 69.4 | 653.2 |
| OFFICE PRODUCTS | 84.0 | 864.3 |
| OFFICE SERVICES | 72.7 | 612.5 |
| **TYPE OF BUYER** | | |
| CONSUMERS | 66.7 | 603.2 |
| DISTRIBUTORS | 73.1 | 760.4 |
| INDUSTRY | 74.6 | 729.8 |
| RETAILERS | 63.6 | 637.9 |
| **INDUSTRY** | | |
| BUSINESS SERVICES | 72.7 | 671.4 |
| ELECTRONICS | 55.0 | 673.3 |
| FABRICATED METALS | 57.9 | N/R |
| FURNITURE AND FIXTURES | 73.9 | 1,700.0 |
| HEALTH SERVICES | 111.7 | N/R |
| HOTELS & OTHER LODGING PLACES | 36.2 | 566.7 |
| INSURANCE | 72.3 | N/R |
| MACHINERY | 97.5 | N/R |
| MANUFACTURING | 89.3 | 680.0 |
| OFFICE EQUIPMENT | 91.6 | 712.5 |
| PHARMACEUTICALS | 108.3 | 1,433.3 |
| PRINTING AND PUBLISHING | 78.8 | 372.5 |
| RETAIL | 50.8 | 427.5 |
| WHOLESALE (CONSUMER GOODS) | 45.0 | 500.0 |
| WHOLESALE (INDUSTRIAL GOODS) | 63.7 | 706.0 |
| **OVERALL** | **$72.7** | **$677.4** |

*SALES VOLUME FIGURES FOR THIS POSITION ARE A MEASURE OF OVERALL JOB RESPONSIBILITY AND DO NOT NECESSARILY REFLECT ACTUAL SALES MADE.

## FIGURE 50

**SALES COMPENSATION AND VOLUME LEVELS**
**REGIONAL SALES MANAGER**

| | AVERAGE PERFORMER | | BETTER PERFORMER | | BEST PERFORMER | |
|---|---|---|---|---|---|---|
| | TOTAL CASH COMP. FOR ALL PLANS COMBINED ($000) | SALES VOLUME* ($000) | TOTAL CASH COMP. FOR ALL PLANS COMBINED ($000) | SALES VOLUME* ($000) | TOTAL CASH COMP. FOR ALL PLANS COMBINED ($000) | SALES VOLUME* ($000) |
| **COMPANY SIZE** | | | | | | |
| UNDER $5 MILLION | $56.0 | $320.5 | $57.2 | $340.2 | $77.3 | $458.6 |
| **PRODUCT OR SERVICE** | | | | | | |
| CONSUMER PRODUCTS | 56.7 | 356.9 | 59.0 | 450.0 | 67.5 | 690.0 |
| CONSUMER SERVICES | 62.0 | 183.6 | 77.7 | 187.5 | 102.0 | 220.0 |
| INDUSTRIAL PRODUCTS | 56.5 | 260.0 | 57.4 | 315.2 | 78.9 | 520.0 |
| INDUSTRIAL SERVICES | 50.9 | 262.7 | 58.1 | 328.0 | 66.4 | 484.2 |
| OFFICE PRODUCTS | 53.1 | N/R | 56.0 | N/R | 89.0 | 420.0 |
| OFFICE SERVICES | 61.2 | N/R | 70.3 | N/R | 89.0 | N/R |
| **TYPE OF BUYER** | | | | | | |
| CONSUMERS | 59.5 | 255.2 | 68.8 | 257.4 | 102.0 | 415.4 |
| DISTRIBUTORS | 56.0 | 351.0 | 58.8 | 412.5 | 73.8 | 632.5 |
| INDUSTRY | 54.6 | 272.0 | 58.2 | 330.3 | 71.4 | 479.5 |
| RETAILERS | 57.4 | 216.0 | 57.8 | 458.3 | 79.6 | 800.0 |
| **INDUSTRY** | | | | | | |
| BUSINESS SERVICES | 56.3 | N/R | 62.0 | N/R | 73.5 | N/R |
| ELECTRONICS | N/R | N/R | N/R | N/R | 49.5 | 525.0 |
| RETAIL | N/R | 165.0 | N/R | 200.0 | 40.8 | 445.0 |
| WHOLESALE (INDUSTRIAL GOODS) | N/R | N/R | 53.8 | 206.0 | 93.5 | 797.3 |
| **OVERALL** | **$56.0** | **$320.5** | **$57.2** | **$340.2** | **$77.3** | **$458.6** |

*SALES VOLUME FIGURES FOR THIS POSITION ARE A MEASURE OF OVERALL JOB RESPONSIBILITY AND DO NOT NECESSARILY REFLECT ACTUAL SALES MADE.

# FIGURE 51

**SALES COMPENSATION AND VOLUME LEVELS**
**DISTRICT SALES MANAGER**

| | AVERAGE PERFORMER | | BETTER PERFORMER | | BEST PERFORMER | |
| | TOTAL CASH COMP. FOR ALL PLANS COMBINED ($000) | SALES VOLUME* ($000) | TOTAL CASH COMP. FOR ALL PLANS COMBINED ($000) | SALES VOLUME* ($000) | TOTAL CASH COMP. FOR ALL PLANS COMBINED ($000) | SALES VOLUME* ($000) |
|---|---|---|---|---|---|---|
| **COMPANY SIZE** | | | | | | |
| UNDER $5 MILLION | $53.8 | $197.5 | $61.1 | $231.8 | $73.2 | $250.2 |
| **PRODUCT OR SERVICE** | | | | | | |
| CONSUMER PRODUCTS | 59.5 | N/R | 63.9 | N/R | 65.7 | 207.5 |
| CONSUMER SERVICES | 54.4 | 168.3 | 73.1 | 226.2 | 81.8 | 303.8 |
| INDUSTRIAL PRODUCTS | N/R | 190.8 | N/R | N/R | 47.3 | 317.3 |
| INDUSTRIAL SERVICES | 50.5 | 168.3 | 63.0 | 188.3 | 70.0 | 190.0 |
| OFFICE PRODUCTS | N/R | N/R | N/R | N/R | 48.2 | 183.3 |
| OFFICE SERVICES | 46.3 | N/R | N/R | N/R | 60.3 | 141.2 |
| **TYPE OF BUYER** | | | | | | |
| CONSUMERS | 58.0 | 201.7 | 73.1 | 241.7 | 81.8 | 345.0 |
| DISTRIBUTORS | 49.1 | N/R | 50.2 | N/R | 52.3 | 166.0 |
| INDUSTRY | 52.5 | 190.6 | 65.4 | 220.5 | 66.0 | 242.0 |
| RETAILERS | 54.4 | 160.7 | 68.7 | 179.0 | 70.0 | 197.0 |
| **OVERALL** | **$53.8** | **$197.5** | **$61.1** | **$231.8** | **$73.2** | **$250.2** |

*SALES VOLUME FIGURES FOR THIS POSITION ARE A MEASURE OF OVERALL JOB RESPONSIBILITY AND DO NOT NECESSARILY REFLECT ACTUAL SALES MADE.

# FIGURE 52

| | AVERAGE PERFORMER | | BETTER PERFORMER | | BEST PERFORMER | |
| --- | --- | --- | --- | --- | --- | --- |
| | TOTAL CASH COMP. FOR ALL PLANS COMBINED ($000) | SALES VOLUME ($000) | TOTAL CASH COMP. FOR ALL PLANS COMBINED ($000) | SALES VOLUME ($000) | TOTAL CASH COMP. FOR ALL PLANS COMBINED ($000) | SALES VOLUME ($000) |
| **COMPANY SIZE** | | | | | | |
| UNDER $5 MILLION | $45.9 | $396.0 | $50.9 | $435.9 | $64.0 | $ 552.0 |
| **PRODUCT OR SERVICE** | | | | | | |
| CONSUMER PRODUCTS | 42.7 | 412.6 | 54.7 | 461.4 | 56.4 | 539.6 |
| CONSUMER SERVICES | 39.1 | 334.4 | 50.4 | 347.9 | 56.6 | 419.2 |
| INDUSTRIAL PRODUCTS | 46.4 | 429.6 | 52.6 | 526.0 | 65.7 | 594.6 |
| INDUSTRIAL SERVICES | 45.1 | 408.5 | 49.5 | 481.7 | 57.6 | 561.0 |
| OFFICE PRODUCTS | 45.9 | 525.0 | 46.9 | 558.4 | 47.5 | 636.5 |
| OFFICE SERVICES | 45.1 | 564.2 | 46.5 | 590.0 | 53.4 | 624.7 |
| **TYPE OF BUYER** | | | | | | |
| CONSUMERS | 41.9 | 388.0 | 51.8 | 398.4 | 66.8 | 438.6 |
| DISTRIBUTORS | 42.7 | 387.2 | 46.9 | 425.8 | 56.8 | 596.1 |
| INDUSTRY | 46.7 | 413.5 | 52.4 | 479.8 | 64.0 | 557.9 |
| RETAILERS | 42.4 | 374.1 | 48.1 | 423.6 | 63.9 | 673.8 |
| **INDUSTRY** | | | | | | |
| BUSINESS SERVICES | 45.0 | 275.0 | 47.8 | 352.0 | 55.0 | 448.4 |
| INSTRUMENTS | 54.7 | 566.7 | 58.0 | 800.0 | 63.7 | 975.0 |
| INSURANCE | 36.2 | 142.0 | 53.8 | 185.0 | 84.0 | 275.0 |
| MANUFACTURING | 47.7 | N/R | N/R | N/R | 58.3 | 245.0 |
| PRINTING AND PUBLISHING | 50.7 | 462.5 | 60.5 | 620.0 | 67.5 | 700.0 |
| RETAIL | 37.2 | 241.8 | 41.3 | 281.3 | 52.3 | 363.5 |
| WHOLESALE (CONSUMER GOODS) | 55.7 | 526.7 | N/R | N/R | 61.8 | 640.0 |
| WHOLESALE (INDUSTRIAL GOODS) | 45.6 | 493.3 | 52.6 | N/R | 70.0 | 515.8 |
| **OVERALL** | **$45.9** | **$396.0** | **$50.9** | **$435.9** | **$64.0** | **$552.0** |

# FIGURE 53

SALES COMPENSATION AND VOLUME LEVELS
INTERMEDIATE SALES REP

| | AVERAGE PERFORMER | | BETTER PERFORMER | | BEST PERFORMER | |
| | TOTAL CASH COMP. FOR ALL PLANS COMBINED ($000) | SALES VOLUME ($000) | TOTAL CASH COMP. FOR ALL PLANS COMBINED ($000) | SALES VOLUME ($000) | TOTAL CASH COMP. FOR ALL PLANS COMBINED ($000) | SALES VOLUME ($000) |
|---|---|---|---|---|---|---|
| **COMPANY SIZE** | | | | | | |
| UNDER $5 MILLION | $34.5 | $248.6 | $37.3 | $257.7 | $41.9 | $321.4 |
| **PRODUCT OR SERVICE** | | | | | | |
| CONSUMER PRODUCTS | 33.8 | 280.3 | 38.2 | 282.8 | 47.0 | 344.5 |
| CONSUMER SERVICES | 31.0 | 249.5 | 33.3 | 257.8 | 41.2 | 268.7 |
| INDUSTRIAL PRODUCTS | 35.2 | 238.3 | 40.5 | 261.9 | 45.3 | 340.8 |
| INDUSTRIAL SERVICES | 36.0 | 287.3 | 40.2 | 326.5 | 41.0 | 419.6 |
| OFFICE PRODUCTS | 30.0 | 241.7 | 27.8 | 327.5 | 33.7 | 328.0 |
| OFFICE SERVICES | 36.6 | 368.7 | 36.6 | 421.2 | 36.7 | 537.2 |
| **TYPE OF BUYER** | | | | | | |
| CONSUMERS | 33.6 | 247.8 | 33.9 | 253.8 | 39.7 | 300.7 |
| DISTRIBUTORS | 32.0 | 244.2 | 33.9 | 260.5 | 35.1 | 321.2 |
| INDUSTRY | 34.6 | 247.4 | 39.3 | 279.3 | 43.0 | 362.5 |
| RETAILERS | 32.1 | 236.5 | 34.0 | 338.1 | 35.8 | 369.2 |
| **INDUSTRY** | | | | | | |
| BUSINESS SERVICES | 36.7 | 240.0 | 38.8 | 280.7 | 41.7 | 444.2 |
| PRINTING AND PUBLISHING | 26.0 | 125.0 | 30.7 | 226.0 | 33.5 | 422.3 |
| RETAIL | 24.4 | 166.0 | 25.0 | N/R | 32.0 | 310.0 |
| WHOLESALE (CONSUMER GOODS) | 36.7 | N/R | N/R | N/R | 47.2 | 413.8 |
| WHOLESALE (INDUSTRIAL GOODS) | 33.3 | N/R | 38.3 | N/R | 59.5 | 279.7 |
| **OVERALL** | **$34.5** | **$248.6** | **$37.3** | **$257.7** | **$41.9** | **$321.4** |

# FIGURE 54

**SALES COMPENSATION AND VOLUME LEVELS**
**ENTRY LEVEL SALES REP**

| | AVERAGE PERFORMER | | BETTER PERFORMER | | BEST PERFORMER | |
| --- | --- | --- | --- | --- | --- | --- |
| | TOTAL CASH COMP. FOR ALL PLANS COMBINED ($000) | SALES VOLUME ($000) | TOTAL CASH COMP. FOR ALL PLANS COMBINED ($000) | SALES VOLUME ($000) | TOTAL CASH COMP. FOR ALL PLANS COMBINED ($000) | SALES VOLUME ($000) |
| **COMPANY SIZE** | | | | | | |
| UNDER $5 MILLION | $25.4 | $139.6 | $28.7 | $168.7 | $36.2 | $ 193.2 |
| **PRODUCT OR SERVICE** | | | | | | |
| CONSUMER PRODUCTS | 22.5 | 144.8 | 29.7 | 183.2 | 39.0 | 230.2 |
| CONSUMER SERVICES | 23.9 | 108.8 | 29.4 | 188.7 | 33.8 | 195.2 |
| INDUSTRIAL PRODUCTS | 24.9 | 129.5 | 30.9 | 147.9 | 39.5 | 197.5 |
| INDUSTRIAL SERVICES | 25.7 | 122.9 | 27.2 | 166.0 | 27.6 | 213.3 |
| OFFICE PRODUCTS | 21.6 | 112.5 | 26.7 | 206.7 | 26.8 | 306.7 |
| OFFICE SERVICES | 23.8 | 137.6 | 25.6 | 203.2 | 26.5 | 211.2 |
| **TYPE OF BUYER** | | | | | | |
| CONSUMERS | 24.0 | 131.4 | 27.4 | 195.2 | 29.8 | 213.1 |
| DISTRIBUTORS | 21.9 | 130.3 | 23.0 | 142.5 | 24.2 | 152.5 |
| INDUSTRY | 25.7 | 145.3 | 30.9 | 185.7 | 39.8 | 204.8 |
| RETAILERS | 23.1 | 104.4 | 22.3 | 180.7 | 25.2 | 195.2 |
| **INDUSTRY** | | | | | | |
| BUSINESS SERVICES | 26.8 | 107.0 | N/R | N/R | 42.3 | 253.0 |
| INSTRUMENTS | N/R | N/R | N/R | N/R | 31.0 | 140.0 |
| MANUFACTURING | N/R | N/R | N/R | N/R | 22.5 | 123.3 |
| OFFICE EQUIPMENT | N/R | N/R | N/R | N/R | 21.0 | 160.0 |
| RETAIL | 18.9 | 130.2 | N/R | 233.8 | 20.1 | 307.0 |
| WHOLESALE (CONSUMER GOODS) | N/R | N/R | N/R | N/R | 31.5 | 275.0 |
| WHOLESALE (INDUSTRIAL GOODS) | N/R | N/R | 25.8 | N/R | 33.0 | 206.3 |
| **OVERALL** | **$25.4** | **$139.6** | **$28.7** | **$168.7** | **$36.2** | **$193.2** |

# FIGURE 55

**SALES COMPENSATION AND VOLUME LEVELS**
**NAT'L/MAJ ACCOUNT MANAGER**

| | AVERAGE PERFORMER | | BETTER PERFORMER | | BEST PERFORMER | |
| | TOTAL CASH COMP. FOR ALL PLANS COMBINED ($000) | SALES VOLUME* ($000) | TOTAL CASH COMP. FOR ALL PLANS COMBINED ($000) | SALES VOLUME* ($000) | TOTAL CASH COMP. FOR ALL PLANS COMBINED ($000) | SALES VOLUME* ($000) |
|---|---|---|---|---|---|---|
| **COMPANY SIZE** | | | | | | |
| UNDER $5 MILLION | $54.8 | N/R | N/R | N/R | $79.0 | $366.0 |
| **PRODUCT OR SERVICE** | | | | | | |
| CONSUMER PRODUCTS | N/R | N/R | N/R | N/R | 52.6 | 252.5 |
| CONSUMER SERVICES | N/R | N/R | N/R | N/R | 51.5 | 363.3 |
| INDUSTRIAL PRODUCTS | N/R | N/R | N/R | N/R | 65.0 | 361.5 |
| INDUSTRIAL SERVICES | N/R | N/R | N/R | N/R | 64.8 | 483.3 |
| OFFICE PRODUCTS | N/R | N/R | N/R | N/R | 76.3 | 420.0 |
| OFFICE SERVICES | N/R | N/R | N/R | N/R | 58.7 | 436.7 |
| **TYPE OF BUYER** | | | | | | |
| CONSUMERS | N/R | N/R | N/R | N/R | 51.5 | 155.0 |
| DISTRIBUTORS | N/R | N/R | N/R | N/R | 53.0 | 287.5 |
| INDUSTRY | 56.3 | N/R | N/R | N/R | 79.0 | 374.0 |
| RETAILERS | 55.6 | N/R | N/R | N/R | 79.0 | 177.5 |
| **OVERALL** | **$54.8** | **N/R** | **N/R** | **N/R** | **$79.0** | **$366.0** |

*SALES VOLUME FIGURES FOR THIS POSITION ARE A MEASURE OF OVERALL JOB RESPONSIBILITY AND DO NOT NECESSARILY REFLECT ACTUAL SALES MADE.

# FIGURE 56

**SALES COMPENSATION AND VOLUME LEVELS**
**NATIONAL ACCOUNT REP**

| | AVERAGE PERFORMER | | BETTER PERFORMER | | BEST PERFORMER | |
| --- | --- | --- | --- | --- | --- | --- |
| | TOTAL CASH COMP. FOR ALL PLANS COMBINED ($000) | SALES VOLUME ($000) | TOTAL CASH COMP. FOR ALL PLANS COMBINED ($000) | SALES VOLUME ($000) | TOTAL CASH COMP. FOR ALL PLANS COMBINED ($000) | SALES VOLUME ($000) |
| **COMPANY SIZE** | | | | | | |
| UNDER $5 MILLION | $52.6 | N/R | N/R | $262.6 | $85.3 | $1,650.0 |
| **PRODUCT OR SERVICE** | | | | | | |
| CONSUMER SERVICES | N/R | N/R | N/R | N/R | 52.7 | 204.3 |
| INDUSTRIAL PRODUCTS | N/R | N/R | N/R | N/R | 57.3 | 281.7 |
| INDUSTRIAL SERVICES | N/R | N/R | N/R | 292.0 | 51.2 | 1,122.0 |
| OFFICE SERVICES | N/R | N/R | N/R | N/R | 50.3 | 181.5 |
| **TYPE OF BUYER** | | | | | | |
| CONSUMERS | N/R | N/R | N/R | N/R | 49.0 | 181.5 |
| DISTRIBUTORS | N/R | N/R | N/R | N/R | 54.2 | 265.8 |
| INDUSTRY | 55.0 | N/R | N/R | 292.0 | 85.3 | 1,122.0 |
| **INDUSTRY** | | | | | | |
| BUSINESS SERVICES | N/R | N/R | N/R | N/R | 74.7 | 335.0 |
| **OVERALL** | **$52.6** | **N/R** | **N/R** | **$262.6** | **$85.3** | **$1,650.0** |

# FIGURE 57

**Sales Compensation and Volume Levels**
**Major (Key) Account Rep**

| | Average Performer | | Better Performer | | Best Performer | |
|---|---|---|---|---|---|---|
| | Total Cash Comp. For All Plans Combined ($000) | Sales Volume ($000) | Total Cash Comp. For All Plans Combined ($000) | Sales Volume ($000) | Total Cash Comp. For All Plans Combined ($000) | Sales Volume ($000) |
| **Company Size** | | | | | | |
| Under $5 Million | $45.1 | N/R | $62.5 | $287.5 | $65.0 | $500.0 |
| **Product or Service** | | | | | | |
| Consumer Products | 50.0 | N/R | N/R | N/R | 88.3 | 396.0 |
| Consumer Services | 33.8 | N/R | 80.0 | N/R | 88.3 | N/R |
| Industrial Products | N/R | N/R | N/R | N/R | 41.0 | 275.0 |
| Industrial Services | 43.5 | N/R | 67.5 | N/R | 68.3 | 493.8 |
| Office Products | N/R | N/R | N/R | N/R | 68.7 | 512.7 |
| Office Services | 44.2 | N/R | N/R | N/R | 80.0 | 675.0 |
| **Type of Buyer** | | | | | | |
| Consumers | 37.2 | N/R | 80.0 | N/R | 88.3 | 700.0 |
| Distributors | 45.1 | N/R | N/R | N/R | 80.0 | 300.0 |
| Industry | 49.5 | N/R | 62.5 | N/R | 65.0 | 368.8 |
| **Overall** | **$45.1** | **N/R** | **$62.5** | **$287.5** | **$65.0** | **$500.0** |

## FIGURES 58–67 — SALES COMPENSATION AND VOLUME LEVELS: THIRD QUARTILE (MARKETING, MANAGEMENT, AND ALL SALES POSITIONS)

One of the many advantages of living in the computer age is the ability to quickly look at data in a variety of ways. Figures 58–67 examine the relationship between total compensation and sales volume produced and repeat the data configurations of Figures 48–57, but report third-quartile findings. Again, since the positions of top marketing executive and top sales executive are generally limited to one individual per organization, there is no data for better performers and best performers.

As you look at these tables, bear in mind that you are looking at the top 25 percent range of responses received. If your company is higher paying, these are the tables you should use. But even if your company pays in the "average" range, these tables provide insights into how well the top salespeople in a variety of industries perform.

You may find through an examination of these tables, for example, that your best salespeople are near the top of the scale in terms of the volume they produce, but nearer the middle in terms of the overall compensation they earn. If that's the case, you might want to reexamine your compensation plan, its objectives, and possible implications for the future. Again, use the data in this survey with discretion and judgment.

# FIGURE 58

**SALES COMPENSATION AND VOLUME LEVELS — 3RD QUARTILE**
**TOP MARKETING EXECUTIVE**

| | TOTAL CASH COMPENSATION ALL PLANS COMBINED ($000) | SALES VOLUME* ($000) |
|---|---|---|
| **COMPANY SIZE** | | |
| UNDER $5 MILLION | $100.0 | $1,000.0 |
| **PRODUCT OR SERVICE** | | |
| CONSUMER PRODUCTS | 102.0 | 1,000.0 |
| CONSUMER SERVICES | 102.0 | 1,200.0 |
| INDUSTRIAL PRODUCTS | 95.6 | 1,000.0 |
| INDUSTRIAL SERVICES | 100.0 | 900.0 |
| OFFICE PRODUCTS | 102.0 | 1,200.0 |
| OFFICE SERVICES | 100.0 | 1,000.0 |
| **TYPE OF BUYER** | | |
| CONSUMERS | 102.0 | 1,000.0 |
| DISTRIBUTORS | 100.0 | 1,200.0 |
| INDUSTRY | 100.0 | 1,000.0 |
| RETAILERS | 100.0 | 800.0 |
| **INDUSTRY** | | |
| AMUSEMENT & RECREATION SERVICES | 82.0 | 500.0 |
| BUSINESS SERVICES | 101.6 | 1,500.0 |
| ELECTRONICS | 56.6 | 600.0 |
| FOOD PRODUCTS | 1,000.0 | 300.0 |
| FURNITURE AND FIXTURES | 90.0 | 150.0 |
| HEALTH SERVICES | 140.0 | 450.0 |
| HOLDING & OTHER INVESTMENT OFFICES | 400.0 | 500.0 |
| INSURANCE | 50.0 | 400.0 |
| MACHINERY | 75.0 | N/R |
| MANUFACTURING | 95.0 | 200.0 |
| OFFICE EQUIPMENT | 95.0 | 2,300.0 |
| PHARMACEUTICALS | 196.6 | 100.0 |
| PRINTING AND PUBLISHING | 115.0 | 800.0 |
| RETAIL | 60.0 | 1,500.0 |
| WHOLESALE (CONSUMER GOODS) | 100.0 | 1,000.0 |
| WHOLESALE (INDUSTRIAL GOODS) | 89.0 | 1,000.0 |
| **OVERALL** | **$100.0** | **$1,000.0** |

*SALES VOLUME FIGURES FOR THIS POSITION ARE A MEASURE OF OVERALL JOB RESPONSIBILITY AND DO NOT NECESSARILY REFLECT ACTUAL SALES MADE.

# FIGURE 59

SALES COMPENSATION AND VOLUME LEVELS — 3RD QUARTILE
TOP SALES EXECUTIVE

| | TOTAL CASH COMPENSATION ALL PLANS COMBINED ($000) | SALES VOLUME* ($000) |
|---|---|---|
| **COMPANY SIZE** | | |
| UNDER $5 MILLION | $100.0 | $1,200.0 |
| **PRODUCT OR SERVICE** | | |
| CONSUMER PRODUCTS | 100.0 | 1,250.0 |
| CONSUMER SERVICES | 87.5 | 1,000.0 |
| INDUSTRIAL PRODUCTS | 100.0 | 1,200.0 |
| INDUSTRIAL SERVICES | 100.0 | 1,200.0 |
| OFFICE PRODUCTS | 100.0 | 1,250.0 |
| OFFICE SERVICES | 100.0 | 1,000.0 |
| **TYPE OF BUYER** | | |
| CONSUMERS | 87.9 | 1,000.0 |
| DISTRIBUTORS | 100.0 | 1,250.0 |
| INDUSTRY | 100.0 | 1,250.0 |
| RETAILERS | 87.5 | 1,250.0 |
| **INDUSTRY** | | |
| BUSINESS SERVICES | 100.0 | 1,100.0 |
| ELECTRONICS | 78.0 | 1,000.0 |
| FABRICATED METALS | 73.8 | N/R |
| FURNITURE AND FIXTURES | 90.0 | 3,000.0 |
| HEALTH SERVICES | 190.0 | 2,000.0 |
| HOTELS & OTHER LODGING PLACES | 51.6 | 1,000.0 |
| INSURANCE | 136.0 | 300.0 |
| MACHINERY | 100.0 | 600.0 |
| MANUFACTURING | 125.0 | 950.0 |
| OFFICE EQUIPMENT | 100.0 | 1,000.0 |
| PHARMACEUTICALS | 120.0 | 3,600.0 |
| PRINTING AND PUBLISHING | 100.0 | 900.0 |
| RETAIL | 60.0 | 750.0 |
| WHOLESALE (CONSUMER GOODS) | 50.0 | 500.0 |
| WHOLESALE (INDUSTRIAL GOODS) | 72.0 | 1,000.0 |
| **OVERALL** | **$100.0** | **$1,200.0** |

*SALES VOLUME FIGURES FOR THIS POSITION ARE A MEASURE OF OVERALL JOB RESPONSIBILITY AND DO NOT NECESSARILY REFLECT ACTUAL SALES MADE.

## FIGURE 60

**SALES COMPENSATION AND VOLUME LEVELS — 3RD QUARTILE**
**REGIONAL SALES MANAGER**

| | AVERAGE PERFORMER | | BETTER PERFORMER | | BEST PERFORMER | |
|---|---|---|---|---|---|---|
| | TOTAL CASH COMP. FOR ALL PLANS COMBINED ($000) | SALES VOLUME* ($000) | TOTAL CASH COMP. FOR ALL PLANS COMBINED ($000) | SALES VOLUME* ($000) | TOTAL CASH COMP. FOR ALL PLANS COMBINED ($000) | SALES VOLUME* ($000) |
| **COMPANY SIZE** | | | | | | |
| UNDER $5 MILLION | $70.0 | $500.0 | $80.0 | $550.0 | $110.0 | $880.0 |
| **PRODUCT OR SERVICE** | | | | | | |
| CONSUMER PRODUCTS | 82.4 | 500.0 | 86.0 | 700.0 | 98.0 | 880.0 |
| CONSUMER SERVICES | 85.0 | 200.0 | 100.0 | 250.0 | 120.0 | 260.0 |
| INDUSTRIAL PRODUCTS | 65.0 | 500.0 | 70.0 | 650.0 | 98.0 | 1,100.0 |
| INDUSTRIAL SERVICES | 63.0 | 387.0 | 70.0 | 400.0 | 80.0 | 600.0 |
| OFFICE PRODUCTS | 65.0 | 300.0 | 70.0 | 350.0 | 98.0 | 1,000.0 |
| OFFICE SERVICES | 80.0 | 200.0 | 86.0 | 200.0 | 98.0 | 200.0 |
| **TYPE OF BUYER** | | | | | | |
| CONSUMERS | 80.0 | 387.0 | 95.0 | 400.0 | 120.0 | 880.0 |
| DISTRIBUTORS | 70.0 | 600.0 | 80.0 | 700.0 | 98.0 | 900.0 |
| INDUSTRY | 70.0 | 400.0 | 80.0 | 500.0 | 98.0 | 880.0 |
| RETAILERS | 80.0 | 325.0 | 86.0 | 975.0 | 110.0 | 1,100.0 |
| **INDUSTRY** | | | | | | |
| BUSINESS SERVICES | 70.0 | 200.0 | 86.0 | 200.0 | 98.0 | 300.0 |
| ELECTRONICS | 55.0 | N/R | N/R | N/R | 55.0 | 650.0 |
| HEALTH SERVICES | N/R | N/R | N/R | N/R | 60.0 | 800.0 |
| MACHINERY | N/R | N/R | N/R | N/R | 85.0 | 500.0 |
| MANUFACTURING | N/R | N/R | N/R | N/R | 80.0 | 400.0 |
| OFFICE EQUIPMENT | N/R | N/R | N/R | N/R | 57.0 | 1,000.0 |
| PHARMACEUTICALS | 95.0 | N/R | 110.0 | N/R | 120.0 | 325.0 |
| PRINTING AND PUBLISHING | N/R | N/R | N/R | N/R | 70.0 | 100.0 |
| WHOLESALE (INDUSTRIAL GOODS) | 37.0 | 32.0 | 65.0 | 212.0 | 150.0 | 1,250.0 |
| **OVERALL** | **$70.0** | **$500.0** | **$80.0** | **$550.0** | **$110.0** | **$880.0** |

*SALES VOLUME FIGURES FOR THIS POSITION ARE A MEASURE OF OVERALL JOB RESPONSIBILITY AND DO NOT NECESSARILY REFLECT ACTUAL SALES MADE.

# FIGURE 61

**SALES COMPENSATION AND VOLUME LEVELS — 3RD QUARTILE**
**DISTRICT SALES MANAGER**

| | AVERAGE PERFORMER | | BETTER PERFORMER | | BEST PERFORMER | |
|---|---|---|---|---|---|---|
| | TOTAL CASH COMP. FOR ALL PLANS COMBINED ($000) | SALES VOLUME* ($000) | TOTAL CASH COMP. FOR ALL PLANS COMBINED ($000) | SALES VOLUME* ($000) | TOTAL CASH COMP. FOR ALL PLANS COMBINED ($000) | SALES VOLUME* ($000) |
| **COMPANY SIZE** | | | | | | |
| UNDER $5 MILLION | $68.0 | $300.0 | $80.0 | $286.0 | $95.0 | $300.0 |
| **PRODUCT OR SERVICE** | | | | | | |
| CONSUMER PRODUCTS | 80.0 | 200.0 | 87.0 | 250.0 | 90.0 | 260.0 |
| CONSUMER SERVICES | 60.0 | 200.0 | 90.0 | 300.0 | 95.0 | 500.0 |
| INDUSTRIAL PRODUCTS | 40.0 | 250.0 | 45.0 | 260.0 | 60.0 | 550.0 |
| INDUSTRIAL SERVICES | 60.0 | 200.0 | 73.0 | 250.0 | 80.0 | 260.0 |
| OFFICE SERVICES | 66.0 | 100.0 | 52.0 | 125.0 | 90.0 | 200.0 |
| **TYPE OF BUYER** | | | | | | |
| CONSUMERS | 70.0 | 300.0 | 90.0 | 300.0 | 95.0 | 500.0 |
| DISTRIBUTORS | 66.0 | 100.0 | 60.0 | 125.0 | 70.0 | 250.0 |
| INDUSTRY | 66.0 | 250.0 | 87.0 | 286.0 | 90.0 | 300.0 |
| RETAILERS | 68.0 | 202.0 | 80.0 | 250.0 | 90.0 | 286.0 |
| **INDUSTRY** | | | | | | |
| BUSINESS SERVICES | 45.0 | 100.0 | 52.0 | 125.0 | 66.0 | 180.0 |
| INSURANCE | 60.0 | 150.0 | 90.0 | 225.0 | 115.0 | 275.0 |
| MANUFACTURING | N/R | 165.0 | N/R | 202.0 | 41.0 | 286.0 |
| PHARMACEUTICALS | 80.0 | N/R | 110.0 | N/R | 160.0 | 300.0 |
| WHOLESALE (INDUSTRIAL GOODS) | N/R | N/R | N/R | N/R | 48.0 | 100.0 |
| **OVERALL** | **$68.0** | **$300.0** | **$80.0** | **$286.0** | **$95.0** | **$300.0** |

*SALES VOLUME FIGURES FOR THIS POSITION ARE A MEASURE OF OVERALL JOB RESPONSIBILITY AND DO NOT NECESSARILY REFLECT ACTUAL SALES MADE.

# FIGURE 62

| | AVERAGE PERFORMER | | BETTER PERFORMER | | BEST PERFORMER | |
| --- | --- | --- | --- | --- | --- | --- |
| | TOTAL CASH COMP. FOR ALL PLANS COMBINED ($000) | SALES VOLUME ($000) | TOTAL CASH COMP. FOR ALL PLANS COMBINED ($000) | SALES VOLUME ($000) | TOTAL CASH COMP. FOR ALL PLANS COMBINED ($000) | SALES VOLUME ($000) |
| **COMPANY SIZE** | | | | | | |
| UNDER $5 MILLION | $60.0 | $ 700.0 | $65.0 | $800.0 | $94.0 | $900.0 |
| **PRODUCT OR SERVICE** | | | | | | |
| CONSUMER PRODUCTS | 53.0 | 650.0 | 72.0 | 900.0 | 85.0 | 950.0 |
| CONSUMER SERVICES | 50.5 | 600.0 | 67.0 | 650.0 | 85.0 | 800.0 |
| INDUSTRIAL PRODUCTS | 55.0 | 750.0 | 72.0 | 800.0 | 94.0 | 900.0 |
| INDUSTRIAL SERVICES | 60.0 | 700.0 | 65.0 | 800.0 | 80.0 | 900.0 |
| OFFICE PRODUCTS | 60.0 | 800.0 | 60.0 | 900.0 | 68.0 | 900.0 |
| OFFICE SERVICES | 65.0 | 800.0 | 60.0 | 900.0 | 68.0 | 960.0 |
| **TYPE OF BUYER** | | | | | | |
| CONSUMERS | 53.0 | 600.0 | 72.0 | 650.0 | 100.0 | 800.0 |
| DISTRIBUTORS | 60.0 | 600.0 | 65.0 | 650.0 | 75.0 | 900.0 |
| INDUSTRY | 60.0 | 750.0 | 67.0 | 800.0 | 94.0 | 900.0 |
| RETAILERS | 54.0 | 800.0 | 65.0 | 900.0 | 85.0 | 1,200.0 |
| **INDUSTRY** | | | | | | |
| BUSINESS SERVICES | 50.0 | 375.0 | 60.0 | 506.0 | 60.0 | 800.0 |
| FABRICATED METALS | N/R | 100.0 | N/R | 125.0 | 65.0 | 170.0 |
| HOLDING & OTHER INVESTMENT OFFICES | 53.0 | 667.0 | 56.0 | 700.0 | 64.0 | 800.0 |
| INSTRUMENTS | 65.0 | 700.0 | 90.0 | 1,000.0 | 97.0 | 1,200.0 |
| INSURANCE | 50.0 | 220.0 | 75.0 | 240.0 | 126.0 | 350.0 |
| MACHINERY | 55.0 | 700.0 | 60.0 | 800.0 | 80.0 | 900.0 |
| MANUFACTURING | 55.0 | 202.0 | 65.0 | 286.0 | 75.0 | 290.0 |
| PHARMACEUTICALS | 60.0 | N/R | 60.0 | N/R | 95.0 | 6,000.0 |
| PRINTING AND PUBLISHING | 60.0 | 600.0 | 75.0 | 900.0 | 80.0 | 900.0 |
| RETAIL | 45.0 | 275.0 | 60.0 | 319.0 | 68.0 | 575.0 |
| WHOLESALE (CONSUMER GOODS) | 62.0 | 800.0 | 75.0 | 325.0 | 85.0 | 800.0 |
| WHOLESALE (INDUSTRIAL GOODS) | 60.0 | 500.0 | 75.0 | 700.0 | 100.0 | 785.0 |
| **OVERALL** | **$60.0** | **$700.0** | **$65.0** | **$800.0** | **$94.0** | **$900.0** |

# FIGURE 63

**SALES COMPENSATION AND VOLUME LEVELS — 3RD QUARTILE**
**INTERMEDIATE SALES REP**

| | AVERAGE PERFORMER | | BETTER PERFORMER | | BEST PERFORMER | |
|---|---|---|---|---|---|---|
| | TOTAL CASH COMP. FOR ALL PLANS COMBINED ($000) | SALES VOLUME ($000) | TOTAL CASH COMP. FOR ALL PLANS COMBINED ($000) | SALES VOLUME ($000) | TOTAL CASH COMP. FOR ALL PLANS COMBINED ($000) | SALES VOLUME ($000) |
| **COMPANY SIZE** | | | | | | |
| UNDER $5 MILLION | $43.0 | $350.0 | $50.0 | $400.0 | $59.0 | $500.0 |
| **PRODUCT OR SERVICE** | | | | | | |
| CONSUMER PRODUCTS | 40.0 | 400.0 | 50.0 | 400.0 | 59.0 | 480.0 |
| CONSUMER SERVICES | 39.0 | 410.0 | 43.0 | 392.0 | 55.0 | 480.0 |
| INDUSTRIAL PRODUCTS | 41.0 | 350.0 | 52.0 | 400.0 | 62.0 | 400.0 |
| INDUSTRIAL SERVICES | 43.0 | 500.0 | 52.0 | 700.0 | 55.0 | 750.0 |
| OFFICE PRODUCTS | 40.0 | 360.0 | 40.5 | 400.0 | 54.0 | 480.0 |
| OFFICE SERVICES | 45.0 | 600.0 | 50.0 | 700.0 | 55.0 | 911.0 |
| **TYPE OF BUYER** | | | | | | |
| CONSUMERS | 40.0 | 350.0 | 45.0 | 400.0 | 55.0 | 410.0 |
| DISTRIBUTORS | 45.0 | 400.0 | 49.5 | 480.0 | 55.0 | 625.0 |
| INDUSTRY | 41.0 | 410.0 | 50.0 | 500.0 | 59.0 | 625.0 |
| RETAILERS | 40.0 | 400.0 | 45.0 | 500.0 | 55.0 | 650.0 |
| **INDUSTRY** | | | | | | |
| BUSINESS SERVICES | 46.0 | 260.0 | 54.0 | 392.0 | 55.0 | 720.0 |
| FABRICATED METALS | 31.0 | 30.0 | N/R | 40.0 | 40.0 | 750.0 |
| FOOD PRODUCTS | 35.0 | N/R | N/R | N/R | 100.0 | 100.0 |
| HEALTH SERVICES | N/R | 150.0 | N/R | N/R | 45.0 | 350.0 |
| HOLDING & OTHER INVESTMENT OFFICES | 48.0 | N/R | N/R | 400.0 | 56.0 | 500.0 |
| INSTRUMENTS | 42.0 | 400.0 | 52.0 | 300.0 | 74.0 | 500.0 |
| MANUFACTURING | N/R | N/R | N/R | 90.0 | 36.0 | 120.0 |
| OFFICE EQUIPMENT | 31.0 | 230.0 | 40.5 | 250.0 | 55.0 | 300.0 |
| PRINTING AND PUBLISHING | 40.0 | 150.0 | 40.5 | 252.0 | 55.0 | 900.0 |
| RETAIL | 30.0 | 250.0 | 36.0 | 225.0 | 38.0 | 480.0 |
| WHOLESALE (CONSUMER GOODS) | 41.0 | 180.0 | 49.0 | 200.0 | 54.0 | 500.0 |
| WHOLESALE (INDUSTRIAL GOODS) | 45.0 | 250.0 | 45.0 | 300.0 | 60.0 | 350.0 |
| **OVERALL** | **$43.0** | **$350.0** | **$50.0** | **$400.0** | **$59.0** | **$500.0** |

# FIGURE 64

**SALES COMPENSATION AND VOLUME LEVELS — 3RD QUARTILE**
**ENTRY LEVEL SALES REP**

| | AVERAGE PERFORMER | | BETTER PERFORMER | | BEST PERFORMER | |
|---|---|---|---|---|---|---|
| | TOTAL CASH COMP. FOR ALL PLANS COMBINED ($000) | SALES VOLUME ($000) | TOTAL CASH COMP. FOR ALL PLANS COMBINED ($000) | SALES VOLUME ($000) | TOTAL CASH COMP. FOR ALL PLANS COMBINED ($000) | SALES VOLUME ($000) |
| **COMPANY SIZE** | | | | | | |
| UNDER $5 MILLION | $33.0 | $250.0 | $41.0 | $250.0 | $51.0 | $350.0 |
| **PRODUCT OR SERVICE** | | | | | | |
| CONSUMER PRODUCTS | 26.0 | 200.0 | 41.0 | 225.0 | 50.0 | 350.0 |
| CONSUMER SERVICES | 31.0 | 200.0 | 35.0 | 326.0 | 50.0 | 400.0 |
| INDUSTRIAL PRODUCTS | 33.0 | 150.0 | 41.2 | 250.0 | 53.0 | 300.0 |
| INDUSTRIAL SERVICES | 33.0 | 200.0 | 41.0 | 250.0 | 51.0 | 400.0 |
| OFFICE PRODUCTS | 25.0 | 200.0 | 41.0 | 300.0 | 45.0 | 400.0 |
| OFFICE SERVICES | 36.0 | 300.0 | N/R | 360.0 | 41.0 | 400.0 |
| **TYPE OF BUYER** | | | | | | |
| CONSUMERS | 30.0 | 200.0 | 35.0 | 326.0 | 50.0 | 400.0 |
| DISTRIBUTORS | 33.0 | 180.0 | 26.0 | 200.0 | 33.0 | 200.0 |
| INDUSTRY | 33.0 | 250.0 | 41.0 | 300.0 | 53.0 | 400.0 |
| RETAILERS | 30.0 | 200.0 | 26.0 | 326.0 | 35.0 | 350.0 |
| **INDUSTRY** | | | | | | |
| BUSINESS SERVICES | 36.0 | 150.0 | 62.0 | N/R | 70.0 | 326.0 |
| INSTRUMENTS | 35.0 | N/R | 45.0 | 150.0 | 55.0 | 250.0 |
| INSURANCE | 40.0 | 120.0 | 45.0 | 140.0 | 47.5 | 180.0 |
| MANUFACTURING | 24.0 | 128.0 | 25.0 | 138.0 | 25.0 | 200.0 |
| PHARMACEUTICALS | 35.0 | 150.0 | 40.0 | 200.0 | 50.0 | 250.0 |
| RETAIL | 23.0 | 200.0 | N/R | 360.0 | 42.0 | 600.0 |
| WHOLESALE (CONSUMER GOODS) | 32.0 | 140.0 | 37.0 | 160.0 | 37.0 | 300.0 |
| **OVERALL** | **$33.0** | **$250.0** | **$41.0** | **$250.0** | **$51.0** | **$350.0** |

# FIGURE 65

**SALES COMPENSATION AND VOLUME LEVELS — 3RD QUARTILE**
**NAT'L/MAJ ACCOUNT MANAGER**

| | AVERAGE PERFORMER | | BETTER PERFORMER | | BEST PERFORMER | |
|---|---|---|---|---|---|---|
| | TOTAL CASH COMP. FOR ALL PLANS COMBINED ($000) | SALES VOLUME* ($000) | TOTAL CASH COMP. FOR ALL PLANS COMBINED ($000) | SALES VOLUME* ($000) | TOTAL CASH COMP. FOR ALL PLANS COMBINED ($000) | SALES VOLUME* ($000) |
| **COMPANY SIZE** | | | | | | |
| UNDER $5 MILLION | $65.0 | $400.0 | $119.0 | $796.0 | $140.0 | $1,500.0 |
| **PRODUCT OR SERVICE** | | | | | | |
| CONSUMER SERVICES | 55.0 | N/R | 65.0 | N/R | 140.0 | 1,000.0 |
| INDUSTRIAL PRODUCTS | 90.0 | 796.0 | 119.0 | 1,500.0 | 140.0 | 1,500.0 |
| INDUSTRIAL SERVICES | 53.0 | 400.0 | 91.0 | 1,000.0 | 140.0 | 1,500.0 |
| OFFICE PRODUCTS | 91.0 | 1,000.0 | 119.0 | 1,500.0 | 140.0 | 1,500.0 |
| OFFICE SERVICES | 53.0 | 400.0 | 91.0 | 1,000.0 | 140.0 | 1,500.0 |
| **TYPE OF BUYER** | | | | | | |
| DISTRIBUTORS | 53.0 | 400.0 | 60.0 | N/R | 140.0 | 500.0 |
| INDUSTRY | 84.0 | 400.0 | 119.0 | 796.0 | 140.0 | 1,500.0 |
| RETAILERS | 65.0 | 250.0 | 119.0 | N/R | 140.0 | 400.0 |
| **OVERALL** | **$65.0** | **$400.0** | **$119.0** | **$796.0** | **$140.0** | **$1,500.0** |

*SALES VOLUME FIGURES FOR THIS POSITION ARE A MEASURE OF OVERALL JOB RESPONSIBILITY AND DO NOT NECESSARILY REFLECT ACTUAL SALES MADE.

# FIGURE 66

**Sales Compensation and Volume Levels — 3rd Quartile**
**National Account Rep**

| | Average Performer | | Better Performer | | Best Performer | |
|---|---|---|---|---|---|---|
| | Total Cash Comp. For All Plans Combined ($000) | Sales Volume ($000) | Total Cash Comp. For All Plans Combined ($000) | Sales Volume ($000) | Total Cash Comp. For All Plans Combined ($000) | Sales Volume ($000) |
| **Company Size** | | | | | | |
| Under $5 Million | $65.0 | $400.0 | $75.0 | $500.0 | $105.0 | $3,000.0 |
| **Product or Service** | | | | | | |
| Consumer Products | 60.0 | N/R | 65.0 | 145.0 | 75.0 | 4,678.4 |
| Industrial Products | 80.0 | N/R | 91.0 | 300.0 | 105.0 | 500.0 |
| Industrial Services | 60.0 | 400.0 | 91.0 | 500.0 | 105.0 | 3,000.0 |
| **Type of Buyer** | | | | | | |
| Consumers | 53.0 | 400.0 | 60.0 | N/R | 75.0 | 218.0 |
| Distributors | 80.0 | 500.0 | 91.0 | 575.0 | 105.0 | 3,000.0 |
| Industry | 80.0 | 400.0 | 75.0 | 500.0 | 105.0 | 3,000.0 |
| Retailers | 60.0 | 400.0 | 65.0 | N/R | 75.0 | 218.0 |
| **Industry** | | | | | | |
| Business Services | 84.0 | 400.0 | 91.0 | N/R | 105.0 | 525.0 |
| Fabricated Metals | N/R | N/R | N/R | N/R | 50.0 | 300.0 |
| Pharmaceuticals | 45.0 | N/R | 60.0 | N/R | 75.0 | 4,678.4 |
| Wholesale (Industrial Goods) | 42.0 | N/R | N/R | 500.0 | 105.0 | 3,000.0 |
| **Overall** | **$65.0** | **$400.0** | **$75.0** | **$500.0** | **$105.0** | **$3,000.0** |

# FIGURE 67

SALES COMPENSATION AND VOLUME LEVELS — 3RD QUARTILE
MAJOR (KEY) ACCOUNT REP

| | AVERAGE PERFORMER | | BETTER PERFORMER | | BEST PERFORMER | |
| --- | --- | --- | --- | --- | --- | --- |
| | TOTAL CASH COMP. FOR ALL PLANS COMBINED ($000) | SALES VOLUME ($000) | TOTAL CASH COMP. FOR ALL PLANS COMBINED ($000) | SALES VOLUME ($000) | TOTAL CASH COMP. FOR ALL PLANS COMBINED ($000) | SALES VOLUME ($000) |
| **COMPANY SIZE** | | | | | | |
| UNDER $5 MILLION | $65.0 | $500.0 | $75.0 | $1,000.0 | $100.0 | $3,446.4 |
| **PRODUCT OR SERVICE** | | | | | | |
| CONSUMER PRODUCTS | 65.0 | N/R | 75.0 | 1,000.0 | 105.0 | 3,446.4 |
| CONSUMER SERVICES | 45.0 | 1,000.0 | 100.0 | 2,000.0 | 140.0 | 5,000.0 |
| INDUSTRIAL SERVICES | 75.0 | 1,000.0 | 100.0 | 225.0 | 140.0 | 1,000.0 |
| OFFICE PRODUCTS | 91.0 | N/R | 105.0 | N/R | 140.0 | 1,000.0 |
| OFFICE SERVICES | 80.0 | 1,000.0 | 90.0 | 1,000.0 | 105.0 | 2,000.0 |
| **TYPE OF BUYER** | | | | | | |
| CONSUMERS | 45.0 | 1,000.0 | 100.0 | 1,000.0 | 140.0 | 2,000.0 |
| DISTRIBUTORS | 75.0 | 500.0 | 50.0 | 1,000.0 | 105.0 | 2,000.0 |
| INDUSTRY | 80.0 | 500.0 | 90.0 | N/R | 100.0 | 1,000.0 |
| RETAILERS | 65.0 | 350.0 | 100.0 | 1,000.0 | 140.0 | 3,446.4 |
| **OVERALL** | **$65.0** | **$500.0** | **$75.0** | **$1,000.0** | **$100.0** | **$3,446.4** |

## FIGURE 68 — SENIOR SALES REP PRODUCTIVITY

How much more productive, in measurable terms, are top sales performers compared to average performers? Survey participants were asked to determine the degree to which their top salespeople outperformed average salespeople in the same company. **Figure 68** takes a look at these estimates. This data represents that group of salespeople who sell *at least more than $1\frac{1}{2}$ times more than average performers.*

To better understand this data, it's helpful to combine the breakouts into different performance categories. By doing so, we see that 66.7% of top-performing salespeople sell $1\frac{1}{2}$ to 2 times more than average salespeople; 21.6% of top performers sell from $2\frac{1}{2}$ to $3\frac{1}{2}$ more than average; and more than 10 percent (11.7%) sell 4 to more than 5 times the average. Just over 4 percent (4.33%) of top-performing salespeople in companies with under $5 million in annual sales sell more than 5 times the volume of the average performer. These are the true top performers, and you can count your blessings if you have one on your team.

This data can provide further guidance in helping you decide who your better and best performers are and what it is reasonable to expect from them. You can also use this data to compare your top performers with the average performance of other top performers.

(Data represents that group of salespeople who sell at least more than $1\frac{1}{2}$ times more than average performers.)

# FIGURE 68

## 1996 Senior Sales Rep Productivity in Companies with Under $5 Million in Annual Sales (All Respondents)

By How Much Do Top Performers
Outshine Average Performers?

| | |
|---|---|
| 37.23% | 1.5 TIMES AVG. |
| 29.44 | 2.0 TIMES AVG. |
| 10.39 | 2.5 TIMES AVG. |
| 9.52 | 3.0 TIMES AVG. |
| 1.73 | 3.5 TIMES AVG. |
| 3.03 | 4.0 TIMES AVG. |
| 0.87 | 4.5 TIMES AVG. |
| 3.46 | 5.0 TIMES AVG. |
| 4.33 | MORE THAN 5.0 TIMES AVG. |

## 1996 Senior Sales Rep Productivity in Companies of All Sizes

By How Much Do Top Performers
Outshine Average Performers?

| | |
|---|---|
| 34.86% | 1.5 TIMES AVG. |
| 31.81 | 2.0 TIMES AVG. |
| 10.69 | 2.5 TIMES AVG. |
| 10.00 | 3.0 TIMES AVG. |
| 3.06 | 3.5 TIMES AVG. |
| 4.03 | 4.0 TIMES AVG. |
| 1.39 | 4.5 TIMES AVG. |
| 2.36 | 5.0 TIMES AVG. |
| 1.80 | MORE THAN 5.0 TIMES AVG. |

## 1994 Senior Sales Rep Productivity in Companies of All Sizes

By How Much Do Top Performers
Outshine Average Performers?

| | |
|---|---|
| 39.01% | 1.5 TIMES AVG. |
| 31.08 | 2.0 TIMES AVG. |
| 10.23 | 2.5 TIMES AVG. |
| 8.30 | 3.0 TIMES AVG. |
| 1.35 | 3.5 TIMES AVG. |
| 4.05 | 4.0 TIMES AVG. |
| 2.12 | 4.5 TIMES AVG. |
| 2.32 | 5.0 TIMES AVG. |
| 1.54 | MORE THAN 5.0 TIMES AVG. |

## FIGURE 69 — SENIOR SALES REP PRODUCTIVITY: 'BETTER' AND 'BEST' PERFORMERS

**Figure 69** takes another look at just how much more annual sales volume is generated by better and best performers compared with average sales performers. (See Terminology Used in This Survey, page 108, for a definition of "better" and "best" performers.) The data is broken out by type of product or service sold; type of buyer; and selected industries.

For comparison purposes, you might want to calculate these ratios in your own company.

To do this, first determine average sales volume for the average senior performers in your company. Then determine how much more sales volume your top performers generate as a percentage increase over average performers.

Finally, determine how much more the top performers in your company make as a percentage increase over average performers. While these figures and ratios can differ dramatically from company to company even within the same industry, this exercise does serve to emphasize the importance of nurturing and cultivating top-performing salespeople. Often, two average salespeople will cost more and deliver less than one superstar.

**FIGURE 69**

**Senior Sales Rep Productivity —
"Better" and "Best" Performers**

|  | Better Performer Increase Over Average Performer (Percent) | Best Performer Increase over Average Performer (Percent) |
|---|---|---|
| **Company Size** | | |
| Under $5 Million | 41.1% | 73.6% |
| **Product or Service** | | |
| Industrial Products | 54.2 | 83.6 |
| Industrial Services | 38.8 | 60.8 |
| Office Products | 50.0 | 83.7 |
| Office Services | 36.1 | 64.4 |
| Consumer Products | 36.0 | 49.4 |
| Consumer Services | 30.3 | 61.3 |
| **Type of Buyer** | | |
| Industry | 45.8 | 78.3 |
| Retailers | 38.8 | 71.4 |
| Consumers | 32.2 | 64.3 |
| Distributors | 39.8 | 85.0 |
| **Industry** | | |
| Business Services | 15.9 | 31.4 |
| Electronics | 23.8 | 50.0 |
| Fabricated Metals | 25.0 | 70.0 |
| Furniture and Fixtures | 16.7 | 33.3 |
| Holding & Other Investment Offices | 4.9 | 19.9 |
| Instruments | 19.8 | 59.5 |
| Insurance | 26.2 | 82.4 |
| Machinery | 14.3 | 28.6 |
| Manufacturing | 7.4 | 52.1 |
| Office Equipment | 12.5 | 25.0 |
| Printing and Publishing | 69.5 | 108.8 |
| Retail | 20.6 | 60.9 |
| Wholesale (Industrial Goods) | 71.0 | 127.3 |
| **Overall** | **41.1%** | **73.6%** |

# EXPENSES, BENEFITS, TRAINING

**W**hat do we pay to keep our salespeople out in the field selling? Should we pay for lodging and meals? How about car phones and automobiles? How much do we pay in benefits? And what about training? How much time—and money—do we spend getting our new hires up to speed and then keeping them up to speed once they've become the experienced and productive salespeople we've brought along the way?

This section reviews the costs of sales, field expenses, benefits, and training. The data received from survey respondents on the overall costs of sales efforts, field expenses, benefits, and training is presented through the following exhibits:

- Figure 70 examines sales force total cost as a percent of sales.
- Figure 71 takes a look at how much companies are paying out in field expenses and benefits for senior salespeople.
- Figures 72–85 present pay practices by field expense item.
- Figure 86 lists the specific benefits offered to salespeople.
- Figure 87 looks at the different methods of training used by companies.
- Figure 88 presents data on the cost and length of training for new hires.
- Figure 89 examines the cost, type of training, and number of training hours per year for experienced salespeople.

Companies with under $5 million in annual sales spend less on field expenses and benefits than their larger counterparts. However, in comparing current data with data from previous Dartnell studies, companies with under $5 million in annual sales are now increasing (or restoring) their spending in these areas. In our survey, companies with under $5 million in annual sales are spending an average of $12,016 on field expenses and $4,023 in benefits per rep annually. (1994 data: $7,908 field expenses; $3,503 benefits; 1992 data: $8,789 field expenses; $4,575 benefits.)

**Good news:** Companies both large and small are restoring, and in many cases, increasing spending on such items as laptop PCs, home fax machines, home photocopiers, and car phones. Up until two years ago, we had noticed a growing willingness on the part of companies to pay for these productivity-enhancing, and by extension, revenue-enhancing, high-tech selling tools. Our 1994 survey saw heavy cost-cutting in this area. (See chart on page 205.)

**Encouraging news:** Companies both large and small are spending more on training new hires as well as experienced salespeople. This is a strong indication that companies are willing to invest in the long-term success of their sales staffs. Training costs for new hires in companies with under $5 million in annual sales, which declined from 1992–1994, are up 43.5 percent over 1994 figures and now stand at $5,291 per year per rep. Training costs for experienced salespeople, holding steady from 1992–1994, are up 39 percent from 1994's $2,498 per experienced salesperson. Companies with under $5 million in annual sales now spend, on average, $3,477 per year training an experienced rep.

## FIGURE 70 — COST OF SELLING

Selling costs can wreak havoc with your bottom line, as many companies know only too well. There are plenty of examples of companies that have seen their sales climb only to see profits plummet.

On the other hand, cutting costs to the point of impeding the performance of your salespeople isn't the answer, either. Remember, the ultimate strategy for cutting daily operating expenses is simply to go out of business.

**Figure 70** examines the total cost of sales as a percentage of sales. The overall percentage rate in our current survey is 11.8 percent.

The figures on the accompanying table should be regarded as an indication of the relative cost of operating a field sales force in a variety of industries. Within individual industries, a wide range of figures was reported. If your cost of sales as a percent of sales varies considerably from figures presented here, bear in mind that your costs may well be on target for your particular company.

Included in these calculations are the cost of sales compensation, cost of benefits provided to a salesperson, and field expenses. Not included are the costs of sales management, overhead, and the like.

# FIGURE 70

**COST OF SELLING**
**(AVERAGE OF MEDIAN RANGE)**

|  | SALES FORCE TOTAL COST AS A PERCENT OF SALES |
| --- | --- |
| **COMPANY SIZE** | |
| UNDER $5 MILLION | 11.8% |
| **PRODUCT OR SERVICE** | |
| INDUSTRIAL PRODUCTS | 14.1 |
| INDUSTRIAL SERVICES | 8.9 |
| OFFICE PRODUCTS | 16.5 |
| OFFICE SERVICES | 9.5 |
| CONSUMER PRODUCTS | 9.8 |
| CONSUMER SERVICES | 7.0 |
| **TYPE OF BUYER** | |
| INDUSTRY | 11.7 |
| RETAILERS | 9.8 |
| CONSUMERS | 8.4 |
| DISTRIBUTORS | 10.7 |
| **INDUSTRY** | |
| AMUSEMENT & RECREATION SERVICES | 5.3 |
| BUSINESS SERVICES | 12.3 |
| ELECTRONICS | 18.5 |
| FABRICATED METALS | 7.1 |
| FOOD PRODUCTS | 13.7 |
| FURNITURE AND FIXTURES | 12.0 |
| HEALTH SERVICES | 16.1 |
| HOLDING & OTHER INVESTMENT OFFICES | 17.1 |
| HOTELS & OTHER LODGING PLACES | 5.1 |
| INSTRUMENTS | 19.4 |
| INSURANCE | 11.6 |
| MACHINERY | 12.4 |
| MANUFACTURING | 16.5 |
| OFFICE EQUIPMENT | 15.5 |
| PHARMACEUTICALS | 17.2 |
| PRINTING AND PUBLISHING | 12.0 |
| RETAIL | 15.0 |
| WHOLESALE (CONSUMER GOODS) | 18.7 |
| WHOLESALE (INDUSTRIAL GOODS) | 14.2 |
| **OVERALL** | **11.8%** |

# FIGURE 71 — COST PER EXPERIENCED SALESPERSON: FIELD EXPENSES AND BENEFITS

**Figure 71** examines the cost of field expenses and cost of benefits per experienced salesperson. Companies with under $5 million in annual sales spend an average of $12,016 on field expenses, per salesperson, an increase of 51.9 percent over the $7,908 that was spent on field expenses per rep in 1994. What's going on here? Are companies letting costs get out of control? Is selling really becoming that much more expensive?

Without historical data to fall back on, the real reason behind this whopping increase would be hard to pinpoint. Let's take a look at what was going on in 1990.

Back in 1990, field expenses per salesperson averaged $14,127, or approximately 12 percent less than is currently spent. Rampant cost-cutting in the wake of the recession of the early '90s had cut field expenses to $8,789 by 1992.

By 1994, companies had cut back field expenses about as far as they could and realized that further reductions could start to have a negative impact on productivity. Thus, the apparent dramatic increase in spending on field expenses should be more properly viewed as a move by companies to *restore* spending that had previously been cut.

Today, companies are investing more in those activities that can have a positive impact on the bottom line, such as supplying their salespeople with productivity-enhancing tools. (See Figures 72–85 for what companies are willing to pay for.)

To further put things in perspective, companies with annual sales of under $5 million spend approximately 31.9 percent less on field expenses than companies with over $5 million in annual sales. Companies with under $5 million in annual sales spend $4,023 on benefits per salesperson. The chart below shows how expense and benefit data has fluctuated since 1990.

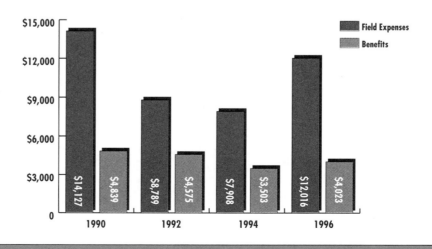

# FIGURE 71

**COST PER EXPERIENCED SALESPERSON**
**FIELD EXPENSES AND BENEFITS**
**(AVERAGE OF MEDIAN RANGE)**

| | FIELD EXPENSES | BENEFITS |
|---|---|---|
| **COMPANY SIZE** | | |
| UNDER $5 MILLION | $12,016 | $4,023 |
| **PRODUCT OR SERVICE** | | |
| CONSUMER PRODUCTS | 9,380 | 4,668 |
| CONSUMER SERVICES | 9,484 | 3,476 |
| INDUSTRIAL PRODUCTS | 13,405 | 4,419 |
| INDUSTRIAL SERVICES | 12,583 | 4,046 |
| OFFICE PRODUCTS | 12,400 | 3,855 |
| OFFICE SERVICES | 13,242 | 3,783 |
| **TYPE OF BUYER** | | |
| CONSUMERS | 8,524 | 3,745 |
| DISTRIBUTORS | 12,549 | 4,710 |
| INDUSTRY | 12,268 | 4,159 |
| RETAILERS | 9,942 | 4,374 |
| **INDUSTRY** | | |
| AMUSEMENT & RECREATION SERVICES | 22,333 | 0 |
| BUSINESS SERVICES | 11,375 | 3,562 |
| ELECTRONICS | 16,400 | 2,220 |
| HEALTH SERVICES | 35,000 | 2,250 |
| HOLDING & OTHER INVESTMENT OFFICES | 22,500 | 3,500 |
| HOTELS & OTHER LODGING PLACES | 11,000 | 4,000 |
| INSTRUMENTS | 24,000 | 5,500 |
| INSURANCE | 7,375 | 3,750 |
| MACHINERY | 7,500 | 5,200 |
| MANUFACTURING | 9,000 | 8,333 |
| OFFICE EQUIPMENT | 12,180 | 2,850 |
| PHARMACEUTICALS | 23,333 | 10,500 |
| PRINTING AND PUBLISHING | 5,200 | 6,250 |
| RETAIL | 4,356 | 3,250 |
| WHOLESALE (CONSUMER GOODS) | 12,120 | 3,288 |
| WHOLESALE (INDUSTRIAL GOODS) | 20,269 | 4,770 |
| **OVERALL** | **$12,016** | **$4,023** |

## FIGURES 72–85 — PERCENTAGE OF COMPANIES THAT PAY FOR ALL OR PART OF EXPENSE ITEMS

Companies of all sizes have ended the across-the-board cost cutting of field expense items and have boosted spending in those areas that they feel will help increase the effectiveness of their salespeople (also see discussion of Figure 71).

Since 1990, we have been tracking what common—and some not so common—expense items companies of all sizes, including those companies with under $5 million in annual sales, are willing to pay for. The 14 items on our list include auto—company owned; auto—company leased; mileage allowance; other travel reimbursement; lodging; telephone; entertainment; product samples; local promotions; office and/or clerical; home photocopier; home fax machine; car phone; and laptop PC.

Figures 72 to 85 provide a detailed picture of what companies with under $5 million in annual sales are willing to pay for. Again, these tables are broken out by product, service, type of buyer, and industry.

In 1990, Dartnell started tracking a growing trend: the willingness of companies to pay for those items that could lead to an increase in salesperson productivity. These expense items included such things as car phones, home fax machines, laptop PCs, and the like. Interestingly, our survey data showed an even stronger trend to pay for these items than had been previously thought. For example, in 1990, nearly 40 percent of responding companies with under $5 million in annual sales said they paid 100 percent of the cost of providing a car phone for their salespeople.

By 1994, however, only 26 percent of responding companies said they paid 100 percent of this cost. Clearly, companies were cutting back and trying to reduce field expenses. In previous Dartnell reports, we noted that companies may have reached the limit of how much they can scale back spending and that further reductions could have a negative impact on salesperson productivity—and the bottom line.

Results from this study suggest that companies had indeed reached the end of spending cuts; they had cut the fat and had started cutting into the bone.

The chart on the facing page dramatically shows how companies with under $5 million in annual sales have cut spending over the past few years and how they are now restoring that spending. We strongly suspect this upward trend will continue, especially as more companies adopt sales automation technology.

It is a significant finding of this survey that nearly one-half (43%) of companies with under $5 million in annual sales pay 100 percent of the cost of supplying their salespeople with laptops. This certainly sets the stage for further expansion of the use of sales automation.

For comparison purposes, we have also included data on how companies of all sizes have allocated field expense costs. You'll note that the *spending trends* over the past few years are quite similar.

## PERCENTAGE OF COMPANIES WITH UNDER $5 MILLION IN ANNUAL SALES
## PAYING 100% OF THE FOLLOWING EXPENSE ITEMS

|  | 1990 | 1992 | 1994 | 1996 |
| --- | --- | --- | --- | --- |
| AUTO — COMPANY OWNED | 29% | 37% | 14% | 35% |
| AUTO — COMPANY LEASED | 30 | 3 | 12 | 26 |
| MILEAGE ALLOWANCE | 52 | 58 | 35 | 58 |
| OTHER TRAVEL REIMBURSEMENT | 84 | 79 | 61 | 72 |
| LODGING | 88 | 88 | 66 | 79 |
| TELEPHONE | 92 | 85 | 71 | 81 |
| ENTERTAINMENT | 70 | 71 | 48 | 78 |
| PRODUCT SAMPLES | 95 | 87 | 52 | 86 |
| LOCAL PROMOTIONS | 83 | 82 | 57 | 66 |
| OFFICE AND/OR CLERICAL | 85 | 83 | 68 | 78 |
| HOME PHOTOCOPIER | 19 | 18 | 10 | 30 |
| HOME FAX MACHINE | 22 | 32 | 11 | 39 |
| CAR PHONE | 39 | 44 | 26 | 43 |
| LAPTOP PC | 25 | 23 | 18 | 43 |

## PERCENTAGE OF COMPANIES OF ALL SIZES
## PAYING 100% OF THE FOLLOWING EXPENSE ITEMS

|  | 1990 | 1992 | 1994 | 1996 |
| --- | --- | --- | --- | --- |
| AUTO — COMPANY OWNED | 39% | 37% | 16% | 31% |
| AUTO — COMPANY LEASED | 59 | 34 | 20 | 40 |
| MILEAGE ALLOWANCE | 51 | 61 | 37 | 57 |
| OTHER TRAVEL REIMBURSEMENT | 88 | 84 | 69 | 79 |
| LODGING | 94 | 92 | 80 | 87 |
| TELEPHONE | 94 | 89 | 81 | 86 |
| ENTERTAINMENT | 83 | 83 | 68 | 77 |
| PRODUCT SAMPLES | 92 | 88 | 63 | 83 |
| LOCAL PROMOTIONS | 85 | 84 | 61 | 79 |
| OFFICE AND/OR CLERICAL | 88 | 85 | 70 | 82 |
| HOME PHOTOCOPIER | 39 | 29 | 16 | 41 |
| HOME FAX MACHINE | 49 | 46 | 25 | 56 |
| CAR PHONE | 48 | 52 | 38 | 53 |
| LAPTOP PC | 37 | 44 | 28 | 66 |

# FIGURE 72

PERCENTAGE OF COMPANIES THAT PAY
FOR ALL OR PART OF EXPENSE ITEMS
AUTO — COMPANY OWNED

|  | ALL | PART | PART<br>% PAID | NONE |
|---|---|---|---|---|
| **COMPANY SIZE** | | | | |
| UNDER $5 MILLION | 35.29% | 5.04% | 72.50% | 59.66% |
| **PRODUCT OR SERVICE** | | | | |
| CONSUMER PRODUCTS | 37.78 | 0.00 | 0.00 | 62.22 |
| CONSUMER SERVICES | 41.94 | 6.45 | 82.50 | 51.61 |
| INDUSTRIAL PRODUCTS | 40.00 | 8.00 | 67.50 | 52.00 |
| INDUSTRIAL SERVICES | 46.51 | 4.65 | 82.50 | 48.84 |
| OFFICE PRODUCTS | 33.33 | 0.00 | 0.00 | 66.67 |
| OFFICE SERVICES | 37.93 | 3.45 | 90.00 | 58.62 |
| **TYPE OF BUYER** | | | | |
| CONSUMERS | 39.13 | 2.17 | 90.00 | 58.70 |
| DISTRIBUTORS | 26.32 | 8.77 | 69.00 | 64.91 |
| INDUSTRY | 41.25 | 7.50 | 72.50 | 51.25 |
| RETAILERS | 32.65 | 4.08 | 82.50 | 63.27 |
| **INDUSTRY** | | | | |
| AMUSEMENT & RECREATION SERVICES | 0.00 | 0.00 | 0.00 | 100.00 |
| BUSINESS SERVICES | 50.00 | 4.55 | 75.00 | 45.45 |
| ELECTRONICS | 20.00 | 0.00 | 0.00 | 80.00 |
| FABRICATED METALS | 66.67 | 0.00 | 0.00 | 33.33 |
| FOOD PRODUCTS | 0.00 | 0.00 | 0.00 | 100.00 |
| FURNITURE AND FIXTURES | 33.33 | 0.00 | 0.00 | 66.67 |
| HEALTH SERVICES | 20.00 | 0.00 | 0.00 | 80.00 |
| HOLDING & OTHER INVESTMENT OFFICES | 0.00 | 0.00 | 0.00 | 100.00 |
| INSTRUMENTS | 0.00 | 0.00 | 0.00 | 100.00 |
| INSURANCE | 0.00 | 0.00 | 0.00 | 100.00 |
| MACHINERY | 100.00 | 0.00 | 0.00 | 0.00 |
| MANUFACTURING | 0.00 | 0.00 | 0.00 | 100.00 |
| OFFICE EQUIPMENT | 20.00 | 0.00 | 0.00 | 80.00 |
| PHARMACEUTICALS | 25.00 | 0.00 | 0.00 | 75.00 |
| PRINTING AND PUBLISHING | 60.00 | 0.00 | 0.00 | 40.00 |
| RETAIL | 28.57 | 14.29 | 90.00 | 57.14 |
| WHOLESALE (CONSUMER GOODS) | 37.50 | 0.00 | 0.00 | 62.50 |
| WHOLESALE (INDUSTRIAL GOODS) | 43.75 | 6.25 | 75.00 | 50.00 |
| **OVERALL** | **35.29%** | **5.04%** | **72.50%** | **59.66%** |

# FIGURE 73

| | ALL | PART | PART<br>% PAID | NONE |
|---|---|---|---|---|
| **COMPANY SIZE** | | | | |
| UNDER $5 MILLION | 25.95% | 7.63% | 66.50% | 66.41% |
| **PRODUCT OR SERVICE** | | | | |
| CONSUMER PRODUCTS | 24.00 | 4.00 | 50.00 | 72.00 |
| CONSUMER SERVICES | 33.33 | 8.33 | 65.00 | 58.33 |
| INDUSTRIAL PRODUCTS | 29.09 | 9.09 | 60.00 | 61.82 |
| INDUSTRIAL SERVICES | 35.42 | 6.25 | 66.67 | 58.33 |
| OFFICE PRODUCTS | 39.13 | 0.00 | 0.00 | 60.87 |
| OFFICE SERVICES | 36.36 | 0.00 | 0.00 | 63.64 |
| **TYPE OF BUYER** | | | | |
| CONSUMERS | 25.00 | 5.77 | 65.00 | 69.23 |
| DISTRIBUTORS | 22.39 | 11.94 | 61.88 | 65.67 |
| INDUSTRY | 32.58 | 6.74 | 50.00 | 60.67 |
| RETAILERS | 19.23 | 7.69 | 71.25 | 73.08 |
| **INDUSTRY** | | | | |
| AMUSEMENT & RECREATION SERVICES | 33.33 | 0.00 | 0.00 | 66.67 |
| BUSINESS SERVICES | 39.29 | 0.00 | 0.00 | 60.71 |
| ELECTRONICS | 33.33 | 0.00 | 0.00 | 66.67 |
| FABRICATED METALS | 33.33 | 0.00 | 0.00 | 66.67 |
| FOOD PRODUCTS | 0.00 | 0.00 | 0.00 | 100.00 |
| FURNITURE AND FIXTURES | 0.00 | 0.00 | 0.00 | 100.00 |
| HEALTH SERVICES | 33.33 | 0.00 | 0.00 | 66.67 |
| HOLDING & OTHER INVESTMENT OFFICES | 0.00 | 0.00 | 0.00 | 100.00 |
| INSTRUMENTS | 50.00 | 0.00 | 0.00 | 50.00 |
| INSURANCE | 0.00 | 40.00 | 92.50 | 60.00 |
| MACHINERY | 100.00 | 0.00 | 0.00 | 0.00 |
| MANUFACTURING | 50.00 | 0.00 | 0.00 | 50.00 |
| OFFICE EQUIPMENT | 25.00 | 0.00 | 0.00 | 75.00 |
| PHARMACEUTICALS | 40.00 | 20.00 | 90.00 | 40.00 |
| PRINTING AND PUBLISHING | 71.43 | 0.00 | 0.00 | 28.57 |
| RETAIL | 0.00 | 12.50 | 10.00 | 87.50 |
| WHOLESALE (CONSUMER GOODS) | 22.22 | 0.00 | 0.00 | 77.78 |
| WHOLESALE (INDUSTRIAL GOODS) | 7.14 | 14.29 | 52.50 | 78.57 |
| **OVERALL** | **25.95%** | **7.63%** | **66.50%** | **66.41%** |

# FIGURE 74

| | ALL | PART | PART % PAID | NONE |
|---|---|---|---|---|
| **COMPANY SIZE** | | | | |
| UNDER $5 MILLION | 58.10% | 12.29% | 51.91% | 29.61% |
| **PRODUCT OR SERVICE** | | | | |
| CONSUMER PRODUCTS | 47.37 | 15.79 | 36.11 | 36.84 |
| CONSUMER SERVICES | 54.90 | 17.65 | 41.78 | 27.45 |
| INDUSTRIAL PRODUCTS | 60.98 | 14.63 | 54.67 | 24.39 |
| INDUSTRIAL SERVICES | 63.89 | 12.50 | 56.33 | 23.61 |
| OFFICE PRODUCTS | 60.00 | 17.14 | 39.17 | 22.86 |
| OFFICE SERVICES | 60.00 | 13.33 | 39.17 | 26.67 |
| **TYPE OF BUYER** | | | | |
| CONSUMERS | 53.62 | 14.49 | 42.10 | 31.88 |
| DISTRIBUTORS | 56.82 | 12.50 | 45.91 | 30.68 |
| INDUSTRY | 62.50 | 14.06 | 51.78 | 23.44 |
| RETAILERS | 49.30 | 12.68 | 51.78 | 38.03 |
| **INDUSTRY** | | | | |
| AMUSEMENT & RECREATION SERVICES | 100.00 | 0.00 | 0.00 | 0.00 |
| BUSINESS SERVICES | 64.10 | 5.13 | 55.50 | 30.77 |
| ELECTRONICS | 85.71 | 14.29 | 10.00 | 0.00 |
| FABRICATED METALS | 50.00 | 0.00 | 0.00 | 50.00 |
| FOOD PRODUCTS | 50.00 | 0.00 | 0.00 | 50.00 |
| FURNITURE AND FIXTURES | 0.00 | 0.00 | 0.00 | 100.00 |
| HEALTH SERVICES | 80.00 | 0.00 | 0.00 | 20.00 |
| HOLDING & OTHER INVESTMENT OFFICES | 33.33 | 0.00 | 0.00 | 66.67 |
| HOTELS & OTHER LODGING PLACES | 100.00 | 0.00 | 0.00 | 0.00 |
| INSTRUMENTS | 80.00 | 20.00 | 90.00 | 0.00 |
| INSURANCE | 20.00 | 0.00 | 0.00 | 80.00 |
| MACHINERY | 75.00 | 0.00 | 0.00 | 25.00 |
| MANUFACTURING | 50.00 | 0.00 | 0.00 | 50.00 |
| OFFICE EQUIPMENT | 57.14 | 28.57 | 50.00 | 14.29 |
| PHARMACEUTICALS | 83.33 | 0.00 | 0.00 | 16.67 |
| PRINTING AND PUBLISHING | 88.89 | 11.11 | 30.00 | 0.00 |
| RETAIL | 25.00 | 41.67 | 32.00 | 33.33 |
| WHOLESALE (CONSUMER GOODS) | 62.50 | 0.00 | 0.00 | 37.50 |
| WHOLESALE (INDUSTRIAL GOODS) | 58.82 | 11.76 | 60.00 | 29.41 |
| **OVERALL** | **58.10%** | **12.29%** | **51.91%** | **29.61%** |

# FIGURE 75

**PERCENTAGE OF COMPANIES THAT PAY
FOR ALL OR PART OF EXPENSE ITEMS
OTHER TRAVEL REIMBURSEMENT**

|  | ALL | PART | PART<br>% PAID | NONE |
|---|---|---|---|---|
| **COMPANY SIZE** | | | | |
| UNDER $5 MILLION | 72.15% | 5.02% | 40.00% | 22.83% |
| **PRODUCT OR SERVICE** | | | | |
| CONSUMER PRODUCTS | 59.42 | 7.25 | 45.00 | 33.33 |
| CONSUMER SERVICES | 75.76 | 10.61 | 46.43 | 13.64 |
| INDUSTRIAL PRODUCTS | 74.00 | 5.00 | 41.00 | 21.00 |
| INDUSTRIAL SERVICES | 77.66 | 6.38 | 37.50 | 15.96 |
| OFFICE PRODUCTS | 69.77 | 9.30 | 37.50 | 20.93 |
| OFFICE SERVICES | 69.49 | 10.17 | 40.00 | 20.34 |
| **TYPE OF BUYER** | | | | |
| CONSUMERS | 68.60 | 6.98 | 52.50 | 24.42 |
| DISTRIBUTORS | 70.48 | 4.76 | 38.00 | 24.76 |
| INDUSTRY | 77.71 | 5.42 | 33.33 | 16.87 |
| RETAILERS | 63.75 | 8.75 | 35.71 | 27.50 |
| **INDUSTRY** | | | | |
| AMUSEMENT & RECREATION SERVICES | 100.00 | 0.00 | 0.00 | 0.00 |
| BUSINESS SERVICES | 77.08 | 12.50 | 52.50 | 10.42 |
| ELECTRONICS | 88.89 | 0.00 | 0.00 | 11.11 |
| FABRICATED METALS | 75.00 | 0.00 | 0.00 | 25.00 |
| FOOD PRODUCTS | 50.00 | 0.00 | 0.00 | 50.00 |
| FURNITURE AND FIXTURES | 33.33 | 0.00 | 0.00 | 66.67 |
| HEALTH SERVICES | 50.00 | 0.00 | 0.00 | 50.00 |
| HOLDING & OTHER INVESTMENT OFFICES | 50.00 | 0.00 | 0.00 | 50.00 |
| HOTELS & OTHER LODGING PLACES | 100.00 | 0.00 | 0.00 | 0.00 |
| INSTRUMENTS | 66.67 | 0.00 | 0.00 | 33.33 |
| INSURANCE | 60.00 | 0.00 | 0.00 | 40.00 |
| MACHINERY | 75.00 | 0.00 | 0.00 | 25.00 |
| MANUFACTURING | 80.00 | 0.00 | 0.00 | 20.00 |
| OFFICE EQUIPMENT | 70.00 | 10.00 | 25.00 | 20.00 |
| PHARMACEUTICALS | 100.00 | 0.00 | 0.00 | 0.00 |
| PRINTING AND PUBLISHING | 60.00 | 10.00 | 40.00 | 30.00 |
| RETAIL | 66.67 | 0.00 | 0.00 | 33.33 |
| WHOLESALE (CONSUMER GOODS) | 55.56 | 11.11 | 10.00 | 33.33 |
| WHOLESALE (INDUSTRIAL GOODS) | 72.73 | 0.00 | 0.00 | 27.27 |
| **OVERALL** | **72.15%** | **5.02%** | **40.00%** | **22.83%** |

# FIGURE 76

**PERCENTAGE OF COMPANIES THAT PAY
FOR ALL OR PART OF EXPENSE ITEMS
LODGING**

|  | ALL | PART | PART<br>% PAID | NONE |
|---|---|---|---|---|
| **COMPANY SIZE** | | | | |
| UNDER $5 MILLION | 79.46% | 3.12% | 60.71% | 17.41% |
| **PRODUCT OR SERVICE** | | | | |
| CONSUMER PRODUCTS | 63.38 | 4.23 | 73.33 | 32.39 |
| CONSUMER SERVICES | 79.41 | 5.88 | 67.50 | 14.71 |
| INDUSTRIAL PRODUCTS | 82.29 | 2.08 | 80.00 | 15.62 |
| INDUSTRIAL SERVICES | 87.10 | 2.15 | 65.00 | 10.75 |
| OFFICE PRODUCTS | 68.29 | 4.88 | 52.50 | 26.83 |
| OFFICE SERVICES | 75.44 | 5.26 | 51.67 | 19.30 |
| **TYPE OF BUYER** | | | | |
| CONSUMERS | 75.00 | 4.55 | 67.50 | 20.45 |
| DISTRIBUTORS | 77.57 | 2.80 | 61.67 | 19.63 |
| INDUSTRY | 85.03 | 2.99 | 57.00 | 11.98 |
| RETAILERS | 73.08 | 3.85 | 51.67 | 23.08 |
| **INDUSTRY** | | | | |
| AMUSEMENT & RECREATION SERVICES | 100.00 | 0.00 | 0.00 | 0.00 |
| BUSINESS SERVICES | 87.23 | 8.51 | 67.50 | 4.26 |
| ELECTRONICS | 100.00 | 0.00 | 0.00 | 0.00 |
| FABRICATED METALS | 100.00 | 0.00 | 0.00 | 0.00 |
| FOOD PRODUCTS | 50.00 | 0.00 | 0.00 | 50.00 |
| FURNITURE AND FIXTURES | 33.33 | 0.00 | 0.00 | 66.67 |
| HEALTH SERVICES | 50.00 | 0.00 | 0.00 | 50.00 |
| HOLDING & OTHER INVESTMENT OFFICES | 60.00 | 0.00 | 0.00 | 40.00 |
| HOTELS & OTHER LODGING PLACES | 100.00 | 0.00 | 0.00 | 0.00 |
| INSTRUMENTS | 100.00 | 0.00 | 0.00 | 0.00 |
| INSURANCE | 71.43 | 0.00 | 0.00 | 28.57 |
| MACHINERY | 75.00 | 0.00 | 0.00 | 25.00 |
| MANUFACTURING | 80.00 | 0.00 | 0.00 | 20.00 |
| OFFICE EQUIPMENT | 77.78 | 11.11 | 25.00 | 11.11 |
| PHARMACEUTICALS | 100.00 | 0.00 | 0.00 | 0.00 |
| PRINTING AND PUBLISHING | 66.67 | 0.00 | 0.00 | 33.33 |
| RETAIL | 83.33 | 0.00 | 0.00 | 16.67 |
| WHOLESALE (CONSUMER GOODS) | 70.00 | 0.00 | 0.00 | 30.00 |
| WHOLESALE (INDUSTRIAL GOODS) | 81.82 | 4.55 | 50.00 | 13.64 |
| **OVERALL** | **79.46%** | **3.12%** | **60.71%** | **17.41%** |

# FIGURE 77

| | ALL | PART | PART % PAID | NONE |
|---|---|---|---|---|
| **COMPANY SIZE** | | | | |
| UNDER $5 MILLION | 81.82% | 5.19% | 54.17% | 12.99% |
| **PRODUCT OR SERVICE** | | | | |
| CONSUMER PRODUCTS | 72.97 | 8.11 | 38.33 | 18.92 |
| CONSUMER SERVICES | 85.92 | 2.82 | 50.00 | 11.27 |
| INDUSTRIAL PRODUCTS | 83.84 | 7.07 | 56.43 | 9.09 |
| INDUSTRIAL SERVICES | 90.62 | 3.12 | 60.00 | 6.25 |
| OFFICE PRODUCTS | 80.49 | 4.88 | 50.00 | 14.63 |
| OFFICE SERVICES | 82.14 | 5.36 | 61.67 | 12.50 |
| **TYPE OF BUYER** | | | | |
| CONSUMERS | 78.02 | 3.30 | 36.67 | 18.68 |
| DISTRIBUTORS | 81.82 | 6.36 | 52.86 | 11.82 |
| INDUSTRY | 87.21 | 5.81 | 58.00 | 6.98 |
| RETAILERS | 80.49 | 4.88 | 58.75 | 14.63 |
| **INDUSTRY** | | | | |
| AMUSEMENT & RECREATION SERVICES | 75.00 | 0.00 | 0.00 | 25.00 |
| BUSINESS SERVICES | 91.67 | 2.08 | 50.00 | 6.25 |
| ELECTRONICS | 100.00 | 0.00 | 0.00 | 0.00 |
| FABRICATED METALS | 100.00 | 0.00 | 0.00 | 0.00 |
| FOOD PRODUCTS | 50.00 | 0.00 | 0.00 | 50.00 |
| FURNITURE AND FIXTURES | 25.00 | 25.00 | 50.00 | 50.00 |
| HEALTH SERVICES | 66.67 | 16.67 | 20.00 | 16.67 |
| HOLDING & OTHER INVESTMENT OFFICES | 50.00 | 25.00 | 85.00 | 25.00 |
| HOTELS & OTHER LODGING PLACES | 100.00 | 0.00 | 0.00 | 0.00 |
| INSTRUMENTS | 100.00 | 0.00 | 0.00 | 0.00 |
| INSURANCE | 57.14 | 0.00 | 0.00 | 42.86 |
| MACHINERY | 75.00 | 25.00 | 50.00 | 0.00 |
| MANUFACTURING | 80.00 | 0.00 | 0.00 | 20.00 |
| OFFICE EQUIPMENT | 88.89 | 0.00 | 0.00 | 11.11 |
| PHARMACEUTICALS | 87.50 | 12.50 | 10.00 | 0.00 |
| PRINTING AND PUBLISHING | 91.67 | 8.33 | 50.00 | 0.00 |
| RETAIL | 85.71 | 0.00 | 0.00 | 14.29 |
| WHOLESALE (CONSUMER GOODS) | 90.91 | 0.00 | 0.00 | 9.09 |
| WHOLESALE (INDUSTRIAL GOODS) | 76.00 | 8.00 | 50.00 | 16.00 |
| **OVERALL** | **81.82%** | **5.19%** | **54.17%** | **12.99%** |

# FIGURE 78

**Percentage of Companies That Pay
for All or Part of Expense Items
Entertainment**

| | ALL | PART | PART % PAID | NONE |
|---|---|---|---|---|
| **COMPANY SIZE** | | | | |
| UNDER $5 MILLION | 69.55% | 9.09% | 40.50% | 21.36% |
| **PRODUCT OR SERVICE** | | | | |
| CONSUMER PRODUCTS | 58.67 | 13.33 | 36.50 | 28.00 |
| CONSUMER SERVICES | 63.38 | 14.08 | 46.00 | 22.54 |
| INDUSTRIAL PRODUCTS | 80.00 | 6.32 | 39.17 | 13.68 |
| INDUSTRIAL SERVICES | 76.84 | 8.42 | 46.88 | 14.74 |
| OFFICE PRODUCTS | 65.12 | 11.63 | 39.00 | 23.26 |
| OFFICE SERVICES | 66.10 | 13.56 | 48.12 | 20.34 |
| **TYPE OF BUYER** | | | | |
| CONSUMERS | 62.92 | 11.24 | 40.00 | 25.84 |
| DISTRIBUTORS | 67.62 | 10.48 | 43.18 | 21.90 |
| INDUSTRY | 75.76 | 9.09 | 38.00 | 15.15 |
| RETAILERS | 63.41 | 9.76 | 40.00 | 26.83 |
| **INDUSTRY** | | | | |
| AMUSEMENT & RECREATION SERVICES | 75.00 | 25.00 | 75.00 | 0.00 |
| BUSINESS SERVICES | 75.00 | 16.67 | 56.25 | 8.33 |
| ELECTRONICS | 66.67 | 33.33 | 15.00 | 0.00 |
| FABRICATED METALS | 100.00 | 0.00 | 0.00 | 0.00 |
| FOOD PRODUCTS | 40.00 | 0.00 | 0.00 | 60.00 |
| FURNITURE AND FIXTURES | 33.33 | 0.00 | 0.00 | 66.67 |
| HEALTH SERVICES | 50.00 | 16.67 | 15.00 | 33.33 |
| HOLDING & OTHER INVESTMENT OFFICES | 50.00 | 0.00 | 0.00 | 50.00 |
| HOTELS & OTHER LODGING PLACES | 100.00 | 0.00 | 0.00 | 0.00 |
| INSTRUMENTS | 100.00 | 0.00 | 0.00 | 0.00 |
| INSURANCE | 14.29 | 0.00 | 0.00 | 85.71 |
| MACHINERY | 75.00 | 0.00 | 0.00 | 25.00 |
| MANUFACTURING | 80.00 | 0.00 | 0.00 | 20.00 |
| OFFICE EQUIPMENT | 62.50 | 12.50 | 25.00 | 25.00 |
| PHARMACEUTICALS | 87.50 | 0.00 | 0.00 | 12.50 |
| PRINTING AND PUBLISHING | 90.00 | 10.00 | 20.00 | 0.00 |
| RETAIL | 64.29 | 0.00 | 0.00 | 35.71 |
| WHOLESALE (CONSUMER GOODS) | 70.00 | 0.00 | 0.00 | 30.00 |
| WHOLESALE (INDUSTRIAL GOODS) | 68.18 | 9.09 | 50.00 | 22.73 |
| **OVERALL** | **69.55%** | **9.09%** | **40.50%** | **21.36%** |

# FIGURE 79

**PERCENTAGE OF COMPANIES THAT PAY
FOR ALL OR PART OF EXPENSE ITEMS
PRODUCT SAMPLES**

|  | ALL | PART | PART<br>% PAID | NONE |
|---|---|---|---|---|
| **COMPANY SIZE** | | | | |
| UNDER $5 MILLION | 70.88% | 4.40% | 41.88% | 24.73% |
| **PRODUCT OR SERVICE** | | | | |
| CONSUMER PRODUCTS | 64.18 | 7.46 | 37.00 | 28.36 |
| CONSUMER SERVICES | 72.00 | 6.00 | 28.33 | 22.00 |
| INDUSTRIAL PRODUCTS | 78.82 | 3.53 | 50.00 | 17.65 |
| INDUSTRIAL SERVICES | 80.60 | 0.00 | 0.00 | 19.40 |
| OFFICE PRODUCTS | 53.33 | 6.67 | 35.00 | 40.00 |
| OFFICE SERVICES | 56.41 | 2.56 | 20.00 | 41.03 |
| **TYPE OF BUYER** | | | | |
| CONSUMERS | 62.12 | 7.58 | 37.00 | 30.30 |
| DISTRIBUTORS | 68.89 | 4.44 | 33.75 | 26.67 |
| INDUSTRY | 77.44 | 5.26 | 40.71 | 17.29 |
| RETAILERS | 65.62 | 3.12 | 35.00 | 31.25 |
| **INDUSTRY** | | | | |
| AMUSEMENT & RECREATION SERVICES | 50.00 | 0.00 | 0.00 | 50.00 |
| BUSINESS SERVICES | 66.67 | 6.67 | 50.00 | 26.67 |
| ELECTRONICS | 66.67 | 16.67 | 15.00 | 16.67 |
| FABRICATED METALS | 75.00 | 0.00 | 0.00 | 25.00 |
| FOOD PRODUCTS | 50.00 | 0.00 | 0.00 | 50.00 |
| FURNITURE AND FIXTURES | 75.00 | 0.00 | 0.00 | 25.00 |
| HEALTH SERVICES | 40.00 | 0.00 | 0.00 | 60.00 |
| HOLDING & OTHER INVESTMENT OFFICES | 0.00 | 0.00 | 0.00 | 100.00 |
| HOTELS & OTHER LODGING PLACES | 100.00 | 0.00 | 0.00 | 0.00 |
| INSTRUMENTS | 100.00 | 0.00 | 0.00 | 0.00 |
| INSURANCE | 42.86 | 0.00 | 0.00 | 57.14 |
| MACHINERY | 100.00 | 0.00 | 0.00 | 0.00 |
| MANUFACTURING | 100.00 | 0.00 | 0.00 | 0.00 |
| OFFICE EQUIPMENT | 40.00 | 0.00 | 0.00 | 60.00 |
| PHARMACEUTICALS | 87.50 | 0.00 | 0.00 | 12.50 |
| PRINTING AND PUBLISHING | 62.50 | 12.50 | 20.00 | 25.00 |
| RETAIL | 69.23 | 7.69 | 50.00 | 23.08 |
| WHOLESALE (CONSUMER GOODS) | 80.00 | 10.00 | 50.00 | 10.00 |
| WHOLESALE (INDUSTRIAL GOODS) | 83.33 | 8.33 | 50.00 | 8.33 |
| **OVERALL** | **70.88%** | **4.40%** | **41.88%** | **24.73%** |

# FIGURE 80

**PERCENTAGE OF COMPANIES THAT PAY**
**FOR ALL OR PART OF EXPENSE ITEMS**
**LOCAL PROMOTIONS**

| | ALL | PART | PART<br>% PAID | NONE |
|---|---|---|---|---|
| **COMPANY SIZE** | | | | |
| UNDER $5 MILLION | 66.30% | 7.73% | 50.71% | 26.52% |
| **PRODUCT OR SERVICE** | | | | |
| CONSUMER PRODUCTS | 61.76 | 10.29 | 40.71 | 27.94 |
| CONSUMER SERVICES | 69.49 | 11.86 | 40.71 | 20.34 |
| INDUSTRIAL PRODUCTS | 64.38 | 10.96 | 58.75 | 24.66 |
| INDUSTRIAL SERVICES | 73.91 | 7.25 | 54.00 | 20.29 |
| OFFICE PRODUCTS | 54.55 | 9.09 | 31.67 | 36.36 |
| OFFICE SERVICES | 59.57 | 6.38 | 31.67 | 34.04 |
| **TYPE OF BUYER** | | | | |
| CONSUMERS | 66.67 | 6.67 | 37.00 | 28.00 |
| DISTRIBUTORS | 67.05 | 7.95 | 43.57 | 26.14 |
| INDUSTRY | 68.25 | 10.32 | 50.77 | 22.22 |
| RETAILERS | 64.71 | 5.88 | 36.25 | 29.41 |
| **INDUSTRY** | | | | |
| AMUSEMENT & RECREATION SERVICES | 100.00 | 0.00 | 0.00 | 0.00 |
| BUSINESS SERVICES | 68.57 | 8.57 | 38.33 | 22.86 |
| ELECTRONICS | 71.43 | 14.29 | 10.00 | 14.29 |
| FABRICATED METALS | 100.00 | 0.00 | 0.00 | 33.33 |
| FOOD PRODUCTS | 50.00 | 0.00 | 0.00 | 50.00 |
| FURNITURE AND FIXTURES | 75.00 | 0.00 | 0.00 | 25.00 |
| HEALTH SERVICES | 50.00 | 0.00 | 0.00 | 50.00 |
| HOLDING & OTHER INVESTMENT OFFICES | 33.33 | 0.00 | 0.00 | 66.67 |
| HOTELS & OTHER LODGING PLACES | 100.00 | 0.00 | 0.00 | 0.00 |
| INSTRUMENTS | 100.00 | 0.00 | 0.00 | 0.00 |
| INSURANCE | 14.29 | 0.00 | 0.00 | 85.71 |
| MACHINERY | 100.00 | 0.00 | 0.00 | 0.00 |
| MANUFACTURING | 100.00 | 0.00 | 0.00 | 0.00 |
| OFFICE EQUIPMENT | 28.57 | 14.29 | 50.00 | 57.14 |
| PHARMACEUTICALS | 100.00 | 0.00 | 0.00 | 0.00 |
| PRINTING AND PUBLISHING | 57.14 | 28.57 | 40.00 | 14.29 |
| RETAIL | 73.33 | 6.67 | 80.00 | 20.00 |
| WHOLESALE (CONSUMER GOODS) | 42.86 | 14.29 | 50.00 | 42.86 |
| WHOLESALE (INDUSTRIAL GOODS) | 71.43 | 9.52 | 50.00 | 19.05 |
| **OVERALL** | **66.30%** | **7.73%** | **50.71%** | **26.52%** |

# FIGURE 81

**PERCENTAGE OF COMPANIES THAT PAY**
**FOR ALL OR PART OF EXPENSE ITEMS**
**OFFICE AND/OR CLERICAL**

| | ALL | PART | PART % PAID | NONE |
|---|---|---|---|---|
| **COMPANY SIZE** | | | | |
| UNDER $5 MILLION | 77.78% | 3.38% | 39.29% | 18.84% |
| **PRODUCT OR SERVICE** | | | | |
| CONSUMER PRODUCTS | 76.39 | 2.78 | 42.50 | 20.83 |
| CONSUMER SERVICES | 84.85 | 3.03 | 62.50 | 12.12 |
| INDUSTRIAL PRODUCTS | 80.68 | 2.27 | 35.00 | 17.05 |
| INDUSTRIAL SERVICES | 84.52 | 2.38 | 62.50 | 13.10 |
| OFFICE PRODUCTS | 75.00 | 0.00 | 0.00 | 25.00 |
| OFFICE SERVICES | 75.47 | 1.89 | 75.00 | 22.64 |
| **TYPE OF BUYER** | | | | |
| CONSUMERS | 80.72 | 3.61 | 45.00 | 15.66 |
| DISTRIBUTORS | 74.00 | 4.00 | 41.25 | 22.00 |
| INDUSTRY | 83.55 | 2.63 | 48.75 | 13.82 |
| RETAILERS | 72.00 | 4.00 | 48.33 | 24.00 |
| **INDUSTRY** | | | | |
| AMUSEMENT & RECREATION SERVICES | 100.00 | 0.00 | 0.00 | 0.00 |
| BUSINESS SERVICES | 77.27 | 4.55 | 50.00 | 18.18 |
| ELECTRONICS | 75.00 | 0.00 | 0.00 | 25.00 |
| FABRICATED METALS | 75.00 | 0.00 | 0.00 | 25.00 |
| FOOD PRODUCTS | 50.00 | 0.00 | 0.00 | 50.00 |
| FURNITURE AND FIXTURES | 50.00 | 25.00 | 20.00 | 25.00 |
| HEALTH SERVICES | 83.33 | 0.00 | 0.00 | 16.67 |
| HOLDING & OTHER INVESTMENT OFFICES | 100.00 | 0.00 | 0.00 | 0.00 |
| HOTELS & OTHER LODGING PLACES | 100.00 | 0.00 | 0.00 | 0.00 |
| INSTRUMENTS | 100.00 | 0.00 | 0.00 | 0.00 |
| INSURANCE | 71.43 | 14.29 | 10.00 | 14.29 |
| MACHINERY | 100.00 | 0.00 | 0.00 | 0.00 |
| MANUFACTURING | 83.33 | 0.00 | 0.00 | 16.67 |
| OFFICE EQUIPMENT | 55.56 | 11.11 | 50.00 | 33.33 |
| PHARMACEUTICALS | 80.00 | 0.00 | 0.00 | 20.00 |
| PRINTING AND PUBLISHING | 77.78 | 11.11 | 75.00 | 11.11 |
| RETAIL | 80.00 | 0.00 | 0.00 | 20.00 |
| WHOLESALE (CONSUMER GOODS) | 81.82 | 0.00 | 0.00 | 18.18 |
| WHOLESALE (INDUSTRIAL GOODS) | 81.82 | 0.00 | 0.00 | 18.18 |
| **OVERALL** | **77.78%** | **3.38%** | **39.29%** | **18.84%** |

# FIGURE 82

PERCENTAGE OF COMPANIES THAT PAY
FOR ALL OR PART OF EXPENSE ITEMS
HOME PHOTOCOPIER

|  | ALL | PART | PART<br>% PAID | NONE |
|---|---|---|---|---|
| **COMPANY SIZE** | | | | |
| UNDER $5 MILLION | 30.33% | 4.10% | 50.00% | 65.57% |
| **PRODUCT OR SERVICE** | | | | |
| CONSUMER PRODUCTS | 29.79 | 4.26 | 45.00 | 65.96 |
| CONSUMER SERVICES | 33.33 | 8.33 | 53.33 | 58.33 |
| INDUSTRIAL PRODUCTS | 27.66 | 4.26 | 45.00 | 68.09 |
| INDUSTRIAL SERVICES | 30.00 | 5.00 | 50.00 | 65.00 |
| OFFICE PRODUCTS | 20.83 | 4.17 | 50.00 | 75.00 |
| OFFICE SERVICES | 25.00 | 3.12 | 50.00 | 71.88 |
| **TYPE OF BUYER** | | | | |
| CONSUMERS | 27.08 | 8.33 | 50.00 | 64.58 |
| DISTRIBUTORS | 34.38 | 3.12 | 50.00 | 62.50 |
| INDUSTRY | 31.71 | 4.88 | 50.00 | 63.41 |
| RETAILERS | 31.11 | 2.22 | 50.00 | 66.67 |
| **INDUSTRY** | | | | |
| AMUSEMENT & RECREATION SERVICES | 0.00 | 0.00 | 0.00 | 100.00 |
| BUSINESS SERVICES | 30.00 | 5.00 | 50.00 | 65.00 |
| ELECTRONICS | 33.33 | 0.00 | 0.00 | 66.67 |
| FABRICATED METALS | 33.33 | 0.00 | 0.00 | 66.67 |
| FOOD PRODUCTS | 16.67 | 0.00 | 0.00 | 83.33 |
| FURNITURE AND FIXTURES | 0.00 | 0.00 | 0.00 | 100.00 |
| HEALTH SERVICES | 0.00 | 0.00 | 0.00 | 100.00 |
| HOLDING & OTHER INVESTMENT OFFICES | 33.33 | 0.00 | 0.00 | 66.67 |
| HOTELS & OTHER LODGING PLACES | 100.00 | 0.00 | 0.00 | 0.00 |
| INSTRUMENTS | 100.00 | 0.00 | 0.00 | 0.00 |
| INSURANCE | 25.00 | 12.50 | 60.00 | 62.50 |
| MANUFACTURING | 66.67 | 0.00 | 0.00 | 33.33 |
| OFFICE EQUIPMENT | 0.00 | 0.00 | 0.00 | 100.00 |
| PHARMACEUTICALS | 75.00 | 0.00 | 0.00 | 25.00 |
| PRINTING AND PUBLISHING | 20.00 | 20.00 | 50.00 | 60.00 |
| RETAIL | 33.33 | 0.00 | 0.00 | 66.67 |
| WHOLESALE (CONSUMER GOODS) | 28.57 | 0.00 | 0.00 | 71.43 |
| WHOLESALE (INDUSTRIAL GOODS) | 36.36 | 0.00 | 0.00 | 63.64 |
| **OVERALL** | **30.33%** | **4.10%** | **50.00%** | **65.57%** |

# FIGURE 83

PERCENTAGE OF COMPANIES THAT PAY
FOR ALL OR PART OF EXPENSE ITEMS
HOME FAX MACHINE

| | ALL | PART | PART<br>% PAID | NONE |
|---|---|---|---|---|
| **COMPANY SIZE** | | | | |
| UNDER $5 MILLION | 39.10% | 3.76% | 40.00% | 57.14% |
| **PRODUCT OR SERVICE** | | | | |
| CONSUMER PRODUCTS | 33.33 | 3.92 | 55.00 | 62.75 |
| CONSUMER SERVICES | 35.14 | 8.11 | 40.00 | 56.76 |
| INDUSTRIAL PRODUCTS | 45.45 | 3.64 | 40.00 | 50.91 |
| INDUSTRIAL SERVICES | 43.18 | 2.27 | 60.00 | 54.55 |
| OFFICE PRODUCTS | 38.46 | 3.85 | 50.00 | 57.69 |
| OFFICE SERVICES | 38.24 | 2.94 | 50.00 | 58.82 |
| **TYPE OF BUYER** | | | | |
| CONSUMERS | 29.17 | 8.33 | 45.00 | 62.50 |
| DISTRIBUTORS | 40.58 | 2.90 | 35.00 | 56.52 |
| INDUSTRY | 46.15 | 3.30 | 43.33 | 50.55 |
| RETAILERS | 31.25 | 2.08 | 50.00 | 66.67 |
| **INDUSTRY** | | | | |
| AMUSEMENT & RECREATION SERVICES | 0.00 | 0.00 | 0.00 | 100.00 |
| BUSINESS SERVICES | 35.00 | 5.00 | 50.00 | 60.00 |
| ELECTRONICS | 50.00 | 0.00 | 0.00 | 50.00 |
| FABRICATED METALS | 33.33 | 0.00 | 0.00 | 66.67 |
| FOOD PRODUCTS | 16.67 | 0.00 | 0.00 | 83.33 |
| FURNITURE AND FIXTURES | 0.00 | 0.00 | 0.00 | 100.00 |
| HEALTH SERVICES | 0.00 | 0.00 | 0.00 | 100.00 |
| HOLDING & OTHER INVESTMENT OFFICES | 33.33 | 0.00 | 0.00 | 66.67 |
| HOTELS & OTHER LODGING PLACES | 100.00 | 0.00 | 0.00 | 0.00 |
| INSTRUMENTS | 100.00 | 0.00 | 0.00 | 0.00 |
| INSURANCE | 16.67 | 0.00 | 0.00 | 83.33 |
| MANUFACTURING | 33.33 | 0.00 | 0.00 | 66.67 |
| OFFICE EQUIPMENT | 66.67 | 0.00 | 0.00 | 33.33 |
| PHARMACEUTICALS | 80.00 | 0.00 | 0.00 | 20.00 |
| PRINTING AND PUBLISHING | 25.00 | 25.00 | 50.00 | 50.00 |
| RETAIL | 20.00 | 10.00 | 20.00 | 70.00 |
| WHOLESALE (CONSUMER GOODS) | 37.50 | 0.00 | 0.00 | 62.50 |
| WHOLESALE (INDUSTRIAL GOODS) | 50.00 | 0.00 | 0.00 | 50.00 |
| **OVERALL** | **39.10%** | **3.76%** | **40.00%** | **57.14%** |

# FIGURE 84

PERCENTAGE OF COMPANIES THAT PAY
FOR ALL OR PART OF EXPENSE ITEMS
CAR PHONE

| | ALL | PART | PART<br>% PAID | NONE |
|---|---|---|---|---|
| **COMPANY SIZE** | | | | |
| UNDER $5 MILLION | 43.43% | 16.00% | 45.00% | 40.57% |
| **PRODUCT OR SERVICE** | | | | |
| CONSUMER PRODUCTS | 33.33 | 15.00 | 40.56 | 51.67 |
| CONSUMER SERVICES | 44.64 | 19.64 | 35.91 | 35.71 |
| INDUSTRIAL PRODUCTS | 49.32 | 17.81 | 50.77 | 32.88 |
| INDUSTRIAL SERVICES | 56.58 | 22.37 | 46.76 | 21.05 |
| OFFICE PRODUCTS | 37.14 | 17.14 | 39.17 | 45.71 |
| OFFICE SERVICES | 38.78 | 22.45 | 39.09 | 38.78 |
| **TYPE OF BUYER** | | | | |
| CONSUMERS | 38.03 | 19.72 | 41.07 | 42.25 |
| DISTRIBUTORS | 41.38 | 17.24 | 50.67 | 41.38 |
| INDUSTRY | 50.40 | 17.60 | 47.05 | 32.00 |
| RETAILERS | 38.24 | 19.12 | 48.46 | 42.65 |
| **INDUSTRY** | | | | |
| AMUSEMENT & RECREATION SERVICES | 66.67 | 0.00 | 0.00 | 33.33 |
| BUSINESS SERVICES | 45.95 | 24.32 | 42.78 | 29.73 |
| ELECTRONICS | 28.57 | 14.29 | 50.00 | 57.14 |
| FABRICATED METALS | 33.33 | 0.00 | 0.00 | 66.67 |
| FOOD PRODUCTS | 33.33 | 0.00 | 0.00 | 66.67 |
| FURNITURE AND FIXTURES | 0.00 | 33.33 | 25.00 | 66.67 |
| HEALTH SERVICES | 50.00 | 0.00 | 0.00 | 50.00 |
| HOLDING & OTHER INVESTMENT OFFICES | 33.33 | 0.00 | 0.00 | 66.67 |
| HOTELS & OTHER LODGING PLACES | 100.00 | 0.00 | 0.00 | 0.00 |
| INSTRUMENTS | 100.00 | 0.00 | 0.00 | 0.00 |
| INSURANCE | 42.86 | 0.00 | 0.00 | 57.14 |
| MACHINERY | 66.67 | 33.33 | 50.00 | 0.00 |
| MANUFACTURING | 0.00 | 33.33 | 75.00 | 66.67 |
| OFFICE EQUIPMENT | 0.00 | 16.67 | 50.00 | 83.33 |
| PHARMACEUTICALS | 40.00 | 40.00 | 37.50 | 20.00 |
| PRINTING AND PUBLISHING | 75.00 | 12.50 | 30.00 | 12.50 |
| RETAIL | 30.00 | 10.00 | 20.00 | 60.00 |
| WHOLESALE (CONSUMER GOODS) | 55.56 | 0.00 | 0.00 | 44.44 |
| WHOLESALE (INDUSTRIAL GOODS) | 50.00 | 11.11 | 37.50 | 38.89 |
| **OVERALL** | **43.43%** | **16.00%** | **45.00%** | **40.57%** |

## FIGURE 85

| | ALL | PART | PART<br>% PAID | NONE |
|---|---|---|---|---|
| **COMPANY SIZE** | | | | |
| UNDER $5 MILLION | 42.96% | 3.52% | 57.00% | 53.52% |
| **PRODUCT OR SERVICE** | | | | |
| CONSUMER PRODUCTS | 28.57 | 4.08 | 55.00 | 67.35 |
| CONSUMER SERVICES | 34.15 | 2.44 | 50.00 | 63.41 |
| INDUSTRIAL PRODUCTS | 50.00 | 3.57 | 55.00 | 46.43 |
| INDUSTRIAL SERVICES | 51.85 | 7.41 | 58.75 | 40.74 |
| OFFICE PRODUCTS | 50.00 | 3.33 | 50.00 | 46.67 |
| OFFICE SERVICES | 37.84 | 5.41 | 62.50 | 56.76 |
| **TYPE OF BUYER** | | | | |
| CONSUMERS | 38.60 | 5.26 | 53.33 | 56.14 |
| DISTRIBUTORS | 35.29 | 2.94 | 62.50 | 61.76 |
| INDUSTRY | 49.48 | 4.12 | 58.75 | 46.39 |
| RETAILERS | 25.49 | 5.88 | 58.33 | 68.63 |
| **INDUSTRY** | | | | |
| AMUSEMENT & RECREATION SERVICES | 50.00 | 0.00 | 0.00 | 50.00 |
| BUSINESS SERVICES | 33.33 | 4.17 | 75.00 | 62.50 |
| ELECTRONICS | 57.14 | 0.00 | 0.00 | 42.86 |
| FABRICATED METALS | 25.00 | 0.00 | 0.00 | 75.00 |
| FOOD PRODUCTS | 16.67 | 0.00 | 0.00 | 83.33 |
| FURNITURE AND FIXTURES | 0.00 | 0.00 | 0.00 | 100.00 |
| HEALTH SERVICES | 50.00 | 0.00 | 0.00 | 50.00 |
| HOLDING & OTHER INVESTMENT OFFICES | 0.00 | 0.00 | 0.00 | 100.00 |
| INSTRUMENTS | 100.00 | 0.00 | 0.00 | 0.00 |
| INSURANCE | 42.86 | 0.00 | 0.00 | 57.14 |
| MACHINERY | 100.00 | 0.00 | 0.00 | 0.00 |
| MANUFACTURING | 66.67 | 0.00 | 0.00 | 33.33 |
| OFFICE EQUIPMENT | 71.43 | 0.00 | 0.00 | 28.57 |
| PHARMACEUTICALS | 80.00 | 0.00 | 0.00 | 20.00 |
| PRINTING AND PUBLISHING | 20.00 | 20.00 | 50.00 | 60.00 |
| RETAIL | 12.50 | 0.00 | 0.00 | 87.50 |
| WHOLESALE (CONSUMER GOODS) | 28.57 | 0.00 | 0.00 | 71.43 |
| WHOLESALE (INDUSTRIAL GOODS) | 38.46 | 0.00 | 0.00 | 61.54 |
| **OVERALL** | **42.96%** | **3.52%** | **57.00%** | **53.52%** |

## FIGURE 86 — PERCENTAGE OF COMPANIES OFFERING SPECIFIC BENEFITS

While nearly 100 percent of survey respondents offer their salespeople some sort of medical plan, just 11 percent offer an Employee Stock Option Plan (ESOP). Previous Dartnell studies have commented on the fact that smaller firms traditionally provide fewer benefits in short- and long-term disability, dental, and pension plans, which reduces their overall cost of benefits. Companies with under $5 million in annual sales continue to spend the least on benefits (see Figure 71).

Based on Dartnell's historical data, spending allocations on various benefits have not fluctuated significantly over the years, an indication that companies are comfortable with current spending practices. We expect that companies will continue to allocate the money spent on benefits as they have in the past.

In passing, it's worth noting that smaller companies that want to attract top talent could look to their benefit plans as an area to improve. All too often, the true monetary value of benefit plans is not communicated effectively to employees, including sales personnel. If your benefit plan is something special, make sure your employees know it. Bear in mind that an attractive benefit plan can sometimes compensate for perceived company drawbacks.

# FIGURE 86

**PERCENTAGE OF COMPANIES OFFERING SPECIFIC BENEFITS**

| | GROUP LIFE | L-T DISAB. | MEDICAL PLAN | S-T DISAB. | DENTAL PLAN | PROFIT SHARING | PENSION PLAN | ESOP | THRIFT SAVINGS PLAN |
|---|---|---|---|---|---|---|---|---|---|
| **COMPANY SIZE** | | | | | | | | | |
| UNDER $5 MILLION | 62% | 40% | 90% | 29% | 52% | 41% | 40% | 11% | 12% |
| **PRODUCT OR SERVICE** | | | | | | | | | |
| CONSUMER PRODUCTS | 63 | 44 | 90 | 34 | 50 | 35 | 37 | 18 | 16 |
| CONSUMER SERVICES | 62 | 38 | 86 | 32 | 55 | 39 | 38 | 18 | 18 |
| INDUSTRIAL PRODUCTS | 62 | 33 | 93 | 28 | 50 | 40 | 36 | 8 | 8 |
| INDUSTRIAL SERVICES | 66 | 40 | 89 | 21 | 58 | 47 | 46 | 12 | 16 |
| OFFICE PRODUCTS | 56 | 31 | 89 | 27 | 47 | 42 | 44 | 7 | 13 |
| OFFICE SERVICES | 61 | 39 | 81 | 28 | 43 | 46 | 43 | 9 | 19 |
| **TYPE OF BUYER** | | | | | | | | | |
| CONSUMERS | 62 | 36 | 89 | 31 | 56 | 34 | 36 | 14 | 17 |
| DISTRIBUTORS | 64 | 41 | 91 | 29 | 57 | 39 | 46 | 17 | 15 |
| INDUSTRY | 65 | 42 | 94 | 29 | 54 | 43 | 42 | 8 | 12 |
| RETAILERS | 61 | 39 | 92 | 30 | 53 | 47 | 49 | 17 | 13 |
| **INDUSTRY** | | | | | | | | | |
| AUTO REPAIR, SERVICES, & GARAGES | 67 | 33 | 100 | 0 | 33 | 33 | 0 | 0 | 0 |
| BANKING | 100 | 67 | 100 | 67 | 100 | 67 | 67 | 67 | 33 |
| BUSINESS SERVICES | 72 | 53 | 87 | 23 | 51 | 36 | 49 | 11 | 17 |
| COMMUNICATIONS | 67 | 67 | 67 | 33 | 67 | 67 | 67 | 0 | 0 |
| CONSTRUCTION | 33 | 67 | 100 | 0 | 0 | 33 | 67 | 0 | 0 |
| EDUCATIONAL SERVICES | 67 | 67 | 67 | 0 | 33 | 67 | 33 | 0 | 0 |
| ELECTRONICS | 56 | 11 | 89 | 22 | 56 | 11 | 11 | 11 | 11 |
| FABRICATED METALS | 67 | 67 | 67 | 67 | 67 | 100 | 33 | 0 | 0 |
| FOOD PRODUCTS | 50 | 50 | 100 | 25 | 75 | 50 | 75 | 25 | 0 |
| FURNITURE AND FIXTURES | 67 | 33 | 100 | 0 | 33 | 33 | 33 | 0 | 0 |
| HEALTH SERVICES | 33 | 33 | 67 | 33 | 50 | 17 | 67 | 33 | 17 |
| HOLDING & OTHER INVESTMENT OFFICES | 25 | 0 | 50 | 0 | 25 | 25 | 0 | 0 | 0 |
| HOTELS & OTHER LODGING PLACES | 100 | 0 | 50 | 0 | 0 | 0 | 0 | 0 | 0 |
| INSTRUMENTS | 40 | 40 | 100 | 40 | 40 | 40 | 40 | 0 | 0 |
| INSURANCE | 71 | 43 | 86 | 43 | 71 | 43 | 57 | 14 | 0 |
| MACHINERY | 75 | 50 | 100 | 25 | 50 | 25 | 25 | 0 | 25 |
| MANUFACTURING | 100 | 33 | 100 | 0 | 67 | 67 | 67 | 33 | 0 |
| MOTION PICTURES | 67 | 67 | 100 | 33 | 100 | 33 | 33 | 33 | 0 |
| OFFICE EQUIPMENT | 50 | 20 | 100 | 40 | 40 | 50 | 20 | 20 | 0 |
| PHARMACEUTICALS | 71 | 57 | 86 | 14 | 57 | 57 | 57 | 57 | 0 |
| PRIMARY METAL PRODUCTS | 33 | 33 | 100 | 33 | 0 | 0 | 33 | 0 | 0 |
| PRINTING AND PUBLISHING | 31 | 23 | 92 | 38 | 54 | 38 | 31 | 0 | 23 |
| REAL ESTATE | 0 | 0 | 100 | 0 | 0 | 0 | 0 | 0 | 0 |
| RETAIL | 60 | 47 | 87 | 40 | 60 | 33 | 20 | 7 | 27 |
| WHOLESALE (CONSUMER GOODS) | 30 | 10 | 100 | 20 | 40 | 30 | 10 | 0 | 0 |
| WHOLESALE (INDUSTRIAL GOODS) | 67 | 29 | 96 | 25 | 62 | 50 | 42 | 4 | 8 |
| **OVERALL** | **62%** | **40%** | **90%** | **29%** | **52%** | **41%** | **40%** | **11%** | **12%** |

## FIGURES 87–89 — A LOOK AT CURRENT TRAINING PRACTICES

How effective our salespeople will ultimately be depends in large part on their training. **Figures 87–89** take an in-depth look at the training methods companies use to train their reps, how much time and money is invested in bringing new hires up to speed, and how much time and money is invested in keeping experienced reps as good as they can be.

But while training has always been an important aspect of sales management, the overriding concern of sales force effectiveness is becoming more and more critical in these supercompetitive times.

One area that can have a dramatic effect on how effective a sales force will ultimately be revolves around recruitment and selection of the salespeople — putting the right people in the job to begin with. Over the years, sales managers have debated who makes the best sales candidate: an entry level rep, or a rep with experience. This survey examines this problem and presents its findings in Figure 99.

However, since this is both a training issue and a sales force effectiveness issue, we'll highlight some of the findings here.

When asked what level of experience they preferred in a newly hired sales rep, 42.5 percent of the sales managers of companies with under $5 million in annual sales said they preferred intermediate level reps — those with one to three years of experience. Another 48.4 percent of sales managers said they preferred senior level reps — those with more than three years of experience. Just 9.2 percent of managers said they preferred to hire entry level people. In companies with over $5 million in annual sales, the results and percentages were remarkably similar.

Here are some general observations, reprinted from our full survey covering companies of all sizes:

**Sales managers preferring less than one year of experience** say they want to train new people themselves. A moldable person is best, they say. Another consideration: Lower salaries. Initiative and "being hungry" were other factors deemed important.

**Sales managers preferring one to three years of experience** say it is clear these individuals are good at sales but not stuck in their ways. Hiring trained people also reduces training costs. Additionally, these people have an already existing customer base — a big plus, these managers say. Another plus: These individuals know that they like sales.

**Sales managers preferring more than three years of experience** say they want maturity, stability, and experience in the people they hire. Other considerations: These individuals are aleady trained so the company doesn't have to spend money on training. Furthermore, these individuals can hit the ground running and only have to learn about the company's products. Many sales managers who said they preferred an experienced salesperson also said the company had no sales training program. Another recurring reason for preferring a senior rep: Many companies have specialized product lines or are in highly technical, complex industries.

Selected comments from survey respondents:
**Entry level (less than one year of experience) preferred:**
"They have no preconceived ideas."
"We prefer to train."
"We have a specialized product and need to train from the start on applications."
"We want to train them 'our way' — we don't want their old baggage!"
"We usually hire at entry level and provide on the job training."
"Reasonable salary, willing to be trained, more aggressive at developing new accounts."

"We train them to learn our system."

"We like them to mature with us."

"I look for a sales personality I can train."

**Intermediate level (one to three years of experience) preferred:**

"They need to understand the basics, but we want to train them our way."

"Limited bad habits, yet knows the industry."

"Bad habits can be coached away, but after three years it's very difficult to change people."

"Clear they are good at sales but not stuck in their ways."

"Trainable yet not new."

"Keep salary expenses down and still have some experience."

"We give extensive training."

"Reduces training costs."

"They tend to be more creative with less experience."

"Saves initial training but you have to 'untrain' if they've been selling too long."

"Need the person aware of corporate America and business cultures/climates."

"Established business contacts are important in this business."

"Long selling cycle, account management is very important."

"We need someone with some experience but not so much that we need to pay more for it."

"Must have some sales experience, but if they're too experienced, they are not likely to want to work in a small company."

"Generally have not established a preconceived notion of how to sell — open to change and direction."

"Still can be motivated, open-minded."

"Energetic and conscientious enough to learn and approach customer."

"No experience gives you a difficult task and too much experience is hard to change."

"Just enough experience to allow a quick restructure to fit our sales culture."

"More profitable."

"They have an understanding of the up and down nature of sales."

"Previous experience reduces training and wage requirement is lower."

**Senior level (three or more years of experience) preferred:**

"We prefer selling experience over specific product knowledge. It's quicker to teach product info."

"Less selling skills training required."

"As we will be looking for a fourth person in '97 or '98, we will look for someone with a good track record over at least four or five years."

"Due to specialized nature of health industry, it helps to get staff from the field who have 'relevant' sales in the industry."

"No time to train. It's better to have a following."

"The more experienced, the better qualified."

"Industry experience essential."

"Understanding of technology and customer contacts."

"Need people who will produce now."

"No money for formal training."

"Don't want to babysit."

"Increase in confidence, experience, contacts, and network of businesses that have already done business with the person."

"They can hit the ground running."

"I like as much experience as possible to show that the candidate is dedicated to selling as a career; for we all know, selling isn't for everyone."

"We're a small company and can't afford the time and expense of training a person who can't contribute immediately."

"No internal training program; we 'buy' the best."

"Want highly skilled reps with strong industrial experience and existing customer relationships."

"As a leader in our industry, we want to put the best people in front of the customer."

"Do not want to train."

"Need a solid background — we are not a training ground."

"Too small to hand-hold."

"Highly specialized product line."

## FIGURE 87 — TRAINING METHODS

On-the-job training is the most prevalent method of training salespeople in companies with under $5 million in annual sales and is used by nearly 80 percent of responding companies. Nearly 91 percent of responding companies said they used this method in 1992. Individual instruction, used by 70.7 percent of responding companies, and external seminars, used by 62.7 percent of responding companies, are among the "top three picks" of survey participants. As a training method, "home assignments" are least favored and used by just 18.5 percent of respondents. (Total exceeds 100 percent due to multiple responses.)

A look at our historical data shows a slight decline in companies using some of the training methods tracked by Dartnell studies, as illustrated by the chart below. One explanation for this variation is the number of extremely small companies in this survey that say they do not have the resources to undertake any type of training.

## PERCENTAGE OF COMPANIES WITH UNDER $5 MILLION IN ANNUAL SALES USING THE FOLLOWING TRAINING METHODS

|  | 1990 | 1992 | 1994 |
|---|---|---|---|
| INDIVIDUAL INSTRUCTION | 74.1% | 74.7% | 70% |
| HOME ASSIGNMENTS | 15.6 | 18.4 | 24.3 |
| IN-HOUSE CLASS | 50.0 | 50.6 | 53.6 |
| ON-THE-JOB TRAINING | 90.7 | 82.8 | 82.9 |
| EXTERNAL SEMINARS | 55.6 | 71.3 | 74.3 |
| OTHER | 5.6 | 2.3 | 7.9 |

# FIGURE 87

## TRAINING METHODS — PERCENTAGE OF COMPANIES USING:

| | INDIVIDUAL INSTRUCTION | HOME ASSGNMENTS | IN-HOUSE CLASS | ON THE JOB | EXTERNAL SEMINARS | OTHER |
|---|---|---|---|---|---|---|
| **COMPANY SIZE** | | | | | | |
| UNDER $5 MILLION | 70.7% | 18.5% | 45.0% | 78.7% | 62.7% | 5.6% |
| **PRODUCT OR SERVICE** | | | | | | |
| CONSUMER PRODUCTS | 68.4 | 17.1 | 51.3 | 78.9 | 64.5 | 3.9 |
| CONSUMER SERVICES | 69.6 | 17.7 | 55.7 | 79.7 | 69.6 | 1.3 |
| INDUSTRIAL PRODUCTS | 67.6 | 16.7 | 41.7 | 77.8 | 61.1 | 5.6 |
| INDUSTRIAL SERVICES | 71.8 | 17.5 | 43.7 | 81.6 | 65.0 | 7.8 |
| OFFICE PRODUCTS | 60.4 | 16.7 | 50.0 | 77.1 | 56.2 | 2.1 |
| OFFICE SERVICES | 72.6 | 19.4 | 50.0 | 82.3 | 69.4 | 8.1 |
| **TYPE OF BUYER** | | | | | | |
| CONSUMERS | 72.4 | 14.3 | 57.1 | 78.6 | 64.3 | 2.0 |
| DISTRIBUTORS | 66.7 | 14.9 | 45.6· | 80.7 | 64.0 | 5.3 |
| INDUSTRY | 71.1 | 18.2 | 41.7 | 79.1 | 63.1 | 6.4 |
| RETAILERS | 74.4 | 24.4 | 52.4 | 84.1 | 68.3 | 3.7 |
| **INDUSTRY** | | | | | | |
| AMUSEMENT & RECREATION SERVICES | 25.0 | 25.0 | 50.0 | 50.0 | 75.0 | 0.0 |
| AUTO REPAIR, SERVICES, & GARAGES | 100.0 | 0.0 | 66.7 | 100.0 | 66.7 | 0.0 |
| BANKING | 100.0 | 0.0 | 100.0 | 100.0 | 100.0 | 0.0 |
| BUSINESS SERVICES | 73.1 | 21.2 | 36.5 | 82.7 | 69.2 | 9.6 |
| COMMUNICATIONS | 100.0 | 66.7 | 33.3 | 100.0 | 100.0 | 0.0 |
| CONSTRUCTION | 33.3 | 0.0 | 0.0 | 33.3 | 66.7 | 0.0 |
| EDUCATIONAL SERVICES | 33.3 | 0.0 | 66.7 | 66.7 | 0.0 | 0.0 |
| ELECTRONICS | 75.0 | 25.0 | 50.0 | 75.0 | 62.5 | 0.0 |
| FOOD PRODUCTS | 83.3 | 0.0 | 16.7 | 66.7 | 50.0 | 0.0 |
| FURNITURE AND FIXTURES | 100.0 | 25.0 | 25.0 | 75.0 | 25.0 | 0.0 |
| HEALTH SERVICES | 66.7 | 0.0 | 66.7 | 100.0 | 100.0 | 0.0 |
| HOLDING & OTHER INVESTMENT OFFICES | 60.0 | 20.0 | 40.0 | 20.0 | 60.0 | 0.0 |
| HOTELS & OTHER LODGING PLACES | 50.0 | 0.0 | 50.0 | 50.0 | 100.0 | 0.0 |
| INSTRUMENTS | 80.0 | 20.0 | 40.0 | 100.0 | 40.0 | 0.0 |
| INSURANCE | 66.7 | 22.2 | 66.7 | 66.7 | 77.8 | 0.0 |
| MACHINERY | 75.0 | 25.0 | 0.0 | 100.0 | 25.0 | 0.0 |
| MANUFACTURING | 87.5 | 25.0 | 62.5 | 62.5 | 50.0 | 12.5 |
| OFFICE EQUIPMENT | 63.6 | 27.3 | 63.6 | 72.7 | 54.5 | 18.2 |
| PHARMACEUTICALS | 62.5 | 37.5 | 50.0 | 62.5 | 62.5 | 0.0 |
| PRIMARY METAL PRODUCTS | 0.0 | 0.0 | 50.0 | 100.0 | 0.0 | 0.0 |
| PRINTING AND PUBLISHING | 61.5 | 23.1 | 38.5 | 92.3 | 61.5 | 0.0 |
| REAL ESTATE | 66.7 | 66.7 | 66.7 | 66.7 | 66.7 | 0.0 |
| RETAIL | 81.2 | 0.0 | 56.2 | 87.5 | 50.0 | 0.0 |
| WHOLESALE (CONSUMER GOODS) | 90.9 | 18.2 | 45.5 | 90.9 | 72.7 | 0.0 |
| WHOLESALE (INDUSTRIAL GOODS) | 65.4 | 11.5 | 42.3 | 73.1 | 57.7 | 7.7 |
| **OVERALL** | **70.7%** | **18.5%** | **45.0%** | **78.7%** | **62.7%** | **5.6%** |

## FIGURE 88 — TRAINING NEW HIRES

Companies with under $5 million in annual sales are spending significantly more on training new hires than they did in 1994, but a little less than they spent in 1992. Average spending in smaller companies to train a newly hired sales rep is up 43 percent from 1994 levels, standing now at $5,291 compared with $3,688 in 1994. (See pages 222–223 for data on experience level preferred in newly hired sales reps.)

In 1992, these companies spent $5,530 to train a newly hired sales rep. These fluctuations indicate a renewed commitment to a well-trained sales force and perhaps the realization that cutting costs on training can end up costing more than it saves.

The length of training for new hires in companies with under $5 million in annual sales has increased slightly from 3.3 months in 1994 to 3.5 months in the current survey. This difference does not indicate dramatic changes in this area.

### TRAINING PERIOD AND TRAINING COSTS FOR NEW HIRES 1990–1996

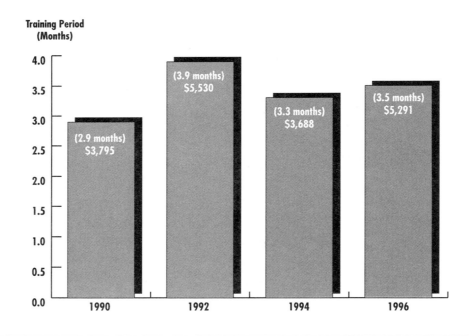

# FIGURE 88

**TRAINING NEW HIRES**
**(AVERAGE OF MEDIAN RANGE)**

| | TRAINING PERIOD FOR NEW HIRES (MONTHS) | COST |
|---|---|---|
| **COMPANY SIZE** | | |
| UNDER $5 MILLION | 3.5 | $5,291.1 |
| **PRODUCT OR SERVICE** | | |
| CONSUMER PRODUCTS | 2.8 | 3,270.4 |
| CONSUMER SERVICES | 3.6 | 4,244.8 |
| INDUSTRIAL PRODUCTS | 4.0 | 6,827.5 |
| INDUSTRIAL SERVICES | 3.9 | 7,765.8 |
| OFFICE PRODUCTS | 2.8 | 4,033.3 |
| OFFICE SERVICES | 2.8 | 4,733.3 |
| **TYPE OF BUYER** | | |
| CONSUMERS | 3.2 | 3,972.2 |
| DISTRIBUTORS | 3.5 | 5,758.1 |
| INDUSTRY | 3.8 | 6,173.4 |
| RETAILERS | 3.8 | 5,128.1 |
| **INDUSTRY** | | |
| AMUSEMENT & RECREATION SERVICES | 5.3 | 4,000.0 |
| BUSINESS SERVICES | 4.2 | 6,750.0 |
| COMMUNICATIONS | 3.3 | 3,416.7 |
| ELECTRONICS | 3.0 | 8,450.0 |
| FABRICATED METALS | 3.7 | 4,666.7 |
| FOOD PRODUCTS | 3.7 | 4,333.3 |
| FURNITURE AND FIXTURES | 3.0 | 6,666.7 |
| HEALTH SERVICES | 6.0 | 5,333.3 |
| HOLDING & OTHER INVESTMENT OFFICES | 3.0 | 2,750.0 |
| INSURANCE | 4.2 | 3,700.0 |
| MACHINERY | 8.5 | 5,500.0 |
| MANUFACTURING | 2.5 | 3,375.0 |
| OFFICE EQUIPMENT | 2.5 | 10,750.0 |
| PHARMACEUTICALS | 1.7 | 6,500.0 |
| PRINTING AND PUBLISHING | 2.5 | 2,200.0 |
| RETAIL | 3.5 | 4,166.7 |
| WHOLESALE (CONSUMER GOODS) | 2.8 | 5,700.0 |
| WHOLESALE (INDUSTRIAL GOODS) | 4.5 | 6,125.0 |
| **OVERALL** | **3.5** | **$5,291.1** |

## FIGURE 89 — TRAINING EXPERIENCED REPS

Experienced sales reps, those with three or more years of experience, are given an average of 35.9 hours of ongoing training per year at a cost of $3,477 per rep. This compares with 35.1 hours of training at a cost of $2,498 per rep in 1994. This year's training dollar figure represents nearly a 39 percent increase over 1994 data. In 1992, experienced reps in companies with under $5 million in annual sales received just 28.4 hours of training per year.

The fact that experienced reps continue to receive increasing amounts of training reflects a continuing commitment on the part of management to provide ongoing learning opportunities for their senior salespeople. Quite simply, companies realize that training is, by and large, an inexpensive way to protect their investments in their sales forces.

Companies with under $5 million in annual sales spend more time on product training (55.6%) than on teaching selling skills (44.2%). It is important to note, however, that selling skills training is an integral part of the experienced rep's training program.

# FIGURE 89

**TRAINING EXPERIENCED REPS**

| | HOURS PER YEAR OF ONGOING TRAINING | TYPE OF TRAINING | | COST |
| | | SELLING SKILLS(%) | PRODUCT(%) | |
|---|---|---|---|---|
| **COMPANY SIZE** | | | | |
| UNDER $5 MILLION | 35.9 | 44.2% | 55.6% | $3,477 |
| **PRODUCT OR SERVICE** | | | | |
| CONSUMER PRODUCTS | 40.1 | 42.9 | 50.2 | 2,210 |
| CONSUMER SERVICES | 38.7 | 51.4 | 47.0 | 2,884 |
| INDUSTRIAL PRODUCTS | 37.1 | 36.6 | 60.6 | 3,956 |
| INDUSTRIAL SERVICES | 35.9 | 46.7 | 55.0 | 4,969 |
| OFFICE PRODUCTS | 39.4 | 45.2 | 52.5 | 3,230 |
| OFFICE SERVICES | 43.9 | 48.6 | 48.0 | 4,516 |
| **TYPE OF BUYER** | | | | |
| CONSUMERS | 38.3 | 45.9 | 51.1 | 2,901 |
| DISTRIBUTORS | 39.4 | 43.2 | 54.0 | 3,840 |
| INDUSTRY | 35.9 | 42.8 | 57.5 | 4,051 |
| RETAILERS | 33.8 | 47.4 | 49.9 | 3,537 |
| **INDUSTRY** | | | | |
| AMUSEMENT & RECREATION SERVICES | 15.0 | 74.5 | 34.0 | 838 |
| AUTO REPAIR, SERVICES, & GARAGES | 100.0 | 63.3 | 22.5 | 10,300 |
| BANKING | 26.7 | 36.7 | 50.0 | 3,500 |
| BUSINESS SERVICES | 44.5 | 48.7 | 49.8 | 4,543 |
| COMMUNICATIONS | 14.0 | 70.0 | 30.0 | 967 |
| EDUCATIONAL SERVICES | 26.7 | 45.0 | 95.0 | 2,280 |
| ELECTRONICS | 58.0 | 34.3 | 64.4 | 4,714 |
| FABRICATED METALS | 15.0 | 53.8 | 46.2 | 2,125 |
| FOOD PRODUCTS | 50.7 | 42.0 | 52.5 | 2,347 |
| FURNITURE AND FIXTURES | 35.0 | 17.5 | 84.0 | 2,625 |
| HEALTH SERVICES | 40.0 | 51.7 | 50.0 | 5,450 |
| HOLDING & OTHER INVESTMENT OFFICES | 25.0 | 48.8 | 60.0 | 1,433 |
| INSTRUMENTS | 46.7 | 30.0 | 76.0 | 8,500 |
| INSURANCE | 31.6 | 47.2 | 52.5 | 3,121 |
| MACHINERY | 40.0 | 22.5 | 61.2 | 2,767 |
| MANUFACTURING | 40.0 | 44.2 | 59.3 | 2,308 |
| OFFICE EQUIPMENT | 54.2 | 48.9 | 46.7 | 7,000 |
| PHARMACEUTICALS | 23.5 | 27.0 | 50.8 | 4,000 |
| PRINTING AND PUBLISHING | 24.0 | 37.0 | 63.3 | 1,869 |
| RETAIL | 35.5 | 40.4 | 59.6 | 2,188 |
| WHOLESALE (CONSUMER GOODS) | 46.7 | 37.7 | 62.3 | 3,155 |
| WHOLESALE (INDUSTRIAL GOODS) | 35.5 | 24.2 | 70.0 | 2,668 |
| **OVERALL** | **35.9** | **44.2%** | **55.6%** | **$3,477** |

# INCENTIVE PLAN DESIGN PRACTICES

How we design our sales compensation plans can have a tremendous effect on their overall success. This section reviews the typical incentive plan design practices of survey participants. In reviewing the data in this section, it is helpful to keep in mind that how you pay your sales force can have a dramatic effect on directing the overall behavior of your salespeople. Enlightened companies are now coming to view sales compensation as a real tool for generating profits, rather than as a "necessary evil" or just another expense item to justify.

In reviewing your compensation plan, ask yourself this question: "Am I getting what I'm paying for?" If you feel you're not getting all you're paying for, determine how you can make your compensation dollars work harder for you.

The tables in this section examine the relationship between incentive pay and performance:

- Figures 90–93 examine the relationship between activities sales managers regard as critically important and whether these performance measures are included in the company's compensation plan design. Specific performance measures looked at include selling to major accounts, retaining existing customers, finding new accounts, and reducing selling costs.
- Figure 94 examines the importance of profit contribution vs. sales rep and sales manager incentives.
- Figures 95–97 focus on the degree of sales force effectiveness and include an examination of how effectively sales forces perform the tasks that sales managers say are important.
- Figure 98 looks at how commissions are paid — on sales volume, profitability of the sale, a combination of sales volume and profitability, or some other measure.
- Figure 99 shows the experience level preferred in new hires.

It's worth noting that independent Dartnell studies show that motivating the sales force is one of the prime concerns of sales managers. Yet often little thought is given to designing the compensation plan so salespeople are motivated to do what the company wants them to do.

Here's an example: Let's say that the XYZ Company, a midsize manufacturer, has determined that company survival depends on dramatically increasing its customer base. While its current customer base is a good source of steady income, these accounts don't have significant growth potential. The word goes out to the sales force: "We need new business, and it's up to you to do the job! We're all counting on you, and we know you can do it!" Sound far-fetched? While there's nothing wrong with a good old-fashioned pep talk, more enlightened companies look to their compensation plan to do the motivating.

Our hypothetical XYZ Company, like many companies, uses a combination (salary plus incentive) compensation plan. Salaries are modest to keep fixed costs down; commissions are based on a percentage of total sales volume achieved to keep the administration costs of the plan low. When the plan was set up, a major concern of the top marketing executive was to keep the plan easy to understand and fair to all concerned. The important point to remember is that the XYZ Company is rewarding all sales the same, i.e., a standard commission rate is paid based on the total dollar amount of the sale made. Whether salary represents 5 percent—or 75 percent—of total compensation received, the incentive value of sales made never varies: All sales are rewarded on the same basis regardless of the difficulty of the sale or whether the sale helps the company reach its overall marketing objectives.

Remember, money motivates, and salespeople are motivated by money. They are also very focused on maximizing their earnings. If "easy" sales are compensated at the same rate as hard-to-make sales, is it likely that your salespeople will spend a significant amount of time going after those tough sales? Not likely at all. But what if your salespeople earned more—far more—for making those tough sales? Now you're talking their language!

Let's go back to our XYZ Company. Now let's suppose its compensation plan paid a significantly higher commission rate on all sales representing new business. In that scenario, you'd find your salespeople going after those accounts because it was now in their best monetary interest to do so.

There's nothing magic going on here. What we're doing is taking a look at what we need our salespeople to do and paying them more to do those specific things. If opening new accounts is important for your salespeople to do, pay them more for opening new accounts. For example, you might consider paying your salespeople twice their standard commission rate on all sales representing new business. This new rate would apply to all sales placed by the new account for a period of six months—or some other predetermined time period at which point the new account would be reclassified as established business.

To further encourage your salespeople to actively seek new business, you might also pay a flat fee for appointments secured at selected accounts—whether or not the appointment resulted in a sale. In this case, we are specifically rewarding those activities that can ultimately lead to additional sales in the future.

The more effectively your compensation plan links pay to performance, the more effectively your compensation plan will influence the behavior of your salespeople.

In looking at the overall design of your compensation plan, determine if you are:
- Overpaying for low-priority salesperson activities.
- Underpaying for high-priority salesperson activities.
- Not distinguishing between high-priority and low-priority salesperson activities.

To rephrase that old cliché, what you pay for—you get.

## FIGURES 90 – 93 — IMPORTANCE OF SALES TASKS VS. SALES REP INCENTIVES

As we discussed in detail earlier in this book, the right incentive program can be the engine that drives your salespeople to success. Or, put another way, the lack of an effective incentive program can derail your best-intentioned sales efforts. It should come as no surprise that salespeople are much more likely to behave in certain ways when there is "something in it for them." But what may be surprising is to realize that many compensation programs are not designed to specifically reward those sales activities that the company believes are important. The data on the following tables looks at this potential problem in detail.

**Figures 90 to 93** focus on the importance of sales tasks vs. sales rep incentives. Sales tasks examined include selling to major accounts, retaining existing customers, finding new accounts, and reducing selling costs. We asked sales managers how they rated these tasks: very important, important, somewhat important, or not important. We then asked sales managers whether their current sales compensation plan specifically included an incentive for performing these particular tasks. The results are displayed on the following four tables. In looking at **Figure 90**, for example, we can see that the overwhelming majority of responding companies (89.8%) consider selling to major accounts an important sales task, yet fewer than 20 percent (18.4%) of responding companies have an incentive that would reward that activity.

It is no secret that salespeople more readily and willingly perform those tasks when there is "something in it for them." It is often a mistake to regard these important-rated activities as "just part of the sales job." The demands on a salesperson's time are immense, and the individual frequently has to decide which task of many he or she should concentrate his or her efforts on. Often a conflict arises.

For example, finding new accounts may be regarded as a very important activity by the company, but by the same token this particular activity requires a greater expenditure of the salesperson's time than is spent securing additional business from long-established existing accounts.

Here's the point: If your salesperson sees the major portion of the job as one of making quota, where is it most likely that those sales will come from? Clearly, the easiest sales to secure are those from existing accounts. Consequently, finding new accounts, while it may be regarded as part of the job, often is neglected.

As you look through these tables, ask yourself whether better results could be obtained from your salespeople if these important-rated activities were included in your overall incentive picture rather than just being regarded as "part of the job." The question you need to answer is, "How important are these activities *really*?"

## FIGURE 90

## Importance of Sales Tasks vs. Sales Rep Incentives/Selling to Major Accounts

| | Percentage Who Consider Important | Percentage With Senior Salesperson Incentive | Gap (%) |
|---|---|---|---|
| **Company Size** | | | |
| Under $5 Million | 89.8% | 18.4% | 71.4% |
| **Product or Service** | | | |
| Consumer Products | 85.9 | 27.3 | 58.6 |
| Consumer Services | 82.3 | 19.5 | 62.8 |
| Industrial Products | 94.7 | 23.1 | 71.7 |
| Industrial Services | 89.7 | 21.2 | 68.5 |
| Office Products | 90.4 | 22.9 | 67.5 |
| Office Services | 86.4 | 19.4 | 67.0 |
| **Type of Buyer** | | | |
| Consumers | 84.2 | 18.6 | 65.6 |
| Distributors | 89.5 | 23.1 | 66.3 |
| Industry | 92.8 | 20.3 | 72.5 |
| Retailers | 95.4 | 28.0 | 67.4 |
| **Industry** | | | |
| Amusement & Recreation Services | 50.0 | 0.0 | 50.0 |
| Auto Repair, Services, & Garages | 100.0 | 50.0 | 50.0 |
| Banking | 50.0 | 33.3 | 16.7 |
| Business Services | 90.9 | 19.6 | 71.3 |
| Communications | 100.0 | 33.3 | 66.7 |
| Construction | 66.7 | 0.0 | 66.7 |
| Educational Services | 100.0 | 0.0 | 100.0 |
| Electronics | 100.0 | 0.0 | 100.0 |
| Fabricated Metals | 100.0 | 25.0 | 75.0 |
| Food Products | 100.0 | 0.0 | 100.0 |
| Furniture and Fixtures | 80.0 | 20.0 | 60.0 |
| Health Services | 80.0 | 0.0 | 80.0 |
| Holding & Other Investment Offices | 60.0 | 0.0 | 60.0 |
| Hotels & Other Lodging Places | 100.0 | 0.0 | 100.0 |
| Instruments | 100.0 | 25.0 | 75.0 |
| Insurance | 77.8 | 12.5 | 65.3 |
| Machinery | 100.0 | 50.0 | 50.0 |
| Manufacturing | 75.0 | 25.0 | 50.0 |
| Motion Pictures | 66.7 | 66.7 | 0.0 |
| Office Equipment | 100.0 | 0.0 | 100.0 |
| Pharmaceuticals | 75.0 | 25.0 | 50.0 |
| Primary Metal Products | 100.0 | 33.3 | 66.7 |
| Printing and Publishing | 100.0 | 23.1 | 76.9 |
| Real Estate | 66.7 | 0.0 | 66.7 |
| Retail | 86.7 | 20.0 | 66.7 |
| Wholesale (Consumer Goods) | 91.7 | 16.7 | 75.0 |
| Wholesale (Industrial Goods) | 96.2 | 25.0 | 71.2 |
| **Overall** | **89.8%** | **18.4%** | **71.4%** |

# FIGURE 91

## Importance of Sales Tasks vs. Sales Rep Incentives/Retaining Existing Customers

| | Percentage Who Consider Important | Percentage With Senior Salesperson Incentive | Gap (%) |
|---|---|---|---|
| **Company Size** | | | |
| Under $5 Million | 98.4% | 23.0% | 75.5% |
| **Product or Service** | | | |
| Consumer Products | 97.5 | 32.5 | 65.1 |
| Consumer Services | 97.6 | 23.4 | 74.2 |
| Industrial Products | 99.1 | 27.9 | 71.2 |
| Industrial Services | 100.0 | 23.2 | 76.8 |
| Office Products | 98.0 | 22.9 | 75.1 |
| Office Services | 98.5 | 19.4 | 79.1 |
| **Type of Buyer** | | | |
| Consumers | 97.1 | 26.8 | 70.3 |
| Distributors | 98.3 | 26.9 | 71.4 |
| Industry | 100.0 | 22.5 | 77.5 |
| Retailers | 100.0 | 29.3 | 70.7 |
| **Industry** | | | |
| Amusement & Recreation Services | 100.0 | 0.0 | 100.0 |
| Auto Repair, Services, & Garages | 100.0 | 50.0 | 50.0 |
| Banking | 100.0 | 33.3 | 66.7 |
| Business Services | 98.1 | 23.5 | 74.6 |
| Communications | 100.0 | 33.3 | 66.7 |
| Construction | 100.0 | 0.0 | 100.0 |
| Educational Services | 100.0 | 0.0 | 100.0 |
| Electronics | 100.0 | 0.0 | 100.0 |
| Fabricated Metals | 100.0 | 25.0 | 75.0 |
| Food Products | 100.0 | 16.7 | 83.3 |
| Furniture and Fixtures | 100.0 | 20.0 | 80.0 |
| Health Services | 100.0 | 0.0 | 100.0 |
| Holding & Other Investment Offices | 60.0 | 0.0 | 60.0 |
| Hotels & Other Lodging Places | 100.0 | 0.0 | 100.0 |
| Instruments | 100.0 | 25.0 | 75.0 |
| Insurance | 100.0 | 50.0 | 50.0 |
| Machinery | 100.0 | 50.0 | 50.0 |
| Manufacturing | 87.5 | 25.0 | 62.5 |
| Motion Pictures | 100.0 | 66.7 | 33.3 |
| Office Equipment | 100.0 | 8.3 | 91.7 |
| Pharmaceuticals | 100.0 | 25.0 | 75.0 |
| Primary Metal Products | 100.0 | 33.3 | 66.7 |
| Printing and Publishing | 100.0 | 23.1 | 76.9 |
| Real Estate | 100.0 | 0.0 | 100.0 |
| Retail | 100.0 | 33.3 | 66.7 |
| Wholesale (Consumer Goods) | 100.0 | 25.0 | 75.0 |
| Wholesale (Industrial Goods) | 100.0 | 29.2 | 70.8 |
| **Overall** | **98.4%** | **23.0%** | **75.5%** |

# FIGURE 92

## Importance of Sales Tasks vs. Sales Rep Incentives/Finding New Accounts

|  | Percentage Who Consider Important | Percentage With Senior Salesperson Incentive | Gap (%) |
|---|---|---|---|
| **Company Size** | | | |
| Under $5 Million | 96.9% | 27.0% | 69.9% |
| **Product or Service** | | | |
| Consumer Products | 98.8 | 33.8 | 65.0 |
| Consumer Services | 98.8 | 33.8 | 65.0 |
| Industrial Products | 95.6 | 28.8 | 66.8 |
| Industrial Services | 98.1 | 29.3 | 68.8 |
| Office Products | 92.3 | 29.2 | 63.1 |
| Office Services | 97.0 | 29.0 | 67.9 |
| **Type of Buyer** | | | |
| Consumers | 98.0 | 34.0 | 64.0 |
| Distributors | 98.3 | 29.6 | 68.6 |
| Industry | 96.4 | 26.4 | 70.0 |
| Retailers | 98.9 | 32.9 | 65.9 |
| **Industry** | | | |
| Amusement & Recreation Services | 100.0 | 0.0 | 100.0 |
| Auto Repair, Services, & Garages | 100.0 | 50.0 | 50.0 |
| Banking | 100.0 | 66.7 | 33.3 |
| Business Services | 98.2 | 29.4 | 68.8 |
| Communications | 100.0 | 33.3 | 66.7 |
| Construction | 100.0 | 0.0 | 100.0 |
| Educational Services | 100.0 | 0.0 | 100.0 |
| Electronics | 100.0 | 0.0 | 100.0 |
| Fabricated Metals | 100.0 | 25.0 | 75.0 |
| Food Products | 100.0 | 16.7 | 83.3 |
| Furniture and Fixtures | 100.0 | 20.0 | 80.0 |
| Health Services | 100.0 | 16.7 | 83.3 |
| Holding & Other Investment Offices | 80.0 | 20.0 | 60.0 |
| Hotels & Other Lodging Places | 100.0 | 0.0 | 100.0 |
| Instruments | 80.0 | 25.0 | 55.0 |
| Insurance | 90.0 | 62.5 | 27.5 |
| Machinery | 75.0 | 25.0 | 50.0 |
| Manufacturing | 100.0 | 37.5 | 62.5 |
| Motion Pictures | 100.0 | 100.0 | 0.0 |
| Office Equipment | 91.7 | 8.3 | 83.3 |
| Pharmaceuticals | 100.0 | 25.0 | 75.0 |
| Primary Metal Products | 100.0 | 33.3 | 66.7 |
| Printing and Publishing | 100.0 | 38.5 | 61.5 |
| Real Estate | 100.0 | 0.0 | 100.0 |
| Retail | 93.8 | 26.7 | 67.1 |
| Wholesale (Consumer Goods) | 100.0 | 16.7 | 83.3 |
| Wholesale (Industrial Goods) | 100.0 | 29.2 | 70.8 |
| **Overall** | **96.9%** | **27.0%** | **69.9%** |

# FIGURE 93

## IMPORTANCE OF SALES TASKS VS. SALES REP INCENTIVES/REDUCING SELLING COSTS

| | PERCENTAGE WHO CONSIDER IMPORTANT | PERCENTAGE WITH SENIOR SALESPERSON INCENTIVE | GAP (%) |
|---|---|---|---|
| **COMPANY SIZE** | | | |
| UNDER $5 MILLION | 57.8% | 8.6% | 49.2% |
| **PRODUCT OR SERVICE** | | | |
| CONSUMER PRODUCTS | 65.8 | 13.0 | 52.8 |
| CONSUMER SERVICES | 60.5 | 7.8 | 52.7 |
| INDUSTRIAL PRODUCTS | 59.6 | 10.6 | 49.1 |
| INDUSTRIAL SERVICES | 56.2 | 6.1 | 50.1 |
| OFFICE PRODUCTS | 51.9 | 4.2 | 47.8 |
| OFFICE SERVICES | 59.1 | 3.2 | 55.9 |
| **TYPE OF BUYER** | | | |
| CONSUMERS | 60.8 | 8.2 | 52.5 |
| DISTRIBUTORS | 57.0 | 10.2 | 46.8 |
| INDUSTRY | 56.0 | 7.7 | 48.3 |
| RETAILERS | 64.0 | 13.4 | 50.5 |
| **INDUSTRY** | | | |
| AMUSEMENT & RECREATION SERVICES | 25.0 | 0.0 | 25.0 |
| AUTO REPAIR, SERVICES, & GARAGES | 66.7 | 0.0 | 66.7 |
| BANKING | 100.0 | 0.0 | 100.0 |
| BUSINESS SERVICES | 50.9 | 7.8 | 43.1 |
| COMMUNICATIONS | 66.7 | 0.0 | 66.7 |
| CONSTRUCTION | 100.0 | 0.0 | 100.0 |
| EDUCATIONAL SERVICES | 33.3 | 0.0 | 33.3 |
| ELECTRONICS | 55.6 | 12.5 | 43.1 |
| FABRICATED METALS | 66.7 | 25.0 | 41.7 |
| FOOD PRODUCTS | 66.7 | 16.7 | 50.0 |
| FURNITURE AND FIXTURES | 60.0 | 0.0 | 60.0 |
| HEALTH SERVICES | 20.0 | 0.0 | 20.0 |
| HOLDING & OTHER INVESTMENT OFFICES | 20.0 | 0.0 | 20.0 |
| HOTELS & OTHER LODGING PLACES | 100.0 | 0.0 | 100.0 |
| INSTRUMENTS | 20.0 | 0.0 | 20.0 |
| INSURANCE | 30.0 | 0.0 | 30.0 |
| MACHINERY | 50.0 | 50.0 | 0.0 |
| MANUFACTURING | 87.5 | 0.0 | 87.5 |
| MOTION PICTURES | 66.7 | 0.0 | 66.7 |
| OFFICE EQUIPMENT | 50.0 | 0.0 | 50.0 |
| PHARMACEUTICALS | 62.5 | 37.5 | 25.0 |
| PRIMARY METAL PRODUCTS | 66.7 | 33.3 | 33.3 |
| PRINTING AND PUBLISHING | 53.8 | 0.0 | 53.8 |
| REAL ESTATE | 100.0 | 0.0 | 100.0 |
| RETAIL | 80.0 | 13.3 | 66.7 |
| WHOLESALE (CONSUMER GOODS) | 66.7 | 16.7 | 50.0 |
| WHOLESALE (INDUSTRIAL GOODS) | 70.4 | 8.3 | 62.0 |
| **OVERALL** | **57.8%** | **8.6%** | **49.2%** |

## FIGURE 94 — IMPORTANCE OF PROFIT CONTRIBUTION VS. USE OF INCENTIVES

With companies paying increasingly more attention to bottom-line matters, it is more and more important to examine the role sales incentives play in the overall profit picture.

Every company's ultimate objective is profitability, and **Figure 94** addresses the bottom-line profitability issue head-on. The data on this table examines the importance of profit contribution vs. the use of incentives. Again, it is in the company's best interest to have salespeople sell its products and services to those important large accounts that will contribute the most to the bottom line. Yet, fewer than half of the responding companies (45.1%) said they provided an incentive that would specifically reward more profitable sales. This figure has improved somewhat since we first started tracking this data in 1990. In 1990, 38.9 percent of responding companies with under $5 million in annual sales provided a salesperson incentive based on profitability of the sale; in 1992, 43.4 percent of responding companies said they provided such an incentive, and in 1994 44.7 percent provided an incentive based on sales profitability. Companies with over $5 million in annual sales have exhibited a similar pattern over the years.

Companies appear to be more inclined to offer an incentive to *sales management* for securing more profitable sales. In our current survey, 54.1 percent of responding companies offer such an incentive to their sales managers, up from 41.7 percent two years ago. In 1992, just 27.7 percent of companies with under $5 million in annual sales offered an incentive to sales management based on profitability of sales.

One possible reason companies are slow to include salespeople: Companies are still reluctant to share sensitive financial information with their salespeople, preferring instead to leave final responsibility for profitable sales with sales management.

(See Figure 98 — How Commissions are Determined — for related data on this important topic.)

# FIGURE 94

## IMPORTANCE OF PROFIT CONTRIBUTION VS. USE OF INCENTIVES

| | PERCENTAGE WHO CONSIDER IMPORTANT | PERCENTAGE WITH SALESPERSON INCENTIVE | GAP (%) | PERCENTAGE WITH SALES MANAGER INCENTIVE | GAP (%) |
|---|---|---|---|---|---|
| **COMPANY SIZE** | | | | | |
| UNDER $5 MILLION | 86.3% | 45.1% | 41.2% | 54.1% | 32.2% |
| **PRODUCT OR SERVICE** | | | | | |
| CONSUMER PRODUCTS | 91.1 | 55.8 | 35.3 | 64.9 | 26.2 |
| CONSUMER SERVICES | 87.7 | 40.3 | 47.4 | 63.6 | 24.0 |
| INDUSTRIAL PRODUCTS | 91.2 | 52.9 | 38.3 | 53.8 | 37.3 |
| INDUSTRIAL SERVICES | 91.3 | 41.4 | 49.9 | 57.6 | 33.8 |
| OFFICE PRODUCTS | 84.6 | 47.9 | 36.7 | 52.1 | 32.5 |
| OFFICE SERVICES | 86.4 | 40.3 | 46.0 | 56.5 | 29.9 |
| **TYPE OF BUYER** | | | | | |
| CONSUMERS | 86.3 | 47.4 | 38.9 | 60.8 | 25.4 |
| DISTRIBUTORS | 89.6 | 48.1 | 41.4 | 52.8 | 36.8 |
| INDUSTRY | 88.0 | 44.0 | 44.1 | 52.2 | 35.8 |
| RETAILERS | 88.4 | 51.2 | 37.2 | 59.8 | 28.6 |
| **INDUSTRY** | | | | | |
| AMUSEMENT & RECREATION SERVICES | 75.0 | 66.7 | 8.3 | 66.7 | 8.3 |
| AUTO REPAIR, SERVICES, & GARAGES | 100.0 | 50.0 | 50.0 | 100.0 | 0.0 |
| BANKING | 100.0 | 33.3 | 66.7 | 100.0 | 0.0 |
| BUSINESS SERVICES | 84.9 | 27.5 | 57.5 | 52.9 | 32.0 |
| COMMUNICATIONS | 100.0 | 33.3 | 66.7 | 66.7 | 33.3 |
| CONSTRUCTION | 100.0 | 33.3 | 66.7 | 66.7 | 33.3 |
| EDUCATIONAL SERVICES | 66.7 | 0.0 | 66.7 | 66.7 | 0.0 |
| ELECTRONICS | 100.0 | 50.0 | 50.0 | 50.0 | 50.0 |
| FABRICATED METALS | 83.3 | 25.0 | 58.3 | 25.0 | 58.3 |
| FOOD PRODUCTS | 83.3 | 66.7 | 16.7 | 66.7 | 16.7 |
| FURNITURE AND FIXTURES | 80.0 | 40.0 | 40.0 | 40.0 | 40.0 |
| HEALTH SERVICES | 60.0 | 50.0 | 10.0 | 33.3 | 26.7 |
| HOLDING & OTHER INVESTMENT OFFICES | 40.0 | 60.0 | − 20.0 | 40.0 | 0.0 |
| HOTELS & OTHER LODGING PLACES | 100.0 | 0.0 | 100.0 | 0.0 | 100.0 |
| INSTRUMENTS | 80.0 | 100.0 | − 20.0 | 25.0 | 55.0 |
| INSURANCE | 50.0 | 25.0 | 25.0 | 50.0 | 0.0 |
| MACHINERY | 100.0 | 50.0 | 50.0 | 75.0 | 25.0 |
| MANUFACTURING | 100.0 | 37.5 | 62.5 | 75.0 | 25.0 |
| MOTION PICTURES | 100.0 | 33.3 | 66.7 | 66.7 | 33.3 |
| OFFICE EQUIPMENT | 83.3 | 16.7 | 66.7 | 33.3 | 50.0 |
| PHARMACEUTICALS | 75.0 | 75.0 | 0.0 | 62.5 | 12.5 |
| PRIMARY METAL PRODUCTS | 100.0 | 33.3 | 66.7 | 100.0 | 0.0 |
| PRINTING AND PUBLISHING | 76.9 | 61.5 | 15.4 | 46.2 | 30.8 |
| REAL ESTATE | 66.7 | 0.0 | 66.7 | 33.3 | 33.3 |
| RETAIL | 100.0 | 66.7 | 33.3 | 66.7 | 33.3 |
| WHOLESALE (CONSUMER GOODS) | 83.3 | 58.3 | 25.0 | 50.0 | 33.3 |
| WHOLESALE (INDUSTRIAL GOODS) | 100.0 | 58.3 | 41.7 | 50.0 | 50.0 |
| **OVERALL** | **86.3%** | **45.1%** | **41.2%** | **54.1%** | **32.2%** |

# FIGURE 95—DEGREE OF SALES FORCE EFFECTIVENESS

Just how effective are today's salespeople in the eyes of their sales managers? While such measurements can be subjective, they can nonetheless be enlightening.

**Figure 95** takes a look at the degree of overall sales force effectiveness as perceived by sales managers. We asked survey participants to (1) rate the relative importance of a variety of selling tasks and then (2) rate how well their salespeople performed those tasks. The "gap" is the difference between the importance of the task and how well salespeople perform the task. (For more complete breakouts of this data, see Figure 97.)

Tasks rated included selling to major accounts, finding new accounts, selling new products, integrating new technology, reducing selling costs, retaining existing customers, and improving profit contribution. With the exception of finding new accounts, salespeople are generally perceived as less effective in performing less important tasks. This may be a bias on the part of the sales managers. After all, one is less likely to appreciate how well a task is being done if the overall merit of performing the task in the first place is in question.

Dartnell has been collecting sales force effectiveness data since 1990. Since that time, salespeople have been judged to be most effective at retaining existing customers and least effective at finding new accounts.

If your salespeople have been encountering difficulties in securing new business, now may be the time to take a fresh look at your incentive plan. It's worth repeating that salespeople are less likely to perform well those activities that they are not specifically rewarded for performing. Making sure that your compensation plan rewards the activities that you deem important is one of the keys to boosting sales force effectiveness. Readers interested in further exploring the relationship between incentive pay and performance are encouraged to compare the data in Figures 90–94 with the data in Figures 95 and 97. Alert readers will note that there appears to be a strong correlation between lack of incentive pay and lack of performance.

# FIGURE 95

## Degree of Sales Force Effectiveness

| Sales Task | Importance | Effectiveness | Gap |
|---|---|---|---|
| Retaining existing customers | 98.4% | 83.4% | 15.0% |
| Finding new accounts | 96.9 | 56.3 | 40.6 |
| Selling to major accounts | 89.8 | 62.7 | 27.1 |
| Improving profit contribution | 86.3 | 51.2 | 35.1 |
| Selling new products | 66.4 | 53.1 | 13.3 |
| Integrating new technology | 58.1 | 48.0 | 10.1 |
| Reducing selling costs | 57.8 | 41.9 | 15.9 |

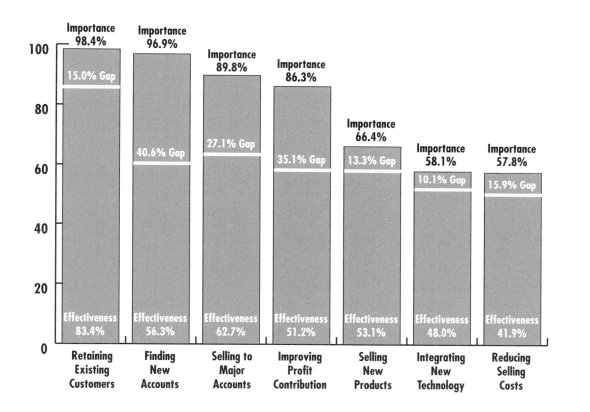

## FIGURE 96 — DEGREE OF SALES FORCE EFFECTIVENESS: PERCENTAGE OF FIRMS INDICATING THEIR SALES FORCE IS EFFECTIVE IN PERFORMING TASKS RATED IMPORTANT

In companies with under $5 million in annual sales, 77.5 percent of respondents say their sales forces are effective in performing tasks rated important. This is a significant improvement over 1990 data, in which just 50.9 percent of the companies gave high marks to their sales forces. In 1994, 76.8 percent of companies with under $5 million in annual sales said their sales forces were effective in performing tasks rated important. Although this data is based on subjective measures, it does seem to indicate that today's salespeople are showing improvement in key task areas.

The data for the degree of sales force effectiveness in larger companies, those with over $5 million in annual sales, is nearly identical to the data posted by smaller companies.

# FIGURE 96

**DEGREE OF SALES FORCE EFFECTIVENESS**

|  | PERCENTAGE OF FIRMS INDICATING THEIR SALES FORCE IS EFFECTIVE IN PERFORMING TASKS RATED IMPORTANT |
|---|---|
| **COMPANY SIZE** | |
| UNDER $5 MILLION | 77.5% |
| **PRODUCT OR SERVICE** | |
| CONSUMER PRODUCTS | 80.7 |
| CONSUMER SERVICES | 78.8 |
| INDUSTRIAL PRODUCTS | 75.2 |
| INDUSTRIAL SERVICES | 74.4 |
| OFFICE PRODUCTS | 81.8 |
| OFFICE SERVICES | 78.7 |
| **TYPE OF BUYER** | |
| CONSUMERS | 79.9 |
| DISTRIBUTORS | 79.6 |
| INDUSTRY | 77.6 |
| RETAILERS | 72.5 |
| **INDUSTRY** | |
| AMUSEMENT & RECREATION SERVICES | 100.0 |
| AUTO REPAIR, SERVICES, & GARAGES | 61.9 |
| BANKING | 85.7 |
| BUSINESS SERVICES | 80.8 |
| COMMUNICATIONS | 38.1 |
| CONSTRUCTION | 81.0 |
| EDUCATIONAL SERVICES | 81.0 |
| ELECTRONICS | 82.5 |
| FABRICATED METALS | 83.3 |
| FOOD PRODUCTS | 71.4 |
| FURNITURE AND FIXTURES | 70.0 |
| HEALTH SERVICES | 68.6 |
| HOLDING & OTHER INVESTMENT OFFICES | 100.0 |
| HOTELS & OTHER LODGING PLACES | 71.4 |
| INSTRUMENTS | 65.7 |
| INSURANCE | 93.6 |
| MACHINERY | 85.7 |
| MANUFACTURING | 57.9 |
| MOTION PICTURES | 52.4 |
| OFFICE EQUIPMENT | 76.5 |
| PHARMACEUTICALS | 76.8 |
| PRIMARY METAL PRODUCTS | 100.0 |
| PRINTING AND PUBLISHING | 68.1 |
| REAL ESTATE | 66.7 |
| RETAIL | 82.1 |
| WHOLESALE (CONSUMER GOODS) | 82.1 |
| WHOLESALE (INDUSTRIAL GOODS) | 66.6 |
| **OVERALL** | **77.5%** |

## FIGURE 97 — IMPROVING OVERALL COMPANY EFFECTIVENESS

The data contained in **Figure 97** is a further breakout of the data presented in Figure 95. Data for Figure 95 was generated by combining the percentage of respondents who rated a particular sales task as either "very important" or "important" and comparing the resulting number with the percentage of respondents rating their sales force either "very effective" or "effective" in performing the task.

Over the years (since 1990, the first year Dartnell collected this data), reps have not scored well in the "very effective" column, with the possible exception of "retaining existing customers." However, the task of retaining existing customers is one of the easier tasks to perform simply because it is easier to obtain business from existing customers than to gain business from new prospects. In any economic climate, one important way to ensure the growth of your company is to expand your number of customers. The data here indicates that this is one area in which companies need to do a better job.

# FIGURE 97

**IMPROVING OVERALL COMPANY EFFECTIVENESS
(ALL RESPONDENTS)**

| | IMPORTANCE TO IMPROVING PERFORMANCE | | | |
|---|---|---|---|---|
| | VERY IMPORTANT | IMPORTANT | SOMEWHAT IMPORTANT | NOT IMPORTANT |
| **SALES TASK** | | | | |
| SELLING TO MAJOR ACCOUNTS | 64.3% | 25.5% | 7.1% | 3.1% |
| FINDING NEW ACCOUNTS | 79.8 | 17.1 | 3.1 | 0.0 |
| SELLING NEW PRODUCTS | 33.6 | 32.8 | 19.4 | 14.2 |
| INTEGRATING NEW TECHNOLOGY | 24.1 | 34.0 | 30.4 | 11.5 |
| REDUCING SELLING COSTS | 24.2 | 33.6 | 30.1 | 12.1 |
| RETAINING EXISTING CUSTOMERS | 83.7 | 14.7 | 1.6 | 0.0 |
| IMPROVING PROFIT CONTRIBUTION | 50.6 | 35.7 | 8.6 | 5.1 |

| | CURRENT EFFECTIVENESS OF SALES FORCE | | | |
|---|---|---|---|---|
| | VERY EFFECTIVE | EFFECTIVE | SOMEWHAT EFFECTIVE | NOT EFFECTIVE |
| **SALES TASK** | | | | |
| SELLING TO MAJOR ACCOUNTS | 14.9% | 47.8% | 30.5% | 6.8% |
| FINDING NEW ACCOUNTS | 15.1 | 41.3 | 38.5 | 5.2 |
| SELLING NEW PRODUCTS | 11.3 | 41.8 | 32.2 | 14.6 |
| INTEGRATING NEW TECHNOLOGY | 13.1 | 34.8 | 35.2 | 16.8 |
| REDUCING SELLING COSTS | 9.8 | 32.1 | 45.1 | 13.0 |
| RETAINING EXISTING CUSTOMERS | 37.2 | 46.2 | 15.4 | 1.2 |
| IMPROVING PROFIT CONTRIBUTION | 9.3 | 41.9 | 40.3 | 8.5 |

# FIGURE 98 — HOW COMMISSIONS ARE DETERMINED

With all the emphasis on bottom-line results (also see Figure 94), we thought it might be interesting to find out how many companies consider the *profitability* of the sale when calculating sales commissions. The data table on the right tells the story.

While nearly half the companies (48.95 percent) continue to determine commission on the basis of sales volume only, a growing number of companies are looking at the profitability of the sale in determining their compensation programs. When the number of companies paying commissions on the "profitability of sale only" are added to those that pay commissions on "sales volume *and* profitability considerations," we see that nearly 46 percent of responding companies are giving some thought to profitability issues when they determine sales commissions.

Respondents checking the "other" category did so in many cases to indicate that they did not pay sales commissions.

However, some respondents listed the following as considerations in determining pay. (These comments are based on Dartnell's sales compensation survey encompassing companies of all sizes. They are included here because all these strategies can be used in all companies regardless of size.)

"Client satisfaction, renewals."
"Market share growth and retention."
"Pay quarterly bonus based on profitability."
"Sales above assigned goal for account base. Two percent paid on all sales above quarterly sales goal."
"Profitability on the entire office. This builds better teamwork."
"Bonus only."
"Market share movement."
"Pay on volume less 50% of commission for bad debt accounts."
"Bonus on sales volume and company profitability."
"Percent of increase in territory."
"Company profitability."
"Product bonuses — bonuses to move key products and inventory."
"Sales volume in excess of base assigned."
"Bonus based on quota and targets."
"Combination of volume, profitability, and target items. We pay a percent of gross profit over a certain level and also a bonus for every account who buys a targeted major line each month, also bonuses for new accounts."
"New accounts."
"Salespeople get 6 percent of their gross profit contribution after they make quota."
"Overall company performance."
"New accounts/existing accounts, maintenance and growth objectives."
"Customer satisfaction."
"Sales volume and personal objectives. All salespeople are geared toward personal growth — less interfighting between sales regions."
"Combination of sales, profit, and product mix."

# FIGURE 98

**HOW COMMISSIONS ARE DETERMINED**

| | PERCENTAGE OF COMPANIES PAYING COMMISSIONS BASED ON | | | |
| --- | --- | --- | --- | --- |
| | SALES VOLUME ONLY | PROFITABILITY OF SALE ONLY | COMBINATION OF SALES VOLUME AND PROFITABILITY OF SALE | OTHER |
| **COMPANY SIZE** | | | | |
| UNDER $5 MILLION | 48.95% | 16.03% | 29.96% | 5.06% |
| **PRODUCT OR SERVICE** | | | | |
| CONSUMER PRODUCTS | 46.58 | 13.70 | 36.99 | 2.74 |
| CONSUMER SERVICES | 45.33 | 14.67 | 37.33 | 2.67 |
| INDUSTRIAL PRODUCTS | 44.76 | 20.95 | 25.71 | 8.57 |
| INDUSTRIAL SERVICES | 45.74 | 18.09 | 28.72 | 7.45 |
| OFFICE PRODUCTS | 44.90 | 26.53 | 26.53 | 2.04 |
| OFFICE SERVICES | 46.77 | 16.13 | 35.48 | 1.61 |
| **TYPE OF BUYER** | | | | |
| CONSUMERS | 47.31 | 15.05 | 36.56 | 1.08 |
| DISTRIBUTORS | 48.11 | 16.04 | 30.19 | 5.66 |
| INDUSTRY | 48.02 | 17.51 | 27.68 | 6.78 |
| RETAILERS | 46.67 | 13.33 | 32.00 | 8.00 |
| **INDUSTRY** | | | | |
| BUSINESS SERVICES | 51.02 | 14.29 | 30.61 | 4.08 |
| ELECTRONICS | 37.50 | 12.50 | 37.50 | 12.50 |
| PRINTING AND PUBLISHING | 45.45 | 9.09 | 36.36 | 9.09 |
| WHOLESALE (CONSUMER GOODS) | 27.27 | 18.18 | 36.36 | 18.18 |
| WHOLESALE (INDUSTRIAL GOODS) | 29.17 | 41.67 | 20.83 | 8.33 |
| **OVERALL** | **48.95%** | **16.03%** | **29.96%** | **5.06%** |

## FIGURE 99 — EXPERIENCE LEVEL PREFERRED IN NEWLY HIRED SALESPEOPLE

**Figure 99** presents full data on the experience level preferred in newly hired salespeople in companies with under $5 million in annual sales. With just 10 percent of survey respondents saying they prefer to hire entry level candidates, the implication may well be that it is getting harder to get into sales. However, as the data suggests, there are a number of industries that entry level reps might investigate for first-time employment to gain the experience they need.

See pages 222–223 for a further discussion of this topic as well as comments from sales managers as to why they prefer a particular level of experience in a sales candidate.

**FIGURE 99**

**EXPERIENCE LEVEL PREFERRED IN NEWLY HIRED SALESPEOPLE**
**(BY PERCENTAGE OF RESPONDENTS)**

|  | ENTRY LEVEL REP (LESS THAN 1 YEAR OF EXPERIENCE) | INTERMEDIATE REP (1–3 YEARS OF EXPERIENCE) | SENIOR REP (MORE THAN 3 YEARS OF EXPERIENCE) |
|---|---|---|---|
| **COMPANY SIZE** | | | |
| UNDER $5 MILLION | 10.36% | 48.21% | 41.43% |
| **PRODUCT OR SERVICE** | | | |
| CONSUMER PRODUCTS | 11.39 | 55.70 | 32.91 |
| CONSUMER SERVICES | 16.25 | 51.25 | 32.50 |
| INDUSTRIAL PRODUCTS | 6.25 | 50.00 | 43.75 |
| INDUSTRIAL SERVICES | 10.68 | 50.49 | 38.83 |
| OFFICE PRODUCTS | 12.00 | 46.00 | 42.00 |
| OFFICE SERVICES | 9.23 | 53.85 | 36.92 |
| **TYPE OF BUYER** | | | |
| CONSUMERS | 16.83 | 55.45 | 27.72 |
| DISTRIBUTORS | 11.30 | 45.22 | 43.48 |
| INDUSTRY | 8.02 | 50.27 | 41.71 |
| RETAILERS | 10.47 | 48.84 | 40.70 |
| **INDUSTRY** | | | |
| AMUSEMENT & RECREATION SERVICES | 25.00 | 25.00 | 50.00 |
| BUSINESS SERVICES | 7.41 | 42.59 | 50.00 |
| ELECTRONICS | 25.00 | 37.50 | 37.50 |
| INSURANCE | 40.00 | 40.00 | 20.00 |
| OFFICE EQUIPMENT | 8.33 | 41.67 | 50.00 |
| PRINTING AND PUBLISHING | 7.69 | 61.54 | 30.77 |
| RETAIL | 18.75 | 62.50 | 18.75 |
| WHOLESALE (CONSUMER GOODS) | 9.09 | 63.64 | 27.27 |
| WHOLESALE (INDUSTRIAL GOODS) | 8.00 | 44.00 | 48.00 |
| **OVERALL** | **10.36%** | **48.21%** | **41.43%** |

# TODAY'S SALES FORCE

This section focuses on today's sales force as a unit. Over the years, the dynamics of the typical sales force and the environment it operates in have brought about dramatic changes. These changes are examined through the following exhibits:

- Figure 100 looks at the percentage of women in the sales force and the percentage of women in sales management positions.
- Figure 101 examines the educational level achieved by sales professionals.
- Figure 102 provides a look at the typical spans of control, that is, the average number of salespeople a sales manager is responsible for in varying industries.
- Figure 103 looks at the amount of time salespeople spend on selling and non-selling activities during a typical week. How many hours they spend on a variety of activities is broken out by product or service sold, type of buyer, and industry.
- Figure 104 looks at face-to-face selling and provides data on the average number of calls per day and the average number of calls required to close the sale broken out by product or service sold, type of buyer, and industry.
- Figure 105 shows how many companies are increasing or decreasing the overall size of their sales force as well as the number of companies that are maintaining the status quo.
- Figure 106 looks at sales force turnover. Turnover data is provided for product or service sold, type of buyer, and industry. In addition, turnover is examined from the various factors that cause it: resignations, terminations, retirements, and corporate restructuring.
- Figure 107 provides data on how many companies use manufacturers' representatives to augment the activities of its direct sales force and also reports the average commission paid.

In reviewing this data, bear in mind that these figures provide indications of general trends and may or may not exactly match the profile of your particular sales force. However, over the years, Dartnell studies have consistently provided sales executives with a comprehensive look at what may be happening "down the road."

## FIGURE 100 — WOMEN IN THE SALES FORCE

One of the most profound changes in the selling profession over the past 14 years has been the relatively steady influx of women into what had been traditionally male-dominated territory. In 1982, the year Dartnell began tracking the number of women in the sales force, less than 9 percent of the total number of salespeople were women. This figure now stands at 24.1 percent for companies with over $5 million in annual sales and 23.7 percent in companies with under $5 million in annual sales. As you can see, women are making significant progress in the selling profession in companies of all sizes.

A word of caution: Percentages can at times be deceiving. Smaller sales forces can often give a distorted view of the picture when percentage figures only are considered. For example, a company employing four salespeople would have 25 percent women on its sales force even if just one member of the sales force was a woman. Thus, use judgment when trying to compare the percentage of women your company employs with the percentages in our survey (**Figure 100**).

The data in **Figure 100** also provides an indication of those industries that tend to hire significant numbers of women in sales positions.

# FIGURE 100

## Women in the Sales Force

| | Percent of Sales Reps | Percent of Sales Managers |
|---|---|---|
| **Company Size** | | |
| Under $5 Million | 23.7% | 10.4% |
| **Product or Service** | | |
| Consumer Products | 24.8 | 9.3 |
| Consumer Services | 26.3 | 14.1 |
| Industrial Products | 19.6 | 6.7 |
| Industrial Services | 25.2 | 11.1 |
| Office Products | 25.0 | 11.1 |
| Office Services | 29.3 | 12.4 |
| **Type of Buyer** | | |
| Consumers | 26.2 | 12.3 |
| Distributors | 25.4 | 7.3 |
| Industry | 23.1 | 9.3 |
| Retailers | 25.1 | 8.7 |
| **Industry** | | |
| Amusement & Recreation Services | 32.5 | 50.0 |
| Auto Repair, Services, & Garages | 29.0 | 22.0 |
| Banking | 32.0 | 0.0 |
| Business Services | 25.2 | 13.6 |
| Communications | 60.0 | 33.3 |
| Educational Services | 26.7 | 16.7 |
| Electronics | 16.9 | 7.3 |
| Fabricated Metals | 21.8 | 16.7 |
| Food Products | 13.7 | 0.0 |
| Furniture and Fixtures | 28.0 | 0.0 |
| Health Services | 41.3 | 8.3 |
| Holding & Other Investment Offices | 22.6 | 20.0 |
| Hotels & Other Lodging Places | 66.5 | 0.0 |
| Instruments | 12.4 | 0.0 |
| Insurance | 18.3 | 16.6 |
| Machinery | 13.2 | 0.0 |
| Manufacturing | 18.9 | 2.5 |
| Motion Pictures | 28.7 | 16.7 |
| Office Equipment | 16.6 | 9.1 |
| Pharmaceuticals | 43.2 | 16.8 |
| Printing and Publishing | 30.6 | 4.8 |
| Real Estate | 67.3 | 33.3 |
| Retail | 24.2 | 1.2 |
| Wholesale (Consumer Goods) | 12.8 | 8.3 |
| Wholesale (Industrial Goods) | 20.1 | 8.6 |
| **Overall** | **23.7%** | **10.4%** |

253

## FIGURE 101 — SALES FORCE EDUCATION LEVEL

The educational level of today's salesperson has never been higher, although more salespeople in companies with over $5 million in annual sales hold college degrees than salespeople in companies with under $5 million in annual sales. Currently, nearly 55 percent (53.5%) of salespeople in companies with under $5 million in annual sales have a college degree, compared to nearly 70 percent (68.2%) of the salespeople in companies with over $5 million in annual sales. In 1982, just 20 percent of U.S. salespeople had attained a college degree.

The number of salespeople holding postgraduate degrees has increased as well. Of today's sales professionals in companies under $5 million in annual sales, 8.6 percent have educational credentials that extend beyond college, compared with 5.2 percent in 1990.

# FIGURE 101

## SALES FORCE EDUCATION LEVEL

| | HIGH SCHOOL | SOME COLLEGE | COLLEGE DEGREE | POST GRAD | TECH. TRAINING |
|---|---|---|---|---|---|
| **COMPANY SIZE** | | | | | |
| UNDER $5 MILLION | 39.5% | 35.9% | 53.5% | 8.6% | 21.1% |
| **PRODUCT OR SERVICE** | | | | | |
| CONSUMER PRODUCTS | 38.8 | 33.8 | 50.0 | 7.5 | 22.5 |
| CONSUMER SERVICES | 43.8 | 33.8 | 47.5 | 10.0 | 22.5 |
| INDUSTRIAL PRODUCTS | 40.2 | 42.0 | 50.0 | 4.5 | 25.0 |
| INDUSTRIAL SERVICES | 41.9 | 39.0 | 55.2 | 8.6 | 27.6 |
| OFFICE PRODUCTS | 38.0 | 38.0 | 58.0 | 14.0 | 24.0 |
| OFFICE SERVICES | 32.8 | 34.4 | 56.2 | 12.5 | 18.8 |
| **TYPE OF BUYER** | | | | | |
| CONSUMERS | 45.5 | 39.6 | 44.6 | 6.9 | 25.7 |
| DISTRIBUTORS | 40.5 | 38.8 | 58.6 | 6.0 | 23.3 |
| INDUSTRY | 40.6 | 35.9 | 55.2 | 9.9 | 22.4 |
| RETAILERS | 43.0 | 40.7 | 59.3 | 5.8 | 14.0 |
| **INDUSTRY** | | | | | |
| AMUSEMENT & RECREATION SERVICES | 0.0 | 50.0 | 50.0 | 25.0 | 0.0 |
| AUTO REPAIR, SERVICES, & GARAGES | 66.7 | 33.3 | 33.3 | 0.0 | 0.0 |
| BANKING | 66.7 | 66.7 | 66.7 | 0.0 | 0.0 |
| BUSINESS SERVICES | 27.3 | 34.5 | 67.3 | 12.7 | 18.2 |
| COMMUNICATIONS | 100.0 | 66.7 | 33.3 | 0.0 | 0.0 |
| CONSTRUCTION | 66.7 | 33.3 | 66.7 | 0.0 | 66.7 |
| EDUCATIONAL SERVICES | 66.7 | 33.3 | 66.7 | 33.3 | 33.3 |
| ELECTRONICS | 55.6 | 44.4 | 33.3 | 0.0 | 55.6 |
| FABRICATED METALS | 33.3 | 33.3 | 50.0 | 0.0 | 16.7 |
| FOOD PRODUCTS | 16.7 | 33.3 | 50.0 | 16.7 | 33.3 |
| FURNITURE AND FIXTURES | 20.0 | 20.0 | 60.0 | 0.0 | 0.0 |
| HEALTH SERVICES | 0.0 | 16.7 | 66.7 | 33.3 | 33.3 |
| HOLDING & OTHER INVESTMENT OFFICES | 20.0 | 20.0 | 60.0 | 20.0 | 20.0 |
| HOTELS & OTHER LODGING PLACES | 50.0 | 0.0 | 50.0 | 0.0 | 50.0 |
| INSTRUMENTS | 60.0 | 40.0 | 60.0 | 0.0 | 20.0 |
| INSURANCE | 55.6 | 44.4 | 44.4 | 0.0 | 11.1 |
| MACHINERY | 25.0 | 25.0 | 75.0 | 0.0 | 25.0 |
| MANUFACTURING | 12.5 | 37.5 | 87.5 | 0.0 | 12.5 |
| MOTION PICTURES | 50.0 | 50.0 | 50.0 | 0.0 | 0.0 |
| OFFICE EQUIPMENT | 45.5 | 27.3 | 72.7 | 9.1 | 18.2 |
| PHARMACEUTICALS | 12.5 | 25.0 | 87.5 | 12.5 | 12.5 |
| PRIMARY METAL PRODUCTS | 66.7 | 33.3 | 66.7 | 0.0 | 0.0 |
| PRINTING AND PUBLISHING | 46.2 | 61.5 | 30.8 | 0.0 | 30.8 |
| REAL ESTATE | 66.7 | 0.0 | 33.3 | 0.0 | 33.3 |
| RETAIL | 75.0 | 18.8 | 31.2 | 6.2 | 25.0 |
| WHOLESALE (CONSUMER GOODS) | 27.3 | 45.5 | 9.1 | 18.2 | 18.2 |
| WHOLESALE (INDUSTRIAL GOODS) | 40.7 | 33.3 | 48.1 | 11.1 | 25.9 |
| **OVERALL*** | **39.5%** | **35.9%** | **53.5%** | **8.6%** | **21.1%** |

*FIGURES TOTAL MORE THAN 100% DUE TO MULTIPLE RESPONSES.

## FIGURE 102—TYPICAL SPANS OF CONTROL

How many salespeople does the average sales manager supervise? According to current survey results, a typical sales manager oversees the activities of approximately six salespeople. **Figure 102** examines the typical spans of control, i.e., the average number of salespeople reporting to a single sales manager. Not surprisingly, the ratio of sales managers to salespeople in smaller companies is lower than in larger companies, where the ratio is 9:1. This makes sense when you realize that a small company may employ just three salespeople, yet also have a need to employ someone to direct sales activities.

# FIGURE 102

## TYPICAL SPANS OF CONTROL

| | TOTAL NUMBER OF SALESPEOPLE | NUMBER OF SALES MANAGERS | SPAN OF CONTROL (RATIO) |
|---|---|---|---|
| **COMPANY SIZE** | | | |
| UNDER $5 MILLION | 2,233 | 336 | 6.6:1 |
| **PRODUCT OR SERVICE** | | | |
| CONSUMER PRODUCTS | 868 | 128 | 6.8:1 |
| CONSUMER SERVICES | 922 | 118 | 7.8:1 |
| INDUSTRIAL PRODUCTS | 860 | 137 | 6.3:1 |
| INDUSTRIAL SERVICES | 853 | 143 | 6.0:1 |
| OFFICE PRODUCTS | 384 | 65 | 5.9:1 |
| OFFICE SERVICES | 576 | 82 | 7.0:1 |
| **TYPE OF BUYER** | | | |
| CONSUMERS | 1,190 | 147 | 8.1:1 |
| DISTRIBUTORS | 1,019 | 162 | 6.3:1 |
| INDUSTRY | 1,439 | 246 | 5.8:1 |
| RETAILERS | 757 | 126 | 6.0:1 |
| **INDUSTRY** | | | |
| AMUSEMENT & RECREATION SERVICES | 56 | 6 | 9.3:1 |
| AUTO REPAIR, SERVICES, & GARAGES | 29 | 8 | 3.6:1 |
| BANKING | 156 | 4 | 39.0:1 |
| BUSINESS SERVICES | 390 | 58 | 6.7:1 |
| COMMUNICATIONS | 14 | 3 | 4.7:1 |
| EDUCATIONAL SERVICES | 20 | 5 | 4.0:1 |
| ELECTRONICS | 32 | 15 | 2.1:1 |
| FURNITURE AND FIXTURES | 45 | 5 | 10.2:1 |
| HEALTH SERVICES | 26 | 6 | 3.2:1 |
| HOLDING & OTHER INVESTMENT OFFICES | 18 | 6 | 3.0:1 |
| HOTELS & OTHER LODGING PLACES | 5 | 1 | 5.0:1 |
| INSTRUMENTS | 29 | 3 | 9.7:1 |
| INSURANCE | 148 | 18 | 8.2:1 |
| MACHINERY | 47 | 4 | 11.8:1 |
| MANUFACTURING | 63 | 11 | 5.7:1 |
| MOTION PICTURES | 49 | 18 | 2.7:1 |
| OFFICE EQUIPMENT | 52 | 9 | 5.7:1 |
| PHARMACEUTICALS | 131 | 16 | 8.2:1 |
| PRIMARY METAL PRODUCTS | 6 | 3 | 2.0:1 |
| PRINTING AND PUBLISHING | 66 | 21 | 3.1:1 |
| REAL ESTATE | 57 | 3 | 19.0:1 |
| RETAIL | 141 | 19 | 7.4:1 |
| WHOLESALE (CONSUMER GOODS) | 64 | 11 | 5.8:1 |
| WHOLESALE (INDUSTRIAL GOODS) | 148 | 25 | 5.9:1 |
| **OVERALL** | **2,233** | **336** | **6.2:1** |

# FIGURE 103 — SELLING AND NONSELLING WORK ACTIVITIES

Today's sales professional in companies with under $5 million in annual sales works, on average, a total of 45.5 hours per week — about the same number of hours as salespeople in companies with over $5 million in annual sales (47.4 hours). Time spent on various job activities is as follows:

| Task | Percent of Weekly Time |
|------|------------------------|
| • Selling face-to-face | 28.4% (12.9 hours) |
| • Selling over the phone | 28.8% (13.1 hours) |
| • Administrative tasks | 14.7% (6.7 hours) |
| • Waiting/traveling | 16.1% (7.3 hours) |
| • Service calls | 12.0% (5.4 hours) |

In looking at the split between hours per week, on average, spent on selling activities (26.1 hours, or 57.4 percent) and nonselling activities (19.4 hours, or 42.6 percent), note that salespeople spend a greater percentage of total working hours on direct selling activities than on nonselling activities.

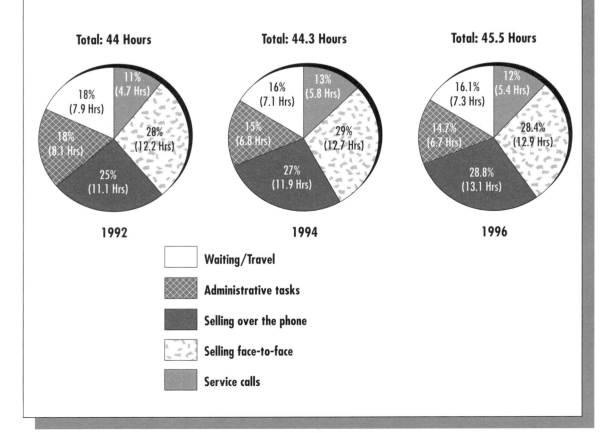

# FIGURE 103

**SELLING AND NONSELLING WORK ACTIVITIES**
**(IN HOURS PER WEEK)**

| | TOTAL WORK HOURS PER WEEK | TIME SPENT SELLING | SELLING TIME SPENT: | | TIME SPENT NON-SELLING | NONSELLING TIME SPENT: | | |
|---|---|---|---|---|---|---|---|---|
| | | | FACE-TO-FACE | ON THE PHONE | | ADMIN. | TRAVEL | SERVICE CALLS |
| **COMPANY SIZE** | | | | | | | | |
| UNDER $5 MILLION | 45.5 | 26.1 | 12.9 | 13.1 | 19.4 | 6.7 | 7.3 | 5.4 |
| **PRODUCT OR SERVICE** | | | | | | | | |
| CONSUMER PRODUCTS | 48.4 | 27.8 | 15.1 | 12.7 | 20.6 | 6.9 | 6.8 | 6.9 |
| CONSUMER SERVICES | 48.5 | 28.0 | 15.6 | 12.4 | 20.5 | 6.3 | 6.7 | 7.4 |
| INDUSTRIAL PRODUCTS | 44.3 | 25.0 | 11.3 | 13.7 | 19.3 | 7.0 | 7.1 | 5.2 |
| INDUSTRIAL SERVICES | 45.3 | 25.3 | 11.8 | 13.5 | 20.0 | 7.0 | 7.4 | 5.7 |
| OFFICE PRODUCTS | 45.0 | 24.3 | 10.7 | 13.6 | 20.7 | 7.3 | 7.3 | 6.1 |
| OFFICE SERVICES | 45.9 | 25.7 | 12.1 | 13.6 | 20.2 | 6.9 | 7.9 | 5.5 |
| **TYPE OF BUYER** | | | | | | | | |
| CONSUMERS | 47.1 | 28.8 | 15.8 | 13.0 | 18.3 | 6.3 | 6.3 | 5.7 |
| DISTRIBUTORS | 47.5 | 27.6 | 12.0 | 15.5 | 19.9 | 6.9 | 7.3 | 5.7 |
| INDUSTRY | 44.8 | 25.2 | 11.3 | 13.9 | 19.6 | 7.1 | 7.3 | 5.2 |
| RETAILERS | 49.1 | 27.7 | 13.9 | 13.9 | 21.4 | 6.9 | 7.5 | 7.0 |
| **INDUSTRY** | | | | | | | | |
| AMUSEMENT & RECREATION SERVICES | 45.8 | 28.0 | 6.8 | 21.2 | 17.8 | 5.8 | 4.0 | 8.0 |
| AUTO REPAIR, SERVICES, & GARAGES | 41.7 | 30.7 | 20.7 | 10.0 | 11.0 | 9.0 | 2.0 | 0.0 |
| BANKING | 60.7 | 32.0 | 25.3 | 6.7 | 28.7 | 10.0 | 7.7 | 11.0 |
| BUSINESS SERVICES | 45.3 | 23.6 | 11.1 | 12.6 | 21.7 | 7.5 | 8.1 | 6.2 |
| COMMUNICATIONS | 54.7 | 35.0 | 18.3 | 16.7 | 19.7 | 6.3 | 5.3 | 8.0 |
| CONSTRUCTION | 37.7 | 20.3 | 9.3 | 11.0 | 17.3 | 1.0 | 14.3 | 2.0 |
| EDUCATIONAL SERVICES | 44.3 | 20.0 | 11.7 | 8.3 | 24.3 | 7.3 | 8.3 | 8.7 |
| ELECTRONICS | 45.4 | 26.3 | 5.9 | 20.4 | 19.1 | 6.1 | 9.8 | 3.2 |
| FABRICATED METALS | 49.0 | 27.7 | 11.8 | 15.8 | 21.3 | 9.0 | 8.2 | 4.2 |
| FOOD PRODUCTS | 53.1 | 34.5 | 15.0 | 19.5 | 18.6 | 10.2 | 5.6 | 2.8 |
| FURNITURE AND FIXTURES | 45.0 | 22.6 | 17.8 | 4.8 | 22.4 | 5.6 | 10.8 | 6.0 |
| HEALTH SERVICES | 44.5 | 23.8 | 12.3 | 11.5 | 20.7 | 7.2 | 7.2 | 6.3 |
| HOLDING & OTHER INVESTMENT OFFICES | 46.8 | 34.0 | 12.0 | 22.0 | 12.8 | 4.8 | 7.2 | 0.8 |
| HOTELS & OTHER LODGING PLACES | 56.5 | 37.5 | 17.5 | 20.0 | 19.0 | 6.0 | 7.5 | 5.5 |
| INSTRUMENTS | 33.4 | 15.6 | 8.0 | 7.6 | 17.8 | 3.2 | 11.0 | 3.6 |
| INSURANCE | 50.7 | 28.9 | 19.2 | 9.7 | 21.8 | 6.7 | 6.1 | 9.0 |
| MACHINERY | 40.0 | 22.5 | 10.2 | 12.2 | 17.5 | 7.2 | 7.5 | 2.8 |
| MANUFACTURING | 43.2 | 19.0 | 10.8 | 8.2 | 24.2 | 3.9 | 12.9 | 7.5 |
| MOTION PICTURES | 59.3 | 40.0 | 14.7 | 25.3 | 19.3 | 7.7 | 7.7 | 4.0 |
| OFFICE EQUIPMENT | 41.7 | 23.5 | 5.3 | 18.2 | 18.3 | 7.2 | 5.7 | 5.4 |
| PHARMACEUTICALS | 46.0 | 28.8 | 18.1 | 10.6 | 17.2 | 6.2 | 7.0 | 4.0 |
| PRIMARY METAL PRODUCTS | 50.3 | 27.7 | 6.7 | 21.0 | 22.7 | 4.7 | 6.0 | 12.0 |
| PRINTING AND PUBLISHING | 42.6 | 27.5 | 12.3 | 15.2 | 15.2 | 5.0 | 5.6 | 4.5 |
| REAL ESTATE | 32.7 | 25.0 | 15.3 | 9.7 | 7.7 | 1.7 | 2.7 | 3.3 |
| RETAIL | 45.5 | 27.1 | 17.8 | 9.3 | 18.4 | 6.5 | 6.3 | 5.6 |
| WHOLESALE (CONSUMER GOODS) | 50.5 | 27.9 | 14.6 | 13.3 | 22.6 | 7.7 | 8.8 | 6.1 |
| WHOLESALE (INDUSTRIAL GOODS) | 43.0 | 26.3 | 13.9 | 12.4 | 16.7 | 7.0 | 5.4 | 4.2 |
| **OVERALL** | **45.5** | **26.1** | **12.9** | **13.1** | **19.4** | **6.7** | **7.3** | **5.4** |

## FIGURE 104 — FACE-TO-FACE SELLING

Since 1990, the average number of sales calls typically needed to close a sale and the average number of sales calls made per day have remained relatively stable in companies with under $5 million in annual sales. The average number of sales calls per day now stands at 3.1.

In 1982, however, salespeople in companies of all sizes made an average of six sales calls per day. Can we infer from this that today's sales professional is less effective? No—and here's why. In the 1980s, it was common for sales managers to set a minimum number of sales calls that their salespeople had to make in any given day. Over the years, sales managers began to realize that the *quality* of the sales calls made was more important than the overall *quantity* of sales calls made. Today's salespeople now go into sales calls much better prepared than they were in the past.

The average number of calls to close a sale, 3.8, is unchanged from 1994.

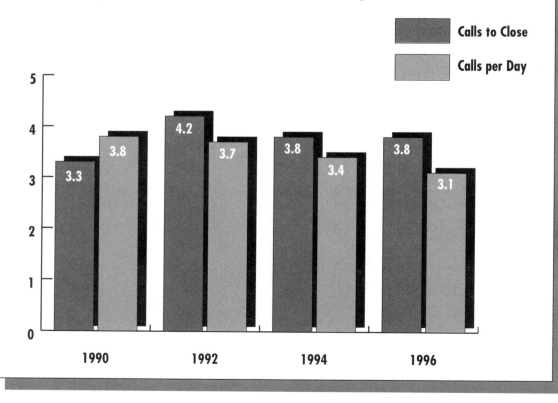

# FIGURE 104

**FACE-TO-FACE SELLING**

|  | AVERAGE NUMBER OF CALLS TO CLOSE SALE | AVERAGE NUMBER OF CALLS PER DAY |
|---|---|---|
| **COMPANY SIZE** | | |
| UNDER $5 MILLION | 3.8 | 3.1 |
| **PRODUCT OR SERVICE** | | |
| CONSUMER PRODUCTS | 3.4 | 3.5 |
| CONSUMER SERVICES | 3.1 | 3.1 |
| INDUSTRIAL PRODUCTS | 3.8 | 3.1 |
| INDUSTRIAL SERVICES | 3.9 | 2.9 |
| OFFICE PRODUCTS | 4.4 | 2.8 |
| OFFICE SERVICES | 3.7 | 2.7 |
| **TYPE OF BUYER** | | |
| CONSUMERS | 3.4 | 3.2 |
| DISTRIBUTORS | 4.0 | 3.2 |
| INDUSTRY | 3.8 | 2.9 |
| RETAILERS | 3.7 | 3.3 |
| **INDUSTRY** | | |
| AMUSEMENT & RECREATION SERVICES | 3.5 | 3.0 |
| BANKING | 0.0 | 3.0 |
| BUSINESS SERVICES | 3.6 | 2.6 |
| COMMUNICATIONS | 5.0 | 3.3 |
| CONSTRUCTION | 5.0 | 0.0 |
| EDUCATIONAL SERVICES | 16.3 | 2.7 |
| ELECTRONICS | 8.3 | 2.0 |
| FABRICATED METALS | 4.0 | 2.5 |
| FOOD PRODUCTS | 3.2 | 3.0 |
| FURNITURE AND FIXTURES | 3.0 | 3.7 |
| HEALTH SERVICES | 4.0 | 3.0 |
| HOLDING & OTHER INVESTMENT OFFICES | 4.3 | 2.5 |
| INSTRUMENTS | 5.0 | 3.0 |
| INSURANCE | 2.5 | 2.8 |
| MACHINERY | 3.5 | 1.5 |
| MANUFACTURING | 3.8 | 4.0 |
| MOTION PICTURES | 4.3 | 0.0 |
| OFFICE EQUIPMENT | 5.2 | 1.7 |
| PHARMACEUTICALS | 5.5 | 5.8 |
| PRIMARY METAL PRODUCTS | 5.0 | 2.7 |
| PRINTING AND PUBLISHING | 4.0 | 3.0 |
| REAL ESTATE | 0.0 | 3.3 |
| RETAIL | 3.2 | 3.2 |
| WHOLESALE (CONSUMER GOODS) | 4.4 | 4.4 |
| WHOLESALE (INDUSTRIAL GOODS) | 4.0 | 4.3 |
| **OVERALL** | **3.8** | **3.1** |

## FIGURE 105 — THE CHANGING SIZE OF THE SALES FORCE

Just 11.6 percent of responding companies said the sizes of their sales forces decreased during the survey period. More than 35 percent of responding companies are increasing the sizes of their sales forces in anticipation of expanding markets and additional growth opportunities. More than half of the companies in the survey (56.2%) say the sizes of their sales forces are expected to remain constant.

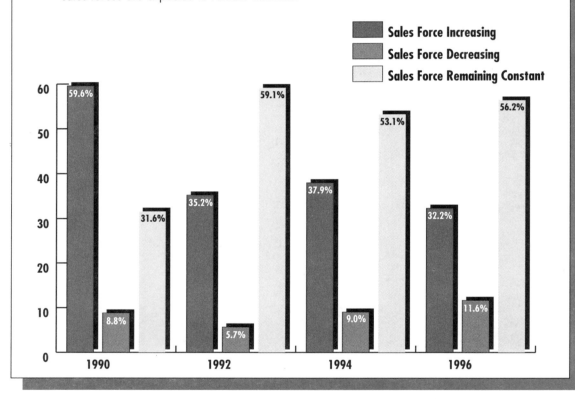

# FIGURE 105

**The Changing Size of the Sales Force**

| | SALES FORCE INCREASING | | SALES FORCE DECREASING | | SALES FORCE REMAINING CONSTANT |
| | PERCENT OF FIRMS | AVERAGE SIZE OF INCREASE (NO. OF PEOPLE) | PERCENT OF FIRMS | AVERAGE SIZE OF DECREASE (NO. OF PEOPLE) | PERCENT OF FIRMS |
|---|---|---|---|---|---|
| **COMPANY SIZE** | | | | | |
| UNDER $5 MILLION | 32.2% | 2 | 11.6% | 2 | 56.2% |
| **PRODUCT OR SERVICE** | | | | | |
| CONSUMER PRODUCTS | 33.3 | 2 | 9.9 | 2 | 56.8 |
| CONSUMER SERVICES | 29.3 | 3 | 12.2 | 1 | 58.5 |
| INDUSTRIAL PRODUCTS | 35.4 | 2 | 14.2 | 1 | 50.4 |
| INDUSTRIAL SERVICES | 30.2 | 2 | 11.3 | 2 | 58.5 |
| OFFICE PRODUCTS | 25.5 | 2 | 11.8 | 2 | 62.7 |
| OFFICE SERVICES | 27.7 | 2 | 9.2 | 2 | 63.1 |
| **TYPE OF BUYER** | | | | | |
| CONSUMERS | 27.2 | 3 | 11.7 | 1 | 61.2 |
| DISTRIBUTORS | 35.9 | 2 | 8.5 | 2 | 55.6 |
| INDUSTRY | 31.1 | 2 | 10.9 | 2 | 58.0 |
| RETAILERS | 34.5 | 2 | 8.0 | 2 | 57.5 |
| **INDUSTRY** | | | | | |
| AUTO REPAIR, SERVICES, & GARAGES | 33.3 | 2 | 0.0 | 0 | 66.7 |
| BANKING | 66.7 | 2 | 33.3 | 1 | 0.0 |
| BUSINESS SERVICES | 25.5 | 2 | 5.5 | 2 | 69.1 |
| COMMUNICATIONS | 33.3 | 1 | 0.0 | 0 | 66.7 |
| CONSTRUCTION | 0.0 | 0 | 0.0 | 0 | 100.0 |
| EDUCATIONAL SERVICES | 0.0 | 0 | 33.3 | 3 | 66.7 |
| ELECTRONICS | 33.3 | 1 | 22.2 | 2 | 44.4 |
| FABRICATED METALS | 16.7 | 2 | 0.0 | 0 | 83.3 |
| FURNITURE AND FIXTURES | 0.0 | 0 | 40.0 | 2 | 60.0 |
| HEALTH SERVICES | 33.3 | 2 | 16.7 | 1 | 50.0 |
| HOLDING & OTHER INVESTMENT OFFICES | 20.0 | 1 | 0.0 | 0 | 80.0 |
| HOTELS & OTHER LODGING PLACES | 50.0 | 1 | 0.0 | 0 | 50.0 |
| INSTRUMENTS | 60.0 | 1 | 0.0 | 0 | 40.0 |
| INSURANCE | 70.0 | 3 | 10.0 | 2 | 20.0 |
| MACHINERY | 25.0 | 2 | 0.0 | 0 | 75.0 |
| MANUFACTURING | 50.0 | 2 | 0.0 | 0 | 50.0 |
| OFFICE EQUIPMENT | 45.5 | 1 | 18.2 | 2 | 36.4 |
| PHARMACEUTICALS | 37.5 | 2 | 0.0 | 0 | 62.5 |
| PRIMARY METAL PRODUCTS | 33.3 | 1 | 0.0 | 0 | 66.7 |
| PRINTING AND PUBLISHING | 38.5 | 2 | 38.5 | 2 | 23.1 |
| REAL ESTATE | 0.0 | 0 | 0.0 | 0 | 100.0 |
| RETAIL | 25.0 | 2 | 12.5 | 1 | 62.5 |
| WHOLESALE (CONSUMER GOODS) | 36.4 | 2 | 9.1 | 1 | 54.5 |
| WHOLESALE (INDUSTRIAL GOODS) | 25.9 | 1 | 14.8 | 1 | 59.3 |
| **OVERALL** | **32.2%** | **2** | **11.6%** | **2** | **56.2%** |

## FIGURE 106 — SALES FORCE TURNOVER

**Figure 106** examines sales force turnover in companies with under $5 million in annual sales and reports an average turnover rate of 20.4 percent. Turnover rates seem to have stabilized from 1990, when poor job prospects kept a significant number of reps from leaving their current employers.

Most reps leave due to resignations, followed by retirements. Terminations and corporate restructurings account for a relatively small number of reps leaving their jobs.

### TURNOVER RATE IN COMPANIES WITH UNDER $5 MILLION IN ANNUAL SALES 1990–1996

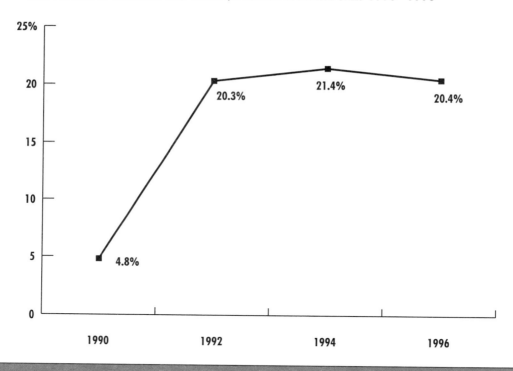

FIGURE 106

## SALES FORCE TURNOVER

| | SALES-PEOPLE | RESIGNA-TIONS | TERMINA-TIONS | RETIRE-MENT | CORP. RESTRUC-TURING | TOTAL TURNOVER (%) |
|---|---|---|---|---|---|---|
| **COMPANY SIZE** | | | | | | |
| UNDER $5 MILLION | 2,233 | 228 | 26 | 179 | 23 | 20.4% |
| **PRODUCT OR SERVICE** | | | | | | |
| CONSUMER PRODUCTS | 868 | 85 | 9 | 66 | 16 | 20.3 |
| CONSUMER SERVICES | 922 | 63 | 10 | 65 | 9 | 15.9 |
| INDUSTRIAL PRODUCTS | 860 | 110 | 10 | 57 | 6 | 21.3 |
| INDUSTRIAL SERVICES | 853 | 126 | 6 | 73 | 5 | 24.6 |
| OFFICE PRODUCTS | 384 | 33 | 2 | 34 | 7 | 19.8 |
| OFFICE SERVICES | 576 | 59 | 3 | 43 | 14 | 20.7 |
| **TYPE OF BUYER** | | | | | | |
| CONSUMERS | 1,190 | 111 | 11 | 100 | 17 | 20.1 |
| DISTRIBUTORS | 1,019 | 87 | 8 | 74 | 15 | 18.1 |
| INDUSTRY | 1,439 | 182 | 17 | 112 | 10 | 22.3 |
| RETAILERS | 757 | 75 | 14 | 48 | 5 | 18.8 |
| **INDUSTRY** | | | | | | |
| AMUSEMENT & RECREATION SERVICES | 56 | 3 | 0 | 11 | 0 | 25.0 |
| AUTO REPAIR, SERVICES, & GARAGES | 29 | 0 | 0 | 0 | 1 | 3.4 |
| BANKING | 156 | 4 | 2 | 3 | 0 | 5.8 |
| BUSINESS SERVICES | 390 | 55 | 5 | 32 | 1 | 23.8 |
| COMMUNICATIONS | 14 | 1 | 0 | 1 | 0 | 14.3 |
| CONSTRUCTION | 8 | 3 | 0 | 1 | 0 | 50.0 |
| EDUCATIONAL SERVICES | 20 | 3 | 0 | 3 | 0 | 30.0 |
| ELECTRONICS | 32 | 2 | 0 | 2 | 6 | 31.2 |
| FABRICATED METALS | 102 | 3 | 0 | 3 | 0 | 5.9 |
| FOOD PRODUCTS | 133 | 2 | 1 | 5 | 5 | 9.8 |
| FURNITURE AND FIXTURES | 45 | 2 | 1 | 5 | 0 | 17.8 |
| HEALTH SERVICES | 26 | 2 | 0 | 0 | 1 | 11.5 |
| HOLDING & OTHER INVESTMENT OFFICES | 18 | 0 | 1 | 0 | 0 | 5.6 |
| HOTELS & OTHER LODGING PLACES | 5 | 1 | 0 | 0 | 0 | 20.0 |
| INSTRUMENTS | 29 | 3 | 0 | 0 | 0 | 10.3 |
| INSURANCE | 148 | 10 | 3 | 21 | 2 | 24.3 |
| MACHINERY | 47 | 1 | 2 | 1 | 0 | 8.5 |
| MANUFACTURING | 63 | 8 | 2 | 8 | 0 | 28.6 |
| MOTION PICTURES | 49 | 8 | 1 | 4 | 1 | 28.6 |
| OFFICE EQUIPMENT | 52 | 5 | 1 | 4 | 2 | 23.1 |
| PHARMACEUTICALS | 131 | 4 | 2 | 0 | 0 | 4.6 |
| PRIMARY METAL PRODUCTS | 6 | 0 | 0 | 1 | 0 | 16.7 |
| PRINTING AND PUBLISHING | 66 | 9 | 0 | 13 | 1 | 34.8 |
| REAL ESTATE | 57 | 2 | 0 | 1 | 0 | 5.3 |
| RETAIL | 141 | 15 | 0 | 24 | 0 | 27.7 |
| WHOLESALE (CONSUMER GOODS) | 64 | 5 | 0 | 7 | 0 | 18.8 |
| WHOLESALE (INDUSTRIAL GOODS) | 148 | 9 | 1 | 10 | 2 | 14.9 |
| **OVERALL** | **2,233** | **228** | **26** | **179** | **23** | **20.4%** |

## FIGURE 107 — USE OF MANUFACTURERS' REPRESENTATIVES

Approximately 25 percent of companies participating in this survey use manufacturers' representatives solely or to augment the efforts of the company's direct sales force. In 1994, 22.6 percent used manufacturers' reps. The average commission rate paid is 12.7 percent.

# FIGURE 107

**USE OF MANUFACTURERS' REPRESENTATIVES**

| | PERCENT USING MANUFACTURERS' REPS | AVERAGE COMMISSION (PERCENT OF SALES) |
|---|---|---|
| **COMPANY SIZE** | | |
| UNDER $5 MILLION | 24.7% | 12.7% |
| **PRODUCT OR SERVICE** | | |
| CONSUMER PRODUCTS | 28.4 | 12.4 |
| CONSUMER SERVICES | 13.4 | 16.2 |
| INDUSTRIAL PRODUCTS | 33.3 | 13.3 |
| INDUSTRIAL SERVICES | 23.4 | 12.4 |
| OFFICE PRODUCTS | 28.8 | 10.1 |
| OFFICE SERVICES | 19.7 | 11.6 |
| **TYPE OF BUYER** | | |
| CONSUMERS | 16.5 | 13.1 |
| DISTRIBUTORS | 33.6 | 13.8 |
| INDUSTRY | 23.7 | 12.7 |
| RETAILERS | 18.4 | 11.3 |
| **INDUSTRY** | | |
| AMUSEMENT & RECREATION SERVICES | 25.0 | 10.0 |
| BUSINESS SERVICES | 9.1 | 14.6 |
| EDUCATIONAL SERVICES | 66.7 | 16.5 |
| ELECTRONICS | 33.3 | 10.7 |
| FABRICATED METALS | 66.7 | 8.8 |
| FOOD PRODUCTS | 100.0 | 10.7 |
| FURNITURE AND FIXTURES | 100.0 | 6.2 |
| HOLDING & OTHER INVESTMENT OFFICES | 20.0 | 35.0 |
| INSTRUMENTS | 60.0 | 24.3 |
| INSURANCE | 10.0 | 30.0 |
| MACHINERY | 100.0 | 11.8 |
| MANUFACTURING | 62.5 | 13.9 |
| MOTION PICTURES | 33.3 | 10.0 |
| OFFICE EQUIPMENT | 25.0 | 5.3 |
| PHARMACEUTICALS | 37.5 | 14.0 |
| PRIMARY METAL PRODUCTS | 100.0 | 4.4 |
| PRINTING AND PUBLISHING | 7.7 | 10.0 |
| RETAIL | 12.5 | 27.5 |
| WHOLESALE (CONSUMER GOODS) | 8.3 | 2.0 |
| WHOLESALE (INDUSTRIAL GOODS) | 19.2 | 17.6 |
| **OVERALL** | **24.7%** | **12.7%** |

## SECTION 7

# PARTICIPATING COMPANIES BY STANDARD INDUSTRIAL CLASSIFICATION (SIC) CODE — FOUR-DIGIT LISTINGS

To help users of this data select relevant comparator groups when comparing their company's data with data in this survey, we have expanded the standard SIC reporting method to include four digits. The three-digit listing immediately follows our expanded listing. Data tables list our broader three-digit SIC industry categories. The four-digit listings are best thought of as subgroups of the three-digit listing. The following types of companies are represented by the compensation data appearing in *What America's Small Companies Pay Their Sales Forces...And How They Make It Pay Off*.

### Construction
*Construction — Special Trade Contractors*
1731   Electrical Work

### Manufacturing
*Food and Kindred Products*
2037   Frozen Fruits & Vegetables
2038   Frozen Specialties, Not Elsewhere Classified
2066   Chocolate & Cocoa Products
2099   Food Preparations, Not Elsewhere Classified

*Tobacco Products*
2131   Chewing and Smoking Tobacco and Snuff

*Textile Mill Products*
2231   Broadwoven Fabric Mills, Wool

*Lumber and Wood Products, Except Furniture*
2499   Wood Products

*Furniture and Fixtures*
2542   Office and Store Fixtures, Partitions, Shelving, and Lockers, Except Wood
2599   Furniture and Fixtures, Not Elsewhere Classified

*Paper and Allied Products*
2679   Converted Paper and Paperboard Products, Not Elsewhere Classified

*Printing, Publishing, and Allied Industries*
2731   Book Publishing
2732   Book Printing
2741   Miscellaneous Publishing
2789   Bookbinding & Related Work

## Chemicals and Allied Products

2834    Pharmaceutical Preparations
2835    Diagnostic Substances
2842    Specialty Cleaning, Polishing, and Sanitation Preparations
2899    Chemicals and Chemical Preparations, Not Elsewhere Classified

## Petroleum Refining and Related Industries

2911    Petroleum Refining

## Rubber and Miscellaneous Plastic Products

3053    Gaskets, Packing, and Sealing Devices
3086    Plastics Foam Products
3089    Plastics Products, Not Elsewhere Classified

## Primary Metal Industries

3369    Nonferrous Foundries
3399    Primary Metal Products, Not Elsewhere Classified

## Fabricated Metal Products, Except Machinery and Transportation Equipment

3442    Metal Doors, Sash, Frames, Molding, and Trim
3443    Fabricated Plate Work (Boiler Shops)
3499    Fabricated Metal Products, Not Elsewhere Classified

## Industrial and Commercial Machinery and Computer Equipment

3549    Metalworking Machinery, Not Elsewhere Classified
3555    Printing Trades Machinery
3561    Pumps and Pumping Equipment
3565    Packaging Machinery
3569    General Industrial Machinery and Equipment, Not Elsewhere Classified
3571    Electronic Computers
3572    Computer Storage Devices
3575    Computer Terminals
3577    Computer Peripheral Equipment, Not Elsewhere Classified
3578    Calculating and Accounting Machines, Except Electronic Computers
3579    Office Machines, Not Elsewhere Classified
3589    Service Industry Machinery
3599    Industrial and Commercial Machinery and Equipment, Not Elsewhere Classified

## Electronic and Other Electrical Equipment and Components, Except Computer Equipment

3621    Motors and Generators
3663    Radio and Television Broadcasting and Communications Equipment
3669    Communications Equipment, Not Elsewhere Classified
3699    Electrical Equipment & Supplies

## Transportation Equipment

3711    Motor Vehicles & Car Bodies
3714    Motor Vehicle Parts and Accessories
3732    Boatbuilding & Repairing
3799    Transportation Equipment, Not Elsewhere Classified

*Measuring, Analyzing, and Controlling Instruments, Photographic, Medical, and Optical Goods;*
*Watches and Clocks*

3821    Laboratory Apparatus & Furniture
3822    Automatic Controls for Regulating Residential and
         Commercial Environments and Appliances
3823    Industrial Instruments for Measurement, Display,
         and Control of Process Variables; and Related Products
3826    Laboratory Analytical Instruments
3827    Optical Instruments and Lenses
3829    Measuring and Controlling Devices, Not Elsewhere Classified
3841    Surgical and Medical Instruments and Apparatus
3842    Orthopedic, Prosthetic, and Surgical Appliances and Supplies
3845    Electromedical Equipment
3861    Photographic Equipment

*Miscellaneous Manufacturing Industries*

3914    Silverware & Plated Ware
3944    Games/Toys/Children's Vehicles
3965    Fasteners, Buttons, Needles
3993    Signs and Advertising Specialties
3999    Manufacturing Industries, Not Elsewhere Classified

## Transportation, Communications, Electric, Gas, and Sanitary Service
*Motor Freight Transportation and Warehousing*

4212    Local Trucking Without Storage

*Transportation Services*

4724    Travel Agencies
4729    Arrangement of Passenger Transportations

*Communications*

4899    Communication Services, Not Elsewhere Classified

*Electric, Gas, and Sanitary Services*

4952    Sewerage Systems
4953    Refuse Systems
4959    Sanitary Services, Not Elsewhere Classified

## Wholesale Trade
*Wholesale Trade — Durable Goods*

5012    Automobiles and Other Motor Vehicles
5013    Motor Vehicle Supplies and New Parts
5014    Tires and Tubes
5015    Motor Vehicle Parts, Used
5023    Home Furnishings
5031    Lumber, Plywood, and Millwork
5032    Brick, Stone, and Related
5043    Photographic Equipment/Supplies

| 5044 | Office Equipment |
|---|---|
| 5045 | Computers and Computer Peripheral Equipment and Software |
| 5046 | Commercial Equipment, Not Elsewhere Classified |
| 5047 | Medical, Dental, and Hospital Equipment and Supplies |
| 5051 | Metals Service Centers and Offices |
| 5052 | Coal/Minerals and Ores |
| 5063 | Electrical Apparatus and Equipment, Wiring Supplies, and Construction Materials |
| 5064 | Electrical Appliances |
| 5065 | Electronic Parts/Equipment |
| 5074 | Plumbing/Hydronic Heat Supplies |
| 5075 | Warm Air Heating and Air-Conditioning Equipment and Supplies |
| 5082 | Construction and Mining (Except Petroleum) Machinery and Equipment |
| 5084 | Industrial Machinery and Equipment |
| 5085 | Industrial Supplies |
| 5087 | Service Establishment Equipment and Supplies |
| 5092 | Toys and Hobby Goods and Supplies |
| 5094 | Jewelry and Precious Stones |
| 5099 | Durable Goods, Not Elsewhere Classified |

*Wholesale Trade — Nondurable Goods*

| 5199 | Nondurable Goods, Not Elsewhere Classified |
|---|---|

## Retail Trade

*Building Materials, Hardware, Garden Supplies*

| 5261 | Retail Nurseries and Garden Stores |
|---|---|

*General Merchandise Stores*

| 5399 | Miscellaneous General Merchandise Stores |
|---|---|

*Food Stores*

| 5421 | Meat and Fish Markets |
|---|---|
| 5499 | Miscellaneous Food Stores |

*Automotive Dealers and Gasoline Service Stations*

| 5599 | Automotive Dealers |
|---|---|

*Home Furniture, Furnishings, and Equipment Stores*

| 5719 | Miscellaneous Home Furnishings |
|---|---|
| 5731 | Radio, Television, and Electronics |

*Miscellaneous Retail*

| 5932 | Used Merchandise Stores |
|---|---|
| 5944 | Jewelry Stores |
| 5947 | Gift, Novelty, and Souvenir Shops |
| 5962 | Automatic Merchandising Machine Operators |
| 5963 | Direct Selling Establishments |
| 5992 | Florists |
| 5999 | Miscellaneous Retail Stores, Not Elsewhere Classified |

## Finance, Insurance, and Real Estate

*Depository Institutions*

| | |
|---|---|
| 6021 | National Commercial Banks |
| 6035 | Federal Savings Institutions |
| 6061 | Federal Credit Unions |

*Nondepository Credit Institutions*

| | |
|---|---|
| 6162 | Mortgage Bankers/Correspondents |

*Insurance Carriers*

| | |
|---|---|
| 6311 | Life Insurance |
| 6321 | Accident and Health Insurance |
| 6324 | Hospital and Medical Service Plans |
| 6331 | Fire, Marine, and Casualty Insurance |
| 6361 | Title Insurance |
| 6399 | Insurance Carriers, Not Elsewhere Classified |

*Insurance Agents, Brokers, and Service*

| | |
|---|---|
| 6411 | Insurance Agents, Brokers, and Service |

*Real Estate*

| | |
|---|---|
| 6515 | Mobile Home Site Operators |
| 6531 | Real Estate Agents and Managers |

*Holding and Other Investment Offices*

| | |
|---|---|
| 6722 | Management Investment Offices, Open-End |
| 6726 | Investment Offices |
| 6732 | Trusts: Educational, Religious |
| 6733 | Trusts |
| 6792 | Oil Royalty Traders |
| 6794 | Patent Owners & Lessors |
| 6799 | Investors, Not Elsewhere Classified |

## Services

*Hotels, Rooming Houses, Camps, and Other Lodging Places*

| | |
|---|---|
| 7011 | Hotels and Motels |

*Personal Services*

| | |
|---|---|
| 7219 | Laundry and Garment Services |
| 7251 | Shoe Repair/Shoeshine Parlors |

*Business Services*

| | |
|---|---|
| 7311 | Advertising Agencies |
| 7313 | Radio/Television/Publisher Representative |
| 7319 | Advertising, Not Elsewhere Classified |
| 7322 | Adjustment and Collection Services |
| 7334 | Photocopying and Duplicating Services |

| 7342 | Disinfecting and Pest Control Services |
|---|---|
| 7349 | Building Cleaning and Maintenance Services, Not Elsewhere Classified |
| 7359 | Equipment Rental and Leasing, Not Elsewhere Classified |
| 7361 | Employment Agencies |
| 7363 | Help Supply Services |
| 7371 | Computer Programming Services |
| 7372 | Prepackaged Software |
| 7373 | Computer Integrated Systems Design |
| 7374 | Data Processing and Preparation |
| 7375 | Information Retrieval Services |
| 7377 | Computer Rental and Leasing |
| 7378 | Computer Maintenance and Repair |
| 7379 | Computer Related Services, Not Elsewhere Classified |
| 7382 | Security Systems Services |
| 7389 | Business Services, Not Elsewhere Classified |

*Automotive Repair, Services, and Parking*
| 7539 | Automotive Repair Shops |
|---|---|
| 7549 | Automotive Services |

*Miscellaneous Repair Services*
| 7699 | Repair Shops and Related Services, Not Elsewhere Classified |
|---|---|

*Movies*
| 7812 | Movie and Video Production |
|---|---|
| 7822 | Movie and Tape Distribution |

*Amusement and Recreation Services*
| 7929 | Bands, Orchestras, Actors, and Other Entertainers and Entertainment Groups |
|---|---|
| 7941 | Sports Clubs, Managers, Pro |
| 7996 | Amusement Parks |

*Health Services*
| 8011 | Offices/Clinics, Medical Doctors |
|---|---|
| 8021 | Offices/Clinics, Dentists |
| 8071 | Medical Laboratories |
| 8099 | Health and Allied Services, Not Elsewhere Classified |

*Educational Services*
| 8211 | Elementary and Secondary Schools |
|---|---|
| 8249 | Vocational Schools, Not Elsewhere Classified |

*Membership Organizations*
| 8611 | Business Associations |
|---|---|
| 8641 | Civic, Social, and Fraternal Associations |

*Engineering, Accounting, Research, Management, and Related Services*

| | |
|---|---|
| 8711 | Engineering Services |
| 8712 | Architectural Services |
| 8721 | Accounting, Auditing, and Bookkeeping Services |
| 8732 | Commercial Nonphysical Research |
| 8734 | Testing Laboratories |
| 8741 | Management Services |
| 8742 | Management Consulting Services |
| 8744 | Facilities Support Services |
| 8748 | Business Consulting Services, Not Elsewhere Classified |

## Standard Industrial Classification (SIC) Codes

Code    Industrial Classification

010    *Agriculture, Forestry, and Fishing*

*Mining*

| | |
|---|---|
| 110 | Metal Mining |
| 120 | Anthracite, Bituminous Coal, and Lignite Mining |
| 130 | Oil and Gas Extraction |
| 140 | Nonmetallic Minerals, except Fuels |

150    *Construction*

*Manufacturing*

| | |
|---|---|
| 200 | Food and Kindred Products |
| 208 | Beverages |
| 210 | Tobacco Manufacturers |
| 220 | Textile Mill Products |
| 230 | Apparel and Other Textile Products |
| 240 | Lumber and Wood Products |
| 250 | Furniture and Fixtures |
| 260 | Paper and Allied Products |
| 270 | Printing and Publishing |
| 280 | Chemicals and Allied Products |
| 283 | Pharmaceuticals |
| 284 | Cosmetics and Toilet Preparations |
| 290 | Petroleum and Coal Products |
| 300 | Rubber and Misc. Plastics Products |
| 310 | Leather and Leather Products |
| 320 | Stone, Clay, and Glass Products |
| 330 | Primary Metal Industries |

| 340 | Fabricated Metal Products |
| 350 | Machinery, except Electric |
| 357 | Computers and Office Equipment |
| 360 | Electric and Electronic Equipment |
| 363 | Household Appliances |
| 367 | Electronic Components |
| 370 | Transportation Equipment |
| 376 | Aerospace Equipment |
| | |
| 380 | Instruments and Related Products |
| | |
| 390 | Miscellaneous Manufacturing Industries |

*Transportation and Public Utilities*

| 400 | Railroad Transportation |
| 420 | Trucking and Warehousing |
| 450 | Transportation by Air |
| 480 | Communication |
| 490 | Electric, Gas, and Sanitary Services |
| | |
| 500 C | *Wholesale Trade (Consumer Goods)* |
| | |
| 500 I | *Wholesale Trade (Industrial Goods)* |
| | |
| 520 | *Retail Trade* |

*Finance, Insurance, and Real Estate*

| 600 | Banking |
| 630 | Insurance |
| 650 | Real Estate |
| 670 | Holding and Other Investment Offices |

*Services*

| 700 | Hotels and Other Lodging Places |
| 730 | Business Services |
| 750 | Auto Repair, Services, and Garages |
| 780 | Motion Pictures |
| 790 | Amusement and Recreation Services |
| 800 | Health Services |
| 820 | Educational Services |

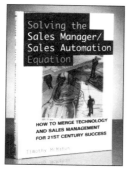

## LEADING YOUR SALES TEAM
### How to Manage a Winning Sales Team

*By Jim Pancero*

Stop being a "doing" sales manager, and start being a "managing" sales manager. Sales management expert Jim Pancero's unique "prescription for success" gives sales managers the courage to examine and improve every facet of their performance as sales managers ... so they can focus 100 percent of their efforts on building and leading motivated, winning teams.

**241 pages; 6" x 9" hardcover; $31.50; Book Code: 1202**

## THE SALES AUTOMATION REPORT

Get ahead and stay ahead with the latest ins and outs of sales automation with *The Sales Automation Report*. Keep on top of an ever-changing area. This timely newsletter will arrive on your desk 10 times a year, offering 12 pages chock-full of advice, information, and ideas about sales automation, written in nontechnical language that is easy to understand.

**Special Charter Subscriber Rate: $175; Order Code: 5017**

Books may be ordered from your local bookseller or from Dartnell. Prices subject to change without notice.

---------------------------------------------------------------------

☑ *YES!* Send me the book(s) and/or newsletter(s) I have indicated. I understand that if I am not completely satisfied, I may return the book(s) and/or cancel the newsletter subscription(s) within 30 days for a full refund. (Shipping and handling charges will be added to your invoice. IL residents please add 8.75% sales tax; IN residents add 5% tax; Canadian residents add 7% GST.)

_____*Solving the Sales Manager/*
*Sales Automation Equation*
$45; Book Code: 1252

_____*The Only Sales Promotion*
*Techniques You'll Ever Need!*
$39.95; Book Code: 1255

_____*Getting Tough Customers to YES*
$24.95; Book Code: 1250

_____*The Greatest Direct Mail Sales*
*Letters of All Time*
$69.95; Book Code: 1239

_____*Leading Your Sales Team*
$31.50; Book Code: 1202

_____*The Sales Automation Report*
$175; Order Code: 5017

Prices are listed in U.S. currency.
To order from Dartnell, call toll free
**(800) 621-5463,**
or fax us your order at
**(800) 327-8635.**
**www.dartnellcorp.com**

Bill my: ❑ Company

Charge my: ❑ VISA   ❑ MasterCard   ❑ American Express

Card No.: _____ Exp. Date: _____

Name: _____ Title: _____

Company: _____

Address: _____

City/State/Province/Zip: _____

Signature: _____

Phone: (\_\_\_\_\_) _____ Fax: (\_\_\_\_\_) _____

E-mail: _____

*(Signature and phone number necessary to process order.)*          97-5504